JEWISH LIFE

IN THE

MIDDLE AGES

by *Israel Abrahams*

A TEMPLE BOOK

ATHENEUM, NEW YORK

Published by Atheneum
Reprinted by arrangement with
The Jewish Publication Society of America

Atheneum
Macmillan Publishing Company
866 Third Avenue, New York, NY 10022
Collier Macmillan Canada, Inc.

Library of Congress catalog card number 58-11933
ISBN *0-689-70001-6*

Macmillan books are available at special discounts for bulk purchases for sales promotions, premiums, fund-raising, or educational use. For details, contact:

    Special Sales Director
    Macmillan Publishing Company
    866 Third Avenue
    New York, N.Y. 10022

15 14 13 12 11 10 9 8 7

Printed in the United States of America

Jewish Life in the Middle Ages

TO MY WIFE

PREFACE

THOUGH I have everywhere referred to the works from which I have derived incidental facts, or from which I have borrowed quotations, there are three writers to whom I should like to express my more general indebtedness. The works of Dr. M. Güdemann, Dr. A. Berliner, and Mr. Joseph Jacobs have been of constant service to me. One thing I have done to justify my frequent use of their works. I have verified their quotations wherever possible. Indeed, I honestly believe that not five in a hundred of the many citations made in the course of the following pages have been set down without reference to the original sources. Moreover, a large proportion of my quotations, and almost all my citations from *Responsa*, have been made at first hand.

Apart from the help that I derived from his published works, I owe to Mr. Jacobs many valuable suggestions made while this book was passing through the printer's hands. A similar remark applies to Professor W. Bacher of Buda-Pesth, who kindly read the proof-sheets and gave me some useful hints. I am deeply grateful to both these gentlemen for the services which they so readily rendered.

My indebtedness to another friend has been of a different character, for it is to him that I owe the very possibility of writing this book.　From Mr. S. Schechter, Reader in Rabbinic in the Cambridge University, I learned in years gone by my first real lessons in research ; he introduced me to authorities, he gave me facts from the store-house of his memory, and theories from the spring of his original thought.　To him my final word of thanks is affectionately offered.

July, 1896.

CONTENTS

CHAPTER I

THE CENTRE OF SOCIAL LIFE

CHAPTER II

LIFE IN THE SYNAGOGUE

CHAPTER III

COMMUNAL ORGANIZATION

CHAPTER IV

INSTITUTION OF THE GHETTO

CHAPTER V

SOCIAL MORALITY

CHAPTER VI

THE SLAVE TRADE

Contents

CHAPTER XXII

MEDIEVAL PASTIMES (*continued*). CHESS AND CARDS

CHAPTER XXIII

PERSONAL RELATIONS BETWEEN JEWS AND CHRISTIANS

CHAPTER XXIV

PERSONAL RELATIONS (*continued*). LITERARY FRIENDSHIPS

INTRODUCTION

THE expression 'middle ages' is often employed in a very elastic sense, but as applied to the inner life of the Jews it has little or no relevancy. There was neither more nor less medievalism about Jewish life in the ninth than there was in the fourteenth century. If medievalism implies moral servitude to a Church and material servitude to a polity, — a polity known in one form as Imperialism and in another as feudalism, — the Jews had no opportunity for the latter and no inclination for the former. The Synagogue was the centre of life, but it was not the custodian of thought. If Judaism ever came to exercise a tyranny over the Jewish mind, it did so not in the middle ages at all, but in the middle of the sixteenth century. A revolt against medievalism such as occurred in Europe during and at the close of the Renaissance may be said to have marked Jewish life towards the close of the eighteenth century.

But this absence of medievalism from Jewish life is quite consistent with the fact that medievalism produced lasting effects on the Jews. On the Jews, the old feudal manners left traces which endured long after Europe had grown to modern ways. As Europe emerges from the medieval period, the Jews pass more and more emphatically into *a special relation towards the government*. Instead of becoming a part of the general population, as the Jews had often been in the earlier centuries of the Christian era, they are thrust out of the general life into a distinct category. One has but to compare the Prayer for the Queen as it still appears in the Anglo-Jewish ritual with its form in the Book of Common Prayer. 'May the supreme King of kings,' says the Jewish version, 'in his mercy put compassion into her heart and into the hearts of her counsellors and nobles, that they may deal kindly with us and with all Israel.' The modern Jew resents this language, but it cannot be denied that its medieval tone remains the keynote of millions of Jewish lives. In Russia to-day the Jews are subject to special, distinctive legislation similar to that under which Jews groaned everywhere from the thirteenth to the eighteenth centuries. At the moment of writing, news comes to hand of a promised amelioration of the circumstances of the Russian Jews. 'It is generally understood,' says the Odessa correspondent of the *Daily News* for July 4, 'that this latest reopening of the Russo-Hebrew question is chiefly due to the generous and sympathetic instincts of the young Empress.' Here, then, we have the old medieval position reproduced. The chattel of the ruler, the Jews had no room for hope but in the ruler's personal clemency and humanity. The fact that this state of things survived all over Europe up to the era of the French Revolution, added to the circumstance that in the sixteenth to eighteenth centuries the Jews fell under a subservience to Rabbinical authority and custom which can only be described as medieval, rendered it impossible for me to confine my attention to the life of the Jews in the middle ages proper. Though, however, I have freely carried on the story in some direction to the beginning of the eighteenth century, I have for the most part avoided details which belong to periods later than the fifteenth century. The great bulk of the material used is far older than this. But I hope that I shall be pardoned for sometimes passing the limits assigned by the most liberal interpretation to the expression 'middle ages.'

Partly by good fortune, the Jews influenced European life in the middle ages proper, despite their exceptional treatment. The year 1492 was the very culminating point of the Renaissance. In 1492 the expedition of Charles VIII to Naples opened Italy to French, Spanish, and German influences. But in the same year the Jews were also driven in large numbers to the Italian coasts, for 1492 by a strange coincidence saw at once some Jews steering Columbus to the New World across the ocean, and others cast adrift from their beloved Spain. How much these Spanish

exiles did for the culture of northern Europe has never yet been
fully told. Baruch Spinoza was but the most eminent of many
influential personalities. In England Jewish influence was
spiritual, not personal. There were no Jews round the table of
King James I's compilers of the Authorized Version, but David
Kimchi was present in spirit. The influence of his Commentary
on the Bible is evident on every page of that noble translation.

It is more important to consider the position of the Jews in
the earlier stages of the progress from old to new forms of life in
Europe. That the Jews played a large part in the transmission of
the Graeco-Arabic philosophy from Islam to Christianity is unanimously admitted. Judaism here filled the mother's function in
seeking to reconcile her two daughters in the spirit. We must
speak less confidently of the Jewish influence on the great
European Universities. But while these remained cosmopolitan,
as they did till the beginning of the fifteenth century, it is obvious
that their doors were not closely shut against Jews and Jewish
ideas. The older Universities were not created by clerics, though
their charters were subsequently confirmed from Rome. ' To the
Jews,' says Professor Andrew White in his recent *Warfare of
Science with Theology* (ii. 33), ' is largely due the building up of
the School of Salerno, which we find flourishing in the tenth
century. . . . Still more important is the rise of the School of
Montpellier ; this was due almost entirely to Jewish physicians,
and it developed medical studies to a yet higher point, doing
much to create a medical profession worthy of the name throughout southern Europe.' Mr. Rashdall, on the other hand, in his
Universities of Europe in the Middle Ages (i. 80), asserts that
Salerno was in its origin, and long continued to be, entirely independent of Oriental influences. But Mr. Rashdall admits (ibid.
p. 85) that ' by the beginning of the fourteenth century Arabic
medicine (i.e. Jewish medicine) was everywhere in full possession
of the Medical Faculties.' Nor was this restricted to Italy. Among
the books prescribed in the Statute of the Faculty of Medicine of
the Paris University, circ. 1270, were ' the works of the Jewish
physician Isaac ' (op. cit. i. 429). It is not easy for a layman
to steer a safe course between these conflicting statements, but

I cannot think that Mr. Rashdall has done justice to Jewish physicians when he dismisses their claims in these words : ' The most valuable Arabic contributions to medicine were chiefly in the region of Medical Botany. The Arabs added some new remedies to the medieval Pharmacopeia, but against their services in this respect must be set their extensive introduction of Astro-logical and Alchemistic fancies into the theory and practice of Medicine.' The researches of Dr. Steinschneider, which seem to have been entirely overlooked by recent writers, would make one pause before accepting this sweeping indictment. If there was one characteristic excellence in Jewish medicine in the middle ages, it was precisely its dependence, not on authority or mystery, but on actual trial or experiment. ' Do not apply a remedy which thou hast not thoroughly tested,' wrote Judah Ibn Tibbon for his son's guidance in the twelfth century. Jewish doctors were placed under such strict and jealous surveillance that they urged one another ' never to use a cure the efficacy of which they could not prove by scientific reasons.' The assertion that the great Jewish doctors of the middle ages were alchemists and astrologers is very far indeed from the truth. So imperfectly are the facts yet known with regard to Jewish scientists in the middle ages, that I feel convinced that further information will render it necessary to revise such strictures as I have made (on p. 234 below) on the unscientific tastes of French Jews. Mr. C. Trice Martin, of the Record Office, informs me that he has found documents proving that Franco-Jewish doctors were in repute in England before the thirteenth century — a fact which implies more knowledge of medicine among French Jews than I have allowed for.

I have written at some length on this subject, for it is obviously of great moment to realize how much or how little the European movements of the middle ages were affected by Jewish influences. It seems to me that far too slighting an attitude is now fashion-able towards the function of intermediation. That the Jews were the great scientific, commercial, and philosophical intermediaries of the middle ages is not denied. But what is not usually admitted is, how much of progress consists simply in the trans-

mission of ideas and the exchange of articles of commerce. Take
the great medieval University of Paris. This became the home
of Scholasticism, but, says Mr. Rashdall (p. 354), 'Aristotle came
to Paris in an orientalized dress.' The matter went far deeper
than the dress, however. The intellectual movement in the
maturity of the nations of Europe was everywhere preceded by
a revolt against the Church. In France the revolt occurred in
the twelfth and thirteenth centuries, and is associated with the
Albigensian heresy. In England the fourteenth century saw the
rise of Lollardism ; in Bohemia the real foundation of the great
Prague University was connected, in the fifteenth century, with
the reforms of the Hussites. Now the second of these movements
was, from the theological point of view, undoubtedly a Judaic
reaction. As to the first and third, it is sufficient to say that
the ruling powers regarded the Jews as the fomenters of the
movements, and paid them in bloody coin for their assumed
participation. To assert for the Jews this claim — that they were
intermediaries of ideas as well as commercial products — is,
I submit, to claim for them a great and not ignoble rôle. The
old familiar notion that the medieval Jew was a ghoul solely
occupied with usury and other blood-sucking pastimes, has been
too often shattered to need a word of further argument. The
real services of Jews to commerce have, however, I hope been
made a little clearer in the course of the present work. Those
who would prefer to read some of the story in the work of
a Christian writer may be recommended to Bédarride's interesting
treatise on *Les Juifs en France, en Italie, et en Espagne* (2d
ed. 1861).

Perhaps of more importance to the Jews themselves is the
reverse phase of this relation. An explanation of certain defects
of Jewish life is often sought in the generalization that the
Jews of the middle ages were what the middle ages made them.
In truth the effect of external pressure was negative rather than
positive. The Jews suffered more from the dispiriting calms of
life within the ghetto than from the passionate storms of death that
raged without it. The anti-social crusade of the medieval Church
against the Jews did more than slay its thousands. It deprived

the Jews of the very conditions necessary for the full development of their genius. The Jewish nature does not produce its rarest fruits in a Jewish environment. I am far from asserting that Judaism is a force so feeble that its children sink into decay so soon as they are robbed of the influence of forces foreign to itself. But it was ancient Alexandria that produced Philo, medieval Spain Maimonides, modern Amsterdam Spinoza. The ghetto had its freaks, but the men just named were not born in ghettos. And how should it be otherwise? The Jew who should influence the world could not arise in the absence of a world to influence. You cannot tie a knot without a cord; you cannot be an intermediary if you have no extremes to join. The Jewish genius is not of the kind that plants its seed, and leaves it for the silent centuries to assimilate it and mature its fruits. It needs living hearts for its soil, and the whole world is only wide enough to provide them. The defects of the Jewish character prove this as well as its virtues. Most of its defects are the result either of isolation, or of reaction after isolation.

Jews themselves are rather weary of the discovery that there nevertheless was life within the walls of the ghettos; life with ideals and aspirations; with passions, and even human nature. Abraham Ibn Ezra, four centuries before Shakespeare, protested that a Jew has eyes; but somehow it has needed Mr. Zangwill to rediscover this for the English world. I confess that in this book I have ventured to take so much for granted. Mr. Zangwill's real discovery is not that there was life, but that there was independent life. It is true that the Jewish mind does not reach its highest in a narrow environment, but it does reach its most characteristic. Several times in the course of this work the familiar contrast has been drawn between the Jews of Spain and those of northern Europe, mostly to the advantage of the former. But it is a striking fact that the 'German' Jews, more characteristically Jewish than their Spanish brethren, ended by gaining control of the whole of European Judaism. The Jewish schools in the Rhineland flourished not, as in Moorish Spain, in imitation of neighbouring illumination, but in contrast to surrounding obscurantism. There was no Christian University in Germany till the middle of

the fourteenth century, but the Rhine-lands had what were practically Jewish Universities in the era of the first Crusade. In
northern Europe generally an age of friars succeeded an age of
monks, and this further made Judaism more Jewish. For the
friars rendered splendid services to education, but their interest
in education was not intellectual. It was purely religious; it was
a means to an end. Hence the very friars who helped Christian
Europe to the Universities drove the Jews into ghettos, in the
hopes of securing for the first, and torturing from the latter,
a saving belief in the dogmas of the Church. The cosmopolitanism of the older European Universities of Bologna and
Paris might have resisted this narrowing of the University ideal,
but in the fifteenth century a provincial spirit grew in Europe, and
the result was — national Universities. The brilliant intellectual
promise of the twelfth-century Renaissance fell before the influence
of the friars and of the national erections which replaced feudalism.
There were no crowds of foreign students at Bologna and Paris in
the fifteenth century, as there had been in the more illustrious
youth of those centres of medieval learning. If feudalism had
no obvious place for the Jews, the nationalism of the fifteenth
century had no place at all for them. The nineteenth century
has seen a new reaction towards local patriotisms, and the intense
territorial nationalism of to-day once more protests against the
possibility of the assimilation of different races into one nationality.
Hence modern anti-Semitism — fanned no doubt by certain
obvious Jewish failings, but fuelled by the provincial fifteenth-
century conception of what a *nation* means.

The effect of this on the Jews was obvious. Great religious
movements, or at least new aspects of old ones, distinguished
Jewish life, but these influenced only the Jews themselves, not
the world at large. Mr. Schechter, in his *Studies in Judaism*, has
recently proved that the religious horizon of the Jews was a very
wide one in the seventeenth and eighteenth centuries. It is
curious that the movements which Mr. Schechter describes all
emanated from the 'German' Jews: from Jews who were not
uninfluenced by foreign ideas, but who were not moved or
dominated by them. The original thought of these Jews was

born with them; but it did not take to travelling. In brief, Judaism, with no hope and no dream of territorial nationalism, nationalized itself. I confess that when I undertook to write of Jewish life in the middle ages, I did so under the impression that Jewish life was everywhere more or less similar, and that it would be possible to present a generic image of it. Deeper research has completely dispelled this belief. Possibly the reader may note with disappointment that my book reveals no central principle, that it is a survey less of Jewish life than of Jewish lives. What misled me into attempting the impossible task of which this work is the result was my perception that, since the fifteenth century, Judaism has worn the same family face all over Europe. But in the middle ages this was certainly not the case. Judaism, I repeat, became nationalized by the fall of feudalism and the rise of the ghettos. The superficial appearance of a national entity has, I fear, originated the movement now popular with some modern Jews in favour of creating a Jewish state, politically independent and perhaps religiously homogeneous. I speak regretfully, because one does not like to see enthusiasm wasted over a conception which has no roots in the past and no fruits to offer for the future. The idealized love of Zion which grew up in the middle ages had no connexion whatever with this process of nationalization through, which Judaism passed. Still less was it connected with an aspiration for religious homogeneity which did not exist in the middle ages, and is not likely to survive in Judaism now that it has once more become denationalized. National aspirations are nursed by persecution, but the medieval longing for the Holy Land grew up not in persecution, but in the sunshine of literature. The Spanish-Jewish poet, to use Heine's famous figure, came to love Jerusalem as the medieval troubadour loved his lady, and the love grew with the lays. Jehuda Halevi uses the very language of medieval love in this passionate address to his ' woe-begone darling.'

> O ! who will lead me on
> To seek the spots where, in far-distant years,
> The angels in their glory dawned upon
> Thy messengers and seers ?

> O! who will give me wings
> That I may fly away,
> And there, at rest from all my wanderings,
> The ruins of my heart among thy ruins lay?

The same Jehuda Halevi who sings thus, declared that Israel was to the nations as the heart to the body — not a nation of the nations, but a vitalizing element to them all.

The change in point of view between Jewish life in the middle ages and in the sixteenth century is well represented in a curious literary phenomenon, viz. the Rabbinical correspondence. If my book be found to possess any originality, it will, I venture to think, be due to the extensive use I have made of the facts revealed in the Responsa literature. The Geonim of Persia who swayed Judaism during the seventh to the eleventh century, and their spiritual successors the Rabbis of North Africa and Spain, carried on a world-wide correspondence. The Answers which they made to questions addressed to them constitute one of the most fertile sources of information for Jewish life in the middle ages. I have explained in a prefatory note to the first Index the use which I have made of these Rabbinical Responses, but a word or two may here be added in illustration of what precedes. The Responses of the later French and German Jews are far more local. Meir of Rothenburg was probably a greater man with a greater mind than some of his Spanish contemporaries, but the latter corresponded with a far wider circle of Jews. True, the codification of Jewish law was inaugurated by Spanish Jews in the 'golden age,' but the Code which finally became the accepted guide of Judaism was the work of the sixteenth century. Codification implies the suppression of local variation, but in the Responsa of the later French and German Rabbis there is already far less heterogeneity of habits than in the Responsa of the Spanish Jews, and certainly of the Geonim. And this is quite natural. If your horizon is narrow, you regard your own conduct as the only normal or praiseworthy scheme of life. Hence, without any conscious resolve to suppress varying customs, these were as a matter of fact much contracted by the local tendencies of the great French Rabbis who became the authority for all Judaism from the fourteenth century onwards. After the end of the twelfth century, even the Spanish Jews relied on their German brethren for guidance in the Talmud. Before, however, a temporary phase of rigidity set in, an era of dissolution intervened. At the end of the fifteenth century local custom was in a very chaotic condition among the Jews, and I have attempted to describe some of the disorganizing effects of it on p. 160 below. Joseph Caro's Code came at an opportune moment. The *Shulchan Aruch* had the good fortune to be written in the age of printing. Compiled in the middle of the sixteenth century, this Code was printed within a decade of its completion and revision by the author. It stimulated that uniformity of religious and social life which was being slowly produced by the German school of Rabbis in earlier centuries. I say social as well as religious uniformity, for the age of the ghettos was the age in which Jewish law most strongly regulated Jewish life. We see in modern times what some Jews lamentingly call a recrudescence of the old chaos, but what is in reality a return to the old cosmopolitanism. It is a process of denationalizing Judaism as a whole in proportion to the nationalization of various groups of Jews in the local patriotisms of the world. It is a completely natural process though its excesses be unnatural, and, to close with a paradox, if not medieval, it strikes the same note of freedom which sounded through the Judaism of the middle ages. This freedom is quite consistent with devotion to the same great ideals, for heterogeneity is the first mark of universalism.

JEWISH LIFE IN THE MIDDLE AGES

CHAPTER I

THE CENTRE OF SOCIAL LIFE

THE medieval life of the Jews had for its centre the synagogue. The concentration of the Jewish populations into separate quarters of Christian and Moslem towns was initially an accident of Jewish communal life. The Jewish quarter seems to have grown up round the synagogue, which was thus the centre of Jewish life, locally as well as religiously.

This concentration round the synagogue may be noted in the social as well as in the material life of the middle ages. The synagogue tended, with ever-increasing rapidity, to absorb and to develop the social life of the community, both when Jews enjoyed free intercourse with their neighbours of other faiths, and when this intercourse was restricted to the narrowest possible bounds. It was the political emancipation, which the close of the eighteenth century witnessed, that first loosened the hold of the synagogue on Jewish life. Emancipation so changed the complexion of that life that the Jewish middle ages cannot

be considered to have ended until the French Revolution
was well in sight. But throughout the middle ages proper
the synagogue held undisputed sway in all the concerns
of Jews. Nor was this absorption a new phenomenon.
Already in Judea the Temple had assumed some social
functions. The tendency first reveals itself amid the
enthusiasm of the Maccabean revival, when the Jews felt
drawn to the house of prayer for social as well as for
religious communion. The Temple itself became the
scene of some festal gatherings which were only in a
secondary sense religious in character.[1] Political meetings were held within its precincts.[2] Its courts resounded
on occasion with cries for the redress of grievances.[3] King
and Rabbi alike addressed the assembled Israelites under
the Colonnade, which was joined to the Temple by a
bridge.[4]

The synagogue in the middle ages filled a place at once
larger and smaller than the Temple. In the middle ages
politics only rarely invaded the synagogue. Bad government, in the Jewish view, was incompatible with the
kingdom of God,[5] but the Jews learned from bitter experience that they must often render unto Caesar the
things that were God's. The Jews of the middle ages
may have been alive to the current corruption, but they
readily administered the public trusts which were sometimes committed to their care. Though they doubtless
used their power at times to the advantage of their co-
religionists, the Jewish holders of financial offices enjoyed
a high, if rather 'unpopular,' reputation for fidelity to

---

[1] Josephus, *Wars*, V. 5.   [2] *Wars*, I. 20.
[3] *Wars*, II. 1.   [4] *Wars*, II. 16.
[5] See S. Schechter, *Jewish Quarterly Review*, vii. p. 209.

their royal employers. Their honesty, as well as their amenability to kingly pressure, may be inferred from the frequency which they were entrusted with confidential posts in Spain and Italy. But the despotic government of the middle ages entailed an insecurity of political status which prevented Jews from participating much in the discussion of public affairs. The Jews gained nothing and lost much by their courageous partisanship of Don Pedro of Castile against his half-brother Henry de Trastamara (1350–1369).[1] Santob de Carrion, a Jewish troubadour of that age, compiled moral and political maxims for the king, but such an incident could hardly be paralleled. The Jews, on the other hand, frequently joined the general population in patriotic movements ; but beyond the regular recitation of a prayer for the sovereign,[2] politics were excluded from the liturgy. Occasionally, special prayers were inserted which involved a partisan attitude on questions of the day. Thus in 1188 the Jews of Canterbury prayed for the monks as against the archbishop in a local dispute.[3] At a much later date, the Jews of Rome erected a trophy in front of one of their synagogues in honour of the temporary establishment of a republican government.[4]

Such instances of political partisanship finding expression in the synagogue were rare in the middle ages, for even under the most favourable circumstances the Jews were subject to sudden and sweeping changes in their relations to the government. But it would be an error to suppose that this fact carried with it as a corollary the exclusion

[1] See Graetz, *History of the Jews* (Eng. Trans.), IV. ch. iv.
[2] Cf. Philo, *Flacc.* § 7.
[3] J. Jacobs, *Jews of Angevin England*, p. 93.
[4] Berliner, *Geschichte der Juden in Rom*, II. ii. p. 120.

from the synagogue of wide and comprehensive social interests. The seventeenth was the gloomiest century in the pre-emancipation history of the Jews, but until the beginning of the sixteenth century they were never for long cut off from the common life around them. Nay, their interests were wider than those of their environment, for they had the exceptional interest of a common religion destitute of a political centre. It is hard to exaggerate the importance of this factor in moulding Jewish life. Thus was begotten that cosmopolitanism which broke through the walls of the ghettos, and prevented the life passed within them from ever becoming quite narrow or sordid.

It was the synagogue that made this influence effective. Owing to the love of travel innate in the Jewish consciousness and stimulated by repeated expulsions, the Jew of many an isolated place became familiar with the manners of foreign co-religionists who would find their way to the local synagogues. The vehicles of this moral traffic were travelling preachers and teachers, bringing new ideas and quaint information as to passing events; beggar-students who, when the conquering Moslems, and later on the Christian Crusaders, demolished the schools in one town, found their way to other schools of repute whereat to continue their studies; merchants and artisans who plodded many a weary mile in search of work,[1] and brought with them new fashions and new handicrafts; strolling cantors who would be hailed by the many for their new hymns and new tunes; pious pilgrims who had set out from home for the Holy Land with but a hazy perception of the length and difficulty of their pro-

[1] E. H. Lindo, *The Jews of Spain and Portugal*, p. 318.

posed journey, but imbued with a rich fund of enthusiasm idealized and communicable ; professional wayfarers, who would bring, by word of mouth or by letter, the moral influence of great Rabbinical authorities, who, with no organized power outside their own local congregations, yet imparted their inspiration to a widespread circle, centring now in Babylon, now in Cordova, at one time in Cairo, at another in the Rhine country ; excited mystics who carried confused but rousing tales of the wondrous doings of ever-new claimants to the Messiahship, and fanned that smouldering dream of an ideal future which brightened the present hideous reality and made it tolerable.

Thus Jewish life was not narrow, though its *locale* was limited. As a legalized institution the ghetto itself was unknown till the beginning of the sixteenth century, the Venetian and Roman ghettos being erected almost con-temporaneously at that period. Hence the predominance of the synagogue in medieval Judaism cannot be alto-gether attributed to the isolation of Jews from the social life of their contemporaries. There were, indeed, influ-ences enough at work to drive the Jews from the world. For centuries they were legally barred from professional careers and honourable trades, though individual Jews contrived to overleap the barriers ; they were forced to become usurers, though at first fully conscious of the obloquy attaching to a traffic banned by the Church and despised by the men of honour of all peoples in all ages. The cruellest result which persecution worked was to produce insensibility to this obloquy on the part of many Israelites. But all these attempts to isolate the Jews from the rest of mankind only partially succeeded. Even when

the persistent efforts of Innocent III had spent themselves
in branding the Jews as a race outside the pale of humanity, when the Inquisition had done its worst, when
the Black Death had spread its baleful cloud between
Jew and Gentile, still the former shared something of the
general life. In Spain and Italy this participation is most
clearly marked, but until the sixteenth century the Jews
were nowhere entirely divorced from the ordinary national
life.

   But this general life lacked centralization. This statement may be illustrated by the phenomenon that no
country in the middle ages possessed a national drama.
National drama needs a national centre, and not even the
concentrating genius of a Charles the Great could bring
homogeneity into the heterogeneous mass over which he
ruled. This lack of a common basis for national life became more marked when feudalism and chivalry fell. The
seething thirteenth and fourteenth centuries show us
national life in the making, not national life made. The
Crescent and the Cross had not yet divided the civilized
world between them. Until the beginning of the sixteenth
century the Jews were hardly subjected to those deep-cut
national prejudices which thenceforward barred them from
the world until the era of the French Revolution. The
only serious exclusion that the Jews suffered occurred at
the Renaissance. Except in Italy the Jews shared little
of the elevating effects which the Renaissance produced.
The causes of this anomaly will be examined hereafter,
but in the middle ages proper, Jewish life, with all the
innate 'provincialism' from which it has never, in all
its long and chequered history, contrived to free itself,
was freshened and affected by every influence of the time,

and the Synagogue, like the Church, attracted to itself and focussed these influences, providing a centre which the ordinary life of the nations failed to create. The life within the synagogue reflected the social life of the Jews in all its essential features. In northern and central Europe, no pursuit or interest was honourable, in the synagogue as in the church, unless it had some religious flavouring. The liturgy of the synagogue created social custom, and the reaction of the latter on the former was at least equally great. Amid a world in which might was right, the Jews learned from their common oppression to respect each other's rights. Any Jew who conceived that he had a grievance against his fellow had the privilege to interrupt the synagogue service until he had gained a public promise of redress.[1] Naturally this privilege was open to abuse, and the right was restricted and eventually suppressed.[2] Whether the synagogue was the scene of flagellations for offences against the moral and religious codes is open to question. Probably this punishment was inflicted in the synagogue precincts, and the statements that the apostles were liable to be 'beaten in the synagogues'[3] may be literally true. It is certain that in the early middle ages flagellation took place in the Beth Din (Jewish Court of Justice),[4] but on the day preceding the Great Fast a symbolical scourging was,[5] and even is, usual in the synagogue itself. When Uriel Acosta did penance in Amsterdam in 1633 he was publicly flogged in the synagogue, but in a retired corner, not on

[1] *Kolbo*, ed. Rimini, fol. 134 a, § 116.
[2] See the quotations in Güdemann's *Quellenschriften*, p. 85.
[3] Matthew x. 17, Mark xiii. 9. Cf. Vitringa, *De Synagoga*, p. 768.
[4] Müller, *Index (Mafteach) to the Responsa of the Geonim*, p. 192.
[5] Maharil, section on *Day of Atonement*.

the central platform. As the culprit always had to strip
to the waist, it was probably regarded as indecorous to
execute the sentence *coram populo*. It was thought no
irreverence, however, to use the synagogue for all kinds
of announcements concerning the just payment of dues.
So fully was this fact understood by the governments of
Europe that it was occasionally utilized for their own purposes. In the thirteenth century, for instance, the English Government compelled the Jews to announce in their
synagogues quittances of debts owing by Christians. In
Spain, by the Castilian Code of 1212, Jews were in certain
cases, in which stolen apparel and furniture had been
pledged with them by Christians, to swear on oath in
synagogue that the transaction had been honest in intention.[1] The ordinary Spaniard made public proclamations
of this nature, not in church but in the squares and market-
places.[2] In Rome, at a later date, it seems that a list of
articles stolen during the year was read out on the eve of
the Day of Atonement to warn Jews against buying or in
any way dealing with the stolen goods.[3] But the voluntary
announcements of this kind were at least as numerous as
the enforced. The inter-communal organization, which
will be described in another chapter, required the periodical proclamation in synagogue of the *Tekanoth*, or Ordinances, which everywhere regulated the moral and social
no less than the religious life of the Jews.

It was an ancient custom in several places for the Shamash or verger to announce every Saturday the results of

---

[1] On the other hand the Cortes of Tarragona in 1234 enacted: 'The oath
is not to be taken in the synagogue or a private place, but in a court of justice,
or the place where oaths are administered to Christians.'

[2] Lindo, p. 118.

[3] Berliner, op. cit. ii. (2), p. 202.

law-suits, and to inform the congregation that certain properties were in the market.[1] The Jews did not exclude their every-day life from the sphere of religion, and felt rather that their business was hallowed by its association with the synagogue than that the synagogue was degraded by the intrusion of worldly concerns. The following incident is typical.[2] Rabbi Meir Halevi of Vienna once had to deal with a Jew who showed a disposition to go back on a business bargain which he had only verbally assented to. This fourteenth-century Rabbi privately remonstrated with the delinquent, but finding him still contumelious, ordered the officiating Reader to make the following public announcement in the synagogue: ' Hear all present, that A. B. refuses to abide by his word, given under such and such circumstances ; thereby he has excited the displeasure of the Rabbis and is unworthy to be regarded as a member of the congregation of Israel, to whom dishonesty and falsehood are an abomination, but A. B. is a liar and a deceiver.' The same moral sensitiveness is manifested in a large class of synagogue announcements, the introduction of which must have begun in the earlier middle ages, though the traces of their existence become more obvious as the eighteenth century approaches. The compulsory institution at Rome of an annual proclamation of stolen goods is less important than the voluntary custom to the same effect which prevailed somewhat later in Frankfort.[3] The

---

[1] Chayim Benveniste in his *Responsa*, § 16, calls it ' an old custom.' R. David Abi Zimri (Radbaz) found the custom established in North Africa, but he suppressed the announcement of sales on Sabbath (Neubauer, *Medieval Jewish Chronicles*, i. p. 158). Cf. Isaac b. Sheshet, *Responsa*, § 388.

[2] Güdemann, *Geschichte des Erziehungswesens und der Cultur der abendländischen Juden*, iii. p. 55.

[3] Schudt, B. VI. § 34. That this was a very old custom may be seen from *Leviticus Rabba*, ch. vi.

' Schulklopfer,' an official of whom more will be said hereafter, took his stand before the ark, proclaimed that certain articles had been stolen or lost, and solemnly ordered
that any worshipper who knew anything of the property
must give instant information to the authorities. Lost
articles were publicly cried in synagogue, and a threat
of excommunication hung over all who withheld information.[1] There is evidence of an earlier custom due to
an even higher sense of honesty. At the end of the
thirteenth century it was necessary for a man who was
about to leave any town in Italy, to publicly announce in
synagogue that he was leaving, and to invite those who
had claims against him to proffer them.[2] Money disputes
were similarly dealt with. Any individual might rise in
his place in synagogue and call upon the congregants to
come forward with evidence on his behalf.[3] It will be more
convenient, however, to deal with other examples of these
synagogue regulations in another connexion, for they belong to the communal organization. Only one other instance will be quoted, because it relates to a custom still
prevalent in some Jewish congregations.[4] ' In our place,
when a man wishes to sell any land, a proclamation is
made in the synagogue three times : " Whoever has any
claim on this land must lay his claim before the Rabbinical
tribunal (Beth Din)." Hereafter, no claim is admitted,
and a record of the threefold proclamation in synagogue
is inserted in the deed of sale.'

It will easily be inferred that the synagogue was freely

[1] Maharil, section on *Ten Ways of Penitence*. Cf. Shulchan Aruch, *Choshen Mishpat*, § 267.

[2] Tashbats, *Responsa*, i. § 11, and iii. § 231.

[3] Shulchan Aruch, ibid. § 28.

[4] *Responsa*, Har Hakarmel, Choshen Mishpat, § 12.

used to enforce obedience to other aspects of the moral law than strict commercial honesty. The conjugal rights of husbands,[1] the prerogatives of fathers with regard to their daughters' marriages, and their claims on their sons' obedience,[2] the duty of women to observe the laws of purity,[3] the obligation to make an honest estimate of one's income in paying the communal taxes[4] which were rated at various percentages, the recital of a special benediction for those who never used bad language nor gossiped during prayer[5] — these are a few instances culled from many in which the synagogue was made a powerful lever to elevate the social morality of the people.

This desirable end was attained with conspicuous success by another feature of the Jewish medieval life. Every Jew found his joy and his sorrow in all Jews' joys and sorrows. He took a personal interest in the family life of the community, for the community was in a very real sense of the word one united and rather inquisitive family. This may be illustrated from an old eastern Jewish custom which had already become stereotyped in Europe by the eleventh century.[6] On the Sabbath following a wedding, the bridegroom attended synagogue accompanied by a concourse of friends. He ascended the reading-desk during the recitation of the weekly portion of the Pentateuch, and as he walked from his place the assembled worshippers, whether related to him or not, broke forth into gleeful Hebrew songs expressing a fourfold greeting

[1] Tashbats, ii. 175.
[2] A very old custom. See Buber's *Tanchuma*, p. לה.
[3] Maimonides, *Responsa*, § 149.
[4] Cf. ch. xvii. below.
[5] Worms, *Pinkas*. See *Jewish Chronicle*, 1850, p. 18.
[6] *Machzor Vitry*, p. 596.

in the name of God, the Law, the Rabbis, and the people.
One such poem — and it is only an average instance —
concludes with these lines :[1] —

> Rejoice, O Bridegroom, in the wife of thy youth, thy comrade!
> Let thy heart be merry now and when thou shalt grow old.
> Sons to thy sons shalt thou see, thine old age's crown;
> Sons who shall prosper and work in place of their pious sires.
> Thy days in good shall be spent, thy years in pleasantness.
> Floweth thy peace as a stream, riseth thy worth as its waves,
> For Peace shall be found in thy home, Rest shall abide in thy dwelling.
> Blessed be each day's work, blessed be thine all,
> And thy bliss this assembly shall share, happy in thee.
> By grace of us all ascend, thou and thy goodly company ;
> Rise we, too, to our feet, lovingly to greet thee ;
> One hope is now in all hearts, one prayer we utter,
> Blessed be thy coming in, blessed be thy going forth.

It would need a very long chapter to collect anything
like a complete list of the synagogal gaieties which accompanied a wedding.   The presence of a bridegroom was
sufficient to cause the excision from the daily prayer of the
passages associated with sorrow.   The ceremony of circumcision was another occasion on which the community
shared a private joy.   So, too, private sorrows were shared,
and a mourner would come to synagogue and be received
with formal expressions of sympathy.   So acutely did all
feel every man's grief, that many objected to the recital of
prayers for the sick on the Sabbath, lest the congregation
be moved to tears on a day which should be all joy.[2]   For
a similar reason no *hesped*, or eulogy of a deceased worthy,
was allowed on the Sabbath day.   Much sympathy was
shown to penitent apostates, and the road back to Judaism
was always made easy in the middle ages by the Jews,
despite that they knew full well the risks which their

---

[1] *Monatsschrift, für Gesch. u. Wissen. d. Judenth*, xxxix. p. 325.
[2] Talmud, Sabbath, ch. i. and Caro, *Abkath Rochel*, § 11.

conduct submitted them to of wholesale persecution and possibly martyrdom. In this respect considerable advance, in point of generous forgetfulness, may be detected as the middle ages advance,[1] for, somewhat earlier, the resentment against returned apostates was unworthily severe.[2] Reverts, at all events in the later middle ages, were admitted to synagogue honours,[3] and though little countenance was shown to the victims of communal excommunication, though no one would come within four paces of them, yet even in the older and more severe days, they were permitted to attend public worship,[4] the rite of the Abrahamic covenant was allowed to their infant sons, and they themselves were buried with sacred rites, but stones were placed on their coffins.[5]

That the communal grief as well as the communal joy on historical anniversaries should lead to outbursts of poignant lamentation or of unbounded merriment goes without saying. Local fasts and feasts, which were not uncommon in the middle ages, perhaps supplied that political element which the Jewish life lacked, for these celebrations mostly turned on events connected with the local politics in so far as they affected the Jews. More pathetic than the fasts themselves were the martyrologies and elegies recited in the synagogue.[6] These sad records are scattered over the medieval history of the Jews with

[1] Cf. particularly *Responsa* of M. Melammed, ii. 9.

[2] Müller, *Mafteach*, p. 8. But contrast *Machzor Vitry*, § 125.

[3] *Responsa*, Chacham Zebi, § 112.

[4] Cf. Müller, *Mafteach*, p. 281.

[5] The last custom was abolished in the middle ages, but was prevalent in the tenth century. Cf. *Shaare Teshuba*, § 41.

[6] Zunz, *Die synagogale Poesie des Mittelalters*, chapter on *Leiden*. An Eng. trans. of this chapter appeared in Publ. of the Soc. of Heb. Literature, Part I. 1872.

an all too lavish hand ; persecution and cruelty, even unto death, knew no bounds of time or place. But the recital of these elegies generated heroic endurance in the worshipper's mind rather than vindictiveness ; they were a call to courage and devotion, and if they appealed to God for revenge, the revenge was idealized almost as much as were the sorrows that demanded it.

> Thy son is once more sold,
> Redeem him, bring Thou relief!
> In mercy say again : My son,
> I know, I know thy grief.[1]

Sometimes the cry for vengeance is harsher than this, but the Jewish poets of the middle ages would have been less than men had they been able to look on unmoved at the murderous attacks from which even the synagogue itself could not protect her sons. Yet these laments were elevating and ennobling. They moved ordinary men and women to play the parts of heroes ; they made devoted priests of them,[2] ready to sacrifice their children to save them from apostasy ; they inspired them with courage to endure all things for that which they held more precious than all things.

> By sorrow's yoke distressed,
> More joy from Him I gain
> Than if rewards of men
> Were glittering on my breast.[3]

A martyr's widow usually remained faithful to his memory : indeed, the re-marriage of such a woman would have outraged the public opinion of any Jewish community in the middle ages.

---

[1] Zunz, *Die synagogale Poesie des Mittelalters*, loc. cit.
[2] The fathers are often compared to priests in these elegies.
[3] Zunz, ibid.

CHAPTER II

LIFE IN THE SYNAGOGUE

THE attitude of the medieval Jew towards his House of God was characteristic of his attitude towards life. Though the Jew and the Greek gave very different expressions to the conception, the Jew shared with the Greek a belief in the essential unity of life amidst its detailed obligations. It is not enough to say that the Jew's religion absorbed his life, for in quite as real a sense his life absorbed his religion. Hence the synagogue was not a mere place in which he prayed, it was a place in which he lived; and just as life has its earnest and its frivolous moments, so the Jew in synagogue was at times rigorously reverent and at others quite at his ease. In this respect no doubt the medieval Church agreed with the Synagogue. 'Be one of the first in synagogue,' writes a fourteenth-century Jew in his last testament to his children. 'Do not speak during prayers, but repeat the responses, and after the service do acts of kindness. . . . Wash me clean, comb my hair as in my lifetime, in order that I may go clean to my eternal resting place, just as I used to go every Sabbath evening to the synagogue.' [1] This writer's sensitiveness was by no means exceptional. Medieval

[1] *Jewish Quarterly Review*, iii. p. 463.

Europe was insanitary and dirty, and the Jewish quarters
were in many respects the dirtiest. Epidemics made
havoc in the Jewries just as they did in the other parts
of the towns. The ghetto streets were the narrowest in
the narrow towns of the middle ages. But all these dis-
advantages were to a large extent balanced by a strong
sense of personal dignity. It was not until three centuries
of life in the ghettos had made their Jewish inhabitants
callous to the demands of fashion, indifferent to their
personal appearance, careless in their speech and general
bearing, that this old characteristic of the Jews ceased to
distinguish them. In the middle ages, however, the Jews
justly prided themselves on their regard for the amenities
of cleanly living and gentle mannerliness. [1]

This cleanliness in person and speech, this — unique
for its age — complete sense of personal dignity, was a
direct consequence of the religion, and it was the synagogue again which enforced a valuable social influence.
Cleanly habits were in fact codified, and, as we shall see
in a later chapter, the medieval code-books of the Jewish
religion contain a systematized scheme of etiquette, of
cleanly custom, and of good taste. The codification of
these habits had the evil effect of reducing them to a formality, and later on even the ritual hand-washing, essential
in many Jewish ceremonies, became a perfunctory rite,
compatible with much personal uncleanliness. But in the
middle ages this was not yet the case. A quaint detail or
two must suffice here. Jacob Molin [2] had a bag suspended

---

[1] Jews needed the special sanction of Rabbis to permit them to dress
inelegantly even while travelling. Thus Maharil advises such a course to
avoid temptation to robbers. Cf. ch. xv. below.
[2] Maharil.

on the wall near his seat in synagogue, containing a pocket-handkerchief for use during prayer, an article of attire unknown in the ordinary life of the middle ages. A medieval Jew had, as already remarked, a special synagogue coat, called in some parts a *Sarabal.*[1] It was a tunic which hung down from the neck, and formed part of the gifts bestowed by parents on their sons when the latter married. Gloves were forbidden in prayer because humility was essential to a proper devotional demeanour, and much vexing of spirit was caused by young men and old who would carry walking-sticks with them to synagogue.[2] There was an iron scraper at the synagogue doors so that worshippers might wipe their feet on entering. Indeed, special synagogue shoes were *de rigueur*, for a regard to decent foot-gear was a very old Jewish characteristic. He who yawned in synagogue or during prayers was ordered to place his hand in front of his mouth.[3] Men did not go to synagogue with the small cap worn in the house, but changed it for a more costly one.

With regard to the feet, it was customary to pray barefooted or in list slippers on the ninth of Ab or on the Day of Atonement, on the 'eve' of which many passed the night in the synagogue. Talmud students in the thirteenth century often went barefooted in the streets [4] — from poverty, however, rather than from piety; but there are indications that in the East Jews habitually prayed

---

[1] For a full account of this see Joseph Nördlingen (Hahn), *Yosef Ometz*, § 3. The term itself occurs already in the Talmud.

[2] Ibid. § 16. There was a Talmudic prohibition against appearing on the Temple Mount with staff and girdle.

[3] A Talmudic custom. Cf. *Or Zarua*, i. p. 37.

[4] Güdemann, i. p. 83.

with bare feet. At all events the wooden sandals of the
fifteenth century in Germany were forbidden except to
keep the feet clean, and in some places Jewish worshippers
were forced to leave their shoes in the vestibule before
entering the House of God, under penalty of excommunication. From reverential motives a space was left
unprinted on the wall facing the synagogue door, to recall
the glory of Zion trailing in the dust.[1] In many private
homes a similar custom prevailed.

But there was another motive at the back of the
prohibition against a few worshippers using cushioned
seats while the others sat on the bare wood. ' It is
unseemly to make such distinctions, but the whole congregation may use cushions.'[2] So, too, we find whole
congregations denying themselves the luxury of wearing
the *Sargenos* — or white surplice — on the Day of Atonement, for fear of putting to the blush the poor who were
unable to provide themselves with the attire. This
regard for the feelings of the poor was extended to
the unlearned. In Palestine the worshipper who was
called to the Law read his section from the scroll. But
very early there were many Jews who were unable to do
this, and though the practice continued in force right
through the middle ages, it had already been modified in
Babylon, where the *Chazan*, or officiating reader, always
helped in the reading whether the individual were learned
or not,[3] in order to avoid putting the unlearned to the blush.
There is indeed some evidence that the general level of
Hebrew knowledge among Jews was higher in the middle

---

[1] יוסף אומץ, § 892.
[2] *Responsa* of Geonim, ed. Müller, § 106.
[3] Müller, *Chilluf Minhagim*, § 47.

ages than it is to-day. There were more professed students of Hebrew, but some of the general Jewish public seem to have been unable to understand any but the most familiar prayers.[1]

To these details must be added the general principle that in the synagogue the worshipper was to be at his best, dignified, simple-hearted, respectful, and attentive. But the inroad of the wider conception of the functions of the synagogue, to which allusion has already been made, inevitably produced breaches of decorum, which, however, were not tolerated without vigorous and often effective protest. To some extent the more educated classes were to blame. The Rabbis themselves were not regular attendants at public worship, and only preached at rare intervals.[2] This was due to their habit of holding semi-public services in their own houses, primarily for the special benefit of their pupils. But the custom of praying at home naturally led to late arrival at synagogue, or total abstinence from it.

Attendance at synagogue was enforced by penalties in some places,[3] but they were ineffective in preventing late arrival. When there, learned men would often prove inattentive, for they had already prayed, and they would while away the time over their learned books while the *Chazan* trilled his airs.[4] It was not unusual for the whole congregation to talk while the Precentor sang or read the Pentateuch,[5] or, what must have been equally

---

[1] See *Machzor Vitry*, p. 1.

[2] Güdemann, iii. p. 49.

[3] E.g. in Candia in the year 1228.

[4] *Or Zarua*, i. p. 22, § 10.

[5] Alami, *Iggereth Ha-musar* (ed. Jellinek), p. 10; *Responsa* of Solomon ben Adret (ed. Venice), § 380; N. Gabay Responsa Peath Negeb, § 2.

disturbing to decorum, the worshippers recited their prayers aloud, going their own way while the Precentor went his. Praying aloud was a long-standing grievance of the synagogue authorities,[1] and has never been quite eradicated. Coming late was a source of disturbance which it was also hard to remove, for no food might be eaten in the morning until after the morning prayer, and many must perforce pray at home and breakfast before going to synagogue. In synagogue, on the other hand, the service could not be begun late, because the rubrics required that the chief part of the prayer be recited within three hours after early dawn. Late arrival was thus so far an admitted necessity that a special chapter in the code-book provides for the case.[2] This feature was more marked on the Sabbath ; on week-days, when the synagogue service was held at a very early hour, workmen would take their breakfasts with them to synagogue, and, after praying, would eat their meal in the courtyard before proceeding to their work. Still, a large number of worshippers went to prayer early on Sabbaths, and waited till the close of the service before taking any food. This class had claims on communal recognition which seriously interfered with one of the chief elements of divine worship, viz. the homiletical discourse. Throughout the later middle ages the sermon falls into the background. In the Talmudic and Gaonic eras[3] the sermon invariably formed part of the morning service, but in Europe the sermon gradually sank into the low position from which the Mendelssohnian revival raised it at the end of the eighteenth century.

---

[1] Müller, *Mafteach*, p. 21.

[2] Shulchan Aruch, *Orach Chayim*, § 52.

[3] Roughly speaking, this covers the period up till the eleventh century.

Sermons were not given every week, were transferred as a luxury to the afternoon, and the place in which they were delivered became the school and not the synagogue, a fact which tended to convert the homily into a learned lecture. The sermon was spoken in the vernacular, but was far from popular, especially in Germany.[1] The preacher was frequently interrupted by questions, as was indeed the custom in some medieval churches. It is interesting to contrast the effect of suffering on Jews and other sects in regard to the sermon. With, say, the Covenanters, persecution gave a new point to the homily and placed in the preacher's hand a sharpened two-edged sword. The German Jew was too overwhelmed by his fate to listen patiently to hopeful prophecies of peace. Yet the contrast is more formal than real, for the Covenanter could be roused to armed revolt, a resource denied to Jewish victims of oppression. Hence to the Covenanter the love of homilies was political rather than religious ; and just because the Jew had no political hopes, so he placed less reliance in the religious consolation provided by homiletical discourses. Never ceasing to be the teacher, the Rabbi ceased almost entirely to preach, and the delivery of sermons was left to a class of itinerant preachers known as *Maggidim*, of considerable eloquence and power. With emancipation came a considerable outburst of Jewish pulpit eloquence ; the Rabbi resumed his old rôle of preacher.

The decay of the sermon in the middle ages was, moreover, closely connected with the debasement of the language of the Jews. A jargon began to be spoken widely in Germany in the middle of the fifteenth

[1] Maybaum, *Jüdische Homiletik*, p. 13.

century,[1] and this no doubt had its effect in killing pulpit eloquence. Style and art are only possible with a classical idiom. To complete the contrast between the Synagogue and the Conventicle, the elegy or *Selicha* flourished in the former as luxuriantly as the sermon did in the latter. The poetical form was assumed, for Hebrew was the medium of prayer, and though the Hebrew used at times was rugged, it was never debased. What the Jews lacked in political hopes they partly made up by their love for an idealized Zion. This love for Zion was created anew by the medieval poets of the synagogue ; and in many a gloomy hour Israel found solace in the hope that once more the Law would go forth from Zion.

But even the best of motives are not always efficient in rendering conduct free from blame. One of the noblest principles of Judaism was its insistence on *effort* in well-doing. A Jew of the middle ages would thus be as anxious as the Jews of Temple times to expend his means in the service of God. He would always value more highly an act that needed a sacrifice of his time and money than one which made no such claim. Hence it came that he would buy the right to participate in the synagogue service, since he could no longer spend his means at the Temple celebrations in Jerusalem. The Jewish layman, if the term can be used when there was no clerical caste, performed certain of the religious rites in the synagogue, and the privilege was so coveted that though, in later times, occasionally apportioned by lot,[2] in the middle ages it went literally to the highest bidder.[3] The *mitsvoth*, as these coveted

---

[1] *Kore Hadoroth* (ed. Cassel), p. 29 a.
[2] Menachem Mendel. *Responsa*, צמח צדק, § 25.
[3] *Or Zarua*, i. p. 41.

rites were named, were sold by auction in synagogue, and each congregation had its fixed rules regulating the method and time of sale. Sometimes the *mitsvoth* were sold once or twice a year, sometimes once or thrice a week, most often once a month. Disputes occasionally arose as to these auctions,[1] and the function led to considerable disorder. Moreover, the poorer members of the congregation were debarred from the coveted honour, though these sometimes made special efforts and sacrifices to secure the privilege.

Again, the announcement in synagogue of money offerings for benevolent or religious purposes gave opportunity for gossip and comment.[2] In the early Church, the offerings of Christians were made publicly, not privately. The presiding officer of the church received the gifts, and solemnly dedicated them to God with words of thanksgiving and benediction.[3] Yet it must be remembered that a free and easy attitude in worship was associated with a very sincere piety. The same authority[4] who applauds the sale of *mitsvoth* enforces the strictest rules for reverent behaviour during prayer. Pray with head bent, with soft utterance, with feet placed neatly together. Spend an hour in the synagogue in silent meditation before venturing to pray — and so forth. Other sources of disturbance, especially among Oriental Jews, were the custom of utilizing the synagogue for inviting guests to semi-religious festivities, the putting on and off of the *sargenos*,[5] laving

[1] See e.g. Meir b. Isaac, *Responsa*, ii. 25.
[2] Mr. Zangwill's *King of the Schnorrers* amusingly illustrates this curious fact. Cf. ch. xvii. below.
[3] Hatch, *Organization of Early Christian Churches*, p. 40.
[4] Or Zarua.
[5] See p. 18, above.

the hands of the *Cohanim*, or descendants of Aaron, previous to their recitation of the Priestly Benediction.[1] Yet, on the whole, the abuses of the great principle that the Jew was at home in his place of worship, did not appreciably lessen devotion. It was only at the close of the eighteenth century, when the Jews hovered between the old and the new, that this familiar attitude towards God became indecorous ; for the old sense of ease was retained, but there was a loss of the thoroughgoing piety which, seeing God everywhere and in all things, looked upon him as a partner in the business of life, rather than as a superior Being to be approached with formal etiquette. In Oriental lands the sense of incongruousness does not strike the observer so strongly as it does in Europe, and this difference in itself amounts to a justification of the synagogue of the middle ages, especially in France and Germany, where the warmth of Oriental emotion was retained. In Italy and Spain there was, perhaps, a more stately demeanour in synagogue; there was unquestionably less warmth and religious intensity.

Gossip was inevitable in synagogue, for the latter was the chief meeting-place of Jews. The licensed conversation, however, occurred in the courtyard,[2] not in the synagogue itself ; and, perhaps to encourage the people to congregate there rather than in the sacred building, the courtyard was sometimes laid out as a garden. It became a fashion, even with the most punctilious Jews, to reassemble after the service for the purpose of talking over the news of the hour, military and political.[3] But those were

---

[1] Numbers, vi. 22-27.
[2] Müller, *Index*, p. 21.
[3] Isserlein, *Responsa*, תרומת הדשן, § 61.

forbidden to join the concourse to whom such gossip proved tedious, for as 'the Sabbath is a delight,' says my authority, 'none should participate in the function if it wearies or bores them.'

Probably the most serious difficulty in maintaining decorum arose from the children.[1] The Jews were not the only sect so troubled, for one frequently meets with Puritan diatribes against the 'wretched boys.' In New England churches the tithing-man used to rap the knuckles of boys (and even of elders) to wake them up or keep them well-behaved during divine service.[2] Occasionally a similar measure was resorted to in synagogue, and, especially with the Sephardic Jews (i.e. those using the Spanish Jewish ritual), the children were kept in order by an official, stick in hand. Some authorities resented the intrusion of young children into the synagogue at all ; indeed the trouble must have been increased by the separation of the boys from their mothers.

In the separation of the sexes, the synagogue only reflected their isolation in the social life outside. The sexes were separated at Jewish banquets and home feasts not less than in the synagogue. If they did not pray together neither did they play together. The rigid separation of the sexes in prayer seems not to have been earlier, however, than the thirteenth century. The women had their own 'court' in the Temple, yet it is not impossible that they prayed together with the men in Talmudic times.[3] Possibly the rigid separation grew out of the medieval custom —more common as the thirteenth century advances—which

[1] Löw, *Lebensalter in der Jüd. Literatur*, pp. 133, 134.
[2] Alice M. Earle, *The Sabbath in Puritan New England*, p. 231.
[3] Löw, *Monatsschrift*, 1884, pp. 304, 463.

induced men and women to spend the eve of the Great Fast in synagogue. By the end of the thirteenth century, and perhaps earlier, Jewish women had their own prayer-meetings in rooms at the side of and a little above the men's synagogue, with which the rooms communicated by a small window or balcony. Or if the women had no separate apartments, they sat at the back of the men's synagogue in reserved places, screened by curtains. There were no galleries for women as at present.[1] In their own prayer-meetings, the women were led by female precentors, some of whom acquired considerable reputation. The epitaph of one of them, Urania of Worms, belonging perhaps to the thirteenth century, runs thus :[2] —

'This headstone commemorates the eminent and excellent lady Urania, the daughter of R. Abraham, who was the chief of the synagogue singers. His prayer for his people rose up unto glory.

'And as to her, she, too, with sweet tunefulness, officiated before the female worshippers to whom she sang the hymnal portions. In devout service her memory shall be preserved.'

The tender regard for woman, despite her inequality as regards legal and religious status, was shown in one or two features of which considerations of space cannot justify the omission. Women, when away from home, were allowed to light their Sabbath candles in the synagogue.[3] It was not an unknown thing even in the seventeenth and eighteenth centuries, when the exclusion of women from active participation in the public worship was most rigid, to use a woman's gold-embroidered cloak or silver-braided apron as a curtain

[1] Some authorities (on *Mishnah Succah*, v. 2, and *Middoth*, ii. 5) believe that temporary galleries were erected for the women in the Temple itself during the festivities of the water-drawing.

[2] A. Löwy, *Jewish Chronicle*, December 30, 1892, p. 11.

[3] Maharil, *Responsa*, § 53.

for the ark, a mantle for the scroll of the Law, or a cover for the reading-desk.[1] The decoration of the synagogue was not severely simple. 'The Jews may not enlarge, elevate, or beautify their synagogues' enacted Alfonso X in 1261.[2] Thus the Talmudic prescription to elevate the synagogue beyond the highest building in the town was impossible in Spain. The difficulty was evaded by making a small symbolical addition to the height of the synagogue whenever a higher house was newly built,[3] and it is barely possible that this cause, besides imitation of the ancient Jewish temple and of the medieval mosque, tended to preserve the old custom of the leaving the synagogues in the East without roof as late as the fifteenth century. Occasionally, however, European synagogues were very high; and a complaint is recorded that the synagogue at Sens in the time of Innocent III was higher than the neighbouring church. Complaints are also recorded in London that, owing to the proximity of the synagogue, the church prayers were interfered with by the noise of the Hebrew hymns.[4] But in Rome in the fourteenth century churches were erected quite close to synagogues and the relations between the two sets of worshippers were not strained by any such recriminations.

The number of windows in a synagogue was by preference twelve,[5] but this feature was neither common nor

[1] *Responsa*, Chavvath Yair, § 161; Joel b. S. Sirkes, § 17.
[2] Lindo, p. 99.
[3] Löw, *Monatsschrift*, 1884, p. 217.
[4] Tovey, *Anglia Judaica*, p. 192. Cf. also Güdemann, ii. pp. 27 and 224. On the other hand, in the fourteenth century, church and synagogue were built in close proximity to one another in Rome, and no complaints were made (Berliner, *Rom*, ii. p. 12).
[5] No synagogue was built without windows; all Jews followed the example of Daniel (Dan. vi. 10).

general. More regard was paid to the Orientation of European synagogues. The decorations of the synagogue were
often costly; and legend has recorded many wonders of the
Alexandrian synagogue, among others. Separate parts of
that building are said to have been reserved for special
trades, and in the middle ages synagogues for Jews of
different nationalities were common especially in Italy and
on the Mediterranean coasts. Spanish and Italian synagogues were noted for their beauty, and even elsewhere the
floors were often of stone or marble.[1] The doors of the
ark were sometimes ornamented with figures of vines or
candlesticks, or stone lions graced the steps leading to it.[2]
The lion was, indeed, a favourite Jewish decorative ornament. It appears in the modern synagogue in every available place, on the ark, whether in relief or painted, in
precious metal on the plates which adorn the scrolls of the
Law, and in gold embroidery on the mantels and curtains,
and even as supports to tables designed for semi-religious
use.[3]

The lamp, burning constantly in front of the ark, was of
gold or silver, but burnished brass, ‘such as is found only in
the houses of princes’[4] was not excluded. So popular was
the presentation of such gifts to the synagogue that it
became necessary to restrict the liberality of individuals,
and no lamp was admitted as a gift without the special
permission of the council.[5] The privilege of supplying
lights for the Sabbath was even inherited.[6] That the

[1] *Or Zarua*, i. p. 35.

[2] Kaufmann, *J. Q. R.*, vol. ix.

[3] See S. Krauss in Bloch's *Wochenschrift* (1896), p. 91. Cf. *Der ungarische
Israelit*, No. 4 (1896). The lion was *protective* and reminiscent of Gen. xlix. 9.

[4] *Chavvath Yair*, § 68.

[5] Ibid.   [6] *Responsa*, Radbaz, i. 387.

synagogue was not Puritanically averse to sensuous attractions, may be seen from the fact that rose-water was, later on, used for washing the hands of the 'Priests' on public festivals.[1] On semi-private festivities rose-leaves were strewn in the ark among the very scrolls of the Law. On the 'Rejoicing of the Law' the 'Bridegroom,' as the layman selected to read the last section in the Pentateuch was named, held a reception in synagogue and his guests were sprinkled from scented sprays.[2] These remarks apply more to the East than to Europe : but on the subject of artistic decoration in synagogue one general remark must suffice. There grew up a strong feeling against ornamenting the synagogue with representations of animals other than lions. Some authorities applied the restriction only to the human figure, or to designs in relief, or to the decoration of the side of the synagogue which worshippers faced during prayer. Others forbade all representations of natural objects. Still, as we have seen, these sentiments were not universal, and in the twelfth century the Cologne Synagogue had painted glass windows, and it was not an unknown thing for birds and snakes, probably grotesques rather than accurate representations, to appear on the walls of the synagogue without the Rabbinical sanction.[3] But these grotesques, like the seal of a thirteenth century Jew, cannot, as Tovey wittily says,[4] ' be thought a breach of the second commandment, for it is the

---

[1] The simplest Jewish praying-room had some decoration. See e.g. Kahn *Les Juifs de Paris au XVIIIe siècle*, p. 73.

[2] *Responsa*, Beth David, § 293.

[3] Zunz, *Zur Geschichte*, p. 175; Berliner, *Aus dem inneren Leben*, etc., p. 20. Cf. Meir of Rothenberg, *Responsa* (ed. Mekitse Nirdamim), § 547. See Caro's *Abkath Rochel*, § 63, for a very enlightened opinion.

[4] *Anglia Judaica*, p. 183. See *Jewish Quarterly Review*, iii. 777.

likeness of nothing that is in heaven, earth, or water.'
Prayer-books were illuminated and pictorially embellished,
and after the invention of printing, wood-cuts depicting the
signs of the Zodiac and the ten plagues of Exodus appeared
in many an edition of the Hebrew prayer-book used in
synagogue.[1] On the feast of Pentecost, again, the synagogue was decorated with flowers. Grass was strewn on
the synagogue floor on the Day of Atonement, less however as an ornament than to serve as a softer ground on
which the worshippers might prostrate themselves.[2]

As to the shape of synagogues, no special form can be
called Jewish. A famous authority of last century maintained that no Jewish law, old or new, restricted the fancy
of synagogue architects[3] in this respect. He himself
authorized the choice of an octagonal form, and this shape
is now rather popular on the continent.

But the oblong or square was the favourite form for
Jewish houses of prayer from very early times. The tem-
ple-courts — which were used for prayer-meetings — were
oblong or square, but there was at one time a prevalent
notion in England that synagogues were round. Thomas
Fuller (circ. 1650) remarks that the 'Round Church in
the Jewry is conjectured, *by the rotundity of the structure*,
to have been built as a synagogue.' Fuller is here referring to the Cambridge Round Church ; while Stow[4] declined to admit that Bakewell Hall was once a synagogue,
because forsooth it was *not* round! There are few round

---

[1] Meir of Rothenberg mildly disapproved of the appearance of figures of
birds and beasts in prayer-books and on walls (*Responsa*, ed. Cremona, 24).

[2] Tur, *Orach Chayim*, § 131.

[3] E. Landau, *Noda Biyudah*, i. § 18.

[4] Jacobs, *London Jewry*, 26.

churches in England altogether, but hardly any of these have not at some time or other been pronounced to have been built by Jews. These round churches really are due to the activity of the Templars.[1] The Church of the Holy Sepulchre in Jerusalem was round, and it would seem likely enough that this design was imitated in England during the Crusading ages. Epiphanius indeed says that the Samaritans, like the Jews, built synagogues 'theatre-like' without roofs ; but he does not make it clear whether he was alluding to the rooflessness as 'theatre-like,' or intended to imply that Jewish places of worship were, 'theatre-like,' round in shape. But the only design which could arouse religious opposition from Jews would be the cruci-form.[2]

The synagogue music does not seem to have been very ornate or refined ; volume of sound being ascribed to it rather than delicacy. The singing Precentor (*Chazan*) was not tolerated without a struggle, though he eventually became a marked feature of the synagogue. Much conservatism prevailed regarding synagogue tunes ;[3] and each locality possessed its own melodies. No serious compunction was felt, however, against introducing popular airs into the synagogue, though there was no doubt some feeling against it. The congregational singing was vigorous and probably general, for we find in later times some resentment at the introduction of boy choirs.[4]

---

[1] James Essex, *Archaeologia*, vol. vi.

[2] On the shape of the Prague synagogue, M. Popper (*Die Inschriften des alten Prager Judenfriedhofs*, p. 23) says that the Pinkas synagogue is a simple round domed edifice ; the Meisel synagogue (built 1590) is more ornate, with a cross-vaulted central roof and side domes.

[3] See Maharil, passim. On synagogue melodies cf. Steinschneider, *Jewish Literature*, pp. 154, 155.

[4] E.g. Steinhart, *Responsa*, Zichron Yosef, § 5.

This leads us back from our digression. The boys had their rights in the synagogue long before they attained their thirteenth year, after which they were accounted, from a religious point of view, as adults. The Barmitzvah rites, which accompanied the completion of a boy's thirteenth year, cannot be clearly traced earlier than the fourteenth century.[1] From early times, however, young boys were encouraged to recite in synagogue the Hallel and the weekly lesson from the Prophets;[2] boys sometimes lit the synagogue candles on the eve of the festivals;[3] in the fifteenth century boys read part of the regular service to congregations of adults.[4] Boys sometimes made announcements in synagogue, a function afterwards filled by the shamash or beadle.[5] Flags in hand, boys headed the procession of the bearers of the scrolls on the ' Rejoicing of the Law,' they ascended the reading-desk *en masse* on that occasion during the reading of the Pentateuch lesson, some of them even bare-headed.[6] On every Sabbath they stood by the steps of the Almemor (reading-desk) and reverently kissed the sacred Scroll.[7] When they were nine or ten years old, they fasted a few hours on the Day of Atonement, and some authorities included them among the ten adults requisite for *minyan*, the ritual quorum for public worship.

The boys were even allowed to preach ; and, as some authorities assume, were admitted to administrative

---

[1] Löw, *Lebensalter*, p. 210.

[2] *Responsa*, Tashbats, iii. 171.

[3] *Responsa*, Beer Esek, § 38.

[4] S. b. Eleazar, Preface to *Baruch Sheamar*.

[5] Maharil informs us that the boys announced יעלה ויבא.

[6] Adults prayed bare-headed in France. See Geiger's *Jüdische Zeitschrift*, iii. 142.

[7] Schechter, *Jewish Quarterly Review*, ii. p. 21.

honours. An epitaph of the third century describes an eight-year-old Roman boy as an *Archon* of the synagogue.[1] But the title of Archon seems to have been hereditary at Rome,[2] and this particular boy may have borne the title in virtue of his descent. Boys were taught to show the greatest respect to their parents in synagogue; they carried their fathers' prayer-books for them; they never occupied their fathers' seats; they stood while their fathers stood, and their fathers blessed them after the reading of the Law, or at the close of the Sabbath eve service. Fathers refrained from kissing their boys in synagogue,[3] but when the service was over the children kissed the Rabbi's hand, which he raised to the children's heads, uttering meanwhile a prayer for their welfare. The mother was not excluded from these tokens of respect, and on Friday, in the interval between the afternoon and evening services, the boys were sent home to their mothers, to intimate that the Sabbath was about to begin,[4] and that the Sabbath candles must be kindled. For the children's sake certain verses from the book of Esther were sung in chorus on Purim, and, despite the trouble they caused there, the young were treated as though the synagogue was their second home. Indeed, up till the ninth or tenth centuries, Asiatic synagogues were homes for travellers, who lodged in the synagogues and took their meals there.[5] The Kiddush or Sanctification over the wine which has, quaintly enough, survived in the modern synagogue ritual, was thus in its

---

[1] Schürer, *Die Gemeindeverfassung der Juden in Rom*, p. 24.
[2] Berliner, *Rom*, i. p. 68.
[3] *Sefer Chassidim*, § 255.
[4] *Ra-ben*, § 342.
[5] Löw, p. 205.

origin part of the Sabbath meal, which was spread in the synagogue itself or in its immediate precincts for passing strangers.   In the European synagogues no such meals took place ; the Sanctification over the wine became a symbol rather than part of the meal, and, instead of the Precentor, a boy sipped the wine from the full cup handed to him.

No doubt there was, as the middle ages closed, a tendency to specialize, and subtract from the synagogue some of its functions.   Yet the association between the school and the synagogue always remained an intimate one.   It was a very old custom for pious worshippers to repair to synagogue early before the services, with the object of studying the Bible and the Rabbinical writings.[1]   Still, the school and the synagogue were independent institutions, though praying was usual in the school, and learning took place in the synagogue.   The term *schule*, now commonly used by Jews to mean the synagogue, was, according to Dr. Güdemann,[2] not of Jewish invention, being first applied to the synagogue by Christians, who found it inconvenient to designate the synagogue a Church.   In England the Norwich school, built before 1189, was not identical with the synagogue,[3] and the same remark applies to the capital.   In Worms, to cite only one other instance, the school was located behind the synagogue.[4]   Hence, some interesting synagogue rites connected with the school will be reserved for the chapter on education.

---

[1] *Responsa* of Geonim (ed. Lyck), p. 87.
[2] iii. p. 94, note.
[3] Jacobs, *Angevin England*, p. 275; cf. ibid. p. 245.
[4] Güdemann, *Quellenschriften*, p. 219.

CHAPTER III

COMMUNAL ORGANIZATION

THE original identity between the organizations of Synagogue and Church was obliterated by the earlier growth within the latter of *institutions*. The Jewish communal organization provided for everything that the Church supplied, but it did so without specialization, without delegating its duties to semi-independent bodies. Thus, while the deacons soon ceased to be the general relieving officers of the Church in cases of sickness and poverty,[1] their Jewish prototypes, the *Parnassim*, or lay directors of the Synagogue, retained very wide functions throughout the middle ages. Until the thirteenth century, there were no Jewish poor-houses or hospitals, no orphanages for the young or almshouses for the aged; but the Synagogue organization fully supplied the place of all these, and, through lack of differentiation of its functions, strengthened its hold on the course of medieval Judaism.

There was, moreover, nothing in European Judaism parallel to the Christian diocese. It was impossible that such a parallel should exist, for the bishop[2] rapidly acquired

---

[1] The monasteries revived something of the Jewish system in the eleventh century.

[2] The Jewish *bishops*, of whom we read in medieval English documents, were not ecclesiastics, but probably were lay heads or *Parnassim*. Mr. Jacobs, however (*Angevin England*, p. 43), believes that they were *Dayanim* or Rabbinical judges.

political power, and in the eighth century, under Boniface's vigorous reforms, the bishop became permanently possessed of disciplinary powers such as no Rabbi ever wielded or claimed. Even the Geonim, who enjoyed a unique sway over the medieval Jews between the seventh and the eleventh centuries, and while resident in Persia ruled the Jewries of Europe, rarely interfered with local custom, nay, they were so anxious to allow local freedom that they even advocated the retention of local *minhagim*, or minor rules of life, of which they personally disapproved.[1] Moreover the Geonim never forced their decrees on foreign congregations; it may be doubted indeed whether they ever interfered in Jewish affairs beyond their own neighbourhood, unless their opinions were specifically invited. It was only the latest of the Geonim, Hai, that displayed some anxiety to have his ritual and legal decisions widely published, and this eagerness for extensive acceptance was one of the presages of the decaying authority of the Geonim. As the centuries rolled on these differences in local custom increased rather than lessened. By the middle of the thirteenth century,[2] the number of independent cycles of customs or *minhagim* — most of them well defined by communal enactments — was so large that Dr. Güdemann is able to enumerate more than twenty, though his list is imperfect even for Europe (for Italy and Spain are omitted), and the East could have added its quotum to the imposing array. *Custom* became master, and custom is a tyrant. Custom survives the circumstances which give it birth, and because the retention of it is based on sentiment, it is not amenable to the assaults of reason. But despite the evils resulting from this multiplicity of cus-

[1] Müller, *Mafteach*, p. 211.　　　　[2] Cf. Güdemann, iii. 12.

toms;[1] despite the disorder accruing, for instance, from the constant presence in a town of immigrant Jews, who were held free to follow their own imported *minhagim ;* Jewish life gained more than it lost by the freedom of the individual, the freshening of the atmosphere, and the avoidance of clerical arrogance, by the co-existence of many smaller varieties within the body general of Judaism.

There were, moreover, several alleviations of this anarchy in customary Judaism of the middle ages. Individual Rabbis won so world-wide a reputation that they often left their impress on the practices of several generations of Jews all the world over.[2] The responses which they sent to correspondents often formed a link between the scattered congregations of Jews in many parts of the globe. Then came to the aid of union, the codification of Jewish law and custom which flourished in Spain in the thirteenth century. Finally, unity of custom on great moral questions was almost completely established by a series of Rabbinical synods. These synods were attended by representatives of many congregations, and the resolutions arrived at dealt with many great problems, such as monogamy, the marriage and divorce laws, the laws against

---

[1] Cf. ch. viii., towards the end of the chapter.

[2] A noteworthy instance was Simon ben Zemach Duran, of Algiers, whose twelve regulations (or tekanoth), issued in 1391, were widely accepted, יקבלום עליהם יהר הקהלות. These regulations were drawn up by Duran in conjunction with Isaac ben Sheshet and Isaac Bonastruc. The most important of them were these : — i. and ii. A maiden's settlement shall amount to 50 per cent. more than her dowry (this was to make divorce expensive). vi. Further additions to the settlement by way of gift are the inalienable property of the wife. viii. In any case of dispute between husband and wife, the case must be tried by the *Jewish* court. x. Any one may contract himself out of these tekanoth provided that he does so *before* the betrothal (ישו"ת ח ההשב"ץ, ii. 292).

informers, the laws of inheritance, and the attitude to be assumed in general in face of the aggressions of the civil government. Jews needed to present something like a united front if they were to face the storms which raged around their homes and lives, and the synods were honourably distinguished by the spirit of unselfishness which they introduced into Jewish communal life. Burdens were to be shared, not shirked. These synods chiefly succeeded in introducing unity of practice on the greater questions of life, and from the eleventh century they became fairly continuous, depending no doubt for their authority on the great regulations of their presidents, foremost among them Jacob Tam (1100–1171). Combined action of a more or less imperfect kind was attempted in the thirteenth century with regard, for instance, to the exclusion of philosophy from Jewish education, but the attempt utterly failed. Alliances for giving practical expression to the religious unity of Judaism were indeed not so common after as they were until the thirteenth century. The later alliances were almost purely local, or were confined to the Jews of a particular nation. A typical instance occurred in Italy in 1416, when a synod held in Bologna created an alliance for internal communal purposes between the Jewish congregations of Rome, Padua, Ferrara, Bologna, and the Romagna and Toscana districts. This union was caused by the papal schism and the consequent insecurity of the Italian Jews.[1] In the sixteenth century a somewhat similar, though more lasting, alliance for communal purposes was the famous *Vaad Arba Aratsoth*, or the 'Union of the Four Districts,' which for a long time ruled Polish Judaism and its organization. At its head

---

[1] Berliner, *Rom*, ii. p. 66.

was an elective president, and the tribunal over which he ruled had even criminal jurisdiction. But this *Vaad* or alliance had no control over the details of communal life; each congregation retained its own Rabbi and its own court or *Beth Din.*[1] Neighbouring congregations, naturally enough, frequently combined for some general purposes in a more or less formal manner. Speyer, Worms, and Mayence offer a noteworthy instance, but the famous regulations of this union are in no sense administrative.[2]

These synods and unions, therefore, did not attempt to set up a central authority as regards the ordinary communal organization. The local Rabbi claimed local allegiance, and, as I have said, it was his reputation, and not his official position, which won him any power beyond his own congregation. He was removable from his post, though depositions were very rare. But until the end of the thirteenth century the Rabbi enjoyed a certain independence of his flock, for, though he was an officer of the synagogue, he was not a regularly salaried servant until the period just named.[3] Often the election of a Rabbi was subject to external interference and needed at least confirmation by the civil power, and the 'Prince of the Captivity' in Persia and the *Nagid* in Egypt, until the beginning of the sixteenth century, were entrusted by the State with powers unknown to the Rabbis of Europe. In Poland, indeed, in the reign of Sigismund I (1506–1548) the Rabbi was confirmed by the king, and was, in a sense, an agent for the crown, collecting the poll-tax and enjoying large powers of civil and criminal

[1] Graetz, *History* (E. T.), V. ch. i.   For title of 'Rabbi' see p. 356 below.
[2] The שו״ם תקנות begin to date from the thirteenth century.
[3] Very interesting particulars on this subject are given in the *Tashbats*, I. 142 seq., and in the Testaments of the Asheri family (ed. Schechter, 1885).

jurisdiction.[1] Napoleon I so completely organized French
Judaism that the Rabbis of France are now practically
government officers, but the State has never once interfered in France to override the wishes of the Jews
themselves. So, in the middle ages, even when the governments ostensibly claimed the right to a voice in the
election of Rabbis, the Jews strongly resented the assumption by their Rabbis of privileges derived from any sanction but their own expressed wishes.[2] A good case in
point may be cited from what happened in Algiers in
the early part of the fifteenth century. Simon Duran
was elected Rabbi on the express condition that he
waived the formality of seeking the ratification of his
appointment from the government.

Though, however, the Jews were jealous of the right
to manage their own communal affairs, their internal organization was largely affected by their relations to the
external civil powers. Their organization, indeed, revolved
on the pivot of the taxes. Wherever and whenever one
casts his eye on the Jewish communities of the middle
ages, the observer always finds the Jew in the clutches
of extortionate tax-collectors. How did the State levy
these exactions, which were mostly of three kinds — poll-
taxes, communal taxes, and particular fines and dues for
individual transactions and privileges ? The age at which
Jews and Jewesses became liable to the poll-tax varied
considerably, but the age was very young, and in Spain,

---

[1] Graetz, *History* (Eng. Trans.), IV. ch. xiii.

[2] A high-spirited precentor (חזן) in the middle ages refused to accept his
office at the hands of the Archbishop of Cologne (*Responsa* of Meir of
Rothenburg, Cremona, § 190). Galician Rabbis were confirmed in their
offices by the government ; an interesting document dated 1741 may be
found in Buber's אנשי שם, p. 236.

as in England in 1273, every Jew above the age of ten was ratable. There is no general information on the subject of the manner in which these taxes were raised, but a careful consideration of many details leads me to the conclusion that in most cases, if not in all, the various medieval governments exacted the taxes *en masse* from the Jewish community, and left the collection of this lump sum to the officials of the synagogue.[1] This method was not confined to England, where the early centralization of government and the peculiar form of feudalism prevalent there placed the Jews in a unique position towards the king. In England we hear of 'Chief Rabbis' and Jewish presbyters with central authority such as was unknown amid the unsettled and decentralized feudalisms of the continent. Despite this difference, however, the English mode of levying the Jewish contributions to the royal revenue did not vary essentially from the system prevailing in Spain and elsewhere. Briefly told, the English method was this. The tallage, which constituted the main source of the crown revenue from the Jewries, was a purely arbitrary tax. Only occasionally was it levied as a poll-tax at all, mostly it was levied collectively, each Jew

---

[1] A good instance of how the two methods worked together is supplied by an ordinance passed at Anagni in 1271. In Anjou every Jew or Jewess was ordered to pay 10 *sols tournois* as a poll-tax. Besides this, the community as a whole 200 *livres tournois* as a general contribution. But — and this is the interesting point — some Jews, like the *non podientes* in Spain, claimed to be too poor to pay this poll-tax. Hence the ordinance decreed that the town bailiff was to hold the Jewish community as a whole responsible for the payment of the poll-tax for 1000 individuals, even though the number of Jews in Anjou be less than 1000. The Jews were represented by a communal official of their own called *sindicus et procurator universitatis judeorum*, an officer no doubt necessitated by the method of collecting the taxes just described (Brunschvicg, *Juifs d'Angers*, pp. 12–13).

contributing according to his power or his reputed wealth.[1] Jewish assessors were appointed because they would be able to estimate each man's property, and these assessors or tallagers were expected, under penalty of severe fines, to perform their duty inexorably, and were sometimes forced to aid the sheriff in levying distress on Jewish defaulters.[2] When there were no Jewish assessors, but — as in the reign of Edward I — Christian collectors were appointed, a few wealthy Jews were nominated as sureties, and were held responsible for the payment of the collective tax. The total sums exacted were enormous. In England the Jews provided one-twelfth of the royal revenue. In another country the Jews, who formed a tenth of the population, supplied a fourth of the public funds.[3] It was often resolved to throw as much as half the total sums raised on to the shoulders of the wealthy.[4]

[1] How thoroughly this method became ingrained on the Jewish organization may be seen from its survival to our own times in *Sephardic* congregations. Thus, in London an appreciable part of the revenue of the Spanish and Portuguese congregation consists of a *Finta* levied by assessors appointed for the purpose. In this method of raising the internal revenue of Jewish congregations, Jews over the age of fifteen were liable to contribute (Eskapa's *Tekanoth*, § 2).

[2] Gross, *Exchequer of Jews of England* (in ' Papers read at Anglo-Jewish Exhibition,' 1887), p. 196, etc. This method of grouping the Jews for purposes of taxation and leaving the collection to Jews themselves was also existent in Spain (Jacobs, *Spain*, p. xxiii). An equally representative instance may be cited in Germany in 1381, where the congregations of Heidelberg, Weinheim, Lindenfels, Eberbach, Mosbach, Sinsheim, Wiesloch, Eppingen, Bretten, and Ladenberg were taxed *en masse* for the ' protection ' rate (Löwenstein, *Kurpfalz*, p. 12). The chain of evidence is completed by the statement of Aaron Perachiah (פרח מטה אהרן, § 123), that in Mohammedan countries the same system prevailed. Cf. the information on the taxes levied in Turkey in A. Danon's essay in *Revue des Études Juives*, vol. xxxi. p. 52. Madox (*Exchequer*, i. 221) speaks of Jews answerable for one another's tallages.

[3] Zunz, *Zur Geschichte*, p. 497; J. Jacobs, *Angevin England*, p. 328.

[4] This must have been the result of the decision to exact the communal burdens half as a poll-tax and half by assessment (Juda Minz, § 42).

My purpose is, however, less to enter into details of this system than to trace its effects on Jewish social life. To sum up these effects in a single sentence, the older Jewish aristocracy of learning was replaced by an aristocracy of wealth. The taxes were paid by the richer for the less rich, or at least the former class contributed more than their share to the communal burdens. As the utility of wealth grew, its privileges were bound to keep pace. Graetz fixes the growth of an aristocracy of wealth among the Jews at the close of the seventeenth century.[1] There is no doubt that the phenomenon then becomes most marked, but it was very gradual in inception. The power of wealth is always seen first in the prestige of Jews who held state offices. In other words, those whose wealth was most useful to the community won a position of influence by it. In the fourteenth century the Jewish organization in Christian Spain was already in the hands of the men who enjoyed Royal favour, but the Jewish population was at the time able to resist this imposition, and sometimes chose its own communal officers in the face of government opposition.[2] Originally, the organization of the Jewry was a thoroughly democratic one; the only aristocracy being one of merit and learning, not of property. Nothing can set the point clearer before the reader than the following contrast between the classes into which the Jews were divided in the fourteenth and the eighteenth centuries. In the former period we hear of a large number of Jews being present in synagogue at a festivity, and the congregation is divided into 'Rabbis, scholars, students, and householders.'[3] In Avignon in 1769 the

---

[1] *History* (Eng. Trans.), V. ch. vi. 　　[2] Zunz, op. cit., p. 511.
[3] This included all the ordinary married men of the community (M. Minz, *Responsa*, § 101).

community is divided into three grades : 'The first grade includes persons possessed of 30,000 livres ; the second, persons possessed of 15,000 livres ; the third, persons possessed of 5000 livres'[1] — and none of lesser wealth were admitted to office. The democratic basis of the Jewish system was never, of course, completely destroyed, and either the ordinary business men of moderate property still had the real control of affairs,[2] or a compromise was reached in which wealth and numbers were equally deferred to[3] — an ideal arrangement which never worked without friction.

Another, less harmful, result was the strength that the system gave to the bonds of the communal organization. It gave the community a strong control over its individual members. The officers appointed by the congregation itself to levy the taxes must have gained an intimate knowledge of each Jew's private affairs and property. The assessment must have led to heart-burning when the grandmotherly official taxed the individual below the latter's own estimate and was deaf to his pleading to be allowed to pay more. Mostly, no doubt, the trouble was of quite an opposite nature, and throughout the middle ages Jewish records are

---

[1] Statutes of Avignon (*Annuaire Études Juives*, 1885, p. 169).

[2] Cf. Shulchan Aruch, *Yore Deah*, § 250, 5.

[3] This principle was that a רוב המון ורוב ממון, ' a majority in votes and a majority in wealth,' was needed to pass a communal resolution ; or, to use another equally alliterative formula, רוב מנין ורוב בנין. Cf. M. Mendel of Nicolsburg, שו"ת צמח צדק, § 1. The same authority, § 2, reports an attempt to appoint a committee of ten to elect Rabbi, Chazan, and Shamash, and to decide all communal affairs. This device for invading the democratic system failed, but no doubt an inner circle often ruled affairs. See below, p. 54, n. 3. At Kremzir (ibid.) one family, we are told, paid three-fifths of the whole communal taxes. At an earlier period in the Rhine-lands, the appointment of Chazan needed a *unanimous* vote (*Or Zarua*, i. 41).

full of complaints of unworthy, if natural, efforts made
by classes and individuals to evade their liability and
throw the whole burden on to a few broad and willing
shoulders. (This remark applies also to the voluntary
taxes raised for internal communal practices.) Professional students, young or old, were exempt from payment ;
Rabbis and sometimes doctors,[1] salaried officers generally
were exempt, though not without an occasional struggle
on the part of the mass of the congregation.[2] The
Rabbi's widow enjoyed immunity, while printers in some
communities were equally spared. Men who lived by the
work of their hands paid the poll-tax, but were excused
from all other burdens.[3] Another source of trouble accrued from the constant immigration of foreign Jews, who
either remained for a short time only, or who attempted
to form independent organizations and refused to contribute to existent burdens.[4]

---

[1] Cf. Moses the Priest's שו"ת כהונת עולם, § 33. A spirited denunciation of
those who attempted to subject every one to the taxes, irrespective of his
profession, may be seen in J. Caro's אבקת רוכל, p. 1.

[2] Much controversy raged round the question whether the *Chazan* or
precentor should be included among the classes who enjoyed this customary
privilege of exemption. Duran (*Tashbats*, iii. 254) asserts that in Mohammedan countries the precentor was free, but in Christian countries he was
liable to pay. A similar question was raised about exempting men who
pursued a semi-religious trade, such as a *sofer* or *writer* of the scrolls of the
Law, marriage certificates, divorces, phylacteries, and *mezuzas*. (Cf. Eskapa's
Tekanoth, § 19.)

[3] Danon, *Revue des Études Juives*, loc. cit. p. 59.

[4] Two principles were applied to the case of recent immigrants, dependent on time and circumstance. If the traveller was present when the annual
dues were being fixed, then, unless he declared that his visit was temporary, he
was taxed by the community like the ordinary Jewish inhabitant. (Eskapa's
Tekanoth, § 5, and J. Soncin, נחלה ליהושע, § 10.) If the new settler arrived
at any other time of the year, then for the first three months he paid half the
tax, after which he was liable to the full amount. If, however, he brought

The taxes were of two kinds : those inflicted from without and those levied within by the community itself for general or special purposes.   There was a danger in these voluntary imposts, for the civil government had a way of stepping in and laying hands on the sums thus raised. Quite early in Jewish history in Rome such a case occurred. All the Jews in the diaspora were in the habit of remitting voluntary contributions to the Temple at Jerusalem. After the destruction, the Roman emperors converted this into an iniquitous *fiscus*, to be used for imperial and even idolatrous purposes.[1]   The voluntary contributions to Palestine have, however, continued without break to our own times, and most congregations still make special collections for the poor of the Holy Land.[2]   Another very iniquitous tax was the levy made on the Jews of Rome for the support of the House of Catechumens,[3] which may be compared to the compulsory attendance of Jews three times a year at Christian sermons against Judaism.   The Jews felt themselves fortunate when Sixtus V[4] fixed the total annual tax at twelve Giulii a head on all males between the ages of sixteen and sixty.   Before that time the popes simply extorted what they could.   Other less strange taxes were those levied for military and naval

his wife with him, he was at once fully liable.   One who left the congregation was free from the tax, unless he returned within the year ; if he possessed land in the city, then the absentee owner paid one-quarter of the tax.   Special relaxations were permitted to absentees who had gone to Palestine.   In Metz (*Annuaire*, i. 96), after a stay of eight days, all strangers were subject to the communal dues.

[1] P. Cassel, *Ersch u. Gruber*, vol. xxvii. 6.   So, too, the present Russian Government seizes the Jewish meat-tax, which was intended for internal religious uses.   [2] קופת ארץ ישראל.

[3] Cf. Berliner, *Rom*, ii. (1), 18, 21, 25.

[4] Bull, dated October 22, 1586.

armaments.[1] In Portugal the Jews under Sancho II were mulcted in a *Fleet-tax*, and were required to 'furnish an anchor and a new cable for every new ship fitted out by the crown.'[2] The Jews bore a large part in aiding Columbus' voyages both in money and men. The billeting of soldiers on Jews in times of peace was a frequent species of exaction, the burden of which, however, the rich helped the poor to bear.[3] When rulers were refused special levies by the people, the Jews were at least forced to pay, and did not escape because the rest of the population was recalcitrant.[4] Further, the Jews were made to contribute annually to the costs of the popular sports and entertainments in the Roman circuses, at first (in the middle of the fourteenth century) only twelve gold pieces, but in 1443 it had grown to 1130 pieces.[5] The Jews were also forced to make a personal participation in the pageants which their money helped to present. Many specially galling taxes were also inflicted in England, but the general burdens of the feudal system were so great that it may be doubted whether they were exceptionally oppressed.[6] In Spain, the Jews, among other things, had to pay for the king's dinner; they were subjected to a hearth tax, to a coronation tax, to a tax on meat and bread[7] — but it would be impossible to enumerate all the vexatious dues exacted from the Jews everywhere throughout the middle ages. Whether the tax was termed a 'protection tax' or was called by any other name, whether the king or noble

---

[1] Cf. Jacobs, *MS. Sources of History of Jews in Spain*, p. xxiv. 86, 89.

[2] Kayserling, *Christopher Columbus*, p. 4.

[3] Thus S. b. David, שו"ת נחלת שבעה, § 10.

[4] This happened e.g. in 1307 in Rome.   [5] Berliner, *Rom*, ii. (1) 61.

[6] Mr. Jacobs (see above, p. 42) estimates that the Jews provided one-twelfth of the royal revenue.   [7] Jacobs, *Spain*, Introduction.

saved them from the clutches of all other robbers but
their so-called protector himself, at one time or another
the Jews had to pay for every act of their lives — for leaving or entering towns, for passing through gates or travers-
ing bridges,[1] for crossing the frontiers of the diminutive
Rhine states, for buying or selling, for marriage or sepul-
ture. The tax-collector stood by the sexton and stopped
the burial till his fee of two florins was handed to him.[2] In
Granada, the Jews had to pay the Alfarda or 'strangers'
tax' in 1480, though the Jews were far older settlers in
Andalusia than were they who imposed the fine. A
favourite device for raising money was to grant only temporary licences of residence to Jews, and for the triennial
renewals a large fee was exacted. Similarly in the Rhine-
lands the Rabbi had to be confirmed by the State every
three years, and this not only meant a heavy fine on the
community, but it unfortunately opened the door to internal intrigues.[3] Germany indeed enjoyed the distinction
of exacting more fees on more occasions than any other
medieval State. The Jewish poll-tax lingered on latest
of all in the same State. It was only abolished in 1803
on payment of an indemnity. The taxes outlined above
are closely allied to the communal taxes imposed by Jews
on Jews, to meet the claims of extortionate governments
as well as the costs of their own organization. Meat,
wine, houses, golden and silver ornaments, jewels, wed-
ding-gifts, imports and exports, were all taxed for these

---

[1] At Anjou, in 1162, Henri II enacted 'Judei si detulerint per pontem
vadimonia sua ad vendendum, dabunt *denarium unum*' (*Archives Nationales*
cited in *Juifs d'Angers*, p. 7). No one but a Jew was subject to this tax.

[2] Löwenstein, *Geschichte der Juden in der Kurpfalz*, p. 32.

[3] *Jewish Quarterly Review*, iii. 310.

purposes.[1] Communal officials were even paid from the
proceeds of collections made at weddings in Poland,
Russia, and Hungary.[2]

Amidst all this external interference, the internal government of the Jewries was largely delegated to Jews
themselves. One of the supreme duties of the Jew in
every age, but more especially after the beginning of the
Crusading epoch, was the obligation to keep Jewish affairs
from the ordinary law-courts.[3] Very often they obtained
the right to enforce this paramount duty. In other words,
the Jewish communities were often able to try not only
civil but even criminal cases in which Jews were involved
as litigants or malefactors. The two lines of privilege ran
closely together, no doubt, especially in the case of informers. For the informer the medieval Jews had no pity;
he was outside the pale of humanity.[4] Death was his
penalty, and executions of this kind were far from rare.
The greatest Rabbis of the middle ages fearlessly sen-
tenced informers to death, and cases of this severity
occurred in all parts of the Jewish world. There can be
no doubt that the rigour which culminated in a tragedy
was perfectly justifiable. Denunciation was the canker
of Jewish medieval society, and massacre and exile often
followed the lying evidence brought against Jews by
unprincipled *delatores.* Hence there was no room for
hesitation, and a good old Talmudic maxim — 'If thou
seest a man in the very act of slaying thee, and no alter-

[1] Eskapa's *Tekanoth,* in ספר עבורת משא.
[2] *Or Zarua,* i. p. 40.
[3] The famous *tekanah* of R. Tam on this subject was frequently repeated in
later times. Cf. p. 58 below.
[4] Cf. Prof. Kaufmann's interesting monograph on the subject in the eighth
volume of the *Jewish Quarterly Review.*

native presents itself, thou mayest prevent him, even at the cost of his life '[1] — was put into force as a pure measure of self-defence.   It is said that as late as the close of the eighteenth century a Jewish informer was put to death in Poland, where the dreadful mischief wrought by this class was slowest to be eradicated.   At last the Jews fell back on prayers and imprecations, and 'as a survival of this gloomy phenomenon of medieval history, there long existed in the ritual a prayer, which was repeated on Mondays and Thursdays, and at other times, against this evil of society.'[2]   Finally, however, even this last trace of medievalism has vanished from Jewish life.

But it must not be imagined that these executions of informers were usually secret or illegal.   In Spain we have particular evidence that the capital punishment was not only never inflicted without the sanction of the government, but the sentence was executed by its officers. Indeed, the Jews were hardly allowed to levy taxes upon themselves for their own internal needs without the sanction of the civil authorities.[3]   Much less were they allowed a free hand in criminal matters; but a large measure of

---

[1] On the other hand, it was strictly forbidden, by the Jewish Council held at Lydda under Hadrian, for a Jew to save his own life at the cost of another's. There was a popular proverb to the same effect : ' How knowest thou that thy blood is redder than another's ? ' i.e. how can you tell that your life is the more valuable ?   (*Pesachim*, 25 b.)   [2] Kaufmann, ibid.

[3] Cf. e.g. the Ordinance of Valladolid in 1412, § 8 : 'No Aljama, or community of Jews or Moors, shall presume to levy any tax or contribution on themselves, or impose a duty on any article (meat, merchandise, or any other object), without the royal permission or order . . . under pain of corporal and other punishments, and no Jew or Moor shall pay such contributions as may be levied without the royal licence and order being expressly given for the purpose.'   One other example may be cited; this dates from Avignon, 1779.   The communal statutes, one by one, have to receive the authorization of the Town Council.   (*Annuaire*, 1885, p. 199.)

liberty was undoubtedly possessed by them in Spain at least until the year 1379, up to which date the Jewish courts could inflict the death penalty as well as minor punishments. But the Jews themselves asked that the execution of these sentences should be left to the Christian bailiffs. In 1360 the Jews of Tudela, entreating the continuation of their former privileges, obtained the Viceroy's assent to this proposal : 'That he would be pleased to order that we may continue *the Jewish law as our ancestors have done hitherto ;* that is, that when a Jew or Jewess commits a sin, on our magistrates applying to the bailiff, and notifying to him the sin committed, and the punishment it deserves according to Jewish law, the bailiff shall execute it, and enforce the sentence of our said magistrates, whether of condemnation or acquittal.'[1] The Jewish congregations had either their own prisons, or at least separate rooms in the ordinary prisons[2] were reserved for the use of Jewish offenders. In Spain, the Jewish prisoners are kept apart from the rest ;[3] in Avignon, the Jewish authorities were able to arrest Jewish offenders and have them conveyed to prison with the sanction of the civil powers. Such prisoners were not released without

[1] Lindo, *The Jews in Spain*, p. 150. Jews had their own jurisdiction almost everywhere in the middle ages. For England, cf. Jacobs, *Angevin England*, pp. 43, 49. Criminal cases between Jews, except for the greater felonies, such as homicide and mayhem, might be decided in England (by the charter of Henry II) by the Jews themselves, and in accordance with their own laws. (Jacobs, ibid. p. 331.) Another form of the same privilege was to allot a special Christian judge to try Jewish cases. He would thus be familiar with Jewish law and usages.

[2] See Ephraim b. Jacob, שו"ת שערי אפרים, § 83, in which it is decided that the communal prison must have a *mezuzah* affixed to it.

[3] Jacobs, *Spain*, xxvi. 139. So, too, it was enacted in Majorca in 1273 that Jews and Christians were to be imprisoned in separate *houses* (*Revue des Études Juives*, iv. 34).

the permit of the Jewish officials.[1] In the Bastile, Jewish
prisoners claimed to follow their own religion ; and in the
French prisons generally in the eighteenth century, the
Jews had special food, retained their religious books, and
kept the Sabbath.[2] When Meir of Rothenburg was imprisoned in the tower of Ensisheim in Alsace (June 1286),
he, like R. Akiba before him, was permitted 'to receive
visits, to instruct his pupils, and to perform the functions
of Rabbi.'[3]

Besides these privileges, the Jews were empowered to
maintain discipline within their own communal bounds.
They inflicted corporal punishment and exacted fines.
But their chief weapon was a moral one, terrible no doubt
in its effects, but the wounds it caused were not irremediable. Mostly the excommunication lasted only for a
brief period, the milder form (or *niddui*) enduring for
thirty days, during which the culprit wore mourning garb
and was denied the society of his brethren. Excommunication of the severer kind, the *cherem* proper, lasted longer,
and was a complete social and religious boycott, involving
the culprit's family unless they too renounced him. The
externals of the penalty were awe-inspiring, even to weird-
ness. The formal warning, the public humiliation, the
solemn announcement, with its accompaniment of lighted
candles extinguished to the blast of the *shofar* (or ram's
horn), the Oriental completeness and verbose vindictiveness of the curses pronounced in the synagogue, were a
fitting prelude to the isolation which followed. Similar

---

[1] *Annuaire*, i. p. 215.

[2] Kahn, *Les Juifs de Paris sous Louis XV*, p. 33, and *Les Juifs de Paris au XVIIIe siècle*, pp. 44–46.

[3] Graetz, *History* (Eng. Trans.), III. ch. xviii.

formalities accompanied the administration of a public oath in case of disputes. 'We bring the funeral bier, and place thereon a cock ; we cover the bier with a fringed garment (*tallith*), illuminate the building, strew burnt ashes under the man's feet, introduce bladders to terrify him, while children and horns (*shofars*) add to the din ; then we seat him below the Ark, and the precentor, standing over him with a scroll of the Law, says: so-and-so will not confess the truth.'[1] Some of the features of the later penances inflicted on excommunicated Jews were borrowed from the medieval Church,[2] for excommunication was at least as rife in Christendom as it was in the Jewry. The luxuriant growth of excommunication in Jewish life is not earlier than the tenth century, and it ended by becoming so common that it lost its force, for it ceased to be a terror. On the whole, the effect of excommunication on Jewish life in the middle ages was a salutary one ; it was a useful weapon, and its point could always be blunted at the will of the offender. It was the more serviceable in that its most prominent use was less against individuals than against communities, whose members voluntarily entered into certain undertakings under penalty of excommunication should they disregard their promises. In this way great moral and social reforms were rendered possible, and the whole life of the Jews was organized by a series of such voluntary promises sanctioned by voluntary acceptances of the dreaded isolation in case of disobedience. This system must now be a little more fully described.

[1] *Responsa* of Geonim (*Mafteach*, p. 229).
[2] Graetz, *History* (Eng. Trans.), V. ch. iii. For a long, though hardly satisfactory, history of Jewish excommunication, see Wiesner's *Der Bann* (Leipzig, 1864).

The democratic constitution of Jewish society in the middle ages shows itself in the method of electing the governing body. The elections mostly took place in Germany on the week-days occurring during the great spring and autumn festivals.[1] In Italy another time was chosen, viz. the three weeks which separate the two summer fasts.[2] In Palermo the annual election occurred on May 1 ; in Marsala on Oct. 16.[3] The election was conducted either by lot or by ballot, the voting being always secret. The officials elected were essentially the same in all Jewish congregations, they differed little from those enumerated in the Talmud, or from those familiar to students of the New Testament records.[4] There was the President or *par excellence Parnass*,[5] the Treasurer or *Gabay ;* there were

[1] Maharil, הלכות חול המועד (beginning) ; the אבקת רוכל (of Caro), § 206, implies that it was a widespread custom to hold the elections only on the middle days of Tabernacles. Cf. *Annuaire*, i. p. 206. In Smyrna the elections occurred on the Saturday night after Passover (Eskapa's *Tekanoth*, ספר עבורת משא, § 1).

[2] Berliner, *Rom*, ii. 32. Some congregations fixed the elections for the Thursday preceding Passover and Tabernacles (cf. *Ascamot*, of London, Spanish and Portuguese Jews, § 1).

[3] Zunz, *Zur Geschichte*, p. 509. See ibid. pp. 512 seq. on the various synagogue officials in Spain, and the manner in which the Spanish congregations sometimes delegated their rights to a special trio of respected members or נאמנים, who — themselves chosen by lot from thirty selected names — nominated their three successors in similar fashion triennially.

[4] Cf. on this subject Schürer, *History of Jewish People* (Eng. Trans.), ii. (2) p. 62 seq. ; and Holtzmann, *Neutestamentliche Zeitgeschichte*, p. 147, etc.

[5] Mention is made of a woman entitled *Parnessa* in Rome in the sixteenth century (Berliner, II. (2) 33). She had charge of the charities for poor widows and orphans, for poor brides and sick women. But though the title was rare, the office seems to have been common throughout the middle ages. (See Maharil, beginning of הלכות חול המועד.) In far earlier times there was an honorary official called *mater synagogae* or *Pateressa* (Schürer, ii. 2, p. 65 ; Berliner, I. ch. v.), and women of great heart and intellect, like Donna Gracia Mendesia (1510–68), were admittedly heads of their whole community. (Graetz, *History* (Eng. Trans.), IV. ch. xvi.)

sometimes special officers to whom the care of the poor and the care of the sick were entrusted, and — except that differentiation of functions is now more complete — the modern organization of the synagogue existed in the middle ages with very slight variation. The other unpaid officials were the Council, mostly of seven,[1] and, until the thirteenth century, the Rabbi and two Dayanim (or members of the court). These became later salaried officers, and the class of paid officials included the *Shochet* (or officer to superintend the slaughtering of cattle for Jewish use), the *Chazan* or precentor, and the teacher. But the most powerful officer of all was the *Shamash* or beadle.

This functionary rapidly became ruler of the synagogue. His functions were so varied, his duties placed him in possession of such detailed information of members' private affairs, his presence so permeated the synagogue and the home on public and private occasions, — that the *Shamash*, instead of serving the congregation, became its master. Unlike the parish beadle, the characteristic of the *Shamash* was not pompousness so much as over-familiarity. He did not exaggerate his own importance, but minimized the importance of every one else. He was at once the overseer of the synagogue, and the executor of the sentences of the Jewish tribunal or *Beth Din*.[2] He

---

[1] Cf. the *tekanah* of R. Tam, *Kolbo*, § 117. They were called טובי העיר *boni urbis*, *heads of the congregation* or *Parnassim* (for the term פרנס originally included all the Council). The number of the *boni viri* varied, being mostly seven, sometimes being twelve (Güdemann, iii. 92). A strong feeling prevailed in the middle ages against electing as *boni viri* men related to one another. These *boni urbis* often had great power, and could even force their views on the congregation (*Kolbo*, § 116).

[2] The שמש is identical with the חזן הכנסת often mentioned in the Talmud. The use of the word *Chazan* as equivalent to precentor belongs to the middle

inflicted corporal punishment on those whom the Jewish court condemned to the penalty, using either a stout, doubled rope, or a leather strap.[1] But his functions were usually less violent and more picturesque. From early times the beadle was the public crier. He ascended a high roof on Friday afternoons, and with a blast of the trumpet, thrice repeated at long intervals, notified that work was to cease.[2] This very old Jewish custom was not carried to Babylon, but was retained in Palestine.[3] The favourite substitute for the *shofàr* in the middle ages was a wooden mallet. A series of knocks was dealt by the *Shamash* or other official[4] at the door of the synagogue and at the doors of all the Jews who worshipped thereat. These knocks were three or four in number, and the following passage from the testament of A. Süsskind will indicate some of the emotions which, in course of time,

ages. Another title for *Shamash* common in the Talmud and in the times of the Geonim was שליח בית דין (cf. *Mafteach*, p. 192), no doubt in distinction to the שליח צבור, the older title for precentor. The same man seems not to have served both the synagogue and *Beth Din* in the times of the Geonim.

[1] A passage in *Mafteach*, p. 192, asserts that a strap was not used by the Geonim. But in שערי תשובה, § 16, the contrary is asserted in the name of Hai Gaon.

[2] *Mishnah Succah*, v. 5. Cf. Buber's *Tanchuma*, Numbers, p. 158, where full references are given.

[3] Müller, הלוף מנהגים, § 21.

[4] This official was termed *Schulklopfer*, called also *Campanator*. The title is as old as 1225, for allusion is made to the *Schulklopfer* in Folz's carnival play, *Der Juden Messias*, of that date (Fastnachtspiele aus dem 15 Jahr. Stuttgart, 1853). Schudt (*Merkwürdigkeiten*, ii. p. 218) calls him *Schulklöpper* as well as *Schulklopfer* (p. 287). The office is much older than the name, for *Talm. Jerus.* Beza, ch. v. cites סבי אקושי' רבי כנישתא. Cf. the interesting comment of the Mordecai *ad loc.* For the number of knocks cf. Schudt, ibid., and Güdemann, iii. 95. On Sabbaths the mallet was not used, but the fist. Some Jews appointed special watchmen to summon them individually to prayers (יוסף אומץ, § 487). On the fast of the ninth of Ab, the *Schulklopfer* did not make his usual rounds (Maharil).

these early morning summonses aroused. 'It is a common practice with Jews that when a member of the community has died during the night, the *Shamash*, when he comes to summon us to synagogue, gives only two instead of the usual three knocks, as a sign of death. When he only knocked twice, I sighed; but when thrice, my heart leapt up with joy!' The *Shamash* also made announcements in synagogue, sometimes interrupting the prayers to do so.[1] He carried the invitations to private festivities,[2] and sometimes the Council of the congregation claimed the right to supervise the invitations, and, if they thought fit, might refuse to sanction them. The *Shamash* was despatched to remind congregants of their duties, such as leaving their boots at home on the eve of the Day of Atonement, and observing some mourning rites on the Sabbath on which the ninth of Ab[3] fell. As regards attendance at synagogue, this was mostly voluntary; but on the New Year and the Day of Atonement, the Jewish authorities were empowered to *compel* ten adult males to attend and thus form a congregation.[4]

---

[1] Ibid. § 310.

[2] *Annuaire*, I. pp. 109, 110, 206, 211. He also went to summon the Council to their meetings.

[3] Maharil (ed. Warsaw, 1874), p. 45 a and 33 a.

[4] Maharil, § on ימים הנוראים, Israel b. Chayim of Brünn, שו"ת, § 164, maintain that the congregation must provide a *minyan* (or ten adult male worshippers) throughout the year. The Mishnah assumes that in every large Jewish congregation ten *batlanim* or men of leisure were always available (*Mishnah Megilla*, i. 3). In the middle ages it became customary to appoint certain men to act as a sort of permanent congregation. These were already paid for the service in the time of Israel of Brünn; and no doubt the Bachurim or older Talmud students were chosen for the purpose. At first these official *batlanim* were men of high respectability and deep learning. But after a time the *minyan* man became a lower type, and was indistinguishable from the ne'er-do-well paid to form the religious quorum which the congregants were too indifferent to form by their own presence. It is

Such compulsory adherence to communal regulations lay near the root of the Jewish medieval organization. The communal life was regulated by what was known as the *Tekanah* or Ordinance. The tekanah was never drawn up without the local Rabbi's assent, indeed he was often the originator of the new regulation. When it had been passed by the chiefs of the congregation, the new law was proclaimed in synagogue on a week-day after public notice had been given, and it was held that, unless a formal, verbal protest was immediately lodged, every individual fully submitted to the general agreement, and became liable to the penalties which would accrue in the event of disobedience to the tekanah.[1] The penalties took various forms : fines, public rebuke, deprivation of the right to fill the honorary synagogal offices, flogging, imprisonment, and excommunication. The tekanoth were mostly enacted for a limited term, at the end of which they fell into disuse. Five years formed the favourite duration of a communal enactment, but a clause was frequently added providing for an annual public confirmation.[2] These tekanoth ranged over the whole field of Jewish life. At one time a tekanah would be passed to enforce monogamy :[3] at another, one would prohibit shaving ;[4] one tekanah would stringently restrain a Jew from dragging a litigant before

amusing to see how this tradition of maintaining ten men in idleness is still retained in places where the genuine *batlanim* are already only too numerous. Cf. Smolenski's fine Hebrew novel, קבורת חמור, ch. i.

[1] A full account of this whole process is given at the end of the *Kolbo* (ed. 1526).

[2] The twelve *Tekanoth* of Simon Duran (see above, p. 37) were to hold for twenty years.

[3] This was a permanent *tekanah*. See ch. iv.

[4] In this, as in all these points, there were many *local* differences, some of which will be mentioned in other parts of this book.

the Christian civil courts,[1] another would fix the tax on
meat ; one would restrain gambling, another the promiscuous dancing of men and women ; one tekanah would practically recast the whole of the laws of marriage and divorce,
another would forbid Jews to sell wine to Mohammedans ;
one tekanah would define the dress and the ornaments
which a Jewess might wear, the food she and her family
might eat, the number of visitors they might admit to
their houses ; another tekanah would decide the hour at
which our friend the *Schulklopfer* should begin his communal rounds. A very early tekanah enforced the presence
of ten males at a wedding ceremony ;[2] another, earlier
still, that the widow's marriage settlement was to be paid
from the movable property of the husband.[3] These belong to the ninth century or earlier. Equally early was
the tekanah excommunicating any man who used the
name of God, whether in Hebrew or the vernacular.
Stringent communal tekanoth prevented Jews from attempting to make proselytes, indeed the Jews went so far
as to denounce to the government Christians who were
suspected of leanings towards Judaism.[4] A local tekanah
in Sicily forbade adulteration of wine, raising the prices of
the necessaries of life, and the practice of house-to-house
begging.[5] A local tekanah of later date involved the
excommunication of a correspondent who omitted to add
after the name of a living person the words ' May his life

---

[1] E.g. the great *Tekanah* of R. Tam, *Kolbo*, § 117 ; cf. J. Jacobs' *Jews
of Angevin England*, pp. 47–49.

[2] *Responsa* of Geonim ; Müller, *Mafteach.* § 103.

[3] Ibid. § 101 ; this is described as one of the oldest *tekanoth.*

Güdemann, iii. 155. The Jewish authorities dared not connive at proselytism. Cf. the *Askamoth* of London Sephardim.

[5] Zunz, *Zur Geschichte*, p. 515.

be long!'[1]   Tekanoth were passed against singing secular songs on fast-days,[2] against permitting any one but the local Rabbi to preach on certain days,[3] against electing as Rabbi a man with relatives in the congregation.[4]   A large series of tekanoth dealt with the questions of rent,[5] on the restriction both of foreign immigration and of the emigration of old settlers (parents might not settle their children in other communities) ; there were tekanoth against assisting the poor of other congregations to the detriment of the local poor, against the member of an old congregation attending a new one twice in succession,[6] against playing into the hands of non-Jewish dealers who unfairly raised the prices of commodities for which there was a large Jewish demand,[7] and among other curiosities may be noted a tekanah against drinking imported

[1] This is reported by Chagiz in his שו"ת הלכות קטנות, ii. 17.   Cf. some extraordinary fines in I. of Brunn's שו"ת, § 205, etc.

[2] Chayim Benveniste, שו"ת, § 44.

[3] Sabbath after the ninth of Ab (נחמו ש") and on Chanukah.   E. b. Jacob's שו"ת, § 63.   [4] A. ben Chayim, שו"ת פרח מטה אהרן, § 44.

[5] Rent was not to be raised except for improvements (Abraham b. Mordecai, שו"ת גנת ורדים, ii. 61).   New settlers raised rents, as the Jewish quarters were strictly limited, and no expansion was allowed (N. Gabbay, שו"ת, § 33).   Poor congregations were often solicited by travelling emissaries, and gave them help which they needed at home (S. Morpurgo, שו"ת שמש צדקה, § 19).   Jews were often forbidden by their communal laws to leave their own place, because the taxes then fell with increased burden on those who remained (A. b. Chayim, ibid. § 54).

[6] At Genoa, see Joseph David, בית דוד, ii. 103.   This difficulty greatly increased in modern times, owing to the dwindling of the Sephardic congregations (cf. Samuel b. Ezekiel Landau, שו"ת שיבת ציון, § 5).

[7] See שו"ת צמח צדק, § 28: 'Once the non-Jewish fishmongers raised the price of fish when they saw that the Jews wanted to buy it for Saturdays. The chiefs of the congregation made a *tekanah* that for two months no Jew should buy any fish.'   Similarly the Talmud (Gittim, 45) ordains that Jews should not ransom Jewish slaves at too high a price, lest this would put a premium on the enslavement of Jews.

wine.[1] But tekanoth on all subjects of social morality
have continued to be formulated until the present time.
In the seventeenth century, in Lemberg,[2] for instance,
some most severe penalties were inflicted on absconders,
on those pawnbrokers who lent money on articles of which
the presumption was that they were stolen, while the
commission of an agent who negotiated the sale of a house
was fixed at one per cent from both parties to the contract, and the widow's settlement was made a first charge
on the deceased husband's estate. An interesting Lemberg tekanah[2] forbade the building of houses which
blocked the road to the synagogue. Most of the medieval tekanoth had no retrospective action.[4]

But despite this readiness to enter into voluntary obligations, both communal and (as we shall see elsewhere)
personal, it may be doubted whether the Jewish organization alone could have succeeded as well as it did in keeping
up the tone of Jewish life. The organization was helped
and completed by a sense of equity which became ever a
stronger tradition as the darker ages of ghetto-life drew
nearer. This sense of equity was summed up in the Talmudical principle of *Chazaka*, or the rights of possession.
The same phenomenon reappears in modern life under
the form of Tenant-Right. But for the proper understanding of this principle, a glance must be had at the
new conditions which ensued from the forcible confine-
ment of Jews within ghettos.

---

[1] Samuel de Medina, פסקי הרשד"ם, § 17.

[2] See the *Tekanoth* in Buber's אנשי שם, pp. 222, 226, etc.

[3] Ibid. p. 229.

[4] This is often distinctly stated. Cf. the eleventh clause of Duran's
Tekanoth (יש"ח התשב"ץ, ii. 292), and the much later repetition of the same
clause in the Lemberg *Tekanoth* at the end of Buber's אנשי שם.

CHAPTER IV

INSTITUTION OF THE GHETTO

Long before residence within a restricted quarter or ghetto[1] was compulsory, the Jews almost everywhere had concentrated in separate parts of the towns in which they lived.[2] Though the era of the ghetto proper begins with the sixteenth century, numerous records are extant of the seclusion of Jews in special quarters several centuries earlier.[3] The *voluntary* congregation of Jews in certain parts of the towns, due to the needs of the communal organization, was very common by the thirteenth century.

[1] The word *ghetto* is most probably derived, as Dr. Berliner maintains (*Rom*, ii. (2) p. 26), from the Italian *geto* or *iron-foundry*, in the neighbourhood of which the first ghetto in Italy (in Venice) was constituted in 1516. The word *ghettum* occurs in a document dated 1306 (Rieger, p. 291). Indeed, Dr. Berliner's may now be regarded as the accepted theory. Anyhow, all other suggestions are too fanciful to deserve even a mention.

[2] There were many exceptions, of course, e.g. Lincoln in 1290. From the records published in the *Jewish Quarterly Review*, viii. p. 360, it is clear that was no Jewish quarter then. On the other hand, the 'Jews' Street' in London is mentioned as early as 1115 (Jacobs, *Angevin England*, 13).

[3] Compulsory ghettos seem to have been in vogue in Sicily as early as the fourteenth, and in parts of Germany even in the twelfth and thirteenth centuries. In Angers in the fourteenth century there was a *Juiverie* (Brunschvicg, *Juifs d'Angers*, p. 15). But until after the foundation of the Roman ghetto in 1555, little rigour was shown in preventing the residence of Jews without the Jewish quarter. On the other hand, there were no ghettos in Coblenz and Trier as late as the seventeenth century (*Jewish Quarterly Review*, iii. 310). In Halle there was a *Judendorf* before the ghetto period (Auerbach, *Geschichte der isr. Gememde Halberstadt*, p. 15).

In Cologne there was a Jews' quarter at that period; though in that city, as well as in most places where voluntary Jewish quarters existed, Jews also resided outside the Jewish district.[1] But the distinction one achieves is not as the distinction that is thrust on one. Nowhere is this more strikingly seen than in the case of Prague. There the Jews who lived outside the *Judenstadt*, determined in 1473 to voluntarily throw in their lot with their brethren in the Jewish town. Now, Prague came in for its own sorry share of persecution and massacre, but on the whole the inhabitants of the Prague Judenstadt had a freer and fresher life than was possible in other compulsory ghettos. The Judenstadt, at the close of the sixteenth century, had its Jewish town-hall, and — privilege most prized of all — a small bell summoned the members to deliberations within its walls. A further distinction of the Prague Jews was the right to bear a flag. This was conferred on them in 1357 for their patriotic services, and the flag is still preserved in the synagogue.[2] Perhaps, however, some facts connected with the Roman ghetto and the Spanish juderias will make the difference clearer between a voluntary and a compulsory massing of Jewish inhabitants in one particular part of a town. In 1555, when Paul IV established the ill-omened ghetto in Rome, there were very few Jewish families resident anywhere else than in the *serraglio delli hebrei* or *septus hebraicus*,[3] as the Jewish quarter on the left bank of the Tiber was

---

[1] See *Das Judenschreinbuch der Laurezpf. zu Köln*, pp. 23, 78. There was a *Jews' Street*, רהוב היהודים, but Jews also lived in the צר הם (p. 41) — i.e. in the Christian quarters.

[2] Philipson, *Old European Jewries*, p. 106.

[3] Cf. Rieger, *Geschichte der Juden in Rom*. ii. p. 290. The best account of the Roman ghetto is Berliner's (*Rom*, ii. (2) pp. 26, 27).

called. But though few Jews dwelt elsewhere, many of the noblest Christians resided in the very heart of the Jewish quarter. Stately palaces and churches stood in the near neighbourhood of the synagogue, and the Roman Christians held free and friendly intercourse with their Jewish fellow-inhabitants. When, however, the ghetto was formally constituted, churches and palaces were gradually removed or divided from the contamination of the neighbouring Jewish abodes by huge and menacing walls.[1] This same thing occurred in Spain, where, however, the separation of the Jews from the rest of the inhabitants was never completely successful because the expulsion of the Jews occurred in 1492, just before the dawn of that black age in Jewish life, the sixteenth century, the century of the ghetto and degradation. What happened in Spain is very instructive, and enables us to fix the rival tendencies which led the Church to the device of creating distinct Jewish ghettos. As early as the eleventh century we find mention of a 'Jewish barrier' in Tudela.[2] In Seville in 1248, Ferdinand appropriated three parishes to the Jews, and surrounded it with a wall, 'extending from the Alcazar to the gate of Carmona,' in order to protect the Jews.[3] Within this quarter were the Jewish 'exchanges, markets, courts of justice, and slaughter-houses, and in an adjacent field their cemetery.' This placing of the burial-ground near the Jewish quarter was, by the way, not uncommon all over Europe. It usually lay at the very limit of the *Judengasse*, often right on the rampart, surrounded sometimes by the town-moat.

---

[1] The high wall separating the ruined palace of the Cenci from the Piazza delle Scuole was only removed in 1847. Rieger, 292.

[2] Lindo, *Spain*, p. 71.   [3] Ibid. p. 85.

But to return to the Jewish quarters in Spain. At first the ghetto was rather a privilege than a disability, and sometimes was claimed by the Jews as a right when its demolition was threatened.[1] In 1412 the ordinances of Valladolid take on a more persecuting tone, and all Jews and Moors are ordered to dwell within separate enclosures. But though the Jews of Castile were only granted a term of eight days within which to transfer themselves to their separate enclosures, and though menaces were held out of corporal punishment and confiscation of property should any Jew or Moor be found outside these enclosures after the eight days had passed, only six months later the ordinance at Cifuentes has to repeat the same injunction, this time fixing the period of grace at a full year.[2] In this ordinance we meet with the familiar ghetto arrangement, afterwards common all over Europe, by which the town appointed two officials as gate-keepers of the Jewry.[3] This arrangement, by the way, was certainly no hardship ; it was protective quite as much as disciplinary, and the same remark applies to the closing of the gates in all the ghettos from sunset to sunrise. Closing the gates over-night was a feature of all medieval life, and the Jews never complained of it. Modern writers have here misread his-

[1] Thus, in the year 1300, such a case occurred in Majorca. Cf. *Revue des Études Juives*, iv. 34.   [2] Lindo, *Spain*, p. 202.

[3] The Jews probably paid for these watchmen. They paid the city of Cologne in 1341 twenty marks yearly as fee to the officer who 'locked the gates at sundown and unlocked them at prime.' (Philipson, *Old European Jewries*, p. 29 ; Stobbe, *Die Juden in Deutschland*, p. 94.) The watchmen were sometimes *Jews;* the epitaph of some who died in 1668 seq. at Prague may be seen in Popper's *Inschriften des Prager Judenfriedhofs*, p. 20. Similarly a Jew was secretary of the 'street police' (ibid.). Hence there is no improbability in Travers' assertion that the Jews of Nantes in the thirteenth century had their own *sénéchal* (Brunschvicg, *Nantes*, p. 4).

tory in conjuring up a grievance in this very ordinary
factor of medieval town-life. Still fixing our attention for
the moment on the Iberian peninsula, it is clear that right
up to the initiation of the Inquisition in Spain, the Spanish
Jewries were not rigidly constituted. For the seventy-
sixth paragraph of the decisions arrived at by the Cortes
of Toledo in 1480,[1] held after the union of the crowns of
Aragon and Castile, opens with a clause which proves that
up to that date the attempt to isolate the Jews had utterly
failed : ' As great injury and inconvenience results from
the *constant society* of Jews and Moors *being intermixed
with Christians*, we ordain and command that all Jews and
Moors of every city, town, and place in these our kingdoms . . . shall have their distinct Jewries and Moories
by themselves, and not reside intermixed with Christians,
nor have enclosures together with them, etc.' Herein is
seen the real atrocity of the institution of the ghetto. It
was a device actually to separate Jews from Christians,
though it operated, as a matter of fact, rather by separating Christians from Jews.[2] The old protective motive is

---

[1] Lindo, p. 245.

[2] Very interesting is this enactment of a Council held in Coyanza in
Asturias in 1050 (Lindo's *Spain*, p. 51) :—' CANON 6.—That no Christian
shall reside in the same house with Jews, nor partake of their food ; whoever transgresses this decree shall perform penance for seven days, or,
refusing to do it, *if a person of rank*, he shall be excommunicated for a year;
if of an inferior degree, he shall receive 100 lashes.' It is instructive to
compare this with the decision of the Council of Palencia in 1388 (ibid.
p. 168). ' Christians must not dwell within the quarters assigned to Jews
and Moors, and *those that resided within them* were to remove therefrom
within two months after the publication of this decree in the cathedral, and
if they did not, were to be compelled by ecclesiastical censure.' It is
evident that many Christians lived in the Jewish quarters before the ghetto
days. Since the ghettos have been abolished, the old Jewish quarters in
European towns are now freely used by Christians.

abandoned, the theory and practice of social ostracism begins, and after the fifteenth century we find no pretence that the ghetto was instituted on behalf of the Jews. It was occasionally a protection, no doubt ; the ghetto gates sometimes rolled back outbursts of popular cruelty, and saved the Jews from massacre. But oftener it had the very opposite effect, for when bigots wanted their Jews to kill, they knew where to find them *en masse.* The ghetto enclosed them in one defenceless pen.

Besides the isolation which the ghettos more or less perfectly effected — I say more or less, for it is quite certain that many Jews contrived to secure the privilege of living outside the ghetto gates — the most serious effect of the new persecution was the terrible overcrowding that necessarily followed from herding thousands of Jews in confined spaces. The Jewish population grew, but the ghettos remained practically unchanged. Enlargements were occasionally permitted, but on the whole the original limits of the ghettos were not expanded. Hence even when the localities in which the ghettos were constructed were not slums, they rapidly became so. Sometimes the Jewish quarter, as in Cologne in the thirteenth century, was the narrowest part of the town, and was even called the 'Narrow Street.'[1]

---

[1] רחוב היהורים הנקרא רחוב קצר (*Das Judenschreinbuch,* p. 23). The German equivalent was *Engegasse.* Dr. Philipson frequently alludes with justice to the narrowness of the ghetto streets, the tallness of the houses, and the obscuration of the sunlight, as grievances. But these features were not always peculiar to the ghettos. Old London streets must have been as dark and sombre as any medieval *Judengasse,* and the same remark applies to most continental towns. Daylight and medievalism were hardly compatible notions. The point is, of course, that the Jewish quarters retained their medieval aspect long after the towns in which they were located had widened their streets and added generally to the comforts of life.

In Frankfort the ghetto was situate near the moat, and on the other side of it lived 'gardeners and people employed in the woods by the day.' But when 4000 persons lived in 190 houses,[1] in a gloomy street, twelve feet wide, with its houses meeting at the top; and when persistently the authorities restricted the Jewish population to this one street, in which a wagon could not turn; when, as in some cities, the brothels were placed in the Judengasse to add to their ill-repute[2] — the effects on the population made themselves marked in many ways to be considered hereafter. The effects were almost completely external, however, and produced no serious moral evils. The purity of the Jewish home-life was a constant antidote to the poisonous suggestions of life in slums, and it was even able to resist the terrible squalor and unhealthiness which prevailed in the miserable and infamous Roman ghetto, where at one time as many as 10,000 inhabitants were herded into a space less than a square kilometre.[3] In the poorer streets of this ghetto, several families occupied one and the same room. The sufferings of the Jews in that hell upon earth in the papal city were not diminished by the yearly overflowing of the Tiber, which made the Roman ghetto a dismal and plague-stricken swamp.

The wide development of the doctrine of *chazaka*, or respect to the equitable rights of others, was the salvation of a society thus thrown upon itself. By a variety of severe tekanoth Jews were forbidden to avail themselves of the letter of the civil law against one another. It is only possible to follow out one or two ramifications of this system of equity and loyalty to brethren in misfortune.

[1] Philipson, p. 56.   [2] Stobbe, p. 276.   [3] Rieger, p. 294.

Originating long before the days of the ghetto, the principle of respecting old rights, which the State ignored, survived the fall of the ghetto walls. Thus it was an old tekanah, probably dating from the tenth century, that no Jew should rent a house from a Christian in place of another Jewish tenant, unless the latter assented to the arrangement, or a year has elapsed since the former tenant vacated the house.[1] It must be understood that the houses occupied by Jews, even in the ghettos, were often owned by Christians, who charged exorbitant rents. If the Jewish organization had not enforced some such law as the one just quoted, there would have been no limit to the house-owner's rapacity.[2] A series of tekanoth drawn up at Ferrara, on the very eve of the creation of the Roman ghetto, has so many points of interest that I quote these ordinances in full, though only the fifth article bears on our present point. These enactments were the work of delegates of the Jewish congregations of Rome, Ferrara, Mantua, Romagna, Bologna, Reggio, Modena, and Venice, and hence they applied to the whole of Italy.[3]

'*The following regulations were passed at a general meeting of the undersigned delegates, held in the city of Ferrara, on Thursday, June 21st, 1554.*

' May it be the divine will that God's grace rest on our work, and that his purpose be fulfilled through us. Amen!

' (i) No printer shall print any new book [4] without the

---

[1] *Kolbo*, § 116.

[2] Pope Clement VIII was bound to interfere and fix the rents which might be charged to Jews in the Roman ghetto.

[3] These *Tekanoth* were published in the Hebrew periodical, עברי אנכי, vol. xv., and were republished in 1879 at Brody.

[4] This *tekanah* was often re-enacted. In 1554 the Jews' books in Rome and Venice were confiscated and burnt. The Jewish authorities feared lest some handle to hostile censorship might be supplied by imprudent controversialists. Hence this *tekanah*.

licence and approval of three Rabbis who are themselves possessed of diplomas from three Rabbis. If the publication is issued in a small town, then the licence of the lay-heads of one of the neighbouring congregations must be obtained ; but if the town is large, then the licences of the lay-heads of that town and of the three Rabbis will suffice. At the head of every book the names of the licensors shall be printed. No Jew may buy any book that does not bear these licences, the penalty of infringement of this tekanah shall be a fine of twenty-five golden scudi in each individual case. The fines shall be devoted to the relief of the poor.

'(ii) Should any Jew force another Jew to appear in the Christian civil courts, then the latter may subsequently refuse to transfer the dispute to the Jewish *Beth Din* (or court of justice).

'(iii) No one shall write a decision on a monetary dispute without the consent of the parties to the dispute, or the consent of the two *dayanim* (judges) appointed by the two parties and the third *dayan* appointed as assessor. Such a decision is forbidden, even though the names be disguised as Reuben and Simeon.

'(iv) No Rabbi of one congregation shall interfere with the internal affairs of another congregation, nor shall any of his decisions be valid in a congregation which has its own Rabbi.

'(v) Whereas there are some who infringe the tekanah of Rabbenu Gershom, which forbids any Jew from ousting another Jew from a house rented from a Christian landlord, and whereas such offenders claim that when the landlord sells his house the Jewish tenant thereby also loses his *chazaka* (= his rights of preferential tenancy), we therefore decree that though the Christian owner sell his house, the right of the Jewish tenant to retain possession is unchanged, and any Jew who ousts him is disobeying the tekanah of R. Gershom and also this tekanah, now newly enacted.

'(vi) Seeing that there are men who rely on an authority who declares that if a man has lived ten years with his wife, and has not fulfilled the law of propagation, he may marry a second wife, despite the tekanah of R. Gershom to the contrary, we hereby decree that if he have a son or daughter [and not both], although he has not thereby fulfilled the duty of increase, nevertheless he may not marry a second wife without the assent and pleasure of his wife,[1] and of one of her near relatives, who shall formally authorize the remarriage in the presence of trustworthy witnesses.

' (vii) Whoever marries in the presence of less than ten witnesses, without the consent of her parents, or if she be an orphan, of two of her nearest relatives, is hereby excommunicated, both he and the witnesses present at such a ceremony.'

The fifth clause is perhaps the earliest instance of the *jus casaca*,[2] which gave the Jewish tenant of a Christian's house in the ghetto a right in that house which no other Jew could usurp. This right was inherited, so that the Jews became practically leaseholders in perpetuity of their ghetto homes. They sold their *jus casaca* and bestowed it as dowries on their daughters. The *jus casaca* (also spelt *gazaga*[3]) was transferable, and Clement VIII legalized

---

[1] Cf. p. 116, below.
[2] I.e. Jus חזקה (tenant-right).
[3] Berliner, *Rom*, ii. (2) 71.

this Jewish arrangement by practically making evictions impossible so long as the rent (also fixed by him) was duly paid. The Jew might enlarge or alter the premises at will. But this concession of Clement was dearly bought, for one of his successors as a corollary practically made the community as a whole responsible for the rent of all the houses in the ghetto, whether the houses were occupied or empty.[1] Similar laws of *chazaka* were applicable to Jewish landowners; Duran, for instance, reports a tekanah which rendered it unlawful for a Jew to evict a fellow Israelite by raising the rent or by any other device whatsoever.[2] Further, there was sometimes a communal law against the renting of two houses by one tenant, unless for educational purposes.[3] Naturally, the sale of ghetto houses to Christians was forbidden.[4]

The internal organization of the medieval Jewries held nothing human to be beyond its ken. Some of the special directions into which this ubiquitous gaze strayed can only be briefly indicated here, further details being reserved for other chapters. The congregational authorities were bound to provide an official called a *shochet*, or slaughterer of animals for Jewish use. But they also provided the means for cooking the animals thus slain. Many congregations had a communal *bakehouse* or *oven*, which was used once a year for baking the passover cakes, and once a week,

---

[1] Jews attempted to boycott apostates by refusing to inhabit the houses which were vacated by converts on leaving the ghetto. The popes effectually stopped this proceeding by exacting from the community the rent of all empty houses (cf. Berliner, ibid. p. 72). This led the Jews themselves to put some limitations on the *jus gazaga* (ibid.).

[2] שו״ת התשב״ץ, ii. 61.

[3] Jacob Weil, שו״ת, § 118.

[4] Cf. *Annuaire* (Avignon), i. p. 168.

on Fridays, for cooking the *shalent* or *schalet*.[1] This, as well as other utensils for cooking purposes, was supplied at the communal cost. Thus, a huge copper cauldron belonged to the community, and was at the disposal of any member who had a wedding feast on hand and wished to add stews to the roasts.[2] The community made some provision, too, for a water supply, and when necessary a well was dug within the synagogue enclosure, probably to provide the water for the bath. There were two kinds of communal baths — the ritual bath or *mikveh*, and the ordinary public bath.[3] No congregation was destitute of the former, and

---

[1] This communal oven was possessed by all German congregations. Cf. Güdemann, iii. 91; יוסף אומץ, § 633. See also the references in the *Judenschreinbuch*, p. 17, where mention (date 1266) is made of the 'Great Bakery.'

[2] Maharil יוכן קרירה נחושת גדולה היתה מיוחדת לקהל לבשל בה לנישואין: (Hilchoth, היתר ואסור). The richer members sometimes paid for the use of the oven (cf. *Annuaire*, i. p. 214), the poor used it without charge. Besides, or in place of, this communal oven there was occasionally a house which was a sort of guildhall of the bakers. Cf. Juda Minz, *Responsa*, 7.

[3] When the Jews were expelled from Heidelberg in 1391, the following confiscated properties of the Jews were presented to the University: the *Judenschule* (or synagogue), with its neighbouring houses and the adjacent *garden;* various private houses; and the Jewish *cemetery* with its house, court and garden. This last is not the same garden as the synagogue garden, but was the *hortus Judeorum*, or 'hortus qui fuit olim cimiterium Judeorum.' (The tombstones were sold in 1397.) In the inventory of the property belonging to the synagogue in 1391 are mentioned 'duo candelabra ferrea magna, que fuerunt Judeorum,' and a vaulted chamber which stood near the synagogue and served as a *Jews' bath :* 'pro testudine que quondam nominabatur *balneum Judeorum*.' (Löwenstein, *Geschichte der Juden in der Kurpfalz* (Frankfurt, 1895), p. 17.) The Jews of Augsburg in 1290 also had a special *Badehaus* (*Monatsschrift*, 1861, p. 280). If Mr. Jacobs' suggestion (*Angevin England*, p. 236) be accepted, and *Bakewell Hall* = *Bathwell Hall*, then the Jews' bath of London must have been a noteworthy building. As to the prohibition of Jews from bathing in the rivers, such edicts were very numerous. Thus in the fourteenth century the Jews of Angers were readmitted to the town on several onerous conditions, one being that they would not bathe in the river Maine (Brunschvicg, *Juifs d'Angers*, 1895, p. 15).

since the State often forbade the Jews to bathe in the rivers Christians used, many congregations had perforce to provide an ordinary bath also.   Above the bakehouse, or in near proximity to it, was a large *communal hall* in which marriages were solemnized.   This hall had various names, and the Jews were very keen on preserving their rights with regard to it.   In 1288 the attempt of an individual to deprive the congregation of Cologne of its hall was defeated by the energetic action of the Jews, who declared that 'it had been the property of the congregation for thirty years.'   Whether the wedding banquet was spread, and the ball gaily footed in the same hall, is uncertain, but there are frequent mentions in medieval records of both a *guest-house* and a *dancing-hall*.   The guest-house was sometimes called the Inn, and seems to have been the means of providing for passing travellers, for whom private entertainment was lacking.   The 'Jews' Inn' is found in early Spanish records as well as in late French, and was a source of considerable trouble to the Parisian police in the eighteenth century.   The Jews were then under the surveillance of a special police inspector, to whom every Jew was accountable for every hour of his day.[1]   This inspector was chiefly anxious to extort as much blackmail from the Jews as he possibly could, but by harbouring travellers in the 'Jews' Inn,' or *Auberge Juive*, the community often evaded some of his attempts to squeeze money out of friendless strangers.   Sometimes there were two or three such inns in Paris at the same time, and it is diverting to note the ingenuity of the police in their attempt to draw the guests of these *auberges* within the

[1] Léon Kahn, *Les Juifs de Paris au XVIIIe siècle* (Paris, 1894), whence these particulars are taken.

expansive nets of their extortions. First, they accused
these inns of being 'houses of ill repute,' but finding that
this charge brought in an inadequate revenue, they tried an
opposite tack, and declared that the Jews' Inns were 'a
kind of synagogue,' an institution apparently more obnoxious to the municipality than a brothel![1] These inns,
however, had by the eighteenth century become private
enterprises; the community as a whole no longer provided
them.

A more general adjunct of medieval Jewish communities was the 'dancing-hall' or *Tanzhaus*. Dancing, as we
shall see in a later chapter, was a favourite Jewish pastime.
Even if this *Tanzhaus* was designed only for use at weddings[2] — yet as the festivities on such occasions lasted for
a week, and in a large community not many weeks can
have passed without a wedding — the *Tanzhaus* must have
been in pretty constant occupation by merry parties.
The *Tanzhaus* became very popular, and soon spread
throughout France and Germany; most of the ghettos
had their *dancing-halls*. In Spain and the East the institution does not appear, for the houses of the Jews were
larger in those parts, and great entertainments could be

[1] Ibid. p. 41.
[2] Güdemann, iii. 138. The *Tanzhaus* was probably identical with the
בית חתנות. In the *Judenschreinbuch* of Cologne the same building is termed
בית הנישואין (p. 62), בית החתנות (p. 64), and in the Latin documents *Speilhuz*
or *Speylhuz*. An entry at Speyer of date 1354 speaks of the great 'Schulhof
called Dantzhus oder *Brutehus*' (= bride's house, Frankel's *Monatsschrift*,
1863, 100; Ersch u. Grüber, *Juden*, p. 100). Later evidence of this identity
is provided by Schudt (*Merkwürdigkeiten*, ii. p. 5), where the Frankfort
Tanzhaus is clearly a marriage-hall. The Frankfort *Tanzhaus* is certainly
older than 1349, that in Augsburg dates from 1290 (*Monatsschrift*, 1861,
p. 280). Dr. Berliner in his *Aus dem inneren Leben*, etc., p. 8, takes the
Tanzhaus to have been a public-hall for dancing, not only at weddings.

given in private abodes.[1]   Dancing in these halls took place also on festivals and Sabbaths, but of that more must be reserved for a later chapter.   The latter remark applies also to some far more important features of the communal life, viz. the modes in which provision was made for education and for the relief of the poor.

The Jews possessed no regular organization in the middle ages for the despatch of letters to a distance, but utilized the services of travellers and merchants for this purpose.   In this way excellent communication was maintained between very distant countries and news spread very fast.   The Rabbis frequently corresponded between various parts of Europe, and even between Asia, Africa, and the European Jewries.   Sometimes a special messenger was employed for a special purpose, as when the Jewish court despatched an order or notification.   Except for the transportation of such official documents, Jews employed the services of Christians or Mohammedans who were going on pilgrimages or in caravans.[2]   Some authorities[3] employed the ordinary medium of communication for delivering a decree of divorce.   When the ghettos were established, the German Jews had their own regular letter-carrier, called — like others who possessed the right of free egress — *Schutzjude*, or 'protected Jew.'   So complete were the Jewish means of communication that Jews often acted as intelligencers to the government.   The

---

[1] It is possible that the house 'in Norwich called the Musick House, which, according to Bloomfield (*Norfolk*, iv. 76), can trace to the twelfth or even eleventh century' (Jacobs, *Angevin England*, p. 383), may have been a Jewish marriage-hall.   An interesting reference to a wedding-hall, בית המיוחד לסעוד בו לנישואין, is made in the MS. *Assufoth* (cf. Gaster, *Sefer Assufoth*, p. 48).

[2] *Responsa* of Geonim (ed. Harkavy), p. 146.

[3] E. g. R. Tam.   For a special Jewish post see Brann, *Graetz-Jubelschrift*, p. 226.

Jewish postmen were bound to respect the privacy of the letters they carried, and a special formula often appeared on Jewish despatches, reminding the bearer that he was forbidden to open them.[1]

Complete as was the care for the living, the reverence and affection for the dead showed themselves in even more loving provisions. In every Jewish community, the last refuge from the storms of life was the most sacred spot of all. The cemetery was the *House of Life*, the *Everlasting Abode*, the *Garden of the Jews*.[2] That the cemetery deserved this appellation cannot be doubted. Jews tried to beautify their burial-grounds with shrubs and trees, and, when they could, selected for the repose of the dead sites well placed amidst rural surroundings until the ghetto restrictions made this impossible.[3] Yet this *hortus Judeorum* must not be confused with another Jews' garden,[4] which surrounded the synagogue and was used as a prom-

---

[1] Letters still sometimes bear the abbreviation בהרר"ג, referring to the rule introduced by R. Gershom against permitting the opening of letters by the carriers. Cf. my articles on 'Jews and Letters' in the *Jewish Chronicle* for Jan. 1890.

[2] The title, בית החיים, House of Life, or House of the Living, was at least as old as the fourteenth century. The term may be found in the *Tashbats*, iii. 1. בית עלמין is much older (Targum to Isaiah, xlii. 11; *Koheleth Rabb.* to x. 9; *Sanhedrin*, 19 a). For the title *hortus Judeorum*, see p. 73 above, note 3. For the planting of trees, cf. Shulchan Aruch, *Yore Deah*, 368, 2. In Barcelona and Gerona the Jewish cemetery was on a hill named *Mons Judaicus*. (Kayserling, *Jewish Quarterly Review*, viii. 491.)

[3] In Heidelberg the cemetery in the fourteenth century was close to the royal park. (Cf. Löwenstein, *Kurpfalz*, p. 12.) Later on the cemeteries became so crowded that the dead as well as the living were confined to space, two and sometimes three graves being placed on top of each other. (Cf. Philipson, *Old European Jewries*, p. 78.) The same thing happened in London in the eighteenth century. When the Brady Street Cemetry was full, 'instead of purchasing a new cemetery, earth was carted and thrown over the old' (Report of United Synagogue, London, 1895).

[4] Maharil, near end (ed. Warsaw, p. פה), cites a גן חקהל.

enade. In the ghettos the cemetery was situated at the
end of the street, as far as was convenient from the
houses, in order to fulfil the old Jewish custom of burying
the dead at least fifty paces from the nearest house.[1] A
Jewish intramural cemetery in the city of London, situated
in Wood Street, is mentioned in the Patent Roll of 1285.
It was surrounded with a stone wall to keep off ma-
rauders.[2] Until the reign of Henry II the English Jews
were forced to transport their dead to London, for they
possessed only a single graveyard in the whole kingdom.
In many parts of the continent the Jews were not able
to acquire cemeteries in the immediate vicinity of their
homes. The Hamburg Jews buried their dead in the
neighbouring Altona, the Amsterdam Jews in Audekerke[3]
— a two hours' journey. In North Africa the cemetery
was at a greater distance from the towns. The protective
wall was a usual feature of the Jewish cemetery[4] — a most
necessary precaution, for the desecration and spoliation
of Jewish graves was a common offence in the middle
ages. Sometimes indeed the government itself not only
forbade the use of tombstones, but confiscated existent
monuments and employed them for building the walls of
the town.[5] Nor was this act of profanation confined to

[1] *Mishnah, Baba Bathra*, ii. 9.
[2] Quoted by M. D. Davis in *Notes and Queries*, 8th sect. viii. 26. Tovey,
Anglia Judaica, p. 8, also speaks of the *Jews' Garden*.
[3] Schudt, *Merkwürdigkeiten*, vi. 38, § 2. Cf. Jacobs, *Angevin England*,
p. 62. Many Jews lived in isolation from their family, and on their death
wished to be buried at considerable distances. In 1772 a Jew who died in
Nantes was buried in Bordeaux (Brunschvicg, *Juifs de Nartes*, p. 19). It is
interesting to note that special permission had to be obtained from the police
before the body could be transported.
[4] Cf. Berliner, *Rom*, ii. (2) 62, 86.
[5] This occurred in Rome in 1560–73 (ibid. p. 63).

Europe. In Egypt the Mohammedans stole the Jewish tombstones, obliterated the inscriptions, and re-sold them to Jews. This was at the end of the fifteenth century. The local Rabbis checkmated this ghastly traffic by forbidding their congregants to use any but newly quarried stones for monuments to the dead.[1] The use of inscriptions and epitaphs was not, by the way, a Jewish custom until after the Christian era. The habit was probably copied from the Romans, and it is noteworthy that tombs in the Jewish catacombs bear no Hebrew inscriptions, Greek and more rarely Latin was used,[2] the Greek inscriptions belonging to the first three centuries of the Christian era. The Jews felt a strong reluctance to employ Latin as their vernacular; the memory of Titus was scarcely of the kind to make the Jews love the language which he spoke.

It is of more than passing importance to note some of the peculiar features of these ancient Roman tombs. They display an artistic tendency of which the later middle ages show revived traces. In the Jewish catacombs in Rome the tombs were adorned with a variety of symbols.[3] The most characteristic symbol was a seven-branched *candlestick*, sometimes with red ascending flames. No Christian tomb has been found with this symbol, but it has remained the traditional emblem of the Jews of Rome, probably because of its prominence on the Arch of Titus.[4] A round *fruit*, with an ear springing from it, is another common figure. Where the fruit appears alone, *three*

---

[1] *Radbaz*, i. 741.

[2] Berliner, ibid. i. 52, 58.

[3] For my knowledge of these I am much indebted to Berliner's *Rom*, vol. i. p. 58.

[4] Modern Jewish tombs in Rome are again being adorned with this symbol.

small leaves are present at the top.[1] The *palm-branch* also
is present on the tombs, but it differs from the palm familiar from the Jewish coins. The same floral emblem was
typical of martyrdom, but its presence on the tombs was
probably suggested by the Psalmist's comparison of the
righteous to the palm tree   Other symbols are the *oil
vessel* and a curved object variously interpreted as a *horn*
(shofar) or a *scythe*. On some of the tombs, the ornamentation is elaborate, whole *scenes* being depicted. The
tomb of Alexandra Severa bears three hens by the side of
a fowl-house, a tree, a hut, two cocks in the act of combat,
with a palm-branch in the centre. Among other emblems
are *birds*, once in conjunction with a *beehive, sheep,* the
head of a *ram,* a doubled-handled *ewer,* a *flower-basket,*
an *open book, a calf, snuffers* (by the side of the candlestick and oil vessel above mentioned), the *budding leaf*—
a symbol never absent from Christian tombs.[3]

Quite in keeping with this early adoption of grave
symbols was the series of emblems which distinguish
some of the German Jewish tombs in the later middle
ages. But these more recent symbols represented not
fancies connected with death, but realities of life. Thus
in Prague *a pair of scissors* appears on a tailor's tomb, a
violin or *harp* on a musician's, a *bag* on a trunk-maker's,
a *crown and two chains* on a goldsmith's, *a lion clutching
a sword* on a doctor's, a *mortar* on an apothecary's.[4] At

---

[1] Is this a Christian symbol ?   [2] Psalm xcii.

[3] The beautiful gilded glasses found in the Roman tombs, with their elaborate ornamentations depicting the temple, were no doubt *kiddush* cups used
for the wine on Sabbaths and festivals. The inscription, ' Drink and live,' is
exactly the חמרא וחיא, ' Wine and life,' of the Talmud.

[4] Cf. M. Popper, *Inschriften des alten Prager Judenfriedhofes* (Brunswick, 1893). These tombs belong to the early part of the seventeenth
century, but the emblems are older.

Frankfort the symbols were of yet another type, for the *signs* of the houses in which the departed had lived were often carved on the tombs. The signs included figures of *dragons, bears, lions,* and *stars*.[1] The tombs of *cohanim* or priests have often been distinguished by the two open hands as displayed in the priestly benediction, while a Levite's often bears a water-jug. Family vaults were more common in ancient than in medieval Judaism, but they are not unknown. The family sepulchre of the Maccabeans at Modin (1 Macc. xiii. 27), with its carved armour and ships, recalls the family vaults of the Bible. In the middle ages, however, graves were inherited, but the mother who was bequeathed a share in the family vault was not able to include her own children in the privilege.[2] In Audekerke the Jewish tombs were reached by steps, and this seems to imply that they were large, family vaults.[3] There was no particular shape for the Jewish tombstone, but the ordinary Oriental practice of placing the stones erect and not flat came to be the mark of a Jewish grave in Europe.[4] The monuments varied greatly in size and cost, but the tendency towards uniformity and the avoidance of display was never quite overthrown. Some of the stones were of huge weight and dimensions, one of those recently discovered by Dr. Kaufmann at Buda Pesth, and dating from the thirteenth century, is nearly a foot thick and five feet high.[5] These remarks on the externals of the cemetery must for the present suffice.

[1] Cf. Philipson, *Old European Jewries*, p. 78.
[2] Shulchan Aruch, *Yore Deah*, 366, 2.
[3] Schudt, *Merkwürdigkeiten*, part vi. ch. 38.
[4] Ibid. The flat tombs of the Portuguese Jews in London were probably imitated from Christian usage.
[5] Quoted in the *Jewish Chronicle* of October 11, 1895.

The communal organization regarded the *House of Life* as one of its foremost cares.   Watchmen were provided at the public cost, and a small building or synagogue was attached to the cemetery.   On the other hand, the office of grave-digger does not seem to have existed, ordinary workmen being employed for the purpose.   The grim humours of the sexton, which find their representative in the Talmud in the person of Abba Saul, strike no echo in the medieval Jewries.   Life was altogether too serious for the Jew to jest of death.   But a later opportunity will present itself for giving an account of the loving rites with which the dead were accompanied to their graves.   We must turn aside now into brighter paths, and must consider some of the ways in which the Jews comported themselves towards the living.

CHAPTER V

SOCIAL MORALITY

PRESENT-DAY observers are commonly struck by the domesticity of Jewish men. Even the working man among the Jews spends his leisure at home. This feature of Jewish life dates from the early middle ages, and is easily explained. Judaism demanded devout attention to all the details of life, and the man rather than the woman possessed the knowledge necessary for obeying the minutiae of the home ritual. A large section of these details concerned the preparation of food, the family regulations for the Sabbath, and the more occasional household arrangements, such as the Easter cleansing of the home and the removal of leaven. Rabbi Solomon ben Adret had a lock made to his stove, and kept the key over the Sabbath to prevent his too considerate housemaid from lighting a fire on Saturdays.[1] Thus the Jewish husband played a personal rôle in the kitchen as well as in the market-place. He was especially busy on Thursdays and Fridays. Eagerly would he bargain for Sabbath dainties in the crowded market, though, in order to circumvent the trick of non-Jewish fishmongers who raised the prices on Fridays, he would sometimes reluctantly abstain from pur-

[1] *Responsa*, ed. Venice, § 857.

chasing that most beloved article of Sabbath food — fish.[1] Mostly, however, he would not be deprived of this dainty, and would hurry home with his bargains, breathless and eager for his wife's admiring approval. He knew the prices, he understood qualities, and was an adept in examining fruits and vegetables. He would not be cheated like the ordinary man of to-day. On Friday the husband would help in the cleansing of the crockery and saucepans, and would lovingly join his wife in spreading the table for the adequate reception of the Sabbath Bride. All this anxiety on the part of the husband must have made him something of a nuisance: he must have been rather too much of a critic and too little of an admirer to please thriftless housewives. But I fancy the gain far outweighed the loss. The wife had a home-loving lord, who perhaps derived some of his devotion to his family from his intimate participation in all the pleasures and anxieties of home management. When we add the reflections that the Jewish home was the scene of some of the most touching and inspiring religious rites, that the sanctity of the home was an affectionate tradition linking the Jew with a golden chain to his fathers before him, that amidst the degradations heaped upon him throughout the middle ages he was emancipated at least in one spot on earth, that he learned from his domestic peace to look with pitiful rather than vindictive eyes on his persecutors — we shall realize something of the powerful influence which the home wielded in forming and softening the Jewish character.

This consideration more than any other must give us

---

[1] *Responsa*, Menachem of Nicolsburg, § 28. A similar interference with prices occurred at a very early date. Cf. above, p. 60.

pause when inclined to assent to the harsh judgment current regarding the social morality of the Jews in the middle ages. The tender husband and self-sacrificing father can hardly have been a monster of malignity. And the curious point is that the medieval Jew was not harshly judged by his contemporaries. Under a surface ruffled by prejudice and suspicion there runs a calm current of respect and trustfulness. The populace, when left to its own devices, found the Jews straightforward and companionable, while the Church directed its persecution against the Israelite in the hope of winning him over to itself. Only when the two streams of baffled proselytism and unbridled suspicion coalesced was the character of the Jew blackened beyond recognition. Besides, the opinion formed of the Jews during the sixteenth, seventeenth, and eighteenth centuries has dominated the nineteenth to the obliteration of earlier impressions. Yet these three centuries were just the centuries of ignorance; Europe never knew less of the Jew than it did in the era of the ghettos. I am far from denying the existence of an antipathy to Jews in earlier centuries; but the older antipathy was one of fear, the later was one of contempt. A careful inquiry into the social life of the Jews in the middle ages reveals no records of serious charges against them. Negative evidence on such a subject is surely weighty. Ferdinand and Isabella's edict for the expulsion of the Jews from Spain in 1492 contains absolutely no charge of social offence; this severe measure is based exclusively on the alleged proselytizing energy of the Jews who reclaimed the Marranos, or Hebrew converts to Christianity. We shall see that this general acquittal must be qualified in certain directions, but the fact remains that by almost universal consent the Jews were clear of the more hideous vices which eat at the root of social life in civilized states.

This brings me back to my starting-point. There can be little question that the state of opinion as to the relations of men and women is an index to the social ethics of an age. Now, though there is room for hostile criticism of the mental attitude of medieval Jews on this question, their moral attitude towards the problem is singularly free from reproach. Jewish literature of post-biblical times is distinguished by a most delicate and refined tone in its treatment of the subject of intercourse between husband and wife. Jews have been often described as sensual,[1] but it is strange and thoroughly characteristic of Jewish sentiment to find that the ethical books written in the middle ages contain practical and eloquent pleadings directed towards elevating into a manly virtue of self-restraint the satisfaction of the most animal of instincts. Time after time, as new Messianic dreams flitted over the ghetto horizon, the Jewish wife would ask herself whether she might not be the mother of Israel's harbinger of salvation. The Scriptures had used the relation of husband to wife as a type of God's relation to His world. Jewish mystics of the middle ages compared a man's love to God with a man's love for his wife, using the most sensuous images, but thereby refining the relations from which the images were drawn. If the first duty of a Jew was to beget children, his religion gave the sanction to the obligation and idealized it, transforming a carnal act into a communion with the Spirit of all life.[2] It would be irrelevant

[1] Tacitus, *Hist.* v. 5.
[2] See the marvellous prayer (on שׁוּב) by Nachmanides. It is found in many editions of the Jewish Prayer-Book

to quote against this view the attacks on women and the contemptuous tone assumed towards them in the works of Jewish satirists in the middle ages. These satires were mostly imitated from Arabic and other Oriental originals, and, moreover, the point of the wit was sharpened by the knowledge that the mocking charges of infidelity and fickleness were exaggerated or untrue.[1] So you find the Jewish satirists exhausting all their powers of drollery over the joys of drunkenness. They roar till their sides creak over the humours of the wine-bibber. They laugh at him, but also with him; pleasantly if Ibn Gebirol be the songster, coarsely if Kalonymos take up the parable. In fact wine shares with women the empire over Jewish satirical writers in the middle ages. Yet we know well enough that the authors of these Hebrew Anacreontic lyrics and satires were sober men who rarely indulged in over-much strong drink.

Fidelity was expected from the husband as well as from the wife;[2] he was to love her, to honour her, and be true to her. If there was no love before marriage, there was no infidelity after it. The wife was addressed in terms of respect and endearment.[3] 'Be not cruel or discourteous to your wife,' says a thirteenth-century father;[4] 'if you thrust her from you with your left hand, draw her back to you with your right hand forthwith.' 'Husbands must honour

---

[1] *Jewish Quarterly Review*, vi. 506.

[2] *Rokeach.* At the end of the seventeenth century the modern spirit creeps in, and the man is allowed more licence than the woman. Güdemann, *Quellenschriften*, p. 180. But Lancelot Addison in his *Present State of the Jews* (London, 1675) asserts that in the matter of concubinage the 'Jews in Barbary are very abstemious.' The vice in question was a European one.

[3] Güdemann, iii. 99, 108–110, etc.; Maharil, p. 85 a.

[4] Asheri, died 1327; *Jewish Quarterly Review*, iii. 457.

their wives more than themselves;'[1] but such passages are too numerous to quote. They extend in an unbroken series over the whole medieval Jewish literature, and a seventeenth-century writer[2] says : 'Never quarrel with your wife. If she ask you for too much money, say to her : "My darling, how can I give you what is beyond my means? Shall I, God forbid, acquire wealth by dishonesty or fraud?"' The Jewish husband was warned against severity in his household conduct. He was not to be a terror at home.

The Jew who indulged in the physical ill-usage of his wife was regarded as a monstrosity. The wife-beater was not altogether an unknown figure in Jewish life, but the attitude of public opinion towards him is very instructive. A wife could not obtain a divorce on the ground of her husband's violence, but in the ninth and tenth centuries the wife-beater was fined to the utmost limit of his resources.[3] Or another method was adopted. The wife was urged to forgiveness, and the husband was compelled to add as much as he could to the marriage settlements.[4] Rabbi Tam, of the twelfth century, forced the wife-beater to provide his wife with separate maintenance. At a considerably later period some Jewish tribunals did practically force the husband to free his wife by a divorce in case that he ill-treated her,[5] but it must be admitted that the Jewish law of divorce was never satisfactory. In the fourteenth century occur some rare cases of husbands ill-treating their

---

[1] *Jewish Quarterly Review*, iii. p. 462.

[2] Sheftel Horwitz in his *Testament*.

[3] *Responsa* of Geonim (ed. Constant.), § 137.

[4] *Responsa*, Müller, *Mafteach*, p. 177.

[5] *Responsa*, Tashbats, ii. 8; A. de Boton, § 31; Benjamin of Arla, שו״ת בנימין זאב, 88, but contrast 116.

wives in order to procure divorces. There was, from the tenth century onwards, a growing feeling against permitting a husband to divorce a wife against her will, but men, if sufficiently destitute of humanity, found means to procure the wife's assent to the separation.[1] These cases were isolated. Rabbi Tam, in framing his regulation cited above, says of wife-beating: ' This is a thing not done in Israel ; ' and a little later on Rabbi Meir of Rottenburg (thirteenth century) remarks : ' Jews are not addicted to the prevalent habit of ill-treating wives.' [2] Wife-desertion was an evil which it was harder to deal with, for, owing to the unsettlement of Jewish life under continuous persecution, the husband was frequently bound to leave home in search of a livelihood, and perhaps to contract his services for long periods to foreign employers.[3] The husband endeavoured to make ample provision for his wife's maintenance during his absence,[4] or, if he failed to do so, the wife was supported at the public cost, and the husband compelled to refund the sums so expended.[5] These absences grew to such abnormal lengths that in the twelfth century it became necessary to protect the wife by limiting the absence to eighteen months, an interval which was only permitted to husbands who had obtained the formal sanction of the communal authorities. On his return the husband was compelled to remain at least six months with his family before again starting on his involuntary travels. During

---

[1] *Responsa*, Tashbats, ii. 20.

[2] *Responsa* (ed. Cremona), 291.

[3] He was even forced by Jewish law to do this, if no other means of living were procurable. See *Responsa* of Geonim; Müller, *Mafteach*, p. 285.

[4] Thus we read of a husband who left a house in his wife's possession, the rent of which sufficed for her support (Maimonides, *Responsa*, § 115).

[5] *Mafteach*, p. 90.

the first year of marriage it became a well-established rule of conduct that the husband was not to leave home on any considerable journey.[1]   A curious corollary of these enforced absences must not pass unnoticed.   A husband on leaving home would hand to his wife a *conditional divorce*, which would only take effect if he failed to reappear within a certain term.   This measure was really dictated by affection, for though it is a common libel to assert that the Jewish laws of marriage and divorce were all too elastic, yet as a matter of fact the Jewish courts of justice were very loath to admit any but ocular testimony of a husband's death.   Hence, the conditional divorce preserved the wife from the lamentable position of being neither maid, nor wife, nor widow.   An even more considerate step was the presentation of an *imperfect divorce*, designed to protect the wife against the persecution of rapacious representatives of Government during her husband's absence.   She would be liable to imposts which she had no means of paying, and the production of the imperfect divorce would often be accepted as proof that she had no responsibility[2] — a subterfuge, no doubt, but no one will very strongly condemn the device who recalls what pitiful extortions were perpetrated against the families of absent Jews by the medieval Jacks in office.

The early age at which marriages occurred[3] must have been partly responsible for the chastity of Jews in the middle ages.   In Jerusalem, in particular, no man over twenty and under sixty was allowed to reside without a wife.   A young girl was not married to an old husband — a Tal-

---

[1] See, for instance, ס״ החינוך, § 549. Cf. Deut. xxiv. 5.

[2] Cf. *Responsa* of Geonim (ed. Harkavy), p. 173.

[3] See ch. ix. below.

mudic precaution which unfortunately has not been always adhered to by Jews in modern times.[1] So delicate was the feeling on the inviolability of marital fidelity that a husband who suspected his wife's chastity was not allowed to live with her. Yet some of the language used in medieval Jewish books regarding the temptations of unmarried men, implies that the vices of to-day were, in varying degrees, the vices of all times and all peoples. But it has to be remembered that the unmarried men formed a very small minority. Even the young students at the Talmud schools were often married, and no breath of suspicion ever hovered round them. The fact that the Rabbi, unlike the priest, was not only permissibly married, but was expected and even compelled to take a wife, worked powerfully towards the elevation of the married state. There was one class only against which suspicion pointed its finger — the *Chazan* or Precentor, an official who was more musician than minister, and who shared some of the frailties apparently associated with the artistic disposition. Yet the comparative frequency with which the chazan was suspected of unchastity must not lead us to the supposition that the whole order was tainted with the same vice. Learned precentors, chazanim noted for the piety and purity of their lives, abound in medieval records. If public opinion was occasionally a little lax in condoning the offences of the chazan, the utmost severity was shown in the popular judgments on other officiants. Thus, an unchaste or unmarried *Cohèn* — reputed descendant of Aaron — was not permitted to pronounce the priestly benediction in synagogue.

[1] Naturally, such a union was allowed in ancient times if the girl were strongly desirous of it. Cf. *Aboth de R. Nathan*, ch. xvi., and the interesting discussion in Chayim Azulai's שו"ת חיים שאל, 74.

The separation of the sexes in their amusements and the resulting denial of opportunities for flirtation were, as we shall see in a later chapter, not accepted without very practical protest. Strangely enough, the more nearly we approach modern times, the less effective became the protest, the more rigid the barrier erected against the free intercourse of men and women in Jewish life. Embracing and kissing were forbidden even to betrothed couples in the eighteenth century.[1] During that same century in Rome no Jewess walked abroad without a girl comrade; love-making was by the billet-doux, not by direct verbal address. In 1697 the Jewesses of Metz were forbidden to appear in synagogue unveiled,[2] and half a century later the Rabbis of Amsterdam attempted to prevent betrothed girls from appearing in public with uncovered faces.[3] All this is the more remarkable, seeing that in Oriental lands, where veils were always *de rigueur*, there are many indications that Jewesses were by no means so punctilious as their Mohammedan sisters with regard to concealing their features. In Europe, however, this prudery of the Jews was so well understood that advantage was sometimes taken of it in a very amusing way.[4] In the seventeenth century a Jew, Reuben, allowed Simeon's wife to describe herself momentarily as his own spouse, to enable her to cross the frontier. Mrs. Simeon had no passport, but Reuben's passport was made out for himself and wife, though, as it happened, he was travelling alone. The frontier official had his suspicions. 'If she is your wife,' he said to

---

[1] Landsofer, מעיל צדקה, § 19.

[2] *Annuaire de la Soc. des Études Juives*, 1881, p. 112.

[3] R. Meldola, שו"ת מים רבים, iii. 28.

[4] The author of *My Official Wife* will thus find that a leading incident in his novel had been anticipated in fact.

Reuben, 'then *kiss her.*' Of course this test was rejected, and the deception was detected.[1] To go back several centuries, in travelling, indeed, some licence was permitted to prevent unpleasant consequences. Jewish women were allowed, in defiance of Scripture,[2] to dress as men to escape molestation, and the men were allowed to dress as Christians, even wearing the distinctive garb of clerics. The civil law also came to the assistance of the Jews, and the regulations concerning the wearing of badges were relaxed in the case of travellers who discarded the obnoxious mark on their journeys. But the Jewish wayfarer was not allowed a long immunity. Wherever he stayed one night he was forced to declare himself and resume his tell-tale badge.

Has this device — the badge — any tale to tell on the subject of Jewish social morality? In the late middle ages it was asserted that Jews were forced to brand themselves on their attire in order to diminish the alleged offences between Jews and Christian women. There is no indication in Jewish authorities that these alleged offences actually occurred except in Italy, and it is noteworthy that in the original institution of the badge the reasons assigned express a fear lest the free intercourse of Jews and Christians might lead to intermarriage and conversion to Judaism, but there was no apprehension of sexual offences. Prostitution was an unknown feature in Jewish life until quite recent times, and the evidence of the Church canons proves most conclusively that the restrictions of the Church were aimed less against Jewish than against Christian offenders. It must suffice to record the facts.

[1] J. C. Bacharach, *Responsa*, § 182.
[2] Deut. xxii. 5.

A large number of regulations were published forbidding
Christian women, on pain of severe penalties, sometimes
on pain of death, from entering the Jewries without companions ; while there were a smaller number of rules forbidding Jews to visit the houses of Christian women in the
absence of their husbands, unless the Jews were attended
by two Christian men or women, except 'physicians, surgeons, apothecaries, and mechanics.'[1] It is certainly false
to assume that Jews felt less scruple in violating the laws
of chastity where women of another creed were concerned,
but undoubtedly the opportunity and the temptation was
greater.[2] Yet so was also the danger. Death was the
penalty for such an offence.[3] On the other hand we read
of Jewesses who disguised themselves as men in order to
secure their honour against ill-disposed non-Jews who were
travelling with them.[4] When such offences between Jews
and Christians were found to prevail to any large extent,
they were rigorously suppressed by the Jewish authorities,
who exercised their full powers to purify their community.[5]

---

[1] This was in 1438.   See Lindo, *Spain*, p. 315; but several similar entries
are found in earlier parts of that book.

[2] One hardly knows what inference to draw from Alami's caution on this
subject to his son (אגרת מוסר, ed. Jellinek, p. 17.)

[3] The same dread penalty was inflicted on a Christian who offended with
a Jewess. Cf. Lecky, *Rationalism*, ii. p. 2.   [4] ספר חסידים, § 200.

[5] Cf. the healthy indignation of the· Jewish communal law (1413) against
those Italian Jews who, sharing the lax morality of their day, held הנשים
הנכריות מותרות בעיניהם (*Graetz Jubelschrift*, p. 60, Heb. section).   Solomon
Ibn Parchon (twelfth century) refers to the same subject (s. v. בעל cf. Bacher,
Stade's *Zeitschrift*, x. p. 143).   The Talmud was very severe against the same
offence, *Synhedrin*, 82 a, on the basis of various Biblical texts.   For rare
cases of such offences cf. the incident of the burning alive of a Jew in
Majorca in 1381 (*Revue des Études Juives*, iv. 37), and with regard to the
thirteenth century in Angers, L. Brunschvicg, *Les Juifs d'Angers*, pp. 14, 15;
for eighteenth century, L. Kahn, *Juifs de Paris*, pp. 49, 50.

The Jews received very scant justice from the medieval governments on this question. At one place the law excluded Jews from the houses of ill-fame ;[1] at another place the brothels would be placed in the Jewish quarter, to be occasionally withdrawn as the result of the angry Jewish protest against the presence of an institution so foreign to Jewish ideals.[2] Offences between Jewish masters and their female slaves did occur,[3] but the penalty exacted by the Jewish authorities was a severe one. The slave was taken from her owner, she was sold, and her price was distributed among the poor. Then the offender was flogged, his head was shaved, and he was excommunicated for thirty days.[4] Or the owner, to escape the penalty of his crime, voluntarily gave his slave her liberty and recognized her son as his legitimate offspring.

[1] Sabatier, *Histoire de la Legislation sur les femmes publiques*, p. 103, cites a statute to this effect passed in Avignon in 1347. Mr. Lecky (loc. cit.) defends the authenticity of this statute.

[2] Cf. Stobbe, *Die Juden in Deutschland*, p. 94, for an instance in the fourteenth century.

[3] *Responsa* of Geonim, צדק שערי, § 38, 15.

[4] Ibid. § 13.

CHAPTER VI

THE SLAVE TRADE

THE real blot on the social morality of the middle ages
lies in the attitude both of Church and Synagogue towards
slavery. The holding of slaves and the trade in them, nay,
the direct enslavement of captives, were not made unlawful by the Church until the thirteenth century.[1] Jews
had ceased to enslave Jews long before the Christian era,[2]
and the notion of selling Jews to foreigners was hateful to
the national sentiment of Judea. King Herod greatly outraged public opinion by transporting housebreakers and selling them to foreign masters, 'which punishment,' says Josephus,[3] ' was not only grievous to be borne by the offenders,
but contained in it an infringement of the customs of our
fathers.' The ransoming of slaves early became a primary
duty of Jewish congregations,[4] and as late as the present
century societies for the freeing of slaves were dotted over
the southern shores of Europe and the northern coast of
Africa. Though, however, the holding of Jewish slaves

[1] Biot, *L'abolition de l'Esclavage*, p. 233.
[2] Maimonides, *Abadim*, i. 10. Cf. Ingram, *History of Slavery*, p. 267.
[3] *Antiq.* XVI. i. 1.
[4] Babylonian Talmud, *Baba Bathra*, f. 8. Cf. ch. xviii., below.

was illegal in Jewish custom,[1] the Jews borrowed from the Mohammedans a species of service which was not distinguishable in kind from slavery. The servant was the hereditary possession of the family, yet was in many respects treated as a member of it. A similar remark applies to the Christian slaves held by Jews. A great Jewish authority of the eleventh century indeed advised his brethren to avoid the holding of slaves altogether. The members of the household should be trained to do the necessary domestic service themselves.[2] In theory the Jew had no compunction with regard to holding slaves ; in practice the slave of the Jew became bound to his owner by the ties of affection and mutual consideration.[3] Neither Jew nor Christian looked with equanimity on the enslavement of members of his own religious sect, but neither raised any protest against the sin which slavery commits against the rights of man.[4] The lands of the Church itself were worked by slaves in the middle ages.[5] In the time of Pope Gregory the Great, the attack on Jewish slaveholders begins to grow strong. Pope Gregory does not complain that Jews hold slaves, but that they hold *Christian* slaves. 'Quid enim sunt Christiani omnes nisi membra Christi ?' asks Gregory,[6] and he continues : 'atque ideo petimus . . . quod fideles illius ab inimicis eius absolvitis.' In another place Gregory's fear of conversion to Judaism is the reason he gives for objecting to the hold-

---

[1] Shulchan Aruch, *Yore Deah*, 267, § 14.

[2] *Responsa* of R. Meshullam (ed. J. Müller), p. 5 and p. 12, note 21.

[3] Cf. chap. viii. below.

[4] The finest passage on this subject is still Job xxxi.; Maimonides, *H. Abadim.* ix. 8, insists on kindness to slaves on similar grounds.

[5] Hatch, *Bampton Lectures*, p. 46.

[6] *Letters*, ix. 109.

ing of slaves by Jews :[1] 'Opportebat quippe te respectu loci tui, atque Christianae religionis nullam relinquere occasionem ut superstitione Iudaicae simplices animae non tam suasionibus quam potestatis Iure quodam modo deservirent.' Pope Gelasius formally allowed Jews to introduce into Italy slaves from Gaul,[2] provided that the imported victims were heathens and not Christians. Obviously, by attempting to suppress only one phase of the trade, the Church left a wide loophole for the trade also in Christians. It is abundantly clear that in the early middle ages there was no antipathy to slavery based on the universal brotherhood of man.

The connexion of the Jews with this hideous traffic must be told in brief outline. In the sixth century Italy was the scene of barbarian invasions, which rendered the slave trade at once possible and profitable. The prisoners furnished the means, the desolate fields and depopulated country formed the need. And here is a point to which attention has not yet, to my knowledge, been directed. So far as the Jews are concerned, Christian Europe distinguished between slave-holding and slave-dealing by Jews ; it suppressed the former, but did not set its face against the latter. Charlemagne in the middle of the eighth century readily allowed the Jews to act as intermediaries in the detestable trade in human life.[3] Later on, in the tenth century, the Spanish Jews often owed their wealth to their trade in Slavonian slaves, whom the Caliphs of Andalusia purchased to form their bodyguards.[4] In Bohemia the Jews there purchased these Slavonian slaves for exportation to Spain and the west of Europe,

[1] *Letters*, iv. 21. [2] Graetz, III. ch. ii.
[3] Ibid. ch. v. [4] Ibid. ch. vii.

where they often fell into the kindly hands of Mohammedan masters.[1] The Church stirred itself vigorously to buy
or confiscate these slaves from the Jewish dealers, but
the aristocracy connived at and profited by the trade.
William the Conqueror is reported to have brought Gallo-
Jewish slave-dealers with him from Rouen. There was
good reason for the solicitude of the Church and for its
desire to prevent Jews from retaining Christian slaves in
their houses. The Talmud and all later Jewish codes
forbade a Jew from retaining in his home a slave who was
uncircumcised.

On the other hand, such slaves were only rarely converted to Judaism. No doubt they often drifted into
conformity with the beliefs and practices of their masters, but the chief thing that was expected of the slave
was to abstain from work on Saturdays. The Jewish
owner, in fact, was forbidden to derive any profit from his
slave's disobedience to the Law of Moses. Further, since
no Jew might drink wine touched by an uncircumcised
person, it was obvious that a slave who had not undergone
this rite was a useless incumbrance. But the rite was
never forced on the slave up to the tenth century; curiously enough, the tendency to enforce it grows with the
middle ages, and we find the curious anomaly that the
sixteenth century finds Jews more resolute in this matter
than the tenth century found them.[2] Certainly in the tenth
century any Christian slave could refuse to be circumcised,
and in that case his master was unable to retain him.

---

[1] The mildness of the slavery prevalent under Mohammedans is well
known. See Ingram, *History of Slavery*, p. 221.

[2] Contrast the very interesting statements in the *Responsa* of the Geonim,
שערי צדק, p. 23 a onwards, with the Shulchan Aruch, *Yore Deah*, 267, especially
the superscription.

With the female slave, however, conversion to Judaism was much more frequent and natural. I must find room for one quotation from a Jewish authority[1] of the early part of the eleventh century : ' In certain places,' he says, ' there are only Egyptian[2] female slaves in the market, and the non-Jews permit the Jews, as in Babylon, to buy these and no others. Some of them become Jewesses at once, some after an interval, some refuse altogether to be converted. The Jews have great need of their services in these places, otherwise their own sons and daughters would be compelled to carry the water on their shoulders from the springs, and go to the ovens with the non-Jewish maid-servants, who are of low character, and thus the daughters of Israel might fall into disrepute and danger. In such cases Jews may retain in their services female slaves without converting them, but they must not allow them to do any manner of work on the Sabbath. In places where Jews are afraid lest their slaves should reveal secrets and turn informers to the prejudice of their masters, who, for this reason, abstain from converting them — such slaves must not be retained.' It will be observed that while an infringement of the Jewish law was allowed in order to preserve the morality of Jewish women, no such infringement was allowed in order to serve the convenience of Jewish men. And, out of the mass of Church laws and Jewish records on the subject, one fact emerges prominently. The Jewish owners of slaves were mild and affectionate masters. A Jewish owner would

---

[1] Hai Gaon. For reference, see previous note.

[2] This seems a mistake for Christian; the words נוצרי and מצרי being confused. It would appear that in Mohammedan countries Jews were only allowed to own Christian slaves.

not sell his slave to a harsh master.[1] Slaves entreated
their masters to admit them to Judaism, because they
knew that they would never again pass out of Jewish
hands.[2] Their masters treated their converted slaves,
especially those acquired when young, as their own children, educated them, often freed them, took the same
concern in marrying them as they did where their own
children were concerned, and the slave would mourn for
his former master as for a father.[3] In later centuries,
when in Mohammedan lands slave-owning was not illegal,
one of the last acts of the dying Jew was frequently the
manumission of his slaves. Sometimes the slave was left
by will as a life-servant of the widow, and became free on
the death of the latter.[4] Any slave who escaped to the
Holy Land became, from very early times, *eo ipso* a free
man.[5] A non-Jewish slave who was seriously injured by
his master ceased to belong to the latter.[6] 'Mercy is the
mark of piety,' says the Shulchan Aruch,[7] quoting the
language of far earlier authorities, 'and no man may load
his slave with a grievous yoke. No non-Jewish slave may
be oppressed ; he must receive a portion from every dainty
that his master eats; he must be degraded neither by word
nor act ; he must not be bullied nor scornfully entreated ;
but must be addressed gently, and his reply heard with
courtesy.'

I have given prominence to these considerations on the
moral attitude towards women and on the state of feeling
regarding the rights of man, because these constitute the

---

[1] ספר חסידים, § 668.　　　　[3] Cf. *Responsa,* שער אפרים, § 91.

[2] שערי צדק, § 19.　　　　　[4] *Responsa,* תורת הסר, § 45.

[5] *Responsa* of Geonim, שערי צדק, § 12.

[6] Shulchan Aruch, *Yore Deah,* 267, § 27.

[7] Ibid. § 17. Cf. Maimonides, *H. Abadim,* ix. 8.

essence of the social ethics of any age. But there are many other points which go to make up our estimate of character. Often, indeed, these more superficial features are so pointed that popular judgment relies entirely on them. I have pointed out above that the Jews are no-where charged with serious crimes. There is both negative and positive evidence that murder, theft, rape, false swearing, are offences from which Jews were singularly free. Charges of ritual murder were occasionally raised, but these were never seriously believed by the popes or the educated classes.[1] Of course, on the theory that the unknown is the monstrous — and the Jews were always an unknown quantity in Europe — the Jews of the middle ages were pronounced tricky, vain, proud, ostentatious, luxurious. Their wealth, in the literal sense of the word, was fabulous. They refused to have intercourse with Christians. Their women were sorceresses. But amidst these prejudices, specific and provable offences are conspicuously absent. Charges of forgery were very rare,[2] and in Spain, at least, the more disreputable abuses connected with usury were sometimes the result of the importunate solicitations of the Hidalgos. Temptations do not seem to have been placed in the way of the nobility by Jewish money-lenders of the middle ages,[3] whatever may be the case as regards the Jewish money-lenders of to-day. Italian Christians, indeed, forbidden by the Church to lend money at interest, tempted the Jews to act as interme-

[1] Cf. Strack, *Der Blutaberglaube*, p. 144 seq. (fourth edition, 1892).

[2] Mr. Jacobs, in *The Jews of Angevin England*, only records one case (p. 175).

[3] Lindo, *Spain*, pp. 135, 179. On the other hand, Jews were forbidden to lend money in Spain to university students (Jacobs, *Spain*, p. xxv), a regulation which has an ugly look.

diaries and to become their agents.[1] So little was dishonesty the reputed vice of Jews that we find them constantly employed in financial offices, partly, no doubt, because of their talents for such posts, but also because of their superior trustworthiness.[2] There is a curious sub-current of evidence, moreover, that Jews were less exacting even in their usurious demands than were others who carried on similar trades.[3] A further indication that Jews of the middle ages do not deserve the odious reputation of pandering to other people's vices is supplied by their attitude towards another social virtue — temperance. In Europe the Jews have always been noted for their moderation in drinking intoxicants. Drunkenness was licensed, so to speak, on Purim and less markedly on the Rejoicing of the Law,[4] while on the eve of the Day of Atonement too much alcohol was sometimes taken to fortify the body for the ordeal of the fast.[5] Drunkenness on the Sabbath was an occasional failing of the Jews in later centuries,[6] but it was easily suppressed by Jewish authorities, one of whom quaintly complains that his brethren drank better wine on Sundays than on Saturdays.[7] In Mohammedan countries there is another tale to tell, for there the Jews have, in modern times at least, won an unworthy notoriety for intemperate habits. But the point to which I wish to call

[1] Berliner, *Rom*, ii. 66.

[2] Cf. Lindo, p. 178.

[3] Cf. among several authorities, *Histoire de la Ville a'Alais* (Nîmes, 1894), p. 89; Güdemann, i. 31; ii. 246–248; iii. 188–191. The Caursini were pronounced far more extortionate than their Jewish financial rivals (Mathew Paris, *Chronica Majora*, anno 1253; ed. Luard, v. 404). Cf. ch. xii. below.

[4] See ch. xix. below.

[5] Maharil, ed. Warsaw (1874), p. 45.

[6] E.g. *Yosef Omez*, § 630.

[7] Ibid. § 693.

attention is this : though the Jews enjoyed the right to sell wine in Mohammedan towns,[1] they often refused to sell wine to Mohammedans,[2] to whom wine is a forbidden pleasure.

On two charges brought against the Jews of the middle ages there is some evidence ; these were clipping the coinage and receiving stolen goods. The charge of fraudulently manipulating the coinage is too well attested for me to deny or palliate it. Occasionally we find Jew accusing Jew. Though the penalty for the crime was death or mutilation in England, we find a Jew in 1205 denouncing a co-religionist as guilty of 'falsifying the King's money.'[3] The Jews, moreover, were not the only offenders. In 1125, King Henry sent orders from Normandy that all the English moneyers should be mutilated, and this was done 'with great justice, because they had foredone the land with their great quantity of false money.' The Jews were, in this instance, not named as the offenders at all. A German satirist of the fifteenth century, Hugo of Trimberg, laments the debased condition of the coinage, but does not name the Jews as the offenders. A Jewish Rabbi of the same century utters his complaint of the same abuse ; he asserts that in his day all the so-called silver coins were copper, but he does not hint at the culpability of his own brethren.[4] The threat of excommunication was held over any Israelite who used counterfeit coins, even in the days when a debased coinage was everywhere common,[5] and there is a true ring of moral indignation in the language used by Jewish medieval Rabbis on

[1] Schudt, *Merkwürdigkeiten*, i. 204. [3] Jacobs, *Angevin England*, p. 233.
[2] *Tashbats*, ii. § 139.   [4] Güdemann, iii. 190.
    [5] See e.g. S. de Medina, *Responsa*, i. 124.

the subject.[1] 'What! make a communal regulation against the use of false coins? You must be a scoundrel indeed to need such a regulation to keep you honest.'

Similar remarks apply to receiving and purchasing stolen goods. The Jewish moral code condemned these offences ; the Jew in practice occasionally committed them. ' Not the mouse, but the hole is the thief,' says a Talmudic proverb,[2] and it needed some centuries of restriction to retail trade to foster in a Jew here and there the meanness which lets I dare not wait upon I would. The Jewish record is by no means black even on this black subject. The law in the twelfth century seems to have permitted German Jews to take stolen goods in pledge, but the Jewish authorities indignantly repudiated the privilege.[3] Casting our glance over Asia, our eyes fall upon a strange practice of the Jews in Persia. They bought stolen goods in the tenth century — with the object of returning the articles to their real owners.[4] The gravamen of the charge against the Jews in Europe was that they took in pledge sacred vestments and blood-stained garments — two classes of pledge which were frequently forbidden by statute.[5] The law showed no disposition to protect its subjects by making the reception of stolen goods in general either difficult or dangerous.

Contempt for the *goy*[6] created in the lower minds among the Jews the feeling that a Christian or Mohammedan was fair game for commercial 'cuteness.' There

---

[1] Solomon Hak-kohen, *Responsa*, iii. 108. Against the use of light coins cf. *Responsa* of Geonim, *Mafteach*, p. 99.   [2] Gittin, 45.

[3] Zöpfl, iii. 205 ; Güdemann, i. 262.   [4] *Mafteach*, 197.

[5] The reception of such pledges by Jews was also forbidden by R. Gershom. Cf. פתחי תשובה to *Choshen Mishpat*, § 356, n. 1 ; Jacobs, *Angevin England*, p. 331.   [6] Non-Jew.

is no note of this in Italy, where the Jews were neither the
only nor the most prominent representatives of trade.   It
would be interesting to inquire how far the characteristics
ascribed to Jews in the middle ages are simply the characteristics of the commercial mind as viewed by non-trading
observers.   I have just spoken of the demoralization of
the lower Jewish mind.   Is it not a remarkable phenomenon that never was the average Jewish mind morally higher
than in the centuries during which persecution was most
grinding ?   When the Jews were the recipients of the
most cruel treatment, when they were glad to be received
with a sneer because a gibe is more friendly than a frown
— they were more convinced than ever that to cheat a non-
Jew was a double crime : it was an act of robbery, and it
involved a profanation of God's holiness.   If preferential
treatment was shown by Jews, it was against Jews and not
in their favour.   The prices that they charged their co-religionists were higher than the prices they charged Gentiles.[1]   That it was a greater offence against Judaism to
cheat a Christian than to cheat a Jew is the constant burden of the Jewish moral books of the middle ages.   These
books were not read by mere students; they were the food
on which the ordinary Jewish mind was nourished, and the
maxims enunciated in them were the most familiar of
household words.   I cannot remember a moral book of
those times from which this doctrine is absent.   'A Jew
sins more against God by cheating and robbing a Christian than when he cheats or robs a Jew, because, though
both acts are dishonest and criminal, in the case of a
Christian the Jew offends not only against the moral law,
but *profanes the sacred name of God.*'[2]   'Ah! Ariel,

---

[1] *Tashbats*, iii. 151.   [2] Semak, 85 and 275.   Cf. *Sefer Chassidim*, § 661.

Ariel! Shall men say there is no God in Israel?' cries another Rabbinical denunciant of those who cheated Christians.[1] This was in 1328. Equally stern were Jewish moral books against undetected dishonesty. 'If a man steals property and his heirs knowingly share in his offence, and — because no evidence exists of their crime — they and *their* heirs retain the ill-gotten possessions, let them beware! Hell opens itself wide to receive them all, throughout their generations.'[2] 'A thief is a thief, though he steal a trifle, be the defrauded person Jew or be he Gentile.'[3] There were lapses from this high teaching, but such lapses were not condoned. A Jew was not permitted to withhold evidence against a fellow Jew who was in litigation with a Christian;[4] and well founded as was the antipathy of Jews to summon one another before any but their own tribunals, yet one of the chief medieval formulators of Jewish custom delivered up, of his own initiative, a Jew to justice if he had robbed a non-Jew.[5] In fact, the authorities of the eighth to tenth centuries made it their practice to denounce to the Governments Jews who bought stolen goods.[6] The tendencies of ages of Jewish teaching are finally summed up in the clear and emphatic pronouncements in the sixteenth century code-book, which still largely regulates Jewish life: 'It is forbidden to purchase stolen goods, for such an act is a great iniquity. It encourages crimes and causes dishonesty. If there were no receiver there would be no thief. . . . Any article concerning which there is even a presumption that it is stolen, must not be purchased.

---

[1] Güdemann, ii. 308.　　　[2] *Sefer Chassidim*, ed. Wistinetzki, p. 25, § 21.
[3] Shulchan Aruch, ח"מ.　　　[4] Ibid. 28, § 3.
[5] *Mafteach*, p. 182.　　　[6] Ibid. cf. also 191.

Sheep from a shepherd, household goods from servants, must not be accepted, for the probability is that the property belongs to their masters. . . . It is prohibited to rob or cheat any one, even to the smallest extent, and the same law applies to the case of Jew and non-Jew alike.'[1]

Evasions demoralize, and in a ceremonial religion, whose followers have to maintain old customs in new environments, evasions seem inevitable. The effect of this on the Jewish character has been a bad one as far as it has gone, but in fact it has not gone very far. Two points only need be referred to here; the first deals with the absolution of vows. 'Let no oath rise to your lips;' 'hold thyself far from vows and oaths;' 'swear not at all,' say Rabbis of all centuries in the middle ages.[2] So, too, with the Talmud, on which Jewish custom in this respect was uniformly based. 'The general principle is : Let thy yea be yea, and thy nay be nay (*Baba Mezia*, 49 a) ; and even a silent determination in the heart is considered as the spoken word which must not be withdrawn or changed (*Maccoth*, 24 a), for he who changes his word commits as heavy a sin as he who worships idols (*Sanhedrin*, 92 a), and he who utters an untruth is excluded from the divine presence (*Sotah*, 42 a). We can thus conceive with what abhorrence the Rabbis must have condemned every false or vain oath. Indeed, such offences belong to the seven capital sins which provoke the severest judgment of God on the world (*Aboth*, v. 11). A false oath, even if made unconsciously, involves man in sin and is punished as such (*Gittin*, 35 a).'[3] 'Love truth and

---

[1] Shulchan Aruch, *Choshen Mishpat*, chs. 366–369.
[2] E.g. *Rokeach* (Zunz, *Zur Geschichte*, 131 f. and 147).
[3] S. Schechter: Appendix to Montefiore's *Hibbert Lectures*, 1892, p. 558.

uprightness,' said Maimonides,[1] 'for they are the ornaments of the soul ; cleave to them, prosperity so obtained
is built on a sure rock.   Keep firmly to your words ; let
not a legal contract or the presence of witnesses be more
binding than your verbal promise even privately made.
Disdain reservations and subterfuges, sharp practices and
evasions. Woe to him who builds his house thereon.' No
doubt Jews sometimes fell away from these high counsels,
and used the vow as a prop to a weak will.   It is amusing
to find a Jew of the sixteenth century breaking the maxim
to keep it : swearing that he would never swear.[2] If men
vowed rashly, a door was opened to them for reconsidera-
tion by a Rabbinical absolution for the offender.   Sometimes men would vow to follow certain courses of conduct
which conflicted with their social or domestic duties ;
and the absolution merely implied that the reawakened
sense of duty overrid a rash or impossible undertaking.
Such absolution had no immoral tendency, for it was safe-
guarded and restricted with the utmost care.   Some
Rabbis in the middle ages were very complacent in releas-
ing their congregants from vows, but strong Rabbinical
authorities always set their face against the practice.
And, at the worst, just those vows or oaths which involved
the social relations between a man and his fellows, just
those vows the breach of which might have demoralizing
consequences, were the ones to which absolution was most
strenuously denied.   No Rabbi or Rabbinical tribunal
could absolve an oath or vow which a man was charged
to make by a Jewish court of justice.[3] So, in the age of

---

[1] In his Testament (*Jewish Quarterly Review*, iii. p. 452).
[2] S. b. Isaac Chayim, *Responsa*, בני שמואל, p. 54 c.
[3] Cf. Schechter, ibid. p. 561.

the Geonim, no dissolution of business contracts made on oath was permitted. Oaths uttered over the Scroll of the Law were indissoluble.[1] Jewish law always cast a severer censure on public vice than on private, because public vice involved social as well as religious evil. A public vow was incapable of annulment.[2] This was in the tenth century. It is obvious, however, that the differences which subsequently prevailed in Rabbinical practice were due to irreconcilable theories of human nature. This is seen very clearly with a type of vow which became extremely common in the later middle ages. It was a most ordinary thing for a Jew to undertake an oath that he would not indulge in gambling or games of chance. Could such a vow be annulled? Some authorities resisted the suggestion with a most sturdy disregard of consequences. Others argued: 'The temptation is too strong for this man's will, he will play in despite of his vow; let us annul his promise and save him from an additional sin.' Judaism always sought to make its moral code a *possible* one; its ideals were all attainable by the best life. The Rabbi who argued thus against an intemperate devotion to temperance may not have been weakening the moral sense after all.

More detrimental, however, were the cases of *legal fictions* which grew up luxuriantly in Jewish life. Yet it is hard to see how Jews were to act otherwise than they did. For instance, by a legal fiction groups of houses were combined and considered as one private enclosure with regard to certain aspects of the Sabbath law; without this fiction Jews could not have lived at all in the

---

[1] *Responsa* of Geonim, Prague, 123.
[2] Geonim, *Mafteach*, p. 8. Cf. ibid. 99, 157.

middle ages. In the course of centuries the fiction has been abolished, and Jews, consciously yielding to the pressure of circumstances, have openly abandoned the Jewish law rather than submit to the demoralization of fictions, however legal. Another legal fiction was connected with money-lending. A Jew — as we shall see later on — was forbidden by Rabbinical law to lend money to a brother Jew. Hence a Christian middle-man was inserted, and by this legal fiction the transaction evaded the Rabbinical prohibition.[1] That the Jewish mind has so easily emancipated itself from this moral danger is clear proof that it did not eat deeply into their medieval character. So, too, a strict adherence to the Sabbath and the Passover law was absolutely irreconcilable with those partnerships between Jews and Christians which were far more common in the middle ages than is thought. The Jew would derive no profit from the Sabbath trade, and in the time of the Geonim all the Sabbath profits were scrupulously assigned to the Christian partner.[2] Yet it is easy to see that the compromise, though honest enough in inception, would be practically impossible. Again, the Jewish law forbade in perpetuity the use or enjoyment of any profit from 'leaven which has been kept during the Passover,' and leaven, as the Jewish code understands it, includes a multitude of things. The Jew would sell the contents of his wine-cellar to a Christian before the Passover and buy it back at a nominal price after the festival. This was a distinctly petty evasion; but again the Rabbis insisted that the sale must be an *effective one*, so that if the purchaser held the seller

---

[1] Cf. M. D. Davis, *Shetaroth*, p. 47.
[2] Geonim, *Mafteach*, 153, etc.

to his bargain, the Jew had no legal claim for the return of the property.[1]

All these and similar devices, growing out of the attempt to live an old form of life amid completely new conditions, were temporary and tentative phases in the thousand-years story of Judaism.   The meaner traits which, inflicted from without, marred the medieval Jewish character, and left a brand on the modern Jew, belong to the same category. Above all these defects soars high a practical and elevated sense of duty, which preserved the Jewish race from organic, moral degeneration.[2]

---

[1] A very similar evasion led, in England, to the Statute of Mortmain. Landowners pretended to give their lands to the Church, and then took them back as tenants of the Church, thus freeing themselves of their feudal obligations to lay superiors.   Equally curious were the extraordinary evasions by which Christian merchants sought to escape the impossible canon laws against usury (Lecky, *Rationalism*, ii. 258, etc.).

[2] 'Researching in the *Conversation* of the *Jews*, it seemed to be very regular, and agreeable to the laws of a well-civilized conduct.   For setting aside the *Artifices of Commerce* and *Collusions of Trade*, they cannot be charged with any of those Debauches which are grown into reputation with whole Nations of Christians, to the scandal and contradiction of their Name and Profession.   Fornication, Adultry, Drunkenness, Gluttony, Pride of Apparel, &c., are so far from being in request with them, that they are scandalized at their frequent practice in Christians.   And out of a malitious insinuation, are sorry to hear that any of their Nation should give a Name to, and die for a people of such Vices.'   L. Addison, op. cit., p. 13.

CHAPTER VII

MONOGAMY AND THE HOME

HEINE has familiarized the modern world with an imposing feature of Jewish home life in the middle ages. The Jewish home was a haven of rest from the storms that raged round the very gates of the ghettos, nay, a fairy palace in which the bespattered objects of the mob's derision threw off their garb of shame and resumed the royal attire of freemen. The home was the place where the Jew was at his best. In the market-place he was perhaps hard and sometimes ignoble; in the world he helped his judges to misunderstand him; in the home he was himself.

It is a common mistake to believe that Jewish life derived one of the most civilizing of its elements from the European world in which it moved. I refer to the custom of monogamy. Monogamy was not the condition and basis of a pure home life; the assertion that it was so transposes cause and effect. Monogamy was the result and not the cause of an idealized conception of the family relations. The hallowing of the home was one of the earliest factors in the development of Judaism after the Babylonian exile, and the practice of monogamy grew up then as a flower on the family hearth.[1] The whole of the Talmud is based on monogamous custom.

[1] Z. Frankel, *Grundlinien des mosaisch-talmudischen Eherechts*, xi.

The allusions to women throughout its pages invariably presuppose such a custom, for although the Jewish law permitted polygamy, Jewish practice very early abrogated the licence. The last chapter of the Biblical book of Proverbs, written not later than the fourth century B.C., is obviously monogamous,[1] and the same may be said of the narrative of the Creation in the Book of Genesis, as well as of all the Apocryphal books, notedly Tobit and Judith. Of the array of Rabbis named in the Talmud, not a solitary instance can be found of a bigamist. Constant references are made in Rabbinical literature to a man's *wife*, never once to his *wives*. There is, moreover, the note of a perfect unity of love in the contents of these references to the married state.

Nothing in modern life can excel the courtly respect and single-hearted devotion which the Talmudic husband displays towards his wife. 'He loves her as himself, but honours her more than himself.[2] . . . God's presence dwells in a pure and loving home.[3] . . . In a home where the wife is the daughter of a God-fearing man, the husband has God for a father-in-law.[4] . . . Not money but character is the best dowry of a wife. . . . Who is rich? He whose wife's actions are comely.[5] . . . Who is happy? He whose wife is modest and gentle.[6] . . . When his wife dies, a man's world is darkened, his step is slow, his mind is heavy; she dies in him, he in her. . . . A man must not make a woman weep, for God counts her tears. . . . Marriages are made in heaven.[7] . . . A man's

---

[1] This fact is strangely overlooked by Mr. Lecky in his *European Morals*, i. p. 104.

[2] *Sanh.* 76 b ; *Yebam.* 62 b.   [5] *Sabb.* 25.

[3] *Kiddushin*, 71.   [6] *Aboth de R. Nathan*, i. 7 (ed. Schechter).

[4] Ibid. 70.   [7] *Sabb.* 22 a–b.

happiness is all of his wife's creation.[1] . . . Many go to sea, and the majority come safely home. It is the few who go and return not. Thus many take a wife and most of them prosper. It is only the few who stumble.'[2] Such sentiments as these have always dominated Jewish life, and the anomaly is presented of women filling legally a very low position indeed, but morally a most exalted one, in Jewish esteem.

To all this indirect evidence that the Talmudic scheme of married life is framed on a monogamous basis, some curious direct proofs can be added. In the second century of the present era, the son of Judah the prince, following the custom of his time, left his youthful spouse to go in search of wisdom. His absence, however, at college was unusually prolonged, and when he returned he found his wife prematurely infirm. Rabbi Judah said to him, 'My son, if you divorce her the world will say, "Is this the return for her faithful devotion?" If you marry another wife, they will say, "The one is his wife, and the other his mistress." So he prayed to God on her behalf, and her youth was restored.'[3] This story, whatever else may be said of it, is surely evidence of a strong popular prejudice in favour of monogamy, and the same may be predicated of another curious fact. According to the Mishnah, there was much anxiety that the High Priest should have a wife living on the Day of Atonement, but though it was felt to be a possible accident for her to die suddenly, the suggestion that the High Priest might be expected

---

[1] *B. Mezia*, 59 a.

[2] *Bam. Rabb.* § 9.

[3] *Kethuboth*, 62 a. Cf. Buchholz, *Die Familie, nach mosaisch-talmudischer Lehre*, p. 66.

to possess a second wife was not contemplated as an
escape from the difficulty.[1]

Thus Jewish custom overrid Jewish law and established
monogamy long before Christianity had made the old
Roman view on the question predominant in Europe.   It
is important to follow up this triumph of practice over
theory a little further.   In the ninth century A.D. the
Rabbis of Babylon explained that the law did not permit
a man to marry a second wife without the consent of the
first.[2]   Should she refuse, then the husband might be compelled to restore her to liberty and pay all the settlements.
The dignified position which Jewish practice had always
assigned to women became partially legalized during the
eighth to tenth centuries.[3]   Though the wife was never
placed on an equality with regard to the initiative in
divorce, yet throughout these centuries there may be detected a tendency to refuse to the husband the right to
divorce the wife frivolously without her consent.[4]   These
two tendencies were focussed by one of the greatest Jews
of the middle ages, a man who has gone down to posterity
as 'the light of the exile.'   Rabbi Gershom (960–1028) not
only prohibited bigamy on pain of excommunication, not
only did he forbid the forcible divorce of the wife, but,
without any synodal authority, he won the complete assent
of Western Jews to his views.   Since his day monogamy
has been the law as well as the custom of all Western
Jews.

---

[1] Cf. Maimonides, *Isure Bia*, xvii. 13.   Mishnah, *Yoma*, i. § 1.
[2] *Responsa* of Geonim, ש״ץ, p. 60 ; *Mafteach*, p. 282.
[3] Cf. ibid. pp. 93, 123.
[4] The husband no doubt might practically force this consent by neglecting
or ill-treating his wife (see שו״ת הרשב״ץ, ii. 20), but there is no ground for
believing that such brutality was common.

Thus the institution of monogamy was not borrowed by Judaism from medieval Christianity. The New Testament gives no hint that polygamy was a Jewish practice in early Christian times. In the middle ages the Church was no nearer than the Synagogue to a complete solution of the marriage problem. For, during the first eight or nine centuries of the Christian era, the language of several popes was by no means sternly monogamous, and the 'Church sometimes permitted simultaneous marriage with two persons in case of the wife's infirmity, and was not powerful enough to check them generally in the Carolingian era.'[1] As late as Luther's day, bigamy was permitted to the Landgraf Philip of Hesse, and in the thirteenth and fourteenth centuries it is hard to reconcile the evidence of conjugal infidelity in Europe with the supposition that monogamy was anything more than a name. What are chiefly interesting, however, are the grounds on which the medieval Church occasionally licensed departures from the monogamous principle, for Jewish authorities practically allowed similar licence under similar conditions. The Church Council of Vermene in A.D. 752 enacted that when a wife refused to accompany her husband on a journey, the husband might marry again if he had no hope of returning home. In the second place, the sterility of the wife was regarded by some Christian authorities as sufficient ground for permitting an act of bigamy.[2] Some Rabbis were less compliant in the latter case; but it was generally held that if a wife had been forcibly captured, and thus the husband was robbed of her society, he might marry again. So if she deserted him, declined to join him on a pilgrimage

[1] Smith, *Dict. Chr. Antiq.*, p. 207.
[2] Ibid. Art. *Marriage.* See also p. 1102.

to Jerusalem, or refused to cohabit.[1] If the wife became
insane or infirm and was without children, it was thought,
even in the later middle ages, a kinder act to her to
permit the husband to remarry than to insist on his
divorcing her.[2]

There was evidently a close parallel between the practice
of Synagogue and Church with regard to the legality of
a second marriage under special circumstances. A similar
identity manifests itself in an unpleasant phenomenon which
may be discerned in Mohammedan lands. For though
Christianity had little to do with the inclusion of monogamy
among the customs of the Jews, Mohammedanism unfortunately wielded a deleterious influence on the Jews who
fell under its sway. Serious lapses from rigid monogamy
occurred in Islamic lands, and cases of similar offences are
not unknown at the present day.[3] Herein lies, to my mind,
the cause of the popular error to which I alluded above. It
was the relapse into polygamy which Judaism owed to
external influences, while its acceptance of monogamy had
been an original, not an acquired, virtue. The Church,
too, often found it difficult to enforce strict monogamy on
Eastern Christians.[4] In the East, as well as in Spain under

---

[1] According to the *Resp.* תשב״ץ, ii. 175, the husband was allowed to
forcibly divorce the wife in such a case, but bigamy was forbidden. Samuel
de Medina (*Resp.* ii. 120), on the other hand, permits the double marriage.

[2] *Resp.* I. b. S. Sirkes, § 93 ; in the opposite sense, I. b. S. Adarbi, *Resp.*
§ 294 ; M. Alshec, *Resp.* § 86. D. Pardo in *Resp.* מכתם לדוד א״ע, § 8, supports the first view.

[3] They are, however, rare. In Morocco much contempt is felt by Jews
for one of their number who commits bigamy. He is practically boycotted.

[4] Writing of the Nicene Canons against bigamy, J. M. Ludlow (Smith,
Dict. Chr. Antiq., p. 205) says : 'It is difficult to attribute Nicene authority to
these Canons, which show so vividly the corruptions that grew up in the more
distant Oriental churches. But whether illustrative of the degeneracy of

the Moors, in the Levant and Southern Italy, the monogamous enactment of Rabbi Gershom was never formally recognized by the Jews.

Bigamy was rather common among the Jews of Spain as late as the fourteenth century. In each individual instance it was necessary to obtain the royal assent on penalty of death.[1] It is true that these incidents took place in Christian Spain, but the old Islamic influences still prevailed there. Spanish Jews like Abraham Ibn Ezra, however, maintained, with a tinge of cynicism, that 'one wife was enough for any man.' In Algiers in the fifteenth century it was held by Solomon Duran[2] that polygamy was lawful, but he added the rider that the husband must provide a separate house for each of his wives — thus practically prohibiting what he theoretically allowed. A European Jew who settled in the East was held bound by the monogamous law of Rabbi Gershom. Much ingenuity was expended to prove that the *Cherem*,[3] as it was termed, only extended to about the middle of the thirteenth century, but this attempt to limit the incidence of the law absolutely failed. It must be remembered that the religious duty of begetting a family was so paramount in the Jewish scheme of life that many an Israelite felt himself reluctantly compelled to

Arabian Christendom before the rise of Mohammedanism in the seventh century, or of the influence of Mohammedan polygamy itself upon it at a later period, they are not the less valuable.'

[1] A similar licence was permitted to the Jews of Christian Spain from about 1230 (Lindo, p. 83). But these Jews were probably of Oriental origin, and the Government derived pecuniary advantage from the privilege as the Jews paid for the right to marry another wife. (J. Jacobs, *Jews in Spain*, p. 25, § 104.) Cf. Kayserling, *Jewish Quarterly Review*, viii. 792.

[2] ספר הרשב״ש, § 75.

[3] I.e. 'excommunication.' Many regulations were popularly described by this term *Cherem*.

divorce his first wife if she had not presented him with a son and a daughter, providing that she had remained child-less for ten years. In case the wife refused to accept a divorce, some Rabbis maintained, just as the Church authorities did, that the law of monogamy might be in-fringed. Even so, the road to bigamy was made as hard as possible. Sometimes the husband was forced to pay over the marriage settlement to the Beth Din or Jewish Court before the question of his re-marriage would be entertained.[1]

But the greatest Jewish authorities, the men of light and leading in the middle ages, forbade bigamy under each and every circumstance. Children or no children, one man one wife was the rigid principle enforced by such world-wide authorities as Rabbis Nissim and Judah Minz.[2] The Pentateuchal law of the Levirate marriage was a persistent but not very serious difficulty. But as it was still open to a low-minded individual to argue that the Rabbis were going beyond the letter of the Jewish law in forbidding bigamy, a device was resorted to at least as early as the twelfth century (probably even earlier) by which the bridegroom entered into a voluntary engage-ment on oath which bound him to observe the strict law of monogamy. An oath to this effect was included in the marriage contract, and the following were its exact terms in Africa:[3] 'The said bridegroom, N.N., hereby promises that he will not marry a second wife during the lifetime of the said bride, M.M., except with her consent, and if

---

[1] R. Meldola, שו"ת מים רבים, iii. 4.

[2] *Responsa*, ed. Venice, § 10.

[3] שו"ת חשב"ץ, i. 94. An early document (communicated by Mr. S. Schechter) containing a similar proviso is preserved in the MSS. of the Cambridge University. In that document the marriage occurred in Fostat (Egypt).

he transgress this oath and marries a second wife during her lifetime and without her consent, he shall give her every tittle of what is written in the marriage settlements, together with all the voluntary additions herein detailed, paying all to her up to the last farthing, and he shall free her by regular divorce instantly and with fitting solemnity.' What is of most interest concerning this provision in the marriage contract is this. It was only added in countries *where Mohammedanism prevailed*, and there is full evidence that it was more than a mere formality, but that it was regularly enforced.[1] That divorces were of frequent occurrence is painfully clear. But several facts mitigated the evil.[2] Marriages were contracted at so young an age that divorce often occurred before the marriage was really consummated. Divorced girls easily remarried, for divorce carried no stigma with it. Divorces among adults, who had lived long together, were quite exceptional in Jewish life. When such occurred, the treatment of the divorced wife by her former husband was tender and considerate in the extreme. In most countries, moreover, the Jewish law of divorce has practically assimilated itself to the laws prevailing with the general public. It is perhaps regrettable that this assimilation has not been admitted into the Jewish code books.

The difference in practice between Eastern and Western Jews was less marked than was the variation in theory. It must not be forgotten that in civilized polygamous countries, monogamy necessarily prevails with the

---

[1] Communal regulations were made to this effect. One of the year 1377 is quoted in שו"ת מהרי"ך (Salonica), ii. § 96. Cf. also שו"ת שפת הים (Salonica, 1818), p. 26 d.

[2] Cf. p. 175 below.

majority, for only the rich can afford the luxury of several wives. At all events, among the Jews of the Orient monogamy was and is the rule and polygamy the exception.[1] The taint, however, had some little influence on the Jewish disposition. There was less warmth in the Oriental Jewish home, less of that tenderness which was once a common characteristic of Jews all the world over, but came in process of time to distinguish Western Jews from their gayer but more shallow brethren of the East. One seems to detect a feebler sense of responsibility in the mental attitude of an Oriental father to his offspring, just as one detects more volubility but less intensity in the Oriental Jew's prayers. Yet the difference was only in degree. The Jewish home life was everywhere serene and lovely, for if Judaism had virtue at all it displayed it in the home. We have already seen something of the relations that subsisted between husband and wife. It is more difficult to outline the relations which prevailed between Jewish parents and their children. For here we are dealing with an impalpable sentiment which pervaded the home and but imperfectly materialized itself in quaint and ennobling customs. The full pathos of the love which linked a Jewish father to his son cannot be set down in words. Is it so curious that the Jewish law-books fail us here? If the duties of parents to children and of children to parents were very incompletely codified,[2]

---

[1] 'But the (Barbary) Jews of whom I write,' says L. Addison, *Present State of the Jews*, p. 73 (1675), 'though they greatly magnifie and extol the concession of Polygamy, yet they are not very fond of its practice.'

[2] In the Bible no enactment compels the parents to provide for their children's maintenance. But the love of God to man is constantly compared by the Biblical poets and prophets to the love of mother and father to their offspring. This love implied more than any legal code could have enjoined.

the omission is very instructive. For once, the Jewish heart allowed free play to its emotions.

The Bible itself places the duty of honouring parents in a special category, suggesting longevity as a reward for observance of the obligation, but specifying no penalty for its neglect. The Jewish Prayer-book, quoting the Mishnah, includes 'honouring of parents' among those things, 'the fruits of which a man enjoys in this world, while the stock remains for him for the world to come.'[1] In the middle ages, however, both the rewards and the penalties fell into the background, for the love grew too deep to need legal encouragements or restraints. Yet the love was of its own *genre*. The same courtliness of etiquette which was observed between parents and children in England a generation or two ago prevailed in Jewish life for several centuries.[2] The Jewish son stood in his father's presence, and never on any consideration occupied his seat or left or entered the room before him. In synagogue, while the father was 'called to the Law,' the son reverently rose from his seat and remained stand-

In the second century A.D. the Synod of Hosa first made it legally compulsory for fathers to maintain their children till the age of adolescence ; the duty was legally incident only till the child reached his seventh year (Babyl. Talmud, *Kethuboth*, 49 v). Among other duties incumbent on the father were : the circumcision of the son, the redemption of the firstborn, the initiation of his son in the study of the Torah, the provision for his early marriage (this applied also to the daughter), and for his training as an artisan. Some authorities included instruction in swimming and in politics. Cf. L. Löw, *Die Lebensalter in der Jüdischen Literatur*, p. 129. But these specific enactments by no means exhausted the full import of the paternal love of which Jewish authorities in all ages speak with unmeasured tenderness and enthusiasm.

[1] *Authorized Daily Prayer-book*, ed. S. Singer, p. 5. Mishnah, *Peah*, ch. i.

[2] I regret that space fails for a fuller account of the respect shown by the young to the old. But see Löw, ibid. p. 265.

ing until his father had completed his duty and returned
to his place.[1]   There was little demonstrativeness of affection.   Even in modern times the fondling of children is
somewhat foreign to Jewish sentiment.[2]   Love found a
deeper form of expression.   Yet it is hazardous to gen-
eralize on this subject, for the inroad of mysticism into
Jewish life gave the kiss a new meaning and vitality.
The caressing of children was chiefly held objectionable
during or antecedent to prayer-time.[3]   The kiss was not
a favourite token of love between the sexes.   Kissing on
the lips was unusual between Jewish brothers and sisters ;
between engaged couples it was barred.   Brothers, however, kissed one another on their lips, their sisters they
saluted by a kiss on the hand.[4]

In the middle ages, some slight variation occurred in the
old Hebrew forms of greeting friends and acquaintances.
The ancient Biblical salutation ' Peace be to thee ' was
retained ; in the middle ages the response took the form
' (To thee) a goodly blessing.'[5]   The Jews, indeed, adopted
the ordinary national greetings in German, French, Arabic,
Italian, and Spanish.   They were very punctilious in
greeting Christians, and naturally used the vernacular for
the purpose.   Even among themselves the Jews used the
ordinary appellations, such as *Don* and *Donna* in Spain and
Hausfrau in Germany.   But over and above these forms
of salutation, the medieval Jews not only retained the

---

[1] This and several others of the customs here enumerated are still very
prevalent in Jewish life.

[2] שו״ת דברי מרדכי (Warsaw, 1867), p. 38 a.

[3] *Sefer Chassidim*, § 18.

[4] See *Jewish Quarterly Review*, iii. p. 477.

[5] Zunz, *Zur Geschichte*, p. 304 seq.   Much valuable information on Jewish
salutations and commemorative formulae is there given.

Biblical and Talmudical formulae, but they considerably developed these on their own lines. On entering the room, the visitor paused, drew back two or three paces, and then bowed.[1] A kiss on the forehead and cheeks often followed, but the Jews early adopted the Persian modification of the custom and kissed on the hand.[2] The chief greetings were of the nature of benedictions containing wishes for peace, health, prosperity, and longevity. These were perpetuated not only in verbal greetings, but also as introductory compliments at the head of letters. ' Length of days and years of life, and peace shall they add to thee ' (Prov. iii. 2) was the favourite text cited, and a formula was contrived from the last four words of the Hebrew of this verse.[3]

On occasions of joy, a Jew's friends congratulated him with the words, ' So be it with thee in future and for many years.' When two Jews drank together, the one exclaimed ' For life,' and the other answered ' For a happy life.' Or the good wishes would take the form ' Good luck,' 'Be strong,' ' May thy power increase ' — all in Hebrew. Should a mishap be recounted, or reference made to an unpleasant subject, the speaker would add in a parenthesis, ' Far be it from thee,' or ' God guard thee from it.' In fact, Jewish etiquette became excessively, not to say superstitiously, sensitive on such points. From the end of the eleventh century it grew customary to invariably tack on the wish ' God protect him ' to the name of any one addressed in

---

[1] Müller, *Mafteach*, p. 28. Cf. *Sefer Chassidim*, § 96.

[2] Kissing the hand as a sign of respect comes strongly to the fore in the *Zohar* (thirteenth century). Cf. Bacher, *Revue des Études Juives* (xxii. 137 and xxiii. 133), to which the same writer now adds references to Jehuda Halevi's *Divan* (ed. Brody, p. 150, No. 98, line 22) and Dunash ben Labrat against Menachem, verse 52.

[3] רחו י״ל. Zunz, *Zur Geschichte*, p. 305.

writing. Or the phrase used might be 'May his Rock keep him.' Rabbis, kings, nobles, were not named without the accompanying formula 'May his glory be exalted.' A son never named his father without the epithet 'My lord' or 'My master.' From the fourteenth century the favourite and habitual phrase for all living Israelites was 'May his light shine on.' A Spanish Jewish greeting of this class was, 'May his end be fortunate.' When a woman was named, she was honoured by the Biblical phrase 'Blessed above women' (Judges v. 24). The dead were spoken of with the respectful rider, 'His (or her) memory be for a blessing,' 'Peace be upon him,' 'May his merit protect us,' 'His resting-place is Eden.' Sacred associations clung round certain cities and these were not mentioned without some such hope as 'May God protect it,' 'May it be speedily rebuilt.'

Reverting to the relations of father and son, it must be said that the child life of the middle ages was in many ways a hard one. Discipline was severe and corporal punishment habitual.[1] At the table the utmost self-denial was demanded of the child in the presence of guests, and the latter were forbidden, by a really salutary piece of etiquette, to 'spoil' their entertainer's child. Some parents were naturally more complacent than others, and medieval moral and casuistical books contain frequent laments that the children were allowed too much licence at table, in synagogue, and in the presence of their elders generally. In the school curriculum no regular provision was made for play, but the rule often was from early morning synagogue to school, and from school to bed,[2]

---

[1] Contrast, however, the milder views of Isaac of Posen, לב טוב, ch. ix.

[2] Statutes, חוקי התורה, in Güdemann, i. p. 271.

the only interval being for an early midday dinner. Play was frequent, but not regular. Toys were common, and included balls ornamented with figures.[1] Jewish children were put in a sort of go-cart when learning to walk.[2]

In most of these particulars I hardly think that the life of the Jewish child differed from that of his Gentile brother. But the Jewish view of domesticity showed itself in the success with which life was made lovable to the child, notwithstanding the rigours of the discipline to which he was subjected. By an infinitude of devices he was made to love his home and his religion. On the passover eve the child was the hero of that most ancient of domestic rites extant, a rite in which the departure from Egypt was retold with weeping and with laughter, to the accompaniment of song and good cheer, the boy, like his sire, quaffing the four cups of wine and firing a volley of questions at his elder's head which the elder rejoiced to hear and to answer. The boys were encouraged to do more than ask questions, they were persuaded to act. How ancient some of these customs are cannot easily be said. The boy took a *matsa* or unleavened passover cake, bound it in a cloth, put it on his shoulder and strutted proudly about the room, in symbolic allusion to the escape from Pharaonic bondage. Or, midway in the service, the boy would creep outside the door and stumble mirthfully into the room at the identical moment when the service was resumed after supper, probably to typify the entrance of Elijah as the harbinger of the Messiah. A more elaborate custom, of which, however, I have found no early

---

[1] *Responsa* of Geonim, *Mafteach*, p. 49.
[2] Löw, *Lebensalter*, p. 287.

description, ran somewhat as follows : [1] — A boy, dressed
as a pilgrim with a staff in his hand, and a wallet containing bread on his shoulders, enters, and the master of the
house inquires: 'Whence comest thou, O pilgrim?'
'From Egypt.' 'Art thou delivered from bondage?'
'Yes ; I am free.' 'Whither goest thou?' 'To Jerusalem.' 'Nay, tarry with us to read the recital of the Passover.' The story of the Exodus follows this pretty prelude.

When the house was being searched for leaven on the
previous night, the boys played many a prank. They concealed particles of bread in corners, and great was their
glee when they eluded the vigilance of the searchers, and
triumphantly produced the incriminating morsels. When
the feast of Tabernacles was over, the boys made bonfires
of the boughs and leaves with which the booths were
roofed, and roasted apples in the flames. [2] But a full
treatment of customs like this belongs to a history of
the Jewish religion. The point that concerns us here is
the success with which the influence of religion was lovingly turned to domestic uses. Her religion strengthened
the Jewish mother in her resolve not to have her infant
child sleep with her lest she overlay it. The lower animals
were treated with uniform kindness. Jews did not make
domestic pets of animals — another form of cruelty —
until the fifteenth century. [3] Pious Jews asked Christians

---

[1] Benjamin II, *Eight Years in Asia, etc.*, p. 328. My belief that this custom
is old is based on a comparison with such various hints as are contained in the
Travels, אבן ספיר, i. 89 a, and the יוסף אומץ, § 788.

[2] Maharil.

[3] At least so I gather from my failure to find allusion to such pets earlier
than Isserlein. See his *Responsa*, פסקים וכתבים, § 105 : — 'You may cut a bird's
tongue to make it speak, and crop a dog's ears and tail to make it pretty,

to milk their cows on the Sabbath and retain the milk, for though the Jews would not derive profit from work done on Saturday, they would not let their animals suffer pain.[1] On the other hand, hens were sometimes kept in the house so that the Jew might fulfil the injunction of the law,[2] which bade him to feed his animals before he fed himself. Live fish in bowls of water were also to be found in some houses, but the motive for this was utilitarian ; Jews never ate fish that was not perfectly fresh.[3] Religion lay at the root of the sensitiveness which forbade repetition, to a man who put on a new pair of boots, of the greeting : ' May they get old and may you have a new pair ' — a form of congratulation common when a new article of attire was first worn. In the case of boots, skin was needed, and as this involved the death of an animal, the usual greeting was prohibited. Bread crumbs might be thrown to the birds on the Sabbath.[4] ' The table at which I study,' wrote a Rabbi to Maharil, ' contains a board on which the body of my wife Jutta was washed previous to her interment.' Similarly, the coffins of Rabbis were made out of the wood of the tables at which they studied, or at which their poor guests were seated when receiving the Rabbis' hospitality.[5] There was no detail of the home life that was not thus hallowed, and the medieval Jewish

since all these animals were made for man's good.' Cf. also Berliner, *Inn. Leben*, p. 17, where citations are made in which pets are pronounced useless. ' Spend the money on the poor,' says the *Sefer Chassidim*, § 1042 (see also Mid. Koheleth Rabba, vi. 11).

[1] *Mafteach*, p. 22.

[2] *Sefer Chassidim*, § 531 ; and Güdemann, iii. 216. Deut. xi. 15.

[3] A similar remark applies also to poultry. Maharil, ed. Warsaw (1874), p. 25.

[4] Maharil, p. 29.

[5] Güdemann, iii. 110.

code books teem with instances in the Jew's religion made for decency and gentleness.

In the poorest ghettos of the middle ages, when the houses were mostly large, but each family's accommodation limited, the religious etiquette of Judaism mostly preserved the masses from that degrading indifference to decency which is so terrible a feature of modern poverty. So, too, with regard to cleanliness. The medieval lack of sensitiveness on the subject of personal cleanliness was tempered in the case of Jew by his Semitic instincts. He took a bath every Friday, for here the religion of the Jew worked with elevating effect. Though theological criticism of Judaism has justly seen much to blame in the excessive punctiliousness of Pharisaism regarding ritual purification, nevertheless the medieval Jew gained more than he lost by it. He washed his hands before partaking of bread, and, what is more, this ritual washing included the rubbing off stains and the cleansing of the nails.[1] At large banquets, as in Talmudic times, the handwashing occurred at table, while after the meal bowls of water were passed round and each member of the company dipped his fingers into the liquid, which was sometimes perfumed. The Jews who lived amid Mohammedans were much more punctilious in this respect than were they who resided in Europe. But European as well as Eastern Jews carefully wiped their fingers after the ritual handwashing, for it was a fine principle with Jews not on any pretext to allow food to become loathsome to look upon.[2] No medieval Jew would

[1] This ceremonial washing has degenerated in modern times into a mere *form*, and is unhappily consistent with much lack of cleanliness. One of the most obvious evils of ghetto life has been this change in Jewish habits.

[2] It would need a whole chapter to enumerate the practical conclusions, in the way of cleanliness, that were drawn from this admirable maxim. The

eat raw fruit without first carefully examining it for worms, but in the middle ages a taste for fruit was not general with Jews. Spiders' webs were most conscientiously swept from the corners of the rooms, but for this no doubt a mystical rather than a sanitary motive must be assigned. The Jew did not drink at dinner without first wiping his mouth. He was very moderate in his eating, and, unlike the ordinary diner of his day, felt it disgraceful to rise from table heavy with food, for gluttony was the worst of reproaches.[1] It was a commonplace to call the table the altar of God; hence, around it, the Jews must become pure as priests. The educational exercises common at meal-time grew from the same principle,[2] and there can be no doubt that Jewish life was immensely the gainer from the marriage of Rabbis.

The Rabbi was not only permitted, he was compelled to marry. Hence the Rabbi's home became at once the centre of a bright, cultured circle, and the model which other homes imitated. The patriarchal spirit revived in the middle ages, and the Jewish father has only recently ceased to be a household teacher and domestic moralist. He called his family round him on Friday nights, and blessed his wife and each child individually, and included the servants in the rite.[3] Similarly with the Saturday night. The Bible and the Prayer-book were regularly

maxim was derived from Ezekiel iv. 13. One of its most pretty results was the habit of covering the loaves with an embroidered cloth during the *kiddush* or sanctification over wine, which on Sabbaths and festivals preceded the breaking of the bread. This prevented the wine soiling the bread.

[1] Maimonides said: 'He who habitually shows moderation at his meals is more praiseworthy than the occasional faster.'

[2] Cf. Mishnah, *Aboth*, iii. § 3.

[3] Isserlein had his boys' hats removed before blessing them. *Leket Yosher*, i. 74 b.

studied in family conclave, and the many Jewish moral
books of the middle ages found their public in the Jewish
home.   Special books were indeed reserved for home
reading, but woe betide the child who treated the volumes
with disrespect or soiled them during use at table!   When
the book was finished, a merry *siyum* or family party
marked the event.[1]   The child kissed a Hebrew book
when he opened or closed it, or if it accidentally fell.[2]

All-night sittings for prayer and for reading semi-sacred
books occurred at stated intervals, mostly twice a year.   A
large number of Jews rose regularly at midnight to pray,
and then retired again to rest.   No pious Jew sought his
couch without first seeking to survey the events of the
past twenty-four hours, without first confessing his sins,
not to a priest, but in the silence of his room to his God.
During the month of Elul, roughly our September, such
confession of sins was repeated daily before every meal.[3]
Early rising was habitual, and a ewer of water stood close
to the bedside so that the hands might be washed immediately on waking.

Sermons in the home were a common feature of Jewish
life.[4]   These sermons often took the form of learned discussions, and a distinguished guest repaid his host's hospitality by a *chiddush*.[5]   Boys on their thirteenth birthday
delivered orations at table, but the custom does not present itself much earlier than the sixteenth century.   The
transition from such religious exercises to ordinary table-

---

[1] יוסף אומץ, § 130.

[2] See e.g. Isaac ben Eliakim's לב טוב, ch. ix. ; Maharil, p. פ״ז.

[3] Maharil, 35.

[4] Berliner, *Rom*, 80, 81.

[5] The חדוש = *novelty*, was some new thought on religious topics, or son.e
ingenious explanation of a Biblical difficulty.

talk was easy. Table-talk, the sallies of those licensed jesters, the *Marshallik* and the *Badchan*, short dramatic performances, especially at weddings and on Purim, were all extremely popular. Riddles were a regular table game, and all the great Hebrew poets of the middle ages composed acrostics and enigmas of considerable merit.[1]

But easy as the transition was between a religious discourse and secular table-talk, a bridge was built to make the crossing even more facile. The Jewish table-songs were the bridge between the human and the divine, they were at once serious and jocular, they were at once prayers and merry glees. These table-songs belong entirely to the middle ages, and are all later than the tenth century. On Friday evenings in the winter, the family would remain for hours round the table, singing these curious but beautiful hymns. The women would mostly remain silent, but the mother would see that her boys joined in with vigorous voices. The girls, however, sang choruses of their own, and husband and wife would sometimes inaugurate the Sabbath with a duet sung to musical accompaniment.[2] The quotation that follows is really a composite from several medieval table-hymns sung after the meal on Friday evenings or Saturday mornings.[3]

> This is the sanctified Rest-day ;
> Happy the man who observes it,
> Thinks of it over the wine-cup,
> Feeling no pang at his heart-strings

[1] Cf. ch. xxi. below.

[2] These hymns were sung before the Sabbath commenced so as to permit of musical accompaniment. Bacharach reports such a case, *Jewish Quarterly Review*, iii. 298. Cf. also Popper, *Inschriften des Prager Judenfriedhofes*, pp. 24, 25; Schechter, *Studies in Judaism*, p. 393.

[3] I. Zangwill's *Children of the Ghetto*, ch. xxi. The whole description in that wonderful chapter applies in most details to the middle ages.

For that his purse strings are empty,
Joyous, and if he must borrow,
God will repay the good lender,
Meat, wine, and fish in profusion —
See no delight is deficient.
Let but the table be spread well,
Angels of God answer 'Amen!'
So, when a soul is in dolour,
Cometh the sweet, restful Sabbath,
Singing and joy in its footsteps,
Rapidly floweth Sambatyon
Till that, of God's love the symbol,
Sabbath, the holy, the peaceful,
Husheth its turbulent waters.

                .   .   .   .   .   .

Bless Him, O constant companions,
Rock from whose store we have eaten,
Eaten have we and have left, too,
Just as the Lord hath commanded
Father and Shepherd and feeder.
His is the bread we have eaten,
His is the wine we have drunken,
Wherefore with lips let us laud Him,
Lord of the land of our fathers,
Gratefully, ceaselessly chanting,
'None like Jehovah is holy.'

                .   .   .   .   .   .

Light and rejoicing to Israel,
Sabbath, the soother of sorrows,
Comfort of downtrodden Israel,
Healing the hearts that were broken!
Banish despair!   Here is Hope come.
What!   A soul crushed!   Lo, a stronger
Bringeth the balsamous Sabbath.
Build, O rebuild Thou, Thy temple,
Fill again Zion, Thy city.
Clad with delight will we go there,
Other and new songs to sing there,
Merciful One and All-holy,
Praisèd for ever and ever.

Space unhappily prevents more than one other quotation, which I have translated from a table-hymn composed by

Abraham Ibn Ezra for the feast of Chanukah, commemorative of Judas Maccabeus' victories. It is more rollicking and lighthearted than the songs from which my first quotation was made.

> Eat dainty foods and fine,
>   And bread baked well and white,
> With pigeons, and red wine,
>   On this Sabbath Chanukah night.
>
> CHORUS
> Your chattels and your lands
>   Go and pledge, go and sell!
> Put money in your hands,
>   To feast Chanukah well.
>
> Capons of finest breed
>   From off the well-turned spit,
> The roasts that next succeed
>   Each palate will surely fit.
>
> Joints tender, poultry young,
>   Rich cakes baked brown in pan ;
> ' A-greed ' is on every tongue,
>   ' Set-to ' laughs every man.
>
> No water here they carry,
>   Their steps fade fast away;
> Over wine we all will tarry,
>   Two nights in every day.
>
> Our ears no more shall tingle
>   At sound of the water's fall ;
> But, red wine in cups come mingle,
>   And shout in chorus all,
> Our fields and our lands
>   We will pledge, we will sell,
> To put money in our hands
>   To feast Chanukah well.

It must not be thought that because these early hymns retained their popular hold on the Jewish affections up to the present time, fresh hymns of the same class were

not composed. On the contrary, the later jargon literature is very rich in fine specimens, for one of which space
may be spared.

SONG FOR FRIDAY NIGHT

Thou beautiful Sabbath, thou sanctified day,
That chasest our cares and our sorrows away,
O come with good fortune, with joy and with peace,
To the homes of thy pious, their bliss to increase!

In honour of thee are the tables decked white;
From the clear candelabra shine many a light;
All men in the finest of garments are dress'd,
As far as his purse, each hath got him the best.

For as soon as the Sabbath-hat's put on the head,
New feelings are born and old feelings are dead;
Yea, suddenly vanish black care and grim sorrow,
None troubles concerning the things of to-morrow.

New heavenly powers are given to each;
Of everyday matters now hush'd is all speech;
At rest are all hands that have toil'd with much pain;
Now peace and tranquillity everywhere reign.

Not the choicest of wines at a banqueting board
Can ever such exquisite pleasure afford
As the Friday-night meal when prepared with due zest
To honour thee, Sabbath, thou day of sweet rest!

With thy angels attending thee, one at each side,
Come on Friday betimes in pure homes to abide,
In the homes of the faithful that shine in their bliss,
Like souls from a world which is better than this!

One Angel, the *good* one, is at thy right hand,
At thy left doth the other, the *bad* Angel, stand;
Compell'd 'gainst his will to say ' Amen,' and bless
With the blessing he hears the good Angel express:

That when Sabbath, dear Sabbath, thou comest again,
We may lustily welcome thee, free from all pain,
In the fear of the Lord, and with joy in our heart,
And again keep thee holy till thou shalt depart!

Then come with good fortune, with joy and with peace,
To the homes of thy pious, their bliss to increase!
Already we've now been awaiting thee long,
All eager to greet thee with praise and with song.[1]

The Jewish table-songs were not, however, uniformly of this character. Praises of wine and love, both in Hebrew and in the vernacular, found their way into Jewish circles, especially in Spain, where the example of the Moors was contagious. These secular songs were even interpolated into the grace after meals and were set to Arabian tunes.[2] Naturally many Rabbis were much scandalized by these proceedings, but it does not appear that the puritanical opinion won the day. For, centuries later, we find the same love for sensuous table-songs prevalent in Germany.[3] Yet the favourite Jewish wine-songs were of an altogether different type, they were merry but they contained not one syllable of licentiousness.

Drunkenness was never a prevalent vice.[4] The sanctified use of wine at every Jewish ceremony produced a real *instinct* for temperance without destroying an equally strong instinct for sociability. The early love of Jews for tobacco and coffee emanated on the one hand from their sobriety, on the other hand from their love of social intercourse with their fellows. Coffee, indeed, was known

[1] Translated by the Rev. I. Myers from Winter and Wünsche's *Die Jüdische Litteratur*, iii. p. 588.

[2] Solomon Alami's אגרת מוסר. He lived in the second half of the fourteenth century in Portugal.

[3] See § 133. יוסף אומץ. שבזמנינו זה שרגילין הרבה אנשים לנבל פיהם במשתה היין. In the Talmud some such abuse is also noted (*Sanhedrin*, 91 a).

[4] Still less was indecent talk. Even in the *Targum Sheni*, Vashti boasts: 'My ancestor Belshazzar drank as much wine as 1,000 persons, yet it never made him indecent in his talk.' In the fourth century the people of Mechuza were noted for drunkenness (*Taanith*, 26 a), but they were not regarded as pure Jews.

as the 'Jewish drink' in Egypt in the early part of the eighteenth century,[1] it was drunk at dawn before morning prayers as a safeguard against influenza, and immediately after grace at formal meals.[2] Coffee was introduced into England by Jews.[3] Tobacco, so far as its use in Europe is concerned, was also discovered by a Jew, Luis de Torres, a companion of Columbus.[4] The Church, as is well known, raised many objections to the use of tobacco, and King James I's pedantic treatise only voiced general prejudice. Jewish Rabbis, on the other hand, hailed the use of tobacco as an aid to sobriety.

Owing to this difference in the attitude of Christianity and Judaism, the habit of smoking spread far more rapidly in the East than in Europe. In the seventeenth century it was much more prevalent with the Jews of Cairo than with the Jews of Poland.[5] The only differences of opinion, however, in Jewish circles concerned not the use of tobacco generally, but (*a*) its use on festivals, Sabbaths, and fasts, and (*b*) the necessity for a benediction before beginning to smoke. On fasts it became usual to abstain from tobacco until the afternoon, on Sabbaths smoking was forbidden altogether. But the latter decision was not accepted without a severe struggle. Some filled a hooka overnight on Friday and thus kept the tobacco alight for Sabbath use. Snuff was not forbidden.[6] The devices resorted to by

---

[1] שו״ת זרע אברהם in A. Isaaci's משקה ישראל הנקרא קאוי, i. §§ 2–3. Cf. שו״ת מקור חיים, § 2, where coffee is termed a second nature with some Jews.

[2] שו״ת חינוך בית יהודה, § 2, and M. b. Mordecai Zacut's שו״ת (Venice, 1760), § 59; also גנת ורדים, iii. § 1.

[3] Howell, *Familiar Letters* (ed. Jacobs), p. 662.

[4] Kayserling, *Christopher Columbus and the Participation of the Jews in the Spanish and Portuguese Discoveries*, p. 94.

[5] Cf. Löw, *Lebensalter*, p. 353 seq.

[6] J. Chagiz, שו״ת הלכות קטנות, § 101.

inveterate smokers were often highly amusing. Thus one gentleman used to visit his Mohammedan friend on the Sabbath and sit in his room while the latter smoked.[1] The tobacco of the Eastern Jews was perfumed, and sweetened with honey. It is worth noting that Jews early took to the trade in tobacco, a trade which they almost monopolize in England to-day.[2]

[1] N. Mizrachi's אדמת קדש, § 4.
[2] Busch, *Handb. d. Erf.* 12, 7; Löw, pp. 356, 437, 438.

CHAPTER VIII

HOME LIFE (*continued*)

IF then the synagogue reproduced the home, the home was the analogue of the synagogue. All the ritual ceremonies of the latter had their counterpart in the domestic preparations. Passover, Pentecost, Tabernacles, Chanuka, Purim, were all home feasts.[1] Jewish history, too, was taught in the home by the occasional fast-days, the rites observed tending to fill the child's heart with loyalty to the past and faith in the present. But what I think more remarkable was the series of private family fasts and feasts. Each family had its own mournful anniversaries, its *Jahrzeits*,[2] observed on the death-day of departed rela-

---

[1] Educational home-rites were associated with Pentecost. See p. 348, below.

[2] This commemoration of the dead was probably of Persian origin (cf. Schorr, החלוץ, vol. vi), but in the middle ages the popularity of the custom was strengthened by imitation of the Catholic masses. Besides the fast, two principal rites distinguished the *Jahrzeit:* (*a*) the Kaddish prayer, which was not due to Christian influence, and (*b*) the *Jahrzeit*-light, which was kept burning for twenty-four hours on every anniversary of the death. This light is emphatically pronounced by Dr. Güdemann (iii. 132) to be of Christian origin, and already Bacharach (Index, 94 a) could give no Jewish explanation of it. The very term *Jahrzeit* was used in the Church of the masses in memory of the dead. But I do not think that we have yet got to the bottom of this custom, on which investigators of folklore have not said their last word. R. Judah Hanasi ordered a seat and light to be kept ready in his wonted place after his death (*T. B. Kethuboth*, 103 a). This association of a flame with the soul is certainly pre-Christian. A similar remark applies to the *Day of Atonement candles*, though here Christian influence is much more obvious.

tives year by year. The fast varied in duration, sometimes lasting for half a day only;[1] and the particular
custom became a family tradition. These fasts must not
be confused with the minor communal fasts such as on
Sabbath afternoons[2] — in memory of the death of Moses
— or on Sundays — in memory of the destruction of the
Temple which occurred on that day.[3] The medieval Jew's
calendar was thickly studded with fasts, indeed some must
have abstained from food for quite half the year. But the
feasts were more popular than the fasts, and some most
remarkable sumptuary laws were enacted to curb the hospitable excesses of Jews on festive occasions.

Hospitality was at first a luxury and subsequently a
necessity in Jewish life. The Crusades mark the turning-
point. Impoverishment followed in the wake of the warriors of the Cross, many Jewish communities were ruined,
others reduced to beggary, and a good many schools
were thus forcibly closed. Thus there grew up among the
Jews a class of travelling mendicants and a class of poor
itinerant students, who wandered from place to place to
sell their wares or to learn the Law. On their peregrina-
tions these students suffered terrible privations, and of
necessity lived entirely on fruits and vegetables. The
entertainment of poor wayfarers became a necessary branch
of communal organization, and the strain was met by

---

[1] *J. Q. R.* iii. 469 and 515. David Altaras (in his צו"ק דב ש"ש, Venice, 1714)
orders his children to fast on the following days : — (1) the day of his death,
(2) at the end of the week of mourning, (3) at the end of the month, (4) at
the end of the eleventh month, (5) at the end of the full year. In modern
times there has been a tendency to turn the *Jahrzeit* into a joyous celebration.
See Aryeh Balchuber, שו"ת שם אריה, § 14.

[2] See Prof. Kaufmann's article on this subject in *J. Q. R.* vi. 754. Cf.
Machzor Vitry, § 141.

[3] יוסף אומץ, § 374.

distributing the guests among the various households of the town at which they broke their journeys for awhile.[1] This system, like all humane systems for the relief of the poor, increased the evil which it sought to mitigate, and was no doubt responsible for the creation of that troublesome feature of modern Jewish life, the professional mendicant traveller, who is less a tramp than a licensed blackmailer.

In the middle ages the treatment of poor Jewish travellers was considerate beyond description. Nothing might be done to put the poor guest to shame. In the Jewish Grace after Meals occurs the Psalmist's optimistic saying : 'I have been young, and now am old ; yet have I not seen the righteous forsaken, nor his seed begging their bread' (Ps. xxxvii. 25). This was said in a soft undertone, lest the poor guest, seated at the table, might be put to the blush. In Talmudical times it was usual to keep the door open during meals, so that any hungry person might enter.[2] In the middle ages this was restricted to the custom of opening the door to the hungry on passover eve, but the custom has ended by becoming a mere symbol. The medieval Jew never lost sight of the principle that the table was the altar and the meals provided for the poor were the best of offerings to God.

Under the blended feelings of pity and hospitality,

[1] Earlier than the sixteenth century there grew up a system of *Pletten*, i.e. 'bills for the payment for poor students and travellers to whom hospitality was shown.' Kaufmann, *J. Q. R.* iii. 512.

[2] This is especially mentioned of R. Huna. Already in the time of the Geonim the custom was abrogated (*Mafteach*, p. 138). Another passover-eve rite that became a mere symbol was the reclining at table. Originally this was the ordinary Graeco-Roman style in use at banquets of freemen, the slaves sitting on lower seats. Already, in the time of Maharil, it was seen that in the changed etiquette of Europe reclining, so far from being a token of freedom, was rather indicative of ill-health.

engendered by necessity and sociality, ostentation and luxury were bound to make encroaching inroads on the simplicity of Jewish home life. The 'diner-out' was not a typical figure in Jewish society, for a stigma attached to any man who was observed too often at other people's tables.[1] But it was not merely permissible, it was religiously praiseworthy, to attend certain hospitable assemblages of a semi-religious kind. These opportunities for display and extravagance were only too numerous. They included what were known as 'Commandment meals,'[2] viz. banquets (*a*) at *milah* or circumcision of an infant boy, (*b*) at the redemption of the first-born, (*c*) at a feast of betrothal, (*d*) at a marriage, (*e*) at a *siyum* when a Talmudical tractate was completed or any event of family interest occurred,[3]

---

[1] How unusual it was to take meals away from home in the middle ages may be seen from the language of the Kolbo (§ on *Meals*) : — מיהו כשאדם אוכל בבית חברו כגון בברית מילה ופורים. The diner-out is denounced in the Talmud (*Pesachim*, 49 b).

[2] The Hebrew term for these was סעודת מצוה (see *Talmud Pesachim*, 114). With regard to the *berith milah*, the night before the ceremony, during which Lilith was supposed to be most inimical to the new-born babe, was known as *Wachnacht*. This was already known to Jews in the thirteenth century, but is probably of non-Jewish origin. The night was spent in watching, hence its title *Watchnight*. The suggestion of A. Cahen that the meaning is *Badesnacht* (*bath-night*) has no probability. During the night the watchers feasted and prayed. More Jewish was the visit paid to the boy on the Sabbath before the *berith*, called Sabbath Zachar. This may or may not be identical with the Talmudical 'week of the son' which Löw (*Lebensalter*, pp. 89, 384) connects with the Greek rite of *hebdomenonomena*, observed on the seventh day after the birth of a child. This probably had no connexion originally with *berith milah*, indeed mention is also made of 'the week of the daughter.' In the middle ages the two ceremonies, the Jewish and the Greek, were assimilated, and the rites of the latter carried over to the former. (Cf. Schechter, *Jewish Quarterly Review*, ii. 6.) Regarding the *Pidyon Haben*, see Löw, p. 110 seq. This ceremony was Biblical in origin.

[3] Thus when a boy recited the *haftara* (lesson from the prophets) in synagogue, some fathers invited the whole congregation to a meal, S. Duran, שו"ת, § 160.

(*f*) on the Saturday night preceding the *milah,* called Sabbath *Zachar,* (*g*) at a banquet in honour of the visit paid by a *Chacham* or noted scholar.   Some other occasions for festivities were general but not universal.   In Germany many observed the greater and lesser *Spinholz,* on the two Sabbaths preceding a wedding,[1] while from the fifteenth century large parties were held at the *barmitsvah* or confirmation of the thirteen-year-old boy.[2]   Thus though Jewish authorities set their faces against all banquets except those of a semi-religious character,[3] it early became necessary to curb the hospitable excesses which occurred on the lawful occasions.

The luxury and dimensions of these meals are seen from the sumptuary regulations which were enacted throughout the middle ages.   No restriction was placed on the number of poor students whom the Rabbi might entertain, and it is said that the famous Isaiah Horwitz (1622) had never less than eighty persons at his table.[4]   A tax was frequently levied on other forms of hospitality, especially in Italy, where display was most common.[5]   In 1418, in Forli,

---

[1] Maharil, p. לז, only knew of one such Sabbath, but יוסף אומץ, § 657, mentions two.   Possibly Spinholz = *sponsalia,* though others more probably connect the word with *Spindle.*   See Güdemann, iii. 119, and Abraham Cahen, *Annuaire des Études Juives,* 1881, i. p. 89.

[2] A curious rite was connected with cutting the barmitsvah boy's hair. Schudt (ii. 295) tells us that the boy wore a wig on the occasion.   The hair-cutting on the thirteenth birthday in Tetuan is described in Benjamin II, p. 333 ; perhaps it is modern.   In other parts of the East, in Arabia and Palestine, the first hair-cutting of the boy after his fourth birthday is celebrated with much formality, and all the guests participate in the honour of shearing off a few hairs.   An account may be found in Luncz's *Jerusalem,* vol. ii.   Cf. Schechter, *J. Q. R.* ii. p. 16.

[3] Cf. Güdemann, iii. 260 (f.) and references.

[4] Sheftel Horwitz, in the preface to ווי העמודים.

[5] Cf. the satires of Immanuel of Rome and Kalonymos.

e.g. the Jewish communal authorities resolved that no one might invite to a wedding more than twenty men, ten women, five girls, and all the relatives till the third generation — a sufficiently generous allowance.[1] If the bride came from a distance, the company that escorted her was restricted to ten horsemen and four attendants on foot. To a *milah* (Ceremony of Initiation) only ten men and five women guests might be added to the relatives. Any one who infringed this law had to pay to the synagogue a fine of one ducat for each extra guest invited. Similar *tekanoth* or regulations were very frequently enacted, partly in the interests of thrift, partly to prevent envy, and partly to protect the poorer Jews from the humiliating necessity of foregoing the banquet altogether.

The practical difficulties in the way of collecting such a tax on the luxury of hospitality were not so great as might at first sight appear. In the first place the synagogue authorities, both Rabbinical and secular, were *ex officio* invited to all family festivities, and they were able, therefore, to gauge the extent to which the sumptuary limitations were exceeded. Then the invitations to these banquets were conveyed by the Shamash,[2] and he could keep the authorities well posted. Not only, however, were there communal *tekanoth* to regulate the number of the guests, but in the seventeenth century similar laws applied to the table appointments. At Metz wine goblets might not exceed ten ounces in weight.[3] That the Jews of the middle ages spent a good deal on their table appointments and on furnishing their homes is evident from a

---

[1] See similar regulations made in Metz in 1694 (*Annuaire de la Société des Études Juives*, 1881, p. 108).

[2] See p. 55 above.　　　　[3] *Annuaire*, ibid. p. 94, article 20.

variety of indications. The dietary laws necessitated the appropriation of one set of utensils for meat and another set for butter. A case is recorded of a very punctilious individual who maintained two complete households for this very purpose.[1] But even in ordinary abodes, the Passover must have entailed the possession of a good deal of extra crockery. No doubt the poor borrowed the appointments used at banquets,[2] just as in more modern times; but few Jewish families in the middle ages but possessed their gold or silver drinking-cup for the 'sanctification' (kiddush) on Sabbaths and festivals,[3] and an ornamental seven-branched lamp for Friday nights. These cups and lamps were at first but rarely embossed with figured designs,[4] but painted and inlaid platters were common, and the table-covers (even of the poorer Jews) were richly embroidered and worked with golden birds and fishes. Wooden vessels, dyed and figured, were also used for hot food in Persia as well as in Germany.[5] The inside walls of the richer houses were sometimes decorated with paintings of Old Testament scenes,[6] and on the outside, in the fifteenth century, even secular subjects were similarly displayed. A thirteenth century mystical book, compiled by a Spanish Jew, represents Pharaoh to have had Sarah's portrait painted on the wall of his chamber.[7] The

[1] Maharil, p. ‏ח״פ‎.

[2] See e.g. J. ben Enoch, ‏שו״ת חינוך בית יהודה‎, § 52.

[3] Silver spoons were much rarer, indeed they were termed 'non-Jewish' in *Machzor Vitry*, § 256, ‏כפות של גוים‎.

[4] Embossed lamps were especially forbidden. See Joseph of Trani, ‏שו״ת‎, § 35.

[5] *Responsa* of Geonim (*Mafteach*, 219, 226), and Maharil (‏הלכות ההגדה‎).

[6] Maharil; Rashi to *Sabbath*, 149, and Aruch, s. v. ‏דיוקן‎. Cf. Berliner, *Aus dem inneren Leben*, notes 98 and 99. Isaac and Goliath were favourite figures.

[7] *Zohar* to Gen. xii. 15.

revival of art at the Renaissance left Jews quite untouched except in Italy. In Germany portraits were not to be found in Jewish houses till the seventeenth century ;[1] in Italy, however, these were known almost two centuries earlier.

Before the art of portrait-painting was popular with Europeans other ornamental objects were familiar features of the Jewish abodes. Cut flowers were placed in water on the tables,[2] daggers and swords seem to have adorned the walls, and fancy objects, such as clocks with weights and apparatus for striking the hours, were used by Jews almost as soon as invented.[3] Candlesticks shaped like human heads had in the seventeenth century established themselves as a fashion rendered lawful by antiquity.[4] That these latter remarks apply only to the houses of the rich need hardly be said, for we find some Jews reduced to the use of egg-shells for holding the Sabbath Chanukah lights. So, too, it could only have been the wealthy who were able to display on the Passover the gold and silver ornaments and utensils pledged by non-Jews. Though these might not be worn or used, they might be displayed on the Passover in the dining-rooms.[5]

Similar differences no doubt prevailed with regard to the *houses* of rich and poor. Stone was the favourite

---

[1] Dr. Berliner put them as late as the eighteenth century. But Jair Chayim Bacharach (died 1702) already approved not only of the custom of having a portrait, but hung it in his room, אין איסור לצייר צורת עצמו או צורת אביו ולתלותם בחדרו. See *J. Q. R.* iii. 512. Cf. Schudt, *Jud. Merckw.* iv. 173.

[2] Maharil, p. כ"ט. These were perhaps restricted, as Dr. Berliner, p. 20, asserts, to the Sabbath.

[3] Jacob Weil, שו"ת, § 116. Rabbis in later centuries were much troubled to decide whether alarm clocks might be used on Sabbaths. Cf. A. Rosenbaum, שו"ת בן יהורה (Pressburg, 1871), § 151.

[4] Joseph David of Salonica, שו"ת בית דוד, ii. 75.   [5] Maharil, p. נ"ו.

material used for building the fine houses of Jews. Ihe-
ring rightly [1] calls the preference for stone houses a Semitic instinct, and curiously enough Mr. Joseph Jacobs
has argued that the Jews were the first people in England
to possess dwelling-houses built with stone, 'probably for
purposes of protection as well as comfort.' [2]   This protective use can hardly have been everywhere desired, for
apparently in Spain the Jewish houses were not always
strongly built. [3]

The Jewish houses were of varying sizes, but in central
Europe they were mostly very large, and many families
lived together under the same roof. [4]   The doors were
barred, but could be opened by a latch. [5]   These large
houses were surrounded by court-yards containing vege-
table gardens and buildings suitable for use in warmer
weather. [6]   Jews, indeed, were very successful gardeners
until they were cooped up within their narrow ghettos
in the sixteenth century.   Syria in ancient times was
famous for its gardens : *Multa Syrorum olera* is a proverb
cited by Pliny.   In the thirteenth century the Jews were
noted for their vineyards and their orchards in southern
France, and, as will be seen in a later chapter, also in
other parts of the world.

---

[1] *Vorgeschichten der Indoeuropäer*, p. 139.   Prof. Bacher adds (*J. Q. R.*
viii. 187) that in the Biblical laws regarding leprous houses (Lev. xiv. 33–53),
only stone dwellings are mentioned.   So, too, the beautiful house of Samuel
Belassar of Regensburg in the fifteenth century was of stone.

[2] *Jews of Angevin England*, p. xiv.

[3] See an epitaph on Samuel ben Shealtiel, who died in Valencia in 1097
from the fall of his house.   So R. Chanoch was killed in Cordova in 1014 by
the collapse of the reading-desk in synagogue.

[4] *Das Judenschreinbuch der Laurez. zu Köln*, passim.

[5] Meir of Rothenberg, *Reponsa* (ed. *Mekitse Nirdamim*, § 22).

[6] *Das Judenschreinbuch*, anno 1282.

The ordinary Jewish home of the middle ages had two distinct rooms, the inner and the outer room, the latter being mostly employed in warm weather. The duty of dwelling in booths during the Feast of Tabernacles [1] was joyously performed throughout the middle ages, the booths being decorated with much taste and often with costliness. [2] Decency and even comfort as regards house-room grew up much earlier among ordinary Jews than among the generality of Europeans of the middle ages. [3] So, too, the wealthy Jews seem to have surpassed wealthy Christians of the middle ages in the comfort and luxuriousness of their homes. This is the description given by a fifteenth-century Christian chronicler of a rich Jew's house in Regensburg ; [4] the contrast between the exterior and interior was probably frequent in Jewish residences : —

The house was a dark-grey, moss-covered, hideous pile of stones, provided with closely-barred windows of various sizes, irregularly placed. It seemed scarcely habitable. A passage, more than 80 feet in length, feebly lighted on the Sabbath, led to a dark, partly-decayed, winding staircase, from which one had to grope one's way in the gloom along the walls to reach the structure in the rear. A well-protected door opened, and one entered into an apartment cheerfully decorated with flowers, with costly and splendid furniture, richly and splendidly appointed. Here, the walls panelled and decorated with polished wood, with many-coloured waving and winding hangings and artistic carved work, was the owner's domestic temple, in which the Sabbath festival was celebrated with alternate religious exercises and luxurious regalements. A costly carpet, rich in colour and design, covered the brightly-scrubbed floor. A flame-red cloth of finest wool overlay the round table, which rested on gilt legs, and above it hung, fastened to a shining metal chain, the seven-armed lamp, bright as when fresh from the casting, and streaming with radiance from seven points. The festal board, adorned with heavy silver goblets, the work of a master-hand, was surrounded by high-backed, gilt-decorated chairs,

[1] Leviticus xxiii. [2] Maharil has a long description of the Succah.

[3] See Berliner, *Inn. Leben*, p. 20. In the Mishnah the size of the average dining-room was 15 ft. square (*Baba Bathra*, vi. 4).

[4] Anselm of Parengar in *Jahrbuch* (Wertheimer), 1856, p. 168. Also Berliner, loc. cit., p. 21. This wealthy Jew is described as *Hochmeister*.

and cushions of shorn velvet. In a niche a massive silver urn, with a golden tap, invited you to the ceremonial hand-washing, and the finest linen inter-woven with costly silk, dried the purified hands. A superbly inlaid oak-table, girt with garlands of flowers, was laden with the festive viands and the glittering wine-jug; a couch of oriental design, with swelling side-cushions, and a silver cupboard filled with jewels, golden chains and bangles, gilt and silver vessels, rare and precious antiques, formed the rich frame which worthily embraced this picture of splendour and magnificence — the *Hochmeister's* domestic temple.

Though the quantity and quality of the food naturally varied with the wealth of the family, there was nevertheless an identity of type in the Jewish meals of the middle ages. The chief meal was taken at midday, both on week-days and on Sabbaths. A long evening meal was exclusively reserved for Fridays, festivals, and large gatherings of a formal character. Three meals were *de rigeur* on the Sabbath with rich and poor alike, viz. on Friday evening, on Sabbath at midday, while a third meal was spread before evening on the Saturday.[1] In winter, this third meal was a mere formality and consisted mainly of dessert, in the Rhine-land hard-boiled eggs being preferred in summer.[2] Fish was the favourite delicacy for Friday evenings, and like most Jewish dishes of the middle ages, it was highly seasoned with pepper and garlic.[3] Poultry was likewise much loved, but it hardly seems that the famous Sabbath *schalet* was originally an individual dish, it was rather a generic term for food kept hot in the oven overnight.[4]

Special dishes were reserved for special occasions, thus

[1] Many Jews kept the table-cloth spread throughout the whole of the Sabbath. Maharil, p. 28 a. [2] Ibid.

[3] Mystical reasons were given for the use of fish in the middle ages, but the fondness for it was probably due to the fact that the laws of *Shechita* (slaughtering) did not here apply.

[4] This goes on the supposition that the word is connected with O. F. *chald* = modern *chaud*.

on the New Year's eve a sheep's head was often eaten, and fruit sweetened with honey. On the other hand, nuts were not eaten till the last day of Tabernacles. Of course the thin unleavened cakes or *matsath* were reserved for the Passover. These were almost always round in shape.[1] On Fridays, as well as on the day preceding the Passover, it was customary to eat very sparingly, so as to build up a keen appetite for the evening meal. Special cakes were made for the Sabbath called *pasdida*,[2] they were, however, restricted to Germany, and were certainly unknown in Poland. A fritter, made in the shape of a ladder with seven rungs, was eaten on Pentecost as an emblem of the 'seven heavens which God rent at the giving of the Law to manifest that there was no God but he.'[3]

But with all this care for the delights of the table,[4]

[1] Frankl, in his *Jews of the East* (Eng. Trans.), i. 103, mentions a square variety. Since machinery was introduced an attempt was made to popularize square *motsas*, but without success.

[2] יוסף אומץ, § 616. The story is added (§ 612) of a Jewish child, captured by brigands, who cried so pitifully on Friday night for his Sabbath cake that he was eventually discovered by Jews and ransomed.

[3] Ibid. § 854. Special cakes were also made for Chanuka (Kalonymos, אבן בוחן). The pastry for Pentecost was known as *Sinai Cake* in the middle ages. *Minhagin*, 16 a (Güdemann, iii. 112).

[4] In his witty *Purim tractate*, Kalonymos (fourteenth century), enumerates the following foods as customary with Jews on that merry anniversary : — Pies, chestnuts, turtle-doves, pancakes, small tarts, gingerbread, ragout, venison, roast goose, chicken, stuffed pigeons, ducks, pheasants, partridges, quails, macaroons, and salad. Beef was too ordinary a thing to be used on so festive an occasion. There were, according to Dante's friend, Immanuel of Rome (*Divan*, xxv), many houses in the papal city where this luxury prevailed. Jews were particularly fond of the goose in Germany in the sixteenth century, especially the liver ; as also of what the Poles called *lokshen* or frimsels. Pike was a favourite fish. Roast goose is named as a dainty as early as the *Targum Sheni* to Esther. Cheese was taken on Chanuka, because Judith gave Holofernes milk to drink (in the Hebrew version of the Apocryphal 'Judith,' in the Greek this detail is wanting).

there was an equal fastidiousness with regard to the spiritual accompaniments of eating. Besides the table-hymns described above, there were a large number of special home prayers which were recited before the meal or as an adjunct to the grace which followed it. In presence of the bridal pair, or of a mourner, or in the house blessed with a new-born boy, passages were interpolated into the grace after meals, while some beautiful penitential prayers were uttered by pietists before their regular daily repasts.[1] Some inserted the 23d Psalm, 'The Lord is my shepherd, I shall not want,' before breaking bread. Isaac Loria Ashkenazi (1534–1572), in his short life, originated many customs of this kind, mainly with a mystical significance. Mysticism had some evil effects on Jewish home life and gave a fresh lease of popularity to many superstitions. Blessing the moon, kissing the mezuzah,[2] inscribing angelic and demoniacal charms in the bedroom where a child was just born, carrying the scroll of the Law into the presence of the mother, the recital of Psalm 91 before going to sleep on Sabbath afternoons, the refusal to speak any language but Hebrew on the Sabbath, puerile punctiliousness as to the number of loaves, the seizure of the bread with the whole ten fingers, the covering of the bread during the blessing of the wine and the covering of knives during grace, the choice of foods, the abstention from meat because of a belief in transmigration,[3] the retention of the custom of

---

[1] קיצור של״ה, § *On eating.*

[2] See Deut. vi. 9. For superstitions in general see Güdemann, vol. i. ch. vii. and elsewhere.

[3] The doctrine of transmigration was not accepted by any of the great Jewish writers of the middle ages. The Jewish mystics, however, employed the belief as the corner-stone of their religious structure.

killing a white cock on the day before the great fast of the tenth of Tishri — all these and many more old customs of a semi-religious character, and in origin tainted with no superstitious implications, were seized upon by the mystics and emphasized into full-blown superstitions. The mysticism of the middle ages was responsible for much of that narrowing of the Jewish home life which gives it its *borné* appearance to modern eyes. It out-Judaized Judaism in its insistence on custom here and custom there, until it bound its adherents hand and foot within the coils of a superstitious code. But it had its good side too. If mysticism chained men's hands and feet it never dominated the freedom of their minds ; it lent wings to their imagination and was in the main a powerful spiritualizing force. The mystics were the best prayer-writers of the middle ages, and one would seek in vain for a Jewish Thomas à Kempis outside the ranks of the mystics.

Before, however, I trace the effects of this mysticism on the Jewish home life of the middle ages, I must find space to indicate one other characteristic feature of that life on which sufficient stress has not been laid. The ghetto-life made the Jew a sloven, it never made him a brute. The Jew was beyond everything *considerate* to all with whom he had very intimate relations. This considerateness was inculcated in the child from its earliest years. Envy, jealousy, anger, violence, the use of oaths, were tabooed by the Jewish domestic code. It is true that Jewish law tended, as the centuries rolled on, to lose its elasticity and to disregard the weaknesses of men. But it was always lenient towards women. Relaxations of the ceremonial law were constantly made, from considerateness for the woman's intenser nature and more absorb-

ing cares. Her position in the home was always anoma-
lous, for she was regarded as at once men's inferior and
superior. But, to pass from a straining of contrasts, it
was she who initiated the most marked stage in the approach of the Sabbath, by kindling the Sabbath lamp, ex-
emplifying the old Jewish proverb, 'The lamp is lit, and
sorrows flit.'[1] In her honour the Jewish husband recited
on Friday eve at table the Eulogy of the Virtuous Woman
(Proverbs xxxi. 10). It was the Jewess who had the most
well-defined of the lighter and brighter domestic privileges; she abstained from work, for instance, on the
New Moon,[2] and in the East did not ply her ordinary
occupations after sunset during the *Omer.*[3] She was
excused from participation in the *habdala* or ceremonial
leave-taking of the Sabbath, because her household
duties were particularly absorbing after a complete day
of rest.[4] She joined in the home prayers, read the
grace, and a girl was sometimes the spokesman for the
family. 'Maharil was at his father-in-law's table one
Passover eve, and his daughter said: "Father, why hast
thou raised the dish?" Then he proceeded at once with
the recital: "We were servants of Pharaoh in Egypt."'[5]
Thus this young lady's query was allowed to replace the

[1] Berliner, loc. cit.
[2] It early became usual to abstain merely from certain occupations, such
as spinning. *Tashbats*, iii. 244.
[3] This period extended from Passover to Pentecost. A. b. E. Salem, in his
שו"ת מטה אשר (Salonica, 1748), § 31, describes this custom as already old. For
the abstinence from work on New Moon see *Shulchan Aruch*, א"ח, § 417.
[4] That the usual explanations of this custom are wrong is clear from the
fact that in the time of the Geonim the habdala wine was not drunk by the
household at all. *Mafteach*, 143.
[5] Maharil, section on the *Hagada.* Sometimes she said *Kaddish*,
חות יאיר, 222.

ritual questions set down in the prayer-book, a clear token, moreover, that in the middle ages ritual had not gained that mastery over Jewish life which it enjoyed after the close of the fifteenth century.

It is in connexion with the Passover, too, that we find a general statement regarding men's estimate of women, which ought to be written in letters of gold. By law, a Jewess was not compelled to ' recline at table '[1] unless she were a woman of extraordinary note. '*Nowadays, however,*' says a thirteenth-century authority, '*all Jewesses are women of surpassing merit.*'[2] Again, woman was regarded as less yielding to the lower passions than a man. A Jewish girl never said, 'I am in love with such and such a man, and will marry him.'[3] On the other hand, songs in praise of a woman's beauty were rejected in the middle ages as indecorous, though the Talmud had allowed them.[4] Again, women were in certain cases allowed to light the Chanuka lamp in behalf of their absent husbands, who became freed from the duty by the vicarious act of their wives.[5] Indeed, some women of the middle ages were as skilled as their husbands in the ritual laws of Judaism, and it was said of them, 'if they are not prophetesses, they are the daughters of prophets.'[6] The point to observe in all this is, however, the practical consequence drawn from such a statement. A woman's opinion was to be deferred to, and her statements concerning customs were to be treated with consideration.[7] The Talmud had already appreciated the finer perceptions of women, they were

---

[1] See p. 142, above.

[2] Mordecai : — האירנא כל הנשים שלנו הוויין חשובות. Maharil, p. 14.

[3] Cf. p. 166, below.

[4] *Mafteach*, 49.

[5] Maharil, *Laws of Chanucah.*

[6] Cf. Güdemann, i. 232.

[7] ויש לסמוך על מנהג, ibid.

better judges of a guest's character, said the Rabbis,
than men were. A picture of the ordinary Jewess's home
life of the middle ages is drawn in the Testament of a
Jew, written before 1357.[1] 'My daughters must respect
their husbands exceedingly, and they must be always
amiable to them; husbands must honour their wives
more than themselves. My daughters ought not to laugh
and speak much with strangers, nor to dance. They
ought always to be at home and not gadding about.
They must not stand at the door (to watch what their
neighbours are doing). Most strongly I beg, most strictly
I command, that the daughters of my house be not, God
forbid, without work to do, for idleness leads to sin, but
they must spin, or cook, or sew, and be patient and modest
in all their ways.' This does not tell us the whole truth,
however. For, as we saw in an earlier chapter, the husband was often compelled to leave his wife for considerable periods, either to study or to trade. During his
absence the wife became a business-woman,[2] and she often
supported her husband at ordinary times, despite the contempt in which a Jew was held for allowing his wife to
play the man for him.[3]

I have insisted on the characteristic Jewish virtue of
considerateness. In no point was it more admirably shown
than in the treatment of inferiors. How far this was
carried in the relief of poverty cannot be told here; I
must reserve my space for the behaviour of Jews towards

---

[1] I have given this document in full in *J. Q. R.* iii. 461.

[2] *Raben.* 115, and Meir of Rothenberg *Responsa* (Lemberg), 57; *Chayim Or Zarua*, 250.

[3] This reliance on the wife became more marked in later centuries.
Authors frequently allude to it in the prefaces of their books. Cf. e.g.
Aaron ben Meir, אהרן מנחת (Neuhof, 1792).

those who served them in their homes. The efforts of
zealous Churchmen much diminished the numbers of the
Christian servants who lived in Jewish homes.[1]   Unless,
however, Jews had agreed to accept the Karaitic innovation and spend the Sabbath in darkness and cold, they
were compelled to seek the aid of non-Jews to kindle fires
and attend to the candles and lamps on the Sabbath day.
The question was one of great difficulty, for the Jews
never lost sight of the fact that he who employs another
to work for him is, morally speaking, working himself.
In Spain, a great pietist like Solomon ben Adret (died
about 1310) found it very difficult to evade the attentions of
a kind-hearted Christian housemaid.   Though I have mentioned the incident before, it is worth citing the Rabbi's
own words : ‘Though in France they allow non-Jews to
light a fire on Sabbaths in winter, I do not allow it.
Two or three times I saw that my maidservant heated
the oven though I had repeatedly forbidden it.   So I had
a lock put on, and I remove the key on Friday evening,
and only replace it on Saturday night.’[2]   On the other
hand, an equally celebrated authority freely permitted non-
Jews to do indispensable work for Jews on the Sabbath.[3]
The question resolved itself into a compromise, and the
Sabbath goy, as well as the *Sabbath goya*[4] — itinerant
servitors of the ghettos, who went about stirring fires,

[1] This subject will be dealt with in a subsequent chapter.   The reverse
relations also subsisted, and Jewesses acted as laundresses for Christians,
Iserlein, תרומת הדשן, § 152.
[2] S. ben Adret, שו"ת (ed. Venice), § 857.   An exactly similar story is told
of Meir of Rothenburg (Güdemann, i. p. 255).
[3] תשב"ץ, iii. 225.
[4] The objection to her long continued.   Cf. יוסף אומץ, § 608, B. Wesel,
מקור ברוך (1755), § 2, etc.

snuffing candles, and heating the *schalet* — became recognized necessaries of Jewish life.[1] It led unhappily to a certain amount of hypocrisy, for many Jews somewhat dulled their conscience by the assumption that an *indirect* order to a servant was less culpable than a straightforward and direct injunction. They would hint a command, but they would not speak it.

The Jewish servant was, in every sense, a member of the family, and though the servant did not usually eat with the master, he or she received a portion of every dish before it came to table. 'A man must never put unnecessary burdens on a servant,' says the *Book of the Pious*.[2] A party of bachurim (students) at a drinking-bout in the fifteenth century, in Vienna, were playing practical jokes with one another, and one of the party threw a dish at the servant's head. The miscreant barely escaped excommunication for the offence, and was subjected to most severe penalties. In the Talmud the relations between masters and servants were most amicable. R. Gamliel's attendant Tobi was a special favourite, and his doings are often quoted. A saying of the maidservant of R. Jehuda became the proverbial formula for dismissing guests when the meal was over : 'The can has reached the bottom of the cask, let the eagles hie them to their nests.' When, however, the pause was merely an interval between the courses she remarked : 'Another follows its like, the can floats on the cask like a ship on the sea.'[3] Similar familiarity prevailed in the middle ages. The Jews were always generous masters. Presents were given to servants on Purim, even

---

[1] The employment of a non-Jew to attend to the candles in synagogue on the Day of Atonement was licensed by many authorities. — Maharil, p. 46.

[2] § 665.

[3] *Erubin*, 53 b.

when the servants were not Jews.[1] The treatment of
servants may be inferred from the remark of Bacharach,
that 'it is not the custom for mistresses' to deduct the
cost of broken crockery from the servant's wages.[2]

Naturally the servants shared in the Sabbath rest, and
participated in home prayers and religious rites. Before
they lit the candles on Saturday nights, the servant-girl
said, 'Blessed be he who separates between holy and pro-
fane.' They frequently sat at table with the family on
Sabbaths and on the passover eve, and it was on these
occasions that the innate real Jewish mannerliness revealed itself. The servant was not to be put to shame,[3]
and was not to be asked to perform her ordinary duties
while at table. 'When I was a child,' says I. Lüpschütz,[4]
'and I asked the servant *who was sitting at table with
us* to give me some water, my mother rebuked me.'

I can best indicate the extent to which this quality was
carried by recalling that it was found necessary at Metz,
in 1694, to insert in the communal regulations a clause
restraining masters from too lavish an expenditure at their
servants' weddings. It was forbidden to invite more than
thirty-two guests (besides the communal authorities) to the
festivities which the master organized in celebration of his
servant's nuptials.[5]

To return from this digression. When one thinks what
human life was for the majority of men in the middle
ages, 'how little of a feast for their senses it could possi-

---

[1] Meir of Rothenburg, שו״ת (ed. Lemberg), 184.
[2] חות יאיר, § 103.
[3] *Book of the Pious*, § 665.
[4] See *J. Q. R.* iii. p. 478.
[5] *Annuaire of the Soc. Études Juives*, 1885, p. 109.

bly be, one understands the charm for them of a refuge offered in the heart and the imagination.'[1]   More than to any others, this remark applies to the Jews.   As the middle ages closed for the rest of Europe the material horizon of the Jews narrowed.   Prejudice and proscription robbed them of the attractions of public life and threw them within themselves, to find their happiness in their own idealized hopes.   But the fancies on which they fed were not of the kind that expand the imagination.

Jews were not inaccessible to ideas, for they never confused the land of Philistia with the land of the children of light.   But the ideas which came to them in the really dark ages of Jewish life were not the ideas which freshened Europe and roused it from its mystic medieval dreams. Indeed, Judaism became more mystical as Europe became more rational, it clasped its cloak tighter as the sun burned warmer.   The Renaissance, which drew half its inspiration from Hebraism, left the Jews untouched on the artistic side.   The Protestant Reformation, which took its life-blood from a rational Hebraism, left the Jews unaffected on the moral side.   It was, in a sense, a misfortune for the Synagogue that it had not sunk into the decadence from which the Reformation roused the Church. As it was not corrupt it needed no rousing moral regeneration, and so it escaped, through its own inherent virtues, that general stirring-up of life· which results from great efforts for the redress of great vices.

Moreover, Judaism in the home kept pace with its fortunes in the world, but did not overstep the bounds thus set.   For, without, Judaism at the close of the Renaissance

[1] Matthew Arnold, *Essays in Criticism* (Eversley ed.), p. 213.

had become thoroughly disorganized. The disgraceful persecutions of the fourteenth and fifteenth centuries completed what the Crusades had begun, and split the Jewish communities into national groups. There were in many towns not only Italian, Greek, Spanish, Portuguese, German, and Moorish congregations side by side, but there were innumerable sections within each of these groups. Each of these congregations had its own managers, its own ritual, its own Rabbis, its own charities, its own jealousies, its own prejudices.[1] They were not only independent of one another, they were often antagonistic; they rarely worked together for common aims. These two or three centuries of retrogression or stagnation followed the tremendous blow inflicted on medieval Judaism by the expulsion of its most enlightened representatives from Spain. At a stroke, the Spanish Inquisition cancelled the painfully-earned right of Jews to admission into the wider world, just when the maritime discoveries of the fifteenth century were expanding the material horizon of Europe, and the revival of interest in the old masterpieces of Hebraic and Hellenic literature was enlarging the range of men's minds. Jewish life, like the Jewish organization, became for a while a mass and maze of detail, without starting-point and without goal. The details were clung to the more desperately because the Jews dared not leave them, having lost sense of the central idea which the details exemplified. They could not prune the branches, because root and branch were intermingled. Home religion became an etiquette, a provincial code of manners formalized against foreign intrusions. Then, with

---

[1] Cf. Graetz, *History of the Jews* (Eng. Trans.), IV. ch. xv.

the close of the eighteenth century, came one touch of
the modern spirit, and lo! the evil humours fled one by
one into the night, and the Tree of Life revived, erect
and expansive.   For its roots were fixed in the home, and
the Jewish home, whatever its faults or limitations, was
never tainted with moral corruption.

CHAPTER IX

LOVE AND COURTSHIP

THE prevalence of child-marriages in the middle ages reduced Jewish courtship to an expression of the will of the parents. But the sons of Israel did not quite forget that the noblest of love poems is contained in the Hebrew Bible. The Song of Songs was perhaps the most popular of all the Books of the Old Testament. It was read in synagogue, and its imagery has left its mark on many pages of the Jewish liturgy. Through a happy misunderstanding of its meaning, this idealization of love became a tradition which tinged the most matter-of-fact marriage bargains with some colour of romance. Nay, there has never been an age in which Jewish love-stories have not relieved the monotony of made-up marriages. In the Talmud and the medieval Jewish records may be found genuine cases of courtship, in the modern sense of the word.

There is no need to quote stray instances, for the language of the Jewish poets of the middle ages leaves no room for doubt. Moses Ibn Ezra (born in 1070) was so weighted by the sense of man's misery that his liturgical pieces turn mostly on the subject of sin and reconciliation. This serious Spanish-Jewish writer, surnamed the 'poet of penitence,' was, nevertheless, the author of Hebrew love-songs worthy of the most light-hearted troubadour. His passion, he tells us, was never equalled before; the world had never seen the like of his love or of his loved one. Though she frown on him and smile on others, his life would be a slavery if he were released from her bonds. The more she spurns him, the more ardent grows his flame. He is love-sick, but asks no healing, for death would be more tolerable than the quenching of his passion. 'Live on,' he cries to the irresponsive object of his affection, 'though thy lips drop honey for others to sip; live on breathing myrrh for others to inhale. Though thou art false to me, till the cold earth claims her own again, I shall remain true to thee. My heart loves to hear the nightingale's song, though the songster is above me and afar.' [1]

Jehuda Halevi, the greatest Jewish poet of the middle ages, wrote numerous love-songs which display a similar abandonment to romantic passion. 'Ophrah bathes her garment in the water of my tears, and dries it in the sunshine of her bright eyes.' Of the Hebrew wedding odes, however, an opportunity will soon present itself to speak. Let it be noted that Jehuda Halevi, who sings of love, added scores of fine hymns to the prayer-book, and became the exemplar of Judaism for his own contemporaries and for all later centuries. It is in the works just of the poets of this class, the men who left their impress on their people's sacred liturgy and innermost life, that women are treated with the utmost reverence and love is idealized.[2] It was not till the thirteenth century that a Spanish Jew, Judah ben Sabbatai of Barcelona, composed a diatribe against the fair

[1] Kaempf, *Nichtandalusische Poesie andalusischer Dichter* (Beilagen, p. 209).

[2] These poems found their way into the liturgy itself. Cf. the Yemen Prayer-book, Brit. Mus. MS. Or. 2227, where many of Jehuda Halevi's wedding odes are introduced.

sex. But can one compare him in importance with the writer who replied to Judah's *Woman Hater* with a ponderous yet chivalrous plea in defence of the daughters of Israel? Yedaya Bedaresi, who entered the lists on woman's behalf, was the writer of perhaps the most popular ethical prose-poem written in Hebrew during the whole middle ages! It is undeniable that the wit was on the side of the enemy; it is undeniable that the folk-tales of the Jews, betraying their Indian origin, are misogynist to a degree never exceeded, hardly equalled, in other literature. But the compilers of these satires were simply using good tales and smart epigrams without overmuch thought of their tendency, and reproduced the *Seven Wise Masters* or Honein's *Maxims of the Philosophers*, not because of the sages' sneers against woman's fidelity, but because the stories they told were ingenious and enthralling. The selection of good motives for tales lay within a very restricted area in the thirteenth and fourteenth centuries until Boccaccio and Chaucer went to other fields than India or Arabia for their lore. Thus we find Zabara, writing a *Book of Delight* in Hebrew in 1200, crowding his pages with narratives full of point and sting, stories which tell of women's wickedness and infidelity, of their weakness of intellect and fickleness of will. But there is a marked divergence between Zabara's stories and the moral which he draws from them. His misogynist satires are never without a philogynist tag. And the reason is obvious. Zabara did not invent the tales; they were the common folk-stock of the medieval poets. But he did invent his own morals.[1]

[1] Cf. the writer's remarks in the *Jewish Quarterly Review*, vi. p. 506. See also p. 87 above.

The love of which the Hebrew versifiers of the twelfth and thirteenth centuries sing was, however, the prerogative of the poets. So far as the ordinary Jews shared such feelings, courtship was entirely of the *man's* making. As the Talmud prettily puts it, one who has lost a treasure must seek it again, the treasure does not look for him. Eve was taken from Adam, hence Adam's sons since born go in search of their Eves. That the woman should display pre-nuptial love was repulsive to the Jewish conception of womanliness. Says a tenth or eleventh century authority : [1] — 'It is the habit of all Jewish maidens, even if they be as much as twenty years old, to leave the arrangement of their marriage in the hands of their fathers ; nor are they indelicate or impudent enough to express their own fancies, and to say, "I would like to wed such and such a one." ' There is even more in this sentiment than at first sight appears, for it marks the chasm separating the conception of marriage which the medieval Jews entertained from the views which find expression in the Talmud. In point of fact the Talmudical view is the much nearer allied of the two to the prevailing opinion of modern Europe. 'A man,' says the Talmud, 'must not betrothe his daughter while she is a minor ; he must wait till she attains her majority, and says, "I love this man." ' [2]

[1] Harkavy, *Responsa* of Geonim, p. 87. The passage is so important that I give the original : — מנהגה דכל בנות ישראל אע"ג דהויא ברתא בית אביה בוגרת ואפילו בת עשרים שנה ואיתיה לאב בחיים בתר אביה גרירא · וליכא מירי פריצותא וחוצפא בבנות ישראל לגלויי איהי דעתא ולמימרא לפל' אני רוצה אלא על אביה סמכה :

[2] Talmud, *Kiddushin*, 41 a. The age of marriage was not unanimously agreed upon in Talmudic times. 'In Babylon a man first marries and then studies the Torah, in Palestine he first learns Torah and then marries' (Müller, חלוף מנהגים, § 70. Cf. *Kiddushin*, 29 b). In the Midrash, *Echa Rabbathi* (to

It will readily be seen that from the sentimental objection which grew up in the middle ages against a Jewish maiden expressing her feelings on the subject of love, the step to early marriage was an easy one. For, if her father might choose her husband for her, why should he not tie the bond while she had no power to interfere? The legal minority of a girl extended to the day after she had completed her twelfth year, and by the thirteenth century a large proportion of Jewish girls were married during their minority.[1] The husbands were not much older, though with them the Mishnaic admonition to regard eighteen as normal age for marriage[2] was not altogether abandoned by medieval Jews. Maimonides explained that the Mishnaic phrase 'eighteen years old,' used of the age proper to a Jewish bridegroom, meant 'in his eighteenth year,' thus reducing the marriage age to seventeen. In the recognized Jewish code[3] the following rule is laid down : — ' It is the duty of every Jewish man to marry a wife in his eighteenth year, but he who anticipates and marries earlier is following the more laudable course, but no one should marry before he is thirteen.'

The motive for these early marriages was a moral one, the promotion of chastity being one of the most pronounced

---

Lamentations i. 1, section beginning עם רבתי העיר) occurs this remark : — ' A Jew used to marry his son when he was twelve years old to a maiden who had reached the period of puberty; he would marry his grandson when he too was twelve, and thus a man of twenty-six was already a grandfather.' This was evidently the national ideal — not realized when this passage was written.

[1] Cf. Tosafoth to *Kiddushin*, 41 a, and many authorities, e.g. the לבוש, i. § 3.

[2] *Mishnah Aboth*, v. § 24.

[3] Shulchan Aruch, העזר אבן, i. 3. Cf. Löw's *Lebensalter*, p. 165 seq. for further details on this point.

of Jewish social ideals. At times, however, marriages occurred at an even earlier age than any yet cited. In the second half of the seventeenth century, the bridegroom was frequently not more than ten years old, and the bride was younger still.[1] A deep mystical thought lay behind this epidemic of child-unions. The period was deeply stirred by visionary expectations, and Messianic hopes — never long absent from the day-dreamers of the ghetto — clustered luxuriantly round the person of that arch-impostor, Sabbatai Zevi. Jewish tradition had it that the Messianic era could not dawn until all the souls created by God from the primeval chaos had been fitted to the earthly bodies destined for their reception here below. To hurry on the great day, mothers and fathers eagerly joined their children in wedlock, each mother dreaming perhaps that in the child of her own offspring God would deign to plant the soul of the longed-for redeemer.

Two other reasons, at once more prosaic and more pathetic than the sentimental or moral motives previously considered, are assigned by medieval authorities for encouraging, or at least permitting, marriages to take place at an earlier age than the Talmud regarded as legal or laudable. These justifications are worthy of more than passing attention, for they throw a lurid light on the darkening circumstances of the Jews. Child-marriages, indeed, were not restricted to Jews, nor to the East. Thus, in 1211, St. Elizabeth, the four-year old Hungarian princess, was married to a bridegroom of the mature age of eleven. Her

---

[1] זאת תורת הקנאות 14 b, cited by Löw, p. 402, note 140. For a case of very early marriage, see Jacob Weil שו''ת 112 (the bride was ten). Much earlier, girls were married at the same age. Cf. Müller, *Mafteach*, p. 115.

transportation to her boy-husband's home in a silver cradle gave rise to the oft-quoted lines :[1]—

> 'Eine Hochzeit sie begingen
> Brautlauf sie empfingen,
> Mit den zwei'n jungen Kinden,
> Eine Eh' sie wollten binden,
> Festen und stärken.'

Here, no doubt, political exigencies played their part, but it cannot be maintained that love marriages were usual in Europe until after the Crusades. Now, the same events which gave chivalrous romance a commanding influence in the marriage customs of Christian Europe produced an exactly opposite effect in Jewish circles. There are two ends to a spear, and while the Christian knight handled the butt-end, the Jew was only acquainted with the point. 'As to our custom,' says a twelfth century Jewish authority,[2] 'of betrothing our daughters before they are fully twelve years old, the cause is that persecutions are more frequent every day, and if a man can afford to give his daughter a dowry, he fears that to-morrow he may not be able to do it, and then his daughter would remain for ever unmarried.' In the fourteenth century, to the uncertainty of the dowry was added the scarcity of eligible men. 'The Talmudic prohibition of child-marriages,' says Perez of Corbeil,[3] 'applied only to the period when many Jewish families were settled in the same town. Now, however (after the Crusades), when our numbers are reduced and our people

---

[1] Cf. Emil Friedberg's, *Ehe und Eheschliessung im deutschen Mittelalter*, p. 15.

[2] Tosafoth, as cited above. This is quoted, too, from Mr. S. Schechter's translation, in J. Jacobs' *Angevin England*, p. 52.

[3] Cf. *Kolbo*, § 86 a, לבוש, p. 26 b, § 8, cites both reasons. Cf. Löw, p. 171.

scattered, we are in the habit of marrying girls under the age of twelve, should an eligible husband present himself.' The first stage on the downward road to the made-up marriage was reached when it was held lawful to betrothe a girl without her knowledge, though it remained necessary to seek her assent before completing the wedding.[1] But it is a universal truth that love laughs at rules, and Isaac and Rebekah would often settle their love affairs without the paternal sanction.

The professional match-maker or *shadchan* comes into prominence and enjoys a legal status at least as early as the twelfth century.[2] It is hardly open to doubt that this enterprising professional owed his existence to the same cycle of events which resulted in the systematization of early marriages. When Jewish society became disintegrated by the massacres and expulsions of the Crusading era, its scattered items could only be re-united through the agency of some peripatetic go-between. There was nothing essentially unromantic about the method, for the *shadchan* was often a genuine enthusiast for marriage. The evil came in when, like the Roman *pronuba* or the Moslem *katbeh*, the *shadchan* made up marriages for a fee, or, happening to be a travelling merchant, hawked hearts as well as trinkets. A good deal of misery resulted from the marriages rashly contracted between strangers, for desertion or indigence would fall to the lot of the hapless Jewesses who were wed to men coming they hardly knew whence,

---

[1] Natronai Gaon (ninth cent.) records the fact that in his time such cases were of daily occurrence :— ‏ומעשים בכל יום דכתב איניש שטר אירוסין לרעתו ואינו‎ ‏נמלך בה עד שעת קידושין‎, Müller, *Mafteach*, p. 115.

[2] The fact that the *shadchan* was regarded as an *agent* and could legally exact a fee is already quoted by the ‏מרדכי‎ (*Baba Kamma*, ch. x), from the *Or Zarua* in the name of R. Simchah.

with past records which veiled their less presentable features from the careless scrunity of fathers in a hurry, but
were revealed all too surely at the repentant leisure of the
poor young brides. Neither the marriages nor the brokers,
however, were originally of this type. 'Whenever you are
arranging a marriage between two parties, never exaggerate, but always tell the literal truth,' says a seventeenth
century writer ; [1] and, he adds, ' in earlier times, none but
students of the law were *shadchanim* (or match-makers).'
This statement is undoubtedly true. That famous authority, to whose memoirs I have had and shall have to make
such frequent recourse, Jacob Molin, known as the Maharil,
maintained himself by the income derived from his match-
making operations. On the other hand, he devoted the
whole of his salary as Rabbi to the support of his students.[2]
His reputation as a successful marriage-agent extended
throughout the Rhine-land, and his probity and prudence
endeared him to youths and maidens alike. Such a Rabbi
was the natural go-between in the middle ages, when
fathers were much more anxious to obtain learned and
respectable than wealthy sons-in-law.

With the French and German Jews, the *bachur* or theological student occupied the position filled by the curate
in modern English society. Nay, just as in Bible times
wives were won by bold feats on the battle-field, so in the
middle ages the way to a maiden's heart was often made
by the brilliant exploits of a young, budding Talmudist on

[1] Jonah Landsofer's צוואה. He informs us, moreover, that by his day the
age at which marriages were common had considerably risen. Eighteen is
the age which he recommends. See *Jewish Quarterly Review*, iii. p. 480;
Güdemann, *Quellenschriften*, p. 135.

[2] Another noted Rabbi-shadchan was Jacob Margolis, a contemporary of
M. Minz (see latter's שו''ת, 74).

the field of Rabbinical controversy.[1] For the *shadchan* was not necessarily brought into requisition, as the youths might display their intellectual prowess under the gaze of their future wives. In the Talmud public opportunities for courtship were already a popular institution, or rather were a survival of a primitive folk-custom.[2] There were no more joyous festivals in Israel than the fifteenth of Ab and the Day of Atonement. On these days the maidens of Jerusalem used to pass out in procession, arrayed in white garments, which all borrowed, in order not to put to the blush those who possessed no fitting attire of their own. They went out to the vineyards and danced. Then they sang — 'Young man, lift up thine eyes and see whom thou art about to choose. Fix not thine eyes on beauty, but rather look to the piety of the bride's family. Gracefulness is deceit, and beauty is a vain thing, but the woman who fears the Lord, she is worthy of praise.' The Talmud, perceiving that this appeal would come best from the lips of those devoid of personal charms, provides a different formula for the lovelier daughters of Israel : 'See how fair we are, choose your bride for beauty.' Such a scene would have shocked the medieval notion of propriety, but the young Jews and Jewesses, deprived of all opportunities for meeting amid romantic and rural surroundings, substituted the fairs for the vineyards, and the aggressive fascinations of the daughters of Jerusalem were replaced by the more passive charmings of the girls of Lemberg. 'To the fairs held at Lemberg and Lublin,

[1] Cf. Graetz, vol. IV. ch. xviii. This was specially noteworthy in Poland in the sixteenth century.

[2] For the dance and choruses of girls in the vineyards, see Judges xxi. 21. Cf. Nowack, *Lehrbuch der Hebr. Archäologie,* i. p. 185 ; Benzinger, *Hebr. Arch.,* pp. 271 and 468.

came young students and their teachers in shoals. He who had a son or a daughter to marry journeyed to the fair and there made a match, for every one found his like and his suit. At every fair, hundreds of matches were made up, sometimes thousands ; and the children of Israel, men and women, used to repair to the fair in their finest attire, for they were held in respect by the kings and the people.' ¹

But the *shadchan* was the favourite means of arranging a marriage in the middle ages. Not that his task was an easy one. To but few professional match-makers could it be applied, as it was applied to Maharil in his function as *shadchan*, the passage in Job : ² —

> 'Unto me men gave ear, and waited,
> And kept silence for my counsel.
> After my words they spake not again,
> And my speech dropped upon them.'

Nay, the *shadchan* often toiled in vain,³ and earned his fee by the sweat of his brow. As regards his legal status, the *shadchan* was included in the class of agents,⁴ and his fees became due when the match was arranged, even if the parties afterwards receded from their compact.⁵ It is not clear how large the *shadchan's* fee was, the usual plan was

---

¹ יון מצולה (ed. Venice, 1653). The passage no doubt greatly exaggerates the number of the marriages contracted at these fairs.

² Job xxix. 21, 22.

³ פ״ הגוזל בתרא Mordecai to כמה שרכנים יגעים לריק.

⁴ *Choshen Mishpat*, 185, § 10. Cf. ש״ך, ad loc.

⁵ This was not universally the custom. Isserlein (פסקים וכתבים 85) says : — 'When the match is made, the shadchan's work is done and his wages earned. But in our place we are not wont to pay the shadchan's fee till the marriage is celebrated. Elsewhere they pay immediately the contract is drawn up' (הושם הקנם).

to estimate it at some fixed percentage on the dowry. In the middle of the eighteenth century the *shadchan* in the Black Forest district received one and a half per cent on dowries of 600 gulden, and one per cent on dowries of larger amount; he received this percentage, be it noted, from both sides. Outside the Black Forest country the *shadchan's* fee was two per cent.[1] In earlier times, much more was often paid, for the fee could always be made a matter of special bargain which would override the current rule. It is interesting to note that the Jewish match-maker was almost invariably a male. With the Easterns, generally, the reverse is the fact, the marriage-broker being usually a woman. Rare cases in which women figured as match-makers did, however, occur in Jewish life.[2]

For a moment we must digress to consider one or two social consequences which resulted from the system of child-marriage. It is clear that a boy in his teens would be unable to set up a house of his own. As a matter of necessity, therefore, the youthful husband often resided in the home of his bride's father or was maintained by the latter for a period more or less definitely fixed beforehand. Formal contracts to this effect abound in the Hebrew documents preserved from the middle ages. In the betrothal contract between R. Yomtob ben Moses of Norwich and Solomon ben Eliab, his daughter's bridegroom, drawn up in England in 1249,[3] these clauses occur.: —

---

[1] *Orient Literaturblatt*, 1845, column 308. In the tekanoth of Lemberg (Buber אנשי שם, p. 225) the rate varies between one and three per cent.

[2] Cf. S. Amarillo's כרם שלמה (1719, i. 24). In the case there cited, the shadchanith makes a false representation as to the age of the young lady, whom the agent describes as sixteen though she is really only twelve.

[3] M. D. Davis, *Hebrew Deeds of English Jews before 1290*, p. 32. If there were no father, the brother or brothers of the girl made similar under-

The father gives his daughter Zeuna in marriage, promising a dowry of ten marks at the time of the nuptials and a further sum of five marks a year later. He will provide both with weekday and Sabbath apparel, and give them ample board and lodging. He will support them an entire year in his house, furnish them with all they require, clothe them and 'shoe' them, and discharge their talliage, if any be imposed on them during the aforesaid year. He will likewise engage a teacher to instruct the husband during the twelvemonth after marriage.

The fault of this method was that it often unfitted the husband for the battle of life, and encouraged a habit of dependence. But, on the other hand, marriage would have otherwise been very difficult for Jews in the middle ages. We have just seen that feudal burdens might, in England, fall on the newly wedded pair when they were unable to bear them. Besides, taxes on marriage were so frequent,[1] that their incidence would have been a bar to the tying of the nuptial knot had not the social arrangements relieved the youthful husband of some of his responsibility at the outset of his married life. In the eighteenth century, another motive may have helped to prevent a newly married Jewish pair in central Europe from setting up house for themselves. From 1745 till 1848, by an amazing law, only the eldest son of a Jewish house was allowed to 'build up a family.'[2]

Another consequence of this system was the prevalence of divorce. But, as has already been pointed out, this was a lesser social evil than might at first appear. For the divorce often occurred before the marriage had, in the true sense, been completed, and the wife's re-marriage was practically secure. Further, the treatment of the divorced

takings (ibid. p. 43). This was the most common arrangement; less frequently, if the bride's father was wealthy he presented his daughter with a house on her marriage (ibid. p. 95).

[1] Cf. Zunz, *Zur Geschichte*, p. 504; Graetz, x. 268.

[2] Graetz, *Geschichte*, xi. 393. Cf. I. H. Weiss זכרונותי (near beginning).

wife by her former husband was invariably considerate
and even tender. The Talmud already laid it down as a
rule of conduct that if a man's divorced wife fell into need,
'he should remember that she had been his flesh and must
stretch out his hand to succour her.'[1]   This maxim was in
general force in the middle ages, and some of the anomalies
of the Jewish marriage law were mitigated and rendered
innocuous by it.

Finally, the system encouraged the growth of *marriage
by proxy,* which was, however, common to the whole of
medieval Europe. A formula for such marriages is
included in several medieval Jewish books:— 'Be thou
sanctified to M. the son of N. by this ring, in accordance
with the law of Moses and Israel.'[2]

Whether the preliminaries were conducted through a professional intermediary or not, the first stage in the arrangement of a Jewish marriage lay through the *shidduchin* or
friendly *pourparlers.*[3]   A marriage effected without this
preliminary was hardly held respectable, and a lover who
ventured to travel his own road and wedded a wife without
the usual negotiations received corporal punishment in Talmudic times.[4]   But the *shidduchin* did not constitute a legal

---

[1] *T. Jerus. Kethub.* xi. 3 ; Midrash, *Levit. Rabba,* § xxxiv ; *Bereshit Rabba,*
§ xxxiii. Cf. p. 121 above.

[2] *Machzor Vitry,* p. 586 ; *Rokeach,* § 351.   תהא את מקורשת לפלוני בר פלוני
בטבעת זו כרת משה וישראל:.   Cf. with this formula that given on p. 206 below.
The Talmud permits of marriage by a double set of proxies ; but it gives no
formula.

[3] This is the meaning of שידוכין —sweet, or soothing utterances.   The
שרכן is thus, literally, the 'charmer.' The old Indian marriage rite also
included the same threefold process which Jewish custom long preserved
viz. : (*a*) the arrangement of the marriage, (*b*) the wedding ceremony or
betrothal, and (*c*) the actual reception of the bride in the husband's home.
Cf. Winternitz, *Das altindische Hochzeitsrituell,* p. 3.

[4] T. B. Kiddushin, 12 b.

bond, and the match might be broken off by either party at will. The knot was tied at the ceremony of betrothal or *erusin*.[1] But though the couple were thenceforth man and wife, and could not part company without a regular divorce, the actual marriage[2] — which consisted in the reception of the bride in the husband's abode or in their cohabitation —did not necessarily follow the betrothal till a whole year had elapsed.[3] This Talmudical arrangement did not continue in the middle ages, for a scheme by which a legally united couple went on living apart was obviously a bad one.

The previously insignificant preliminary or *shidduchin* increased in importance owing to this change. In place of a half-complete marriage union, to be consummated after an interval, medieval custom adopted a legal contract binding the couple to marry at some fixed or unfixed date, and defining a monetary penalty to be paid by the party desirous of abandoning the match.[4] Like the English of to-day, the Jews of the middle ages never entered into any important business without a public dinner. Hence the *shidduchin* were accompanied by a banquet provided by the bridegroom. This festivity, at which much excess occurred, was termed *Knas-Mahl* (or *Penalty-feast*) — a hybrid expression, part Hebrew, part German, symbolizing the whole of the Jewish marriage customs of the middle ages, which were a strange combination of the ways of the Orient with the manners of Europe. The *Knas-Mahl*

---

[1] The אירוסין.

[2] The נישואין or קידושין. In the middle ages the wedding ceremony was beautifully known as ' The Blessing' or ברכה (so Maharil).

[3] *Mishnah Kidd.* v. 2.

[4] On the connexion of this fine (קנס) and the betrothal gifts (סבלונות) mentioned below, cf. Perles in the *Graetz Jubelschrift*, p. 6. Cf. Israel Isserlein, *Pesakim*, §§ 67 and 74.

derived its designation from the stipulated sums and penalties mutually agreed upon, as explained above. The process by which the betrothal passed into the mere engagement to pay a fine in case of breach of promise seems to have reached an intermediate stage in the tenth or eleventh century, when both the betrothal and the *Knas* are found side by side.[1] On the other hand, in the eleventh century it was already customary to solemnize both the betrothal and the marriage proper on the same day, either contemporaneously or with an interval of a few hours, during which the bridal party feasted merrily at the new husband's cost. This practice of allowing half the day to elapse between the two ceremonies was abandoned owing to the expense entailed by the double banquet.[2]

The diminution of the interval between ceremonial betrothal and marriage did not carry with it a shortening of engagements. In Italy, in particular, engagements based on a pecuniary contract lasted long,[3] and the same fact may be noted in other parts of the Jewish world. To a certain extent, the longer engagement implied more love-making, and it certainly entailed the frequent exchange of gifts. In one medieval instance recorded in England[4]

---

[1] That there was a *customary* fine in the Gaonic period is clear from this passage: — כותבין על החתן שאם יחזור בו ולא יכנוס יהא עליו קנס כך וכך אע״פ שקבל יותר ממנהג ידוע שבמקומו מחוייב באותו קנס, Müller, *Mafteach*, p. 283. It is equally clear that the older form of אירוסין was prevalent in the same epoch.

[2] Cf. the תשובות מרש״י cited in the *Machzor Vitry* (ed. Hurwitz, p. 587): וששאל מקום שמברכין ברכת אירוסין ונישואין ביום אחד שחרית וערבית · מנהג זה לא ראיתי בשום מקום · אבל במקומינו רגילין לעשותם במקום אחר · אך אין מברכין שתיהן על כוס אחר · Again, ibid. p. 588, the remark is added: שמנהג זה שנהגו לעשות אירוסין ונישואין ביחד לפי שאינם רוצים לעשות סעודה לאירוסין.

[3] Moses ben Mordecai Zacuth שו״ת, § 48. Cf. שו״ת Joseph of Trani. i. § 131. See also *Kolbo*, 87 d; Müller, *Mafteach*, p. 133.

[4] M. D. Davis, *Hebrew Deeds*, etc., p. 299.

an interval of four years is fixed between the engagement and the marriage. But trouble arose over the separation of sexes, of which more anon. The culmination of the feeling was reached in the objection to interviews between engaged couples. In the eighteenth century this sentiment became so marked that an engaged Polish Jew often swore on oath that he would rigidly abjure the pleasure of visiting his intended. Here is a specimen of these most self-denying ordinances : —

I, Aaron ben Ephraim, solemnly agree, on my oath, that from this day forward it is forbidden to me to go to the residence of my intended. I will not go there at any time, whether by day or by night, until my wedding. If I infringe this undertaking, I am to be adjudged as one who breaks his oath and I shall become liable to every penalty, fine, censure, and contempt. Witness my signature, Tuesday, Ellul 26, 1783.[1]

At the bottom of this sensitiveness lay a suspicion which did little credit to those who entertained it. A less prurient ground for the objection is given by an early authority, — 'familiarity breeds contempt.'[2] Engaged couples, however, exchanged gifts at the festivals, and the custom survived the wedding, as recent brides received presents of rings, garments, and money from their friends on the Purim succeeding the marriage.[3] Presents from the bridegroom were so customary in Talmudical times that some authorities regarded the *sablonoth* — as the Jewish *dona sponsalitia* were named — so far presumptive evidence of actual marriage that the recipient could not marry any other man unless she obtained a divorce from the donor.[4] When we come to later times, it is hard to draw a line between these *sablonoth* and another type of

[1] Buber, אנשי שם, p. 232.
[2] *Kolbo*, 87 d, שמא יבואו לירי שנאה מחמת שרואין זה את זה תדיר.
[3] Müller, *Mafteach*, 28.   [4] *T. B. Kiddushin*, 60 b.

offering, the *shoshbinuth*,[1] which were originally bestowed on the bride on the wedding-day by the *shoshbin*, the best man or particular friend (later called *Unterführer*) of the bridegroom. To act as *shoshbin* was a much-prized honour, for did not God himself lead Eve to Adam and act as her best-man?[2]

In the middle ages wedding presents were profusely given. A favourite gift was a prayer-book, an article of so much cost that it sometimes appears in the marriage settlements.[3] The ritual for the passover eve, known as the *haggada*, was coloured and illuminated to serve as a choice wedding gift.[4] It was felt necessary in Italy — the home of luxury in dress and food in the middle ages — to limit the gifts which might be exchanged at betrothals and weddings, but the particulars on these heads belong to the seventeenth and eighteenth centuries.[5] Sweets and confections were a much-prized present, and these in particular were bestowed to excess. Girdles and ornaments for the hair were given to girls immediately on their engagement.[6]

Engagement rings were worn rather by the men than by the women. In Germany a gold ring was presented to the bridegroom by his intended's father some time before the wedding, whereas the lady only received her

[1] *T. B. Baba Bathra*, 144 b.   [2] Genesis ii. 22; *T. B. Erubin*, 18 b.

[3] Cf. M. D. Davis, ibid. p. 298, where a MS. Bible is the chief dowry of the bride. See also the case in the שו״ת חיים אור זרוע, § 2. On the flyleaf of the British Museum copy of M. b. J. Chagiz's שתי הלחם it appears that this particular volume was a wedding present from Hirsch Bondet to Moses Frankl, at Berlin, Ellul 15, 1787.

[4] See the inscription in MS. Additional (British Museum) No. 27210.

[5] Cf. Berliner, *Rom*, ii. (2) p. 197; Buber אנשי שם, p. 231.

[6] Cf. Perles, *Graetz-Jubelschrift*, p. 6. The antiquity of the predilection for sweets as a wedding gift may be seen from Winternitz (op. cit.) p. 71.

engagement ring on her wedding morn. The Greco-Turkish Jewish maiden usually wore a ring immediately on her engagement, and much ceremonial etiquette was connected with the presentation. Some of the elders of the congregation, accompanied by a crowd of members, visited the future bride, and bestowed the ring on her.[1] In Italy the wearing of rings was the delight of both sexes, so much so that in 1416 it was necessary to enact in a communal tekanah or ordinance:[2] —

No man shall bear more than one gold ring, which he may place on any finger of either hand. No woman shall put on more than two rings on the same occasion, or at the utmost she may wear three rings.

These rings, however, were for ordinary use. A large number of genuine betrothal rings are extant in various collections. But these so-called rings were not worn. They are of great size, the huge hoops terminating not in an ordinary bezel, but bearing artistic designs worked in gold, representing a turreted building, often with a moveable weather-cock on the apex.[3] Some of these splendid specimens are said to belong to the thirteenth century, and several, if not most, bear the Hebrew inscription *mazal tob* or 'Good luck!' It is said that a sprig of myrtle was placed inside the ring; the size of the hoop would thus be accounted for. In short these ornaments are possibly not rings at all in the ordinary sense, but are bouquet-holders. This explanation is not improbable, for the medieval episcopal rings also had very large hoops, but to permit of their being worn even over the cleric's gloves,[4] the rings are smooth, while these so-called Jewish

[1] Perles, ibid. 6, note 1.   [2] Ibid. (Hebrew section), p. 59.
[3] Several such rings are described in Jones' *Finger-ring Lore*, p. 299, and in the Catalogue of the *Anglo-Jewish Historical Exhibition*, pp. 115 and 124.
[4] *Encycl. Britannica*, vol. xx. p. 561.

betrothal rings cannot, as a practical experiment proves, be worn without pain.amounting to torture, owing to the projecting points of the ornamentation on some of them. In the middle ages, many rings made by and belonging to Christians were inscribed with cabalistic inscriptions, and were in great request for use at weddings.[1] It may be that the Hebrew inscription *mazal tob* on these betrothal rings belongs to the same category, but it is more probable that the expression 'Good luck' had lost its astrological meaning by the time it was employed to adorn the Jewish betrothal and wedding rings.[2]

The ornamental building worked on the ring always represents the Temple of Jerusalem or one of its more modern counterparts — a synagogue. This was not a medieval design, but can be traced back as far as the fourth century. In a Roman tomb there has been found a glass — probably made by a Jewish artificer — which bears an elaborate picture of the Temple, with the pillared porch of Solomon, the columns known as Jachin and Boaz, the seven-branched candlestick, and other typically Jewish emblems. There are two inscriptions in Greek (the language of the Jews in Rome for several centuries): 'House of Peace, take the blessing,' and 'drink and live with all thine.' This glass may possibly have been a wedding glass, but at all events the Temple design is a very old one.[3]

---

[1] Ibid. p. 562.

[2] Anciently, a talisman or amulet was sometimes given to the Jewish bride to protect her from the 'evil-eye' (*Pesikta R.* § 5, ed. Friedmann, p. 21 b). In much more recent times seal-rings were engraved as charms with the name of God on them (חות יאיר, § 16). Eastern Jews have always been addicted to this species of superstition.

[3] Berliner, *Rom*, i. (1) p. 61. Benzinger, *Hebr. Archaeologie*, p. 251.

Ornate as were the rings referred to in the previous paragraph, the true wedding rings were innocent of jewels. A gemmed ring could not lawfully be used at a Jewish wedding ;[1] it would need a specialist or a dealer to estimate accurately the value of a jewel, and the bride might be easily deceived. This consideration was important. It must be remembered that the ring in Jewish ceremony simply replaced the old gift of money or of some article of value, which itself was a symbolical survival of the yet older acquisition of a bride by direct purchase. The wedding ring is not mentioned in the Talmud, nor was it regularly introduced into Jewish ceremony until the seventh or eighth century. Probably it was used in Palestine somewhat earlier than in Babylon, owing to Roman influence.[2] The Jewish wedding ring was not necessarily made of gold, but no deception might be practised on the bride. It could be silver-gilt or even brazen, but the bride had to be informed that it was com-

---

[1] R. Tam was the author of this rule. Cf. A. de Boton, לחם רב, § 20. 'Nowadays,' said Rashba, ' the daughters of Israel modestly cover their faces with veils and do not look at the ring.' *Kolbo*, 86 d. That some Jewish authorities permitted the use of jewelled rings is clear from cases in which a ring ornamented with two pearls was used. Cf. שו״ת מהרש״ל, ii. 76, and A. de Boton, loc. cit.

[2] This is perhaps the meaning of the statement (Müller, חלוף מנהגים, § 25) that ' in the East they do not regard the marriage ring, in the land of Israel they do regard it.' The difficulty, however, is that in the time of the Geonim the wedding ring was a well-established favourite with the Jews of Babylon (cf. Harkavy, תשובות הגאונים, § 65). Müller suggests an explanation which may be compared with what has been said above concerning the *sablonoth*. In Babylon, the fact that a ring had been presented was not regarded as in itself constituting a complete marriage, whereas in Palestine it would be held evidence of the marriage. Hence the phrase בטבעת זו ' *with this ring*' in the marriage formula, i.e. a specific statement was needed that this particular ring effected the marriage. Yet these significant words were not a fixed part of the formula till a much later period (cf. *Kolbo*, אישות).

posed of baser metal. It seems probable that Jones[1] is correct in stating that the use of the wedding ring appeared as a Jewish marriage custom before the Church adopted it. Pope Nicholas (800 A.D.) is, I believe, the first to distinctly allude to the Christian use of the ring, whereas it must then have been in use among the Palestinian Jews for some centuries. Both Synagogue and Church accepted the ring from heathen Rome, indeed the modern wedding customs of all races and creeds are largely indebted to heathen sources.

The Jews owed other items on their marriage list to Rome. The study of superstitions is often disappointing, because people are too imitative. The Jews had certain notions about lucky and unlucky times for marrying, but the most important of their superstitions on this head was borrowed from the Romans. Between Passover and Pentecost — custom varies as to the days on which an exception is allowed — no Jewish marriage takes place even at the present time. There can be little doubt that we are here in presence of a variant of the Roman superstition which forbade marriages in May.[2] The origin of the Jewish custom was unknown to the Rabbis themselves in the eighth century, and an improbable connexion between this marriage superstition and the recorded mortality of a large number of R. Akiba's pupils in the second century was suggested to explain the prevalence of this mysterious mourning rite. The tendency to give fanciful reasons for

---

[1] *Finger-ring Lore*, p. 297.

[2] Cf. the monograph by Dr. Julius Landsberger in Geiger's *Jüdische Zeitschrift für Wissenschaft und Leben*, vol. vii. His chief references are to the *Tur Orach Chayim*, § 493, R. Jerucham's ספר אדם וחוה 5, 4, שבלי הלקט 7, 74 and the *Responsa* of the Geonim שערי תשובה (ed. Leipzig), § 278. See also 'Aliquis' (Dr. A. Asher) in *The Jewish Pulpit* (London, 1886).

rites of which the origin had faded from memory is characteristically Jewish, and must be held responsible for a good many of those customs which would be honoured in the breach but persist in the observance.

Of similarly non-Jewish origin was a widespread medieval dread of marrying except at the new or full moon. Both these superstitions can be paralleled in ancient Indo-Germanic rites, and at the beginning of the eleventh century Bishop Burchard of Worms castigates those who would neither begin to build a house nor marry except at the new moon.[1] Jews, however, shared this old objection to the full.[2] In Spain the Jews copied the Greek custom of marrying only on the new moon.[3] Elsewhere, many Jews preferred to inaugurate a new enterprise, or to begin a new book, on the new moon.[4] In fact the middle ages encouraged a perfect free trade in superstitions, and Jews and Christians borrowed terrors from one another with the utmost enthusiasm. In Germany, Spain, France, and Italy the same phenomena of imitation present themselves.[5]

---

[1] Winternitz, *Das altindische Hochzeitsrituell*, pp. 4, 27, and 30. See also Grimm, *Deutsche Mythologie*, p. xxxvi. ibid. p. 406.

[2] Cf. נמוקי יוסף to Alfasi, *Synhedrin*, ch. vii; *Yore Deah*, 179, 2; *Eben Haezer*, 64, 3. Possibly, as Landsberger suggests (op. cit. p. 18), the Talmud in *Chulin*, 95 b, already knew of this superstition. See Jost's *Annalen*, 1841, p. 82. R. Akiba (*Synhedrin*, 65) and in later times Maimonides and other authorities did their utmost to suppress these superstitions concerning times and seasons.

[3] Nachmanides, שו″ת § 283.

[4] *Yore Deah*, 179, 2. Cf. par. 4, ibid. Semak, 136, cites another reason for the latter rule: it was to enable travelling students to know when to present themselves at the various schools.

[5] Cf. Güdemann, i. 199 and ii. 229. A current Jewish superstition prevented the marriage of a man with a girl whose father's name was identical with his own (צוואה of Judah Chassid). See Winternitz, op. cit. p. 37, for parallels in Indo-Germanic custom.

CHAPTER X

MARRIAGE CUSTOMS

THE choice of certain days of the week on which to celebrate Jewish marriages was, however, quite free from superstitious motives. The favourite wedding day in the middle ages was Friday.[1] The selection of this day was entirely against the Talmudic prescriptions on the subject,[2] but the convenience of marrying on Friday was so obvious that medieval authorities, while deploring the custom, did not seriously attempt to effect a change. Wednesday was also a not uncommon day for the marriage of virgins, and Thursday for widows, but Friday carried off the palm for popularity.

There were several reasons for this. Though marriage was forbidden on the Sabbath (as well as on festivals), nevertheless the proximity in time to the day of rest, and the opportunity given for associating the wedding with the synagogue service of the following day, gave to Friday a peculiar appropriateness. For the marriage

---

[1] See Mordecai to *Beza* v; *Kolbo*, 87 a: לבוש, *Hilch. Kiddushin*, 63, 3; Maharil (cited in full below); Simeon b. Zemach Duran פי דכתובה (Constant. 1576?); *Rokeach*, § 353; *Machzor* מנהג רומנייאה (ed. Constantinople, 1573).

[2] Wednesday and Thursday were the marriage days of the Mishnah (*Mishnah Kethuboth*, i. 1).

day, amid all its uproarious merrymakings, possessed a solemnity illustrated by many customs. The bride and bridegroom fasted on the wedding morn and regarded the occasion as one on which to make special penitence. Ashes were strewn over the heads of the bridal pair during the wedding ceremony. In Germany the bridegroom wore a cowl — a typical mourning garb. Fur was an ordinary trimming for the wedding dresses: this was equally a sign of grief. The bride wore over her more festive attire a white sargenes or shroud.

These and similar tokens of grief did not imply that marriage was other than a joy, but arose from a twofold sentiment, on the one hand from a desire to keep even men's joys tempered by more serious thoughts, and on the other hand from the never-forgotten memory of the mourning for Zion. As Byron put it : —

> These Oriental writings on the wall,
> Quite common in those countries, are a kind
> Of monitors adapted to recall,
> Like skulls at Memphian banquets, to the mind
> The words which shook Belshazzar in his hall,
> And took his kingdom from him : you will find,
> Though sages may pour out their wisdom's treasure,
> There is no sterner moralist than pleasure.

Probably both these motives, the moralizing of pleasure and the memory of Zion, combined in equal degrees to popularize what has become a most characteristic feature of Jewish weddings, namely the breaking of a glass,[1] the pieces of which were eagerly picked up by unmarried girls. More

---

[1] Cf. *T. B. Berachoth*, 30 b, which suggests that the former reason predominated. 'When the son of Rabina was married the father saw that the Rabbis present at the marriage feast were in an uproarious mood, so he took a costly vase of white porcelain worth 400 zuzim (= £20?) and broke it before them to curb their spirits.' See *Tosafoth*, ad loc.

fanciful explanations have been suggested for the glass breaking, and there is little doubt that sentimental thoughts have encouraged the retention of the practice. A similar association of the serious with the joyous prompted the chorus of a rabbi at a wedding feast : [1] —

> Woe to us, we must die!
> Woe to us, we must die!
> Where is the Law?
> Where is the deed?
> The Law and good deeds will save us from death!

Though the wedding songs of the Jews seldom repeat this dirgeful note, the memory of Zion recurs, especially in the wedding odes of Jehuda Halevi, as a pathetic refrain : —

> A dove of rarest worth
> And sweet exceedingly;
> Alas, why does she turn
> And fly so far from me?
> In my fond heart a tent,
> Should aye preparèd be.
> My poor heart she has caught
> With magic spells and wiles.
> I do not sigh for gold,
> But for her mouth that smiles;
> Her hue it is so bright,
> She half makes blind my sight.
>
> .   .   .   .   .   .
>
> The day at last is here
> Filled full of love's sweet fire;
> The twain shall soon be one,
> Shall stay their fond desire.
> Ah! would my tribe should chance
> On such deliverance ! [2]

---

[1] *Berachoth*, 31 a.

[2] This beautiful translation of Jehuda Halevi's Ode (written by the late Amy Levy) is taken from Lady Magnus' *Jewish Portraits*, p. 24. A reference to the restoration of Zion's glories is made in the ordinary Jewish wedding benedictions cited at the close of this chapter.

Another of this poet's wedding hymns closes with the same idea. I have attempted to preserve the rhyme and rhythm of the original : —

> Thus, with one accord,
> When Zion is restored,
> When, on her hill, the Lord
> Refuge from the sword,
> Granteth ;
>
> Her King, before her face,
> Her captive from disgrace,
> Her victor in the race,
> Each his songs of grace,
> Chanteth.

But from the compositions of the other medieval writers of Hebrew love-songs this mournful memory of Zion's distress is absent. The following epithalamium, by Abraham Ibn Ezra, is a typical specimen of such songs, and it will be seen that this Spanish-Jewish writer is not wanting in passion when treating of love : —

> 'Thy breath is far sweeter than honey,
>   Thy radiance brightens the day;
> Thy voice is e'en softer than lyre-note,
>   Yet hear I its echoes alway.
> Thy wit is as pure as thy witchery,
>   And both in thy face are displayed ;
> Alas! mid the maze of thy pleasaunce,
>   From the path to thy heart I have strayed.'
>
> Soft on my couch sleeping, dreaming,
>   I heard this, my lover's fond word ;
> Blushing a blush of new rapture,
>   Methought that I whispered, ' My lord!
> If thou can'st desire my poor beauty
>   Stand not outside or afar;
> Come, I will lead to thy garden,
>   For thine all my pleasaunces are.'

'Beloved, thy words of allurement,
    Like dew-drops refreshen my heart.
My soul boundeth free from its fetters,
    My life leaves its longing and smart.
Come yield now thy lips to thy lover,
    Come yield me the sweets of thy heart.'

The later wedding odes become more ornate; there is
much punning on the names of the bridegroom and his
bride, there is a much more elaborate use of metaphor.
The finest writer of Hebrew after the decay of the Spanish school of Jewish poets was Moses Chayim Luzzatto.
He belongs, it is true, to the beginning of the eighteenth
century, but his muse was centuries older. His constant model was the Italian poet Guarini, whose dramatic
Pastor Fido was perhaps more imitated than any other
medieval poem.[1]   Luzzatto composed mostly without
rhyme, but his skill in writing metrical Hebrew is inimi-
table.   Like Jehuda Halevi, Luzzatto was much in demand as a turner of marriage verses, and sometimes his
efforts in this direction rise to a considerable height of
merit.   I give an extract from the ode which he composed
in honour of the nuptials of his pupil Isaac Marini and
Judith Italia.[2]   The poet plays round these names, wittily
takes Marini in its literal sense (sea), while Italia represents the land.   The land and sea contend for love's prize,
each asserting its claims to superior notice.   When each
has argued its claim at length, the poet continues : —

Ye daughters of Song, come tell
Wherein doth your Spirit dwell ?
Do you dive to the heart of the Sea for your song,
Or find ye your music Land's high hills among ?

[1] Of course Fletcher's *Faithful Shepherdess* was based on the same
original.
[2] The Hebrew is printed in Schorr's *Hechaluts*, vol. ii. p. 105.

Love wandered o'er the verdured plains,
Love strayed between the rising waters,
To fire the flashing children of his bow,
But held his hand,
Till by the shore, united each to each other,
Land and Water kissed.

'Land and Water,' quoth he,
'Be ye the target both, of these my loving shafts.
Thou son of royal sires, of ancient kings,
From thy sea-depths arise,
With waves of sense and science girt.
And come, too, thou maiden rare,
Beauteous as Tirzah famed,
Come, bring with thee thy crown of virgin sweetness.

'Not Sea or Land alone
May win my wished-for tribute,
But Land and Sea together
Shall share the robe of victory.

'A desert, Earth, art thou and silent,
Dumb till thy fields are laved by freshening dews,
By blessed streams that give thee life.

'Ah! Sea of wasting waters! storm-stricken,
The note thou roarest forth is drear destruction's signal,
Till Earth's fond arms embrace thee;
Then singest thou a rippling song of peace.

'Now bind ye twain your hearts,
Join depths of wisdom's Sea
To height of Earth's adornments,
And sing for e'er in unison,
The song that a flowing river
Sings as it glides through a garden,
In your earthly paradise.'

No more need the daughters of song to roam,
In your heart of hearts they fix their home;
They sing their glees with love and pride,
And enter their heritage with bridegroom and bride.

Songs of this type were sung in the home or in the wedding house rather than in the synagogue, though, as we have seen, the Yemen Jews appear to have chanted the wedding odes of Jehuda Halevi during public worship. But songs of another type were composed in large numbers for actual synagogue use. These songs were *generic*, and date from the tenth century, while the *individual* odes, those I mean written for some particular wedding, are not older than Jehuda Halevi. In making this statement, I am alluding only to medieval Jewish custom, for the Bible already contains in Psalm xlv a magnificent marriage song, obviously written to celebrate some monarch's nuptials with a foreign princess. The *generic* songs to which I have just referred were prayers like the typical one cited above on page 12. They were sung in synagogue on the Sabbath after the wedding, and formed part of the regular liturgy on such occasions. I have little doubt that this habit was confirmed by the solemnization of marriages on Fridays, for the event was then so recent that all the congregation could enter with full heartiness into the spirit of the celebration on the next day.

Some of the prettiest synagogue rites prevailed in the East ; indeed, the Oriental Jewish weddings, though similar in type to those in Europe, were far more picturesque. The Oriental Jews had better eyes for colour, a finer taste for decoration, and a readier flow of cultured wit, if a more shallow humour. The Jews who remained in contact with Easterns imitated their neighbours, just as European Jews did, but somehow they chose the prettier things to adopt as their own. But all the world over the Jewish marriage customs were decidedly dainty, and only occasionally a little gross.

Time refined away **the** grosser elements. The bridal procession — as old as the Bible — was originally the actual transference of the bride to her husband's home, and the *chuppa*, or *canopy*, under which Jewish marriages are still celebrated, was in ancient time either the canopied litter occupied by the bride during the procession, or the actual apartment to which the married couple retired when the wedding had been solemnized.[1] It was this act that marked off the *nissuin* or marriage proper from the *erusin* or betrothal. But the procession changed its character in the middle ages and led to the synagogue rather than to the bridal chamber. The Spanish Jews turned the procession into a mimic tourney with gay crowds of horsemen and lance-breakers.[2] In Egypt the bride wore a helmet and, sword in hand, led the procession and the dance. The bridegroom, not to fail in his share of the frolic, donned feminine attire, and the youths wore girls' clothes and put the favourite *henna* dye on their finger-nails.[3] This was more than medieval Rabbis would allow, and the custom seems never to have become common.[4] The wedding procession was rarely as objectionable as this, but the rites connected with it differed greatly in their antiquity and significance.

To begin with, the bridal pair wore crowns of roses and

[1] This act was originally public (*Semachoth*, ch. viii). As late as the reign of Henry VIII the same indelicacy prevailed in England (Calendar of State Papers, Henry VIII, vol. i. p. 861). It still has a symbolical force in modern India (cf. Winternitz, ibid. p. 92, for some amazing facts). The celebration of Jewish weddings at night still occurs in the East, and in Europe frequently took place late on Friday just before sunset.

[2] Cf. Perles, *Monatsschrift*, 1860. Zunz, *Zur Geschichte*, 174.

[3] Many Jewesses in the East dyed their hands for beauty. Cf. Moses ben Nachman, *Pseud.* שו״ת (Venice, 1519), § 124.

[4] Maimonides חדושים, p. 51 a (cf. Perles, loc. cit.). But the Geonim (Müller, *Mafteach*, p. 49) already complain that in Egypt the women clashed cymbals and danced in public at Jewish weddings. The Geonim especially objected to this being done by women in the presence of men.

myrtles and olive branches, intertwined with salt-stones and pyrites amid threads of gold and crimson.[1] These wreaths were often made by the hands of students and scholars, who thus gave evidence of their sense of the importance and dignity attached to the wedded state.[2] Here we have a very ancient custom, for it is probable that the bridegroom's crown belongs to the oldest of Hebrew wedding ornaments. The wreath worn by the bride was apparently a later introduction, for Isaiah, in a famous though difficult passage,[3] says : ' I will greatly rejoice in the Lord, and my soul shall be joyful in my God ; for He hath clothed me with the garments of salvation, He hath covered me with the robe of righteousness, as a bridegroom decketh himself with a garland and as a bride adorneth herself with her jewels.' Under Hellenistic influence, the garland both of men and women became more conspicuous in Jewish festivities, and just as the Hellenistic boon companions cry in the Wisdom of Solomon, ' Let us crown ourselves with rosebuds before they be withered,' [4] so in the time of the author of the third book of the Maccabees (iv. 8) the garland of the bride comes equally to the fore.

After the final struggle against Vespasian, the garland was discontinued at Jewish weddings,[5] but it was subse-

---

Sota, 49 b; 3 Macc. iv. 8.   Löw, *Gesammelte Schriften,* iii. 415.

[2] *Gittin,* 7 a.

[3] Is. 61, 10.   The קישורים of the bride (Jer. ii. 32) was a *girdle,* not a wreath, as Löw suggests (*Gesammelte Schriften,* iii. 412) ; though in the Talmud the word קשר is employed of head-gear (*Chagiga,* 13 b).   Nor does כלה (bride) mean, as Löw maintains, 'the *garlanded* maiden.'   Delitzsch appears in the right when he supposes that the bride was so called because she became *included* in her husband's family (Nowack, *Hebr. Archäeol.* i. 162–3).   Cf. Song of Solomon iii. 11 ; but this may be due to Greek influence.

[4] Wisdom of Solomon ii. 8.

[5] *Mishnah Sota,* ix. 14.

quently resumed, and the *myrtenkranz*, or wreath of myrtles, became an established feature of the bridal attire in the middle ages. The sufferings endured under the cruelty of Vespasian left their mark, however, on the bride's garland, for no gold or silver trimming was permitted in order to accentuate the bitter memories associated with the older joys.[1]

But I must resist the temptation to devote more space to these attractive details. So many foreign rites found their way into this department of the Jewish wedding that a study of a medieval marriage in the synagogue would be a liberal education in folk-lore. The *faces nuptiales* of the Romans were early introduced, and young maidens met the bridal pair with torches.[2] Later, the Arabian Jews bore a long pole with a burning light poised on high at the head of the procession.[3] In Persia a further modern variation of this custom may be noted, for in Bagdad a crowd accompanies the bridegroom by torchlight to the bride's house, where the canopy is erected. The procession, which starts towards evening, grows at every step. The poor cast live lambs in front of the bridegroom, crying out *korban* (offering). The bridegroom carefully steps over the lamb, and gives the poor half a florin on each occasion.[4] This Indian rite[5] was localized among the Jews of Persia, but another Aryan custom was older and more common. Traces of the well-known stepping of the bride into seven circles

[1] Shulchan Aruch, *Orach Chayim*, 560, § 4. Cf. מקורי מנהגים § 70, p. 100. The bridegroom's crown was altogether discontinued. See e.g. *Machzor* מנהג רומנייאה (Constantinople, 1573).

[2] Matthew xxvi.   [3] Zunz, *Gesch. und Lit.* p. 489.

[4] Schur (Heb.), *Reisebilder*, 51-2. For a full description of an eastern Jewish wedding see *Eben Sappir*, i. 81 a, and ii. 74.

[5] Cf. Winternitz, op. cit. p. 3.

towards the bridegroom appear in some forms of the Jewish wedding service. The Jewish bridegroom was placed in the centre, and the bride turned round him thrice.[1] Or the bride and bridegroom were seated side by side, and the assembled company danced round them, the young being joined by the old,[2] for, as the Talmudic proverb has it, 'the woman of sixty runs to the sound of music like the girl of six.'[3]

In honour of the bridal pair an old Persian custom was followed in Talmudic times, and nuts and wheat were cast about the path on which they strode.[4] Barley was sown in a flower-vase a few days before the wedding as an emblem of fertility,[5] and was thrown over the young couple, as in modern times. When a boy was born a cedar was planted, and at the birth of a girl an acacia. The trees were felled before their wedding to provide the wood for the bridal canopy or litter.[6] The people of Tur Malka, with less delicacy, carried a pair of fowls before the bridal procession. These ancient rites all survived into the middle ages. A live fish played a part in Oriental Jewish weddings, and the newly married pair leapt thrice over the bowl in which the fish disported itself.

It has been seen that wedding odes were characteristic of medieval Jewish weddings. But so were songs and jests of another character, in which wit and merriment scintillated to the end that the 'heart of bridegroom and bride might be rejoiced.' The seven days' wedding feast

---

[1] מקורי מנהגים, p. 104.   [2] *Machzor Vitry*, p. 602.

[3] *Moed Katon*, 9 b.   Cf. Dukes, *Blumenlese*, p. 134.

[4] *Berachoth*, 50 b; *Semachoth*, viii. Cf. Winternitz, ibid. p. 59, for Indo-Germanic parallels.

[5] *Kethub.* 8 a; *Aboda Zara*, 8 b; Maharil; cf. Perles, loc. cit.

[6] *Gittin*, 57 a.

was marked by incessant musical performances, which
not even the Sabbath day itself interrupted. Indeed, as
the Sabbath was the day immediately succeeding the
ceremony, it would have been impossible to prevent the
employment of musicians on the Saturday.[1] Christian
musicians were employed for that purpose, and Christian
guests were entertained — this even after the inauguration
of the ghettos. It was left for modern Oriental governments to permit the invasion of Jewish homes by rowdy
mobs of roughs — a survival perchance of the old detestable claim of the *jus primae noctis*, of which so much complaint is made by early Jewish chroniclers.[2]

The wedding music, to return to a more pleasant topic,
was not abolished even under the ascetic wave which
swept over Judaism after the destruction of the Temple.
In the middle ages the music was provided, Saturdays
excepted, by Jewish professionals. The ghetto musicians
were in much vogue, and were often employed at Christian
banquets. Dramatic performances were a usual feature of
Jewish weddings in the seventeenth century, indeed most
of the Hebrew plays extant were written either for weddings or for the feast of Esther — Purim. But the most

---

[1] Isserlein, הרומת הדשן 7, describes the banquet on the Sabbath as 'the
chief element in the wedding joys.' The employment of Christian musicians
is attested by the Mordecai (*Beza*, v), as well as by Maharil (ה״ עירובי הצרוה).
According to the Radbaz (*Responsa*, iv. 132) this was forbidden in Palestine,
Egypt, and Damascus. Christian musicians seem (ibid.) to have come to
Jewish weddings uninvited, in which case no objections were raised by the
Rabbis. Radbaz himself suppressed the custom. Cf. Neubauer, *Medieval
Jewish Chronicles*, i. p. 157. Many sumptuary enactments had to be made
to restrict extravagant expenditure in this direction.

[2] Cf. on this subject Israel Levi's articles in the *Revue des Études Juives*,
vol. xxx. See Winternitz, p. 88. For the outrages in modern times, cf.
C. Wills, *Persia as it is*, p. 231.

characteristic element in the proceedings was the *jest*. In the later middle ages the *marshallik*[1] became an indispensable guest at every Jewish wedding. He was a merry jester to whom the utmost licence was allowed, none being safe from his ready and often caustic wit. Not even the bride herself was spared, and many a time and oft in the middle ages the marshallik obeyed the stern 'forbear-to-exaggerate' of Shammai and, holding the mirror up to nature, told an ugly bride the truth.[2] 'The litter is his grave,' said the Talmudic jester to a handsome husband wedded to an unattractive bride.[3] But these liberties were rarer than the praises. 'Every bride is beautiful,' said the genial Hillel, and most medieval marshalliks accepted this rose-coloured axiom.

Wit of another kind was displayed at table. The wedding discourse by the Rabbi was a conspicuous function. This discourse was delivered not, as now, during the marriage ceremony, but afterwards, at the banquet.[4] Many objections were felt against the propriety of introducing

---

[1] This word is German, not Hebrew. It is undoubtedly the old German *Marschalk* (see Grimm, p. 1674) or Marshall. The Marshall of the feast easily became the buffoon, as in the Lord of Misrule excesses once so common all over Europe. Grimm quotes a similar sport in which occur the characters of a mock 'Konig und der Marschalk,' which shows that this official was sometimes so named in a playful signification. The suggestion that the word is connected with the Hebrew *mashal* (= proverb, or anecdote) is without foundation.

[2] Cf. *Derech Eretz*, ch. v., *Nedarim*, 51 a, *Yebamoth*, 43 b.

[3] Midrash to Ps. xxiv. 1. Cf. Buber, ad loc. Another jest (*Ber.* 8 a), 'מוצא' or 'מצא?' was a play on two texts, and contrasted the happiness of the husband who had won a good wife with the misery of one who was mated to a shrew (cf. Perles, loc. cit.).

[4] Dähne thinks that the so-called 'Fourth Book of the Maccabees' was such a wedding discourse. But there is no probability in the view. Cf. Freudenthal, *IV Makkabäerbuch*, p. 11.

a religious discourse, with all the medieval ingenuity and elaboration, at a jovial feast.[1] This consideration has, no doubt, led to the transference of the address from the home to the synagogue. In eastern Europe the wedding gifts came to be called *Derashaschenk*, i.e. 'discourse presents,' for the bridegroom delivered a table sermon, and the wedding gifts followed upon its close. An intermediate stage between the wedding ode and the *derasha* or discourse was filled by the *didactic wedding poem*, such as the *Silver Bowl*, written in 1270 in Provence, by Joseph Ezobi. It is a complete ethical code, inculcating a temperate, intellectual, righteous life, in which, however, the emotions are to have a part. That a father should send his son such a wedding gift is surely worthy of note.[2]

The religious concomitants of a Jewish marriage were the subject of continuous development in the middle ages. The priestly benediction is mentioned neither in the Bible nor the Talmud. But the Talmud already recommended that a 'congregation' should be constituted for the purpose of celebrating a wedding, i.e. the presence of ten adult males was regarded as desirable.[3] In the middle ages many Jewish communities converted this desire into a binding statute. In the tenth century marriages were performed before a 'congregation' in the bridegroom's

---

[1] Cf. Israel of Brünn, *Responsa*, 231. That the *derasha* or discourse occurred at the table is shown by the same authority (227), where he alludes to דרישות על הסעודת. Cf. Güdemann, iii. 121; Schudt, ii.* 5.

[2] A complete translation of the *Silver Bowl*, by D. I. Freedman, may be found in the *Jewish Quarterly Review*, vol. viii.

[3] ברכת חתנים בעשרה. *T. J. Kethuboth*, i. 1. Cf. Ruth iv. 2 : 'And he (Boaz) took ten men of the elders of the city.' See also Masecheth כלה, ed. Coronel, p. 1 a. This must not be confused with the legal requirement of the presence of ten in witnessing the betrothal *contract*.

abode, or in the synagogue. In either case the congregational reader was present and officiated,[1] and for a long time it became customary for weddings to be solemnized in the synagogue.

This medieval custom was not universal, for some Jews preferred to perform the ceremony under the open sky, in the courtyard of the synagogue, and not within the synagogue building.[2] A practical reason may be assigned for this, viz. the impossibility of accommodating the numerous guests and spectators within the walls of the synagogue or of the wedding house. The changes which took place in the signification of the *chuppa* point in the same religious direction. In the East the association of the actual cohabitation (chuppa) with the marriage ceremony long continued, but in Europe by the fourteenth century the chuppa had become a mere religious emblem. Instead of a real room, it became a symbolical room,[3] a canopy, or even a veil or garment (tallith) thrown over the heads of the bridal pair, typical of their union. In the tenth century, the introduction of *liturgical* marriage hymns begins to make itself noticeable.[4] Moreover — and this was a feature more marked with Oriental than with Western Jews — a religious turn was given even to a frankly 'made-up' marriage by the practical belief that marriages were really made in heaven.[5] From this motive,

[1] Müller, *Mafteach*, p. 16. The regular presence of a Rabbi at a wedding is not earlier than the fourteenth century.

[2] For the history of this custom see Löw, *Gesammelte Schriften*, iii. 200. The Talmud, *Kidd.* 12 b, tells how Rab had a woman flogged for perpetrating the same custom. Rab regarded an open-air ceremony as indecent.

[3] In Germany this canopy, supported on four poles and richly decorated, was borne by four boys (Schudt, *Merkwürdigkeiten*, ii.* 3).

[4] Cf. above, p. 11.

[5] On this subject cf. my article in the *Jewish Quarterly Review*, ii. 172. On

when the bridegroom visited the synagogue on the Sabbath following his marriage, the congregation chanted the chapter of Genesis in which is narrated the story of Isaac's marriage which, as Abraham's servant claimed, was providentially directed. This chapter was sung not only in Hebrew, but in Arabic-speaking lands, in the language of the country. These special readings seem to have fallen out of use in Europe in the seventeenth century, but they are still retained in the East.

The refining influence of this close association with religion was strengthened by the high ideal which Jews always and everywhere entertained on the subject of marriage. The Jewish moralists of the middle ages with one voice said that character and not gold must be the qualification of a life companion,[1] and the famous *Book of the Pious* emphatically says: 'The offspring of a Jew who married a wife not of the Jewish race, but who was a woman of good heart and modesty and charity, must be preferred to the children of a Jewess by birth who is, however, destitute of the same good qualities.'[2] Jews seem, on the whole, to have been tolerant as regards intermarriage between sects. The Pharisees and Sadducees may have rarely intermarried, but there was no prohibition in the Rabbinical law. Some medieval authorities were, on the other hand, somewhat more emphatic against intermar-

---

the history of the liturgical expression given to the belief that 'marriages are made in heaven,' see the elaborate notes in Reifmann's שלחן הקריאה (Berlin, 1882), p. קכד seq.

[1] Cf. *Kolbo*, 88 c, and ספר הסידים, § 374–377. The Talmud sets an excellent example on this head: 'Marry the daughter of a man of character, for as the tree, so are its fruits' (*Pesachim*, 49); 'A good and virtuous wife expands a man's character' (*Ber.* 57 b).

[2] ספר החסידים, § 377; ed. Wistinetzki, § 1097.

riages between Rabbinical Jews and the Karaites, but opinion was not entirely in favour of prohibition.[1]

But, arising mainly from laudable considerations, a serious difficulty was presented in the middle ages with regard to marriage with strangers, of whose past nothing was definitely known. This, as was seen above, has always been a specifically Jewish trouble, for in no other community were there so many new settlers, driven from their homes by stress of persecution or the innate Jewish love of travel. Social exclusiveness came to the aid here of prudence, and often Jews would disdain to intermarry with the families of new-comers against whom nothing but good was reported.[2] It was long before the Sephardic Jews — those, that is, who were descended from Jews who had lived in Spain — could reconcile themselves to the truth that they did not degrade themselves by intermarriage with their so-called 'German' brethren. But pride of family was always a Jewish characteristic, and in judging the Jewish exclusiveness with regard to other races, it must not be forgotten that a similar feeling prevailed within the racial circle between Jews of different degrees.[3]

But, to combine some of the preceding details into a complete picture, let us imagine ourselves transferred in place to the neighbourhood of the Rhine, and in time to the beginning of the fifteenth century. A Jewish wedding

[1] The famous Gaon, Elijah Wilna (1720–1779), forbade intermarriage with the sect of the new-Chassidim (Graetz, *Geschichte der Juden*, xi. 125).

[2] Cf. a communal enactment in Rome in 1705, which forbade intermarriage with a stranger without the sanction of Rabbi and other communal authorities. Berliner, *Rom*, ii. (2) p. 103.

[3] The Talmud is particular in urging a man to attach great importance to the family position of the wife. See e.g. T. Jerusalem, *Kiddushin*, ii. 5. Cf. Winternitz, op. cit. p. 38, for ancient Indian parallels.

is in progress, and we may see it with the eye of an actual spectator.[1] If we were in the habit of attending Christian weddings in the same time and place, we should find the two types of ceremony identical in essence, though divergent in most of the details.[2] Probably the give-and-take between Church and Synagogue is more marked in the wedding than in any other social rites of the middle ages. Most of the superstitions, even, were common. Thus, in Germany, as in other parts of Europe, the belief was current that if the bridegroom put his foot on the bride's while the nuptial knot was being tied, he was sure of post-marital mastery over her.[3] A Jewish superstition combines this quaint belief with another popular notion associated in this country with the well of St. Keyne.[4]

But our fifteenth century Jewish wedding party is growing impatient, and we must not keep the ceremony waiting for us any longer. The narrative that follows is taken verbally from the report of a pupil of the officiating Rabbi.

[1] Maharil.

[2] Compare, with the following description, E. Freiberg's *Ehe und Eheschliessung in deutschen Mittelalter*, p. 32 seq.

[3] Cf. Freiberg, op. cit. p. 26.

[4] The following passage from the forty-eighth chapter of חסר לאברהם, by Abraham Azulai (died 1644), will interest folk-lorists : 'If the bridegroom places his right foot over the left foot of the bride when the seven blessings are being said, he will rule over her all his days, she will be obedient to him, and will hearken to all his words. If the bride is careful to set her left foot over the bridegroom's right, she will rule over him all her days. Now it happened that the bridegroom put his right foot over the left foot of the bride during the seven blessings, to gain dominion over her, and when the bride told her father what had occurred, he advised her that when the marriage was about to be consummated, she should ask her husband for a glass of water. This gave her the dominion all her days, and the expedient is an excellent antidote for overcoming the influence of the placing of the foot by the bridegroom, and the bride can thereby obtain the mastery.'

'At dawn on Friday, when the beadle called the people to prayer, he summoned the bridegroom to the *Meien*[1] ceremony. The Rabbi led the way with the bridegroom to the courtyard of the synagogue, and a crowd of people followed, brandishing lighted torches and playing on musical instruments. Having escorted the bridegroom, the torch-bearers and musicians retraced their steps and soon returned with the bride and her company.[2] When she reached the entrance of the courtyard, the Rabbi and other notables brought the bridegroom forward to receive her. He took her hand, and as they stood there clasped together, all the assemblage cast wheat over their heads, and said three times "Be fruitful and multiply!" Together the pair walked as far as the door of the synagogue, where they remained seated awhile. Next, the bride was taken home again and dressed herself in a *sargenes* or white shroud which covered all her other attire ; she threw a veil over her face, and put on a fur robe in place of her usual dress or *sarbel*. The bridegroom meantime was led into the synagogue building, dressed in Sabbath attire, with a cowled or hooded garment suspended from his neck,

---

[1] Meien, in M. H. D. = 'to make merry' (cf. Güdemann, iii. 120). As late as in the time of Moses Schreiber (חתם סופר, iii. 98) the *Meien* ceremony was common throughout Germany.

[2] It is impossible to enter into the many variations of custom regarding the etiquette enforced on the bride. In the Gaonic age (Müller, *Mafteach*, p. 49) the bride was taken from her father's house on the evening preceding her marriage. She remained overnight as a guest at one of her kinsmen's abode. Next day she was conducted to her husband's house, and at both places the seven benedictions were recited. A similar custom still prevails with the Jews in some parts of the East. It is almost universally the custom with Jews that the bridegroom and bride shall not meet from sunset of the day before until the wedding. Sometimes neither the Jewish bride nor bridegroom left the house for the eight days preceding the marriage (Schudt, ii. 3).

in memory of the destruction of the Temple, as is the manner in the Rhine-lands.[1]

'The bridegroom was placed by the ark, on the north-east side of the synagogue. Then the congregation chanted the hymn "Lord of the world" and the morning Psalms, but omitted the *techina* (or penitential prayer). While this was proceeding, her friends decorated the bride with garlands and gave her rings.[2] The wedding ceremony occurred directly after the morning service, and the Rabbi wore his Sabbath clothes, as did all the relatives of the bridegroom and bride. The Rabbi wore his week-day tallith or praying-shawl, but when his own daughter was wed, he substituted the tallith which he only used on Sabbaths.

'The bride had by this time been reconducted to the synagogue door, amid musical accompaniments. There, however, she paused while the Rabbi placed the bridegroom on the platform which stood in the middle of the synagogue. The Rabbi strewed ashes from a furnace on the bridegroom's head, under the cowl, in the place where the phylacteries[3] are worn — once more in memory of the destruction of Zion. Joined by the notables, the Rabbi proceeded to the door to receive the bride. He took her

[1] This was a common German mourning garb. Cf. Güdemann, ibid. 121.

[2] A usual gift to the bride was a girdle. This was given to her on the Thursday, by the Rabbi or by a leading lay official (cf. above, p. 180) in the name of the bridegroom. A gift of stringed coins is still made to the bride in the East on the Sabbath before the wedding (cf. C. Pontremoli, צפיחת ברבש, § 5). Some other rites, e.g. *Spinholz* (above, p. 144), also preceded the wedding. These may be likened to the more ancient πρωτογαμία ceremonies which the Jews adopted from the Greeks, including festivities on both the preceding and succeeding Sabbaths (T. Jer. *Demai*, iv; *Shebiith*, iv; and *Levit.* R. ch. xi.). Cf. Fürst, *Glossarium Graeco-Hebraeum*, p. 181.

[3] According to the *Kolbo*, 86 d, p. 181, some Jewish bridegrooms wore their tephillin as an ornament. The bridegroom also wore *white* shoes (ibid.).

by the robe, not by the hand, and they placed the bride at the right of her future husband.[1] The faces of the bridal pair were turned to the south ; their mothers both stood near the bride. Then men took the corner of the bridegroom's hood and placed it over the head of the bride, so as to form a canopy over them twain. But when his own daughter was married, Maharil took the end of her veil and threw it over the bridal pair as a canopy, for, said he, this was the old custom,[2] but it had been forgotten.

'They held in readiness two wineglasses, one for the betrothal, the other for the wedding, using, moreover, one set of glasses for a maiden, another set for the nuptials of a widow. Then the Rabbi sang the blessings of betrothal ;[3] when he had finished, he called for two witnesses, showed them the ring, and asked, —

' "You see this ring, do you think it has some value ? "

' "Yes," answered the witnesses.

'If the bride was a minor (under twelve), the Rabbi questioned her as to her age. Then he bade the witnesses observe that the bridegroom wedded the bride with the formula : —

'*Behold thou art consecrated unto me by this ring, according to the Law of Moses and of Israel.*

'Thereupon the bridegroom placed the ring on the fore-

---

[1] 'At thy right hand doth stand the queen,' says the wedding ode in Psalm xlv. 10. Jewish fancy went further than the mere imitation of this passage, and read the word bride (כלה) in the final letters of the words of the text just quoted, נצבה שגל לימינך (read backwards). Cf. *Rokeach*, § 353.

[2] Cf. Genesis xxiv. 65: 'And she (Rebekah) took her veil and covered herself' when she met her future husband, Isaac.

[3] Cf. S. Singer, *Authorized Daily Prayer-book*, p. 278 seq. In the Karaitic prayer-book (ed. Vienna, 1854) the service occupies twelve large pages. The thirty-first chapter of Proverbs (אשת חיל) was included. The same addition may be found in the Yemen MSS.

finger of the bride's right hand.[1] Two other witnesses were then called to testify to the Kethuba[2] and marriage settlements, but the Rabbi did not read the contents of the document aloud. The Rabbi stood all this time with his face to the East, saying the Seven Benedictions, of which the fourth ran thus : —

' Blessed art Thou, O Lord our God, King of the Universe, who hast made man in Thine image, after Thy likeness, and hast prepared unto him, out of his very self, a perpetual fabric. Blessed art Thou, O Lord, Creator of man.

'But when, in the recitation of the subsequent blessings, the Rabbi reached the words : —

' O make the loved companions greatly to rejoice, even as of old Thou didst gladden Thy creature in the Garden of Eden, he turned his face to the bridal pair and continued : —

'Thou didst create joy and gladness, bridegroom and bride, mirth and exultation, pleasure and delight, love, comradeship, peace and fellowship. Soon may there be heard in the cities of Judah, and in the streets of Jerusalem, the voice of joy and gladness, the voice of the bridegroom, and the voice of the bride, the jubilant notes of bridegrooms from their

---

[1] Cf. *Rokeach*, § 351; M. Minz, § 109. As the ring was intended to be a *token* of marriage, it was worn on the most prominent finger (see מקורי מנהגים, p. 105). At present, Jewesses transfer the ring from the right to the left hand after the ceremony.

[2] The *Kethuba*, or written marriage contract, dates from the Hellenistic period; it was introduced by Simon ben Shetach (first century B.C.). Cf. N. Krochmal, *More Nebuche Hazeman*, p. 185 a. The *Kethuba* included the wife's settlements; indeed, the word *Kethuba* came to mean the settlements themselves. The amount contracted to the bride greatly varied in different parts. Cf. Zunz, *Zur Geschichte*, p. 177. The marriage document was sometimes ornamented with portraits of the bridegroom and bride (A. de Boton, שו"ת לחם רב, § 15), or even with nude figures representing Adam and Eve in Paradise. Reading the *Kethuba* aloud to the bride was at first an eastern Jewish custom (אדרת אליהו, p. 160). It is now general.

canopies, and of youths from their feasts of song. Blessed art Thou, O Lord, who makest the bridegroom to rejoice with the bride.

'At the end of the "blessing" — as the wedding ceremony was aptly termed in the middle ages [1] — the Rabbi passed the wine to the bridegroom and then to the bride. He retained the glass in his hand while they sipped its contents, but he now gave it to the bridegroom, who turned round, faced the north, and threw the glass at the wall, breaking it.[2] Thereupon the assembled company rushed at the bridegroom, uttering expressions of joy, and conveyed him — before the bride — to the wedding house.[3]

'After the ceremony was over,' continues our informant, 'it was an ancient rite for the married couple to eat an egg and a hen in the wedding house by themselves, with only one person — a female relative — in attendance.[4] Then all the relatives and whoever wished entered, in order to increase the merry-making. Now, however,' continues our fourteenth century authority, 'this custom has been forgotten, and all flock in together, and there is no tête-à-tête for the happy pair — a change which is improper. During the seven days after the wedding public entertainments are given,[5] and during all this period, if

[1] Cf. p. 177 above.

[2] It is nowadays usual to have a separate glass for this purpose. The bridegroom breaks it with his foot. See above, p. 187.

[3] Either his own abode or the public hall mentioned above, p. 74.

[4] Sometimes this first meal consisted of milk and honey, and salt (' it is a covenant of salt for ever,' Num. xviii. 19) was strewn in the house (*Rokeach*, § 353). On the second day after the wedding, *fish* was a favourite dish (*Rokeach*, § 354). Special foods on the various days succeeding a marriage were common with the ancient people of India, but salt was avoided (Winternitz, ibid.).

[5] In the Sephardic custom the bride used to remain under the chuppa or canopy all day, receiving the guest's congratulations (Schudt, ii.* p. 5).

a stranger is seated at the table who was not present at the wedding, they repeat the Wedding Benedictions. On the next Friday evening the young men assemble for the evening prayer in the home of the bridal couple, for the latter do not go to synagogue.

‘ On the Sabbath morning, when the congregation have finished the early Psalms, the leading members leave the service and escort the bridegroom to synagogue, with his hat on in the usual manner, not suspended as a hood from his neck as at his marriage. He is placed in the north-east of the synagogue, near the ark. Next, the fathers of the bridegroom and bride choose groomsmen, and seat them by his side. All these men are "called up" to the Law — sometimes there are more than the usual seven (who are "called up" every Sabbath). Then the Precentor sings various special hymns [1] while the bridegroom and his company ascend the reading-desk. More hymns are sung, offerings are made for providing wax candles, for a wrap for the Scroll of the Law, for alms to the poor, for supporting the school, and for providing dowries for poor maidens. In the afternoon of the Sabbath, the bridegroom mostly remains at home, so that certain passages [2] need not be omitted. In some parts the bridegroom for the first time in his life wears a *tallith* (the praying-vestment worn by male worshippers) on the occasion of his wedding.[3] When I was myself wed,’

---

[1] See p. 11 above.

[2] צדקתך צדק. *Authorized Daily Prayer-book*, ed. Rev. S. Singer, ed. iv. p. 176. On this point see Tur, *Orach Chayim*, § 131, where we are told אין נופלים בבית החר׳ן, showing that the service was held in the bridegroom's private house. Later on (cf. Joseph Caro, loc. cit.) the custom was for the bridegroom to go to synagogue.

[3] This would not be unnatural, seeing that marriages were so early. Possibly we have here the origin of a modern custom — the bride presents the

adds our informant, 'a large body of the chief members and a concourse of young men came with me by water for three miles, from Mayence to Oppenheim.'

bridegroom with the silken *tallith* in which he is wed.   In the middle ages the tallith sometimes served as a *chuppa*.   Cf. *Rokeach*, § 353, and above, p. 206.

CHAPTER XI

TRADES AND OCCUPATIONS

In the year 1160, or thereabouts, a Jewish merchant left Tudela, his native town in Navarre, on a journey round the world. Of the incidents of this journey, Benjamin of Tudela's *Itinerary* has preserved the precious record.[1] Benjamin travelled from Saragossa by way of Catalonia, the South of France, Italy, Greece, the Archipelago, Rhodes, Cyprus, and Cilicia, to Syria, Palestine, the lands of the Caliphate, and Persia. His return route took him to the Indian Ocean, the coast towns of Yemen, Egypt, Sicily, and Castile, whither he returned, after an absence of about fourteen years.[2] This Benjamin was a typical Jewish trader of the middle ages, yet he was no financier, usurer, hawker, or dealer in secondhand goods. As a merchant, he records the state of trade, and the nature of the products, of each country which he visited. His *Itinerary* furnishes the oldest material for the history of the commerce of Europe, Asia, and Africa in the twelfth century. But with an almost modern large-mindedness, Benjamin was equally interested in the general life of the peoples into whose midst he strayed. Countries and men interest him as

---

[1] The best edition (Hebrew and English) is *The Itinerary of R. Benjamin of Tudela*, ed. A. Asher, 2 vols. (London, 1840–41).

[2] Cf. Zunz, op. cit. ii. p. 251.

much as their commerce and handicrafts. Courtly gossip, popular superstitions, are entered in his diary side by side with business-like statements concerning trade and traders. Here, says he, may be obtained the brightest pearls. There, he tells us, again, arose the latest new Persian-Jewish Messiah. Art and archaeology have attractions for him. He revels in the picturesque with all the ardour of an enthusiastic sightseer. He invariably tells us the number of Jewish residents in the various parts of the world through which he passed, and reports on their manner of life, their schools, and their trades. But he devotes much of his space to topics of wider interest. He describes the Assassins in Syria and Persia, the dangers of navigating the China seas ; he gives a full account of Rome, with its buildings and relics ; he has several brilliant paragraphs descriptive of Constantinople and Bagdad ; Jerusalem and Damascus are depicted vigorously and vividly. Kings and peoples, their learning and their customs, their dress and their burials, all fall within the purview of this medieval merchant. His Hebrew style is that of a plain merchant, but it says a good deal that a plain merchant could write with so much simplicity and with so many graceful touches.

Jews of the type represented by Benjamin of Tudela were not confined to Spain. The double motive of feeling and preserving the magic bond between Jews scattered to the four corners of the world and of finding new outlets for trade, made the Jewish merchants of Italy and the Levant active and farseeing beyond their *confrères* of other faiths. Greed for information and greed for gain form a not undesirable business combination. But, for the moment, our interest lies in the Jewish mercantile operations, in so far as they brought nation into contact with nation. Montpellier in the twelfth century was a convenient clearing-house for the trade between Italy and the Levant. 'You meet there,' says Benjamin of Tudela,[1] 'with Christian and Mohammedan merchants from all parts: from Portugal, Lombardy, the Roman Empire, from Egypt, Palestine, Greece, France, Spain, and England. People of all tongues are met there, principally in consequence of the traffic of the Genoese and of the Pisans.' Yet Montpellier was the seat of an extremely active and wealthy commercial colony of Jews, as well as of a learned and famous Rabbinical college. A similar remark applies to Marseilles and to all the Mediterranean seaports. Regensburg, to take a typical town of another description, formed one of the chief inland centres from which the products of the East reached central and northern Germany. From Constantinople the cargo boats filled with Eastern commodities worked up the Danube until they reached Regensburg, and the vessels returned laden with the agricultural products and manufactured articles of Germany.[2] In this international trade the Jews took a foremost part, and their extensive wholesale operations had an excellent effect on the traffic, which extended to and from Germany in all directions.

Another characteristic instance is supplied by Narbonne. This southern French town was a noted centre of Jewish learning from the eleventh century onwards. It also stood in direct commercial communication with the East. Literary and industrial intercourse was maintained by way of Kairo- wan and southern Italy. As late as the fifteenth and sixteenth centuries the Jews succeeded in performing a similarly important service to central Europe. In those

---

[1] Ed. Asher, i. p. 33.

[2] Berliner, *Aus dem inneren Leben der deut. Juden*, p. 43.

centuries the nobility and peasantry of Poland had no com-
prehension of the value of their own native products. But
in Silesia the raw materials of Poland found a ready market.
Two-thirds of this very considerable trade was in the hands
of enterprising Jewish merchants, who carried the products
of Poland to Breslau and exchanged them for the products
and manufactures of Germany.[1] This striking fact is
certain. In all the great inland ganglia of commerce in
the middle ages, no less than at the peripheral seaports,
Jewish merchants congregated in large numbers. Indeed,
as Mr. Lecky maintains, Jews were for centuries the only
representatives of international commercial activity. 'By
travelling from land to land till they had become intimately
acquainted both with the wants and the productions of each,
by practising money-lending on a large scale and with
consummate skill, by keeping up a constant and secret[2]
correspondence, and organizing a system of exchange which
was then unparalleled in Europe, the Jews,' says Mr. Lecky,
'succeeded in making themselves absolutely indispensable
to the Christian community.'[3]

Passing from this general question, it is probable that
Oriental products owed a good share of their acclimatization
in Europe to Jewish importers, to the quickness of perception and resourcefulness of the medieval Jewish middle-
men. This is not only true of coffee and tobacco,[4] but
also of sugar. It was the Portuguese Jews who in 1548
transplanted the sugarcane from the island of Madeira to
Brazil.[5] European Jews also imported sugar to Vienna

---

[1] Brann, in the *Graetz-Jubelschrift*, p. 225.

[2] Mr. Lecky is mistaken in supposing that this correspondence was necessarily or usually secret.

[3] *Rationalism in Europe*, ii. p. 283.   [4] Above, p. 137.

[5] G. Kohut in *Publ. Jew. American Hist. Soc.* iv. p. 103.

from Candia.[1] Spices of all descriptions were also imported by Jews, partly because of the ritual laws for the Passover, which required absolute purity in all the condiments used during that festival. Religious needs also induced the Jews of various parts of Europe to import myrtles from France and citrons from the coasts of the Mediterranean.

In all these directions the Jewish mercantile activity was thus useful to the general community and productive of an enlightened spirit among the Jews themselves. The narratives of the Jewish travellers of the middle ages are extraordinarily free from mythical elements [2] and rich in notes useful for the social history of the times. Every Jewish congregation had its ‘travellers’ tales,’ but these tales were records of fact as well as of fiction. This partly accounts for the absence of original Jewish fairy tales in the middle ages. The Jews interpreted to Europe the folk-lore of the East, which they brought with them on their many travels. But as they carried with them facts as well as fancies, they were unwilling or unable to weave fresh imaginative designs in imitation of those already existing. On the other hand, there is in the Jewish satires of the middle ages a remarkable use of folk-lore elements so far as the form is concerned. Joseph Zabara, for instance, is probably the first European to employ the Indian framework and chain of stories for the purposes of satire. Far more, however, than this was acquired by means of the merchant and Rabbi travellers of the middle ages. Not all Jewish scholars were so restless as Abraham Ibn Ezra, who wandered to and fro all over Europe, even

[1] Berliner, loc. cit. p. 45.
[2] Petachia's narrative, it is true, is far more ‘fabulous’ than Benjamin's.

visiting England twice, and leaving behind him as the signposts of his journeys works which breathe the spirit of an observer who has known many men and many lands. But it is worthy of note that scarcely a great Rabbi of the middle ages ended his career in the land in which he was born.

We shall soon see that the Jews suffered in two distinct ways from the opposition between the theological spirit and the commercial which dominated the general thought of the middle ages. For the present we must fix our attention on the fact that the Jews were the only great merchants, practically without rivals in Christian circles, until the great Italian republics reorganized themselves on a commercial basis. The Jews were also intermediaries of the retail, as well as of the wholesale trade of Europe. If the Jew was a familiar figure at the seaports, he was equally in evidence at the fair and the inland market.[1] Just as the enterprising merchant travelled to little-known lands in search of profit as well as of knowledge, so the motives of the lesser Jewish merchants were made generous by the noble alloy of intellectual curiosity. For visitors from Cologne, Mainz, and Worms would betake themselves, say, to the fair at Troyes, not merely in order to display their wares, to introduce fresh commodities, to push a newly imported spice, to arrange a marriage, or buy a trinket for their wives. They would go thither to sit at the feet of Rashi, or at least to breathe the atmosphere purified by the near neighbourhood of that great Rabbinical luminary of the eleventh century. While Eastern Jews were venerating

---

[1] See p. 172 above; Brunschvicg, *Les Juifs d'Angers*, p. 17; Graetz (Eng. Trans.), IV. ch. xviii; Löwenstein, *Kurpfalz*, p. 8 and passim; Bacharach, *Resp.* חות יאיר, p. 230 a; Depping, p. 132.

the relics of dead saints, the Jewish hawker in Europe was expending his heart's overflowing reverence at the shrine of some great living teacher whose reputation and works, and not his dead relics, became the precious heirloom to the Jews of all succeeding ages.

But the ubiquity and the range of Jewish commercial enterprises, their curious combination of religion with everyday life, are not the only object lessons read to us by the narrative of Benjamin of Tudela. He introduces us not only to Jewish traders, but also to Jewish artisans. He shows us not only what Jews did when congregated in large numbers in cities where the arts and handicrafts were more or less completely barred against them, but he also informs us of the manner in which Jews worked with their hands in countries where the guilds or parallel institutions were unknown. Benjamin often came across solitary Jews living in isolation from their brethren. This is, indeed, a noteworthy point. For Benjamin found small congregations of Jews, or even single families, scattered in several places on his route. In later centuries such a phenomenon becomes far rarer. The supposed gregariousness of Jews in large towns was no innate instinct, but was a characteristic enforced by the necessities of European life. In these small congregations of Jews, Benjamin invariably found his brethren engaged in handicrafts. I give a few of Benjamin's entries in his own words, some referring to larger, others to smaller, Jewish congregations : —

One day's journey (from Taranto) to Brindisi on the sea coast, containing about ten Jews, *who are dyers*.[1]

Three days (from Corinth) to the large city of Thebes, with about two thousand Jewish inhabitants. These are the most eminent *manufacturers of silk and purple cloth* in all Greece.[2]

[1] Ed. Asher, p. 45. [2] Ibid. p. 47.

The town of Saluniki . . . contains about five hundred Jęwish inhabitants . . . who live by the exercise of handicrafts.[1]

In Constantinople many of the Jews are *manufacturers of silk cloth*, many others are merchants, some of them being extremely rich; but no Jew is allowed to ride on a horse except R. Solomon the Egyptian, who is the King's physician, and by whose influence the Jews enjoy many advantages, even in their state of oppression.[2]

Antioch stands on the banks of the Makloub . . . and is overlooked by a very high mountain. A wall surrounds this height, on the summit of which is situated a well. The inspector of the well distributes the water by subterranean aqueducts, and provides the houses of the principal inhabitants of the city therewith. . . . Antioch contains about ten Jews, who are *glass manufacturers*.[3]

New Tyre is a very beautiful city, being guarded from the sea by two towers, within which vessels ride at anchor. The officers of the customs draw an iron chain from tower to tower every night, thereby effectually preventing any thieves or robbers to escape by boats. . . . The Jews of Tyre are *shipowners* and *manufacturers of the far-renowned Tyrian glass*. Purple dye is also found in this neighbourhood.[4]

To St. George, the ancient Luz (Judges i. 26), half a day's journey. One Jew only lives there; *he is a dyer*.[5]

The *dyeing house* (in Jerusalem) is rented by the year, and the exclusive privilege of carrying on this trade is purchased by the Jews, two hundred of whom dwell in one corner of the city, under the tower of David.[6]

Two Jews live at Beith Nabi, and both are *dyers*. At Jaffa only one Jew resides; he, too, is a *dyer*. Similarly at Cariateen Benjamin found a solitary Jew, also a dyer (p. 87). One day and a half to Serain, the ancient Jezreel, a city containing a remarkably large fountain; one Jewish inhabitant, a *dyer*.[7]

Thus in several Asiatic and southern European districts Benjamin found Jews engaged in handicrafts. In truth, the same remark applies to the Jews of northern and central Europe. Until the beginning of the thirteenth century, though they were much hampered by distinctive legislation, the Jews pursued the same handicrafts as the rest of the world.[8] Naturally, the Jews had their favourite arts. In

[1] Ed. Asher, p. 50. [2] p. 55. [3] p. 58.
[4] p. 63. [5] p. 65. [6] p. 69. [7] pp. 78, 79, 80.
[8] Renan, *Le Judaisme et le Christianisme*, p. 22.

Asia, as Benjamin shows, the Jews were specially noted as dyers and manufacturers of silk. In Italy the Jewish dyers were only less noted than their Sicilian brethren who plied the same art. It even appears that the Jewish tax in southern Europe was sometimes called *Tignta Judaeorum*, as it was levied as an impost on dyed goods.[1] Subsequent travellers in Syria found the Jews, few and scattered as they were, engaged in the same pursuit — dyeing. When Petachia visited Jerusalem in the twelfth century, and Nachmanides in the thirteenth, the only Jewish residents in the Holy City were dyers. Nachmanides writes,[2] and I quote the whole passage to show the conflicting feelings of this Rabbi, who, driven from Spain because of his unwilling victory in the theological dispute at Barcelona in 1263, passed his last days far from his beloved Spain, but near his beloved Zion : —

A mournful sight I have perceived in thee (Jerusalem). Only one Jew is here, a dyer, persecuted, oppressed, and despised. At his house gather great and small when they can get *Minyan*.[3] They are wretched folk, without occupation and trade, consisting of a few pilgrims and beggars, though the fruit of the land is still magnificent and the harvests rich. Indeed it is still a blessed country, flowing with milk and honey. . . . O! I am a man who have seen affliction. I am banished from my table, removed far away from friend and kinsman, and too long is the distance for me to meet them again . . . I left my family. I forsook my house. And there with my sons and daughters, and with the sweet and dear children whom I have brought up on my knees, I left also my soul. My heart and my eyes will dwell with them for ever. . . . But the loss of all this and of every other glory my eyes saw is compensated by having now the joy of being a day in thy courts, O Jerusalem, visiting the ruins of the Temple, and crying over the desolate sanctuary; where

[1] Cf. Güdemann, ii. p. 312.

[2] Quoted by S. Schechter in his fine article on Nachmanides (in the *Jewish Quarterly Review*, v. 87).

[3] *Minyan* (or *number*) is the technical Hebrew term for a 'congregation' (of at least ten adult males) for public worship.

I am permitted to caress thy stones, to fondle thy dust, and to weep over thy ruins. I wept bitterly, but I found joy in my tears. I tore my garments, but I felt relieved by it.

In Sicily the production of silk was largely in Jewish hands, and the Jews paid heavily for the privilege in contributions to the government exchequer. They exported silk to Italy and France. But they were not left in the quiet enjoyment of the industry which they had created, for when they carried their silks to the annual market at Reggio, the Christian merchants of Lucca and Genoa contrived, after many attempts, to suppress their Jewish rivals by destroying the industry of the latter and exiling the Jewish silk-producers from their homes on the coast and islands of southern Italy.[1] So far, however, as they were allowed to engage in them, the Jews of the middle ages pursued a whole cycle of these handicrafts, in which artistic taste as well as manual skill was needed. Jewish preference was almost always for occupations of that class, and it is strange that, this being so, they developed no originality in art or architecture. But they showed some bent for artistic mechanical inventions, such as the construction of water-clocks. Quite early after the introduction of playing-cards, Jews in the Rhine-lands were engaged in the painting of cards used in that most fascinating pastime of medieval and modern Europe.[2] Artistic bookbinding, and the illumination of manuscripts, were carried to some proficiency by Jews, but these arts they probably learned from the monks. The Hebrew illuminated MSS. are very beautiful, but, characteristically enough, the skill of the Jewish artists is displayed less in figure-work

[1] Güdemann, ii. p. 240.
[2] Mone, see p. 397 below.

than in grotesques and initial and marginal decorations. These do not date earlier than the fourteenth century. The calligraphy of the Jewish scribes was of a very high order. Gold embroidery was another branch of the same decorative art, and here the Jews undoubtedly excelled. They were, naturally, clever gold and silver smiths. Their methods of refining and wire-drawing metals, especially silver, were noted for their excellence. The Jews who in 1446 were expelled from Lyons, established a silver industry in Trevoux which was unrivalled.[1]

It may be best to point out here that in the fifteenth century, Jews found another occupation in which mind and hand were united. The invention of printing found an enthusiastic welcome among the Jews. As Dr. Steinschneider points out[2] several old Hebrew printed books contain poems in praise of the art which 'enables one man to write with many pens.' The Jewish printer was not regarded as a mere artisan, but he was 'the performer of a holy work' — to use the formula which is still prevalent with regard to Jewish compositors. The only restraint on the spread of printing among the Jews arose from the ritual injunction that the scrolls of the law and certain legal documents, such as divorces, must be written by hand. But religious books, including the Bible, were permitted to be printed, and the high estimation in which printing was held by the Jews may be seen from an amusing attempt which was early made to prove that the art was already alluded to in the Talmud. In point of fact the Talmud does refer to various methods of shortening

---

[1] Depping, *Les Juifs au Moyen âge*, p. 315.

[2] Art. Jüdische Typographie in Ersch and Gruber, *Allgemeine Encyklopädie*, ii. vol. 28. Many of the facts which follow are derived from this source.

the labour of writing several copies of the same text ; it also knew of a species of short-hand writing, and it developed the use of abbreviations into a system.[1] But of the art of printing the Talmud was quite ignorant. Printing was begun by Jews about thirty-five years after its invention, the first Jewish press being established in Italy, though the actual compositors were German Jews. From Italy Jewish printing spread to Spain, but enjoyed only a short career there, as the expulsion of the Jews from Spain occurred before the fifteenth century closed. In the sixteenth century the art spread to the Jews of Turkey and the Orient ; a little later to Germany, the Slavic lands, and Holland. Two main species of type were used, the square and the Rabbinical characters ; in the eighteenth century a cursive type for printing Jewish-German books was introduced. The sizes of the oldest Hebrew books were folio and quarto, the paper was stout but somewhat yellow in appearance. Editions de luxe on blue and red papers are also extant, and some of these are as beautiful as the finest handwork. The ink used was nearly always black, but red ink was occasionally substituted. Further details may be found in the authority already cited. It is sufficient to remark that the best of the earliest specimens of Italian and Dutch Hebrew printing have not been excelled in modern times. Jewish women also followed the same occupation, and female compositors were often employed in Jewish printing-houses.

An extensive Jewish trade was carried on in cloth and wool. Here the Jews of Spain came to the front. They had large connexions with the wool and cloth trade which formed the staple industry of England in the middle ages.

[1] Cf. ch. xix. p. 351 below.

References are made in Spanish-Jewish documents [1] to 'cloth of London,' 'cloth of Vristol' (=Bristol), while 'Orabuena, on behalf of the Jews, has to settle with Messrs. Cella and Co. for cloth from England.' In England itself the Jews were deeply interested in the corn and wool crops of the thirteenth century, and appear to have traded largely in these commodities.[2] The cloth trade was also carried on by the Jews of Rome in the fourteenth century.[3] It is not probable that any but the Spanish Jews participated in the *manufacture* of cloth. Two causes — the one compulsory, the other voluntary — combined to restrain the Jews from this industry. In the first place, the Jews were sometimes forbidden to manufacture cloth, as, for instance, in Majorca,[4] where in the fourteenth century only converted Jews were permitted to learn or exercise the art of weaving wool and manufacturing cloth. On the other hand, Jews themselves were loth to engage in this industry. Weaving was regarded in the Talmud as a degraded occupation, and in France in the fifteenth century a similar antipathy was felt.[5] So, too, we know that in very early times the fine cloths used in Palestine were imported and were not of home manufacture. The ground for the objection to weaving was that it brought men into relations with women, the women being the chief spinners and weavers of ancient and medieval times. We know, however, that Jewish women were constantly engaged in spinning in their homes. Though, then, this point must be left doubtful, there is no question

[1] J. Jacobs, *Spain*, p. xxxix.
[2] B. L. Abrahams, *Jews of Hereford* (Transactions of the Jewish Historical Society of England, vol. i. p. 141).
[3] Berliner, *Rom*, ii. (1), p. 60.   [4] *Revue des Études Juives*, iv. 39.
[5] *Tashbats*, i. § 16.

that the medieval Jews were busily occupied in preparing the manufactured cloth for wear. Tailoring became in course of time the most common Jewish occupation, and in the ghettos on a summer day the Jews might be seen seated by hundreds at their doors plying their needles and shears. By the beginning of the eighteenth century three-fourths of the Roman Jews were tailors,[1] and a large proportion of Jews at the present day pursue the same handicraft. The Jewish women at this late period were noted as buttonhole makers, and were employed as such also by Christian tailors in Rome. This state of affairs, however, did not prevail in earlier centuries, and it must be remembered that the Jews often had difficulty in obtaining the right to maintain even one or two Jewish tailors to make clothes for Jewish wear in accordance with the requirements of the Biblical laws.[2] Jewish bakers were also a religious necessity, for few pious Jews of the middle ages would have eaten bread prepared by a non-Jew. A similar remark applies to wine. Indeed Jews often supplied the wine used in the ceremonies of the Church, just as, in the ninth century, they made the vestments of the Roman bishops.[3]

The Jews took a very active part in the manufacture of wine everywhere. In Asia and southern Europe they owned mills and vineyards, and the manufacture of wine was carried on by Jews in Germany and France when permitted. They were stimulated to this activity by the fact just noted that they would not drink wine prepared by non-Jews. But the ritual law showed itself very

---

[1] Berliner, *Rom*, ii. (2), p. 86.
[2] For the Biblical Laws see Lev. xix. 19, Deut. xxii. 11.
[3] Berliner, *Rom*, ii. (1), p. 7. Güdemann, ii. 48.

reasonable on another aspect of this question, and during the middle days of the Feast of Tabernacles the Rabbis permitted Jews to occupy themselves with the vintage,[1] should the various village authorities fix that time for the annual preparation of wine for the market. Even where they did not own the vineyards themselves, and this was not very generally the case, the Jews of Germany carried on a retail trade in wine, horses, poultry, especially geese. The truth is that so far from feeling an antipathy to agricultural pursuits, the Jews were never happier than when they were employing their capital in the trade in natural products. In Persia the Jews were the chief possessors of olive-presses,[2] which they lent on hire to non-Jews on the Sabbaths. The Jewish gardeners of the same country were held in such repute that they were employed by non-Jewish landowners.[3]

The opposition of the medieval guilds was felt in this as well as in all other occupations. The Austrian Jews in 1316 were forbidden to make clothes, on pain of forfeiting all the garments so made. How completely this opposition of the guilds succeeded in driving the Jews to abandon handicrafts in favour of retail trade in second-hand goods or of peddling, how, especially after the Crusades, the Jews were gradually and persistently denied the right of participating in great commercial undertakings, and were restricted to the trade in money, are facts too well known to need repetition here. Their alienation from handicrafts and from commerce naturally was slow and incomplete,

---

[1] Cf. Berliner, *Inn. Leben*, p. 44.

[2] *Responsa* of Geonim, Müller, *Mafteach*, p. 35.

[3] Petachia (ed. Benisch, London, 1856, p. 13) was much struck by the skill of the Jewish gardeners in Persia.

but the exceptions made the rule all the more cruel both against the Jews and the rest of the population, for sometimes the whole of the industries of a people were disorganized and retarded by the alternate permission and prohibition of the Jews to participate in them. Under the Spanish rule, though the Church never allowed the kings for long at a time to deal fairly with the Jews, the latter were nevertheless less violently robbed of their right to work than they were in other parts of Europe. But at the close of the fifteenth century, the Inquisition obtaining full control over the policy of Ferdinand, expulsions of the Jews were everywhere the order of the day in his Catholic majesty's dominions.

Sicily had long been the seat of a wide industry in metal manufactories conducted mainly by Jews. The Jewish acquaintance with chemistry stood them here in good stead, and partly accounts for the skill of medieval Jews in all kinds of metal work. The medieval Jews were largely concerned in *mining*, and in the reign of Elizabeth were instrumental in introducing into England improved methods of reducing copper alloy.

The mining incident alluded to in the previous sentence is worth detailing, as it forms a link in the chain of evidence which proves that Jews resided and worked in England in the sixteenth century. It has moreover several other points of interest. In the year 1581 one Jeochim Gaunz proposed to supply the English Government with information concerning new methods of manufacturing copper, vitriol, and copperas, and of preparing copper for commerce. His plans included suggestions for improvements in smelting copper and lead ores. Gaunz, or Gaunse, actually conducted experiments in Cumberland, in the mining districts of Keswick. 'For some eight or nine years,' says Mr. Lee,[1] 'Gaunz lodged in Blackfriars, but in September, 1589, he visited Bristol, and Richard Crawley, a minister of religion there, discovered that he could speak Hebrew.' Crawley was also something of a Hebrew scholar, and as a result of frequent discussion added to current rumour, Gaunz's Jewish opinions leaked out. The Jew was taken in custody before the Bristol magistrates, and 'in answer to inquiries the prisoner stated that he was a Jew, was born in Prague in Bohemia, was brought up in the Talmud of the Jews, was never baptized, and did not believe any articles of the Christian faith. The magistrates, in doubt how to deal with him, sent him before the Privy Council at Whitehall, and he was probably banished.' In the inroad of foreign merchants which occurred during the reign of Elizabeth, Jews must have found their way into England, and it may well be that they helped considerably to extend English trade with the Levant, as well as to promote English mining. All the fashionable doctors of Elizabethan England were foreigners, and Mr. Lee has detected Jews among them.

But to return to Sicily. When the edict of expulsion reached that island in the fifteenth century, the state counsellors saw the ruin which such an act implied also for the Christians. They entreated Ferdinand to delay the measure he contemplated, for, said they, 'nearly all the artisans in the realm are Jews. In case all of them are expelled at once, we shall lack craftsmen capable of supplying mechanical utensils, especially those made of iron, as

[1] *Calendar of State Papers*, Domestic Series, 1581–90, pp. 49, 617; and S. Lee, *Elizabethan England and the Jews* (Trans., New Shakespeare Soc., 1888, p. 159); Wolf, *Publ. Angl. Jew. Exh.* i. p. 71.

horseshoes, agricultural implements, and equipments for ships, galleys, and other conveyances. Hence, if the Jews are banished *en masse*, it will be impossible for Christian artisans to replace them, except after considerable delay, and apart from the inconvenience which must result from a cessation of the supply of these necessary implements, there will be the further detriment that the few Christian artisans who are able to make the required articles will be in a position to enormously raise the price.' [1]

It is obvious from this, as also from many other indications, that the old Jewish estimation of handicrafts survived in the middle ages. Labour was dignified, not only by the words, but by the acts of Rabbis who practised handicrafts besides eulogizing them. Many a Talmudic Rabbi was an artisan who, so far from using the Law as a spade to dig with, earned his living by hard work in the actual fields that lay in the neighbourhoods where the schools were fixed. Agriculture was the most highly esteemed of occupations; but of all handicrafts the Rabbis said 'Great is labour, for it honours its practisers.' [2] As we have seen above, the medieval Rabbis earned a living as artisans, physicians, merchants, authors, penmen, marriage-brokers, finance ministers, men of science, and it was not till the fourteenth century that the Rabbis became dependent on the support of their congregations. [3] Maimonides, the hard working physician-Rabbi of the twelfth

---

[1] La Lumia, *Gli Ebrei Siciliani* (Palermo, 1870), ii. 38, 50. Cf. Güdemann, ii. 288.

[2] *Nedarim*, 49 b; *B. Kamma*, 79 b.

[3] See above, pp. 39, 55. For a Rabbi who was also engaged in business as late as the end of the eighteenth century, see Chayim J. Eliezer שׁו״ת שמחת יהורה, 19.

century, said 'A single coin earned by one's own manual labour is worth more than the whole revenue of the Prince of the Captivity, derived as it is from the gifts of others.' [1] When Spinoza refused a professorship, and preferred to earn a meagre living as a polisher of lenses, he was continuing a most estimable Jewish tradition.[2]

[1] Maimonides in his letter to Joseph Aknin : Munk, *Notice sur Joseph ben Jehouda* (Paris, 1842), p. 28. Maimonides adds : 'I advise you to devote your attention to commerce and the study of medicine, occupying yourself also with the study of the Torah (Law), in accordance with the right method.'

[2] Pearson, *Mind*, viii. p. 339. Cf. xi. p. 99.

CHAPTER XII

TRADES AND OCCUPATIONS (*continued*)

THE medieval Jews, however, even where they were free to choose their own handicrafts, were not very prone to select those which involved mere physical exertion. They were not so much wanting in endurance, they were not so much given to shirking bodily toil, as they were contemptuous of unskilled labour. The restrictions placed upon them, which more and more converted the Jew into a head-worker, only emphasized an innate inclination to use the body as the servant of the mind. This tendency produced some evil consequences upon the Jewish physique as well as on the Jewish character, and gave point and truth to the jargon proverb which the Jews themselves became wont to use —

'Save me from Christian *Koach*,
Save me from Jewish *Moach*.'[1]

M. Anatole Leroy-Beaulieu is more than just to the Jews when he ascribes all the evils of this tendency to the life in the ghettos. On the other hand, though it be certain that the Jews showed no predilection for arduous physical undertakings, they were by no means averse to

---

[1] *Koach* (כח) = *strength*, and *Moach* (מוח) = *brains*. Both words are Hebrew.

dangerous occupations. One rarely sees a Jewish brick-
layer nowadays, but the reason is to be sought not in
the danger of the occupation, but in the fact that it reduces
the man to a mere instrument for the exertion of brute
strength. A most common Jewish occupation is that of
the glazier, which is not free from danger, but makes less
demand on the strength. So too the Jewish peddler of
recent centuries was no coward; had he lacked courage,
he must have remained at home. The whole array of
Jewish travellers in the middle ages, when a journey was
as hazardous as a battle is now, proves the same possession
of manliness. Jewish soldiers and sailors abounded, and
so did Jewish martyrs. Tradition has it that the first
man to sight America was a Jewish sailor on board one of
Columbus' vessels. It is true that the same qualification
might here again be entered; the Jews were more often
navigators in the theoretical than in the practical sense.
A Jewish astronomer prepared nautical tables or invented
nautical instruments, a Jewish financier would pay for building a ship to use them, but the crew would only contain
a straggling Jewish sailor or two. Yet these generalizations
are very precarious. The Jews of Spain not only fitted out
fleets in the thirteenth and fourteenth centuries, but they
displayed their patriotic zeal personally as well as scienti-
cally and financially.[1] Jayme III, the last king of Mallorca,
testifies in 1334 that Juceff Faquin, a Jew of Barcelona,
'had navigated the whole of the then known world.' In
the Portuguese Armada, which captured Mauritania in 1415,
there were many Jews. Jewish travellers were of direct
service in times of war; they were the Intelligencers of

---

[1] Kayserling, *Christopher Columbus and the Participation of the Jews in
the Spanish and Portuguese Discoveries*, p. 3, etc.

Cromwell as well as of Julius Caesar. But their chief services to the navigation of the middle ages were services of peace. It is no exaggeration to assert that but for Jewish encouragement Columbus would never have sailed. The Jews were noted map-drawers, cartography in the fifteenth century being almost entirely in the hands of the Mallorcan Jews. Jafuda Cresques was called the ' Map-Jew,' just as his friend Moses Rimos was popularly known as the ' parchment-maker.'[1] Besides cosmography Jews were proficient in the manufacture of nautical instruments, and it is commonly asserted that the Portuguese Jews deserve a large share of praise for the most important medieval improvements.

Vasco de Gama was materially aided on his voyages by Jewish pilots and navigators. Another Jew was the constant companion and most intimate friend of another noted Portuguese admiral, Alfonso d'Albuquerque.[2]

Evidence is indeed accumulating to prove that the Jews were personally concerned in most of the great exploring enterprises in the middle ages. A striking instance connected with the East India Company may be here cited. A Jew, born in the Barbary States, but domiciled for some time in England, and well acquainted with the English language, sailed with Captain James Lancaster in 1601 on the first expedition of the East India Company, and rendered great service as an interpreter between the English and the Arabic-speaking Sultan of Achin in Sumatra.[3]

It must not be assumed, therefore, that dangerous occupations were foreign to the Jews. Jewish travellers, such

---

[1] Kayserling, op. cit. p. 6.   [2] Op. cit. pp. 113, 119.
[3] The records bearing on this incident will be published by Mr. B. L. Abrahams in the *Jewish Quarterly Review*, vol. ix.

as those cited above, bring back stirring stories of Hebrew hordes of hardy and indomitable warriors in Asia. The middle ages rang with echoes of the military prowess of the Ten Tribes. These fabulous reports would not have found such ready credence in Christian Europe had the Jews there been notorious cowards. So far from this being the case, the Spanish armies contained a large number of Jewish soldiers who fought under the Cross or the Crescent in the great wars that raged between the Christians and the Moors. The martial spirit of the Jews of Spain showed itself in their constant claim of the right to wear arms and engage in knightly pastimes. Spanish mobs did not attack the Jewish quarters with impunity, and elsewhere in Europe and in the East the Jews occasionally displayed a courage and a proficiency in self-help which, had it been more frequently exercised, would have put an entirely different complexion on the relations between the governments of many States and their Jewish subjects in later centuries. A curious side-light is thrown on the courage of Jews by the fact that the royal lion-tamers in Spain were Jews.[1] The English State Papers of the year 1521 bear witness to the exploits of a notorious dare-devil Jew : ' As to Coron, it was reported at Rome a few days ago that Andrea Doria was informed that the famous Jewish pirate had prepared a strong fleet to meet the Spanish galleys which are to join Doria's nineteen.'[2] We find Jews too in Germany engaged in the dangerous occupation of manufacturing gunpowder.

---

[1] Kayserling, *Revue des Études Juives*, vol. xxv. p. 255. Cf. Jacobs, *MS. Sources of the Hist. of the Jews in Spain*, p. xxxvii.

[2] *Letters and Papers of the Reign of Henry VIII*, vi. 427 (Kayserling, *Christopher Columbus*, p. 121).

When Jews were non-combatants they nevertheless frequently accompanied expeditions as commissaries, providing the armies with food, accoutrements, and often sacrificed their lives as well as their goods. In these partially dangerous occupations the Jews excelled. The close relations which their commercial undertakings established between the Jews of various countries, their knowledge of routes and languages, their rigid fidelity, and, it must be added, their combined cautiousness and daring, equipped the Jews to act as State envoys, as the purveyors of confidential messages, and as the collectors of necessary information.

An occupation in which Jews of the middle ages particularly excelled was medicine. In North France and Germany this was not the case, for there the Jews were altogether indifferent to scientific pursuits. In this they only imitated their neighbours of other faiths, and the Jews, like the Christians, cured sicknesses, especially such as affected women and children, by using charms and specifics of the most superstitious character. Yet even in these countries the Jewish *Mohel* knew some surgery, and the *Shochet* some anatomy. This state of ignorance in North Europe changed after the expulsion of the Jews from Spain. The Jewish physicians of Spain and Italy were unrivalled, except by the Moors. It was their scientific skill which gave Jewish Rabbi-statesmen their peculiar position at the courts of Spain and Portugal. These Jewish ministers of State often started on their career as the Royal physicians, and the influence which they thus won over their patients' minds was, with some justice, resented by the Church. The meaner suspicions of foul play sometimes raised against Jewish doctors were entirely without foundation. The frequency with which the Jewish Rabbis followed the profession of medicine was due in part to the regard which Judaism teaches for bodily health, and in part to the great compatibility of this profession with the Rabbinical function;[1] for a fine feature of the Jewish medical man of the middle ages was his devotion to the poor. In the year 1199 Maimonides thus writes from Cairo in reply to Samuel Ibn Tibbon, who proposed to visit the famous Jewish Rabbi in order to discuss some literary points : —

Now God knows that, in order to write this to you, I have escaped to a secluded spot, where people would not think to find me, sometimes leaning for support against the wall, sometimes lying down on account of my excessive weakness, for I have become old and feeble.

But with respect to your wish to come here to me, I cannot but say how greatly your visit would delight me, for I truly long to commune with you, and would anticipate our meeting with even greater joy than you. Yet I must advise you not to expose yourself to the perils of the voyage, for beyond seeing me, and my doing all I could to honour you, you would not derive any advantage from your visit. Do not expect to be able to confer with me on any scientific subject for even one hour, either by day or by night, for the following is my daily occupation: I dwell in Mizr (Fostat), and the Sultan resides at Kahira (Cairo); these two places are two Sabbath days' journeys (about one mile and a half) distant from each other. My duties to the Sultan are very heavy. I am obliged to visit him every day, early in the morning; and when he or any of his children, or any of the inmates of his Harem, are indisposed, I dare not quit Kahira, but must stay during the greater part of the day in the palace. It also frequently happens that one or two of the royal officers fall sick, and I must attend to their healing. Hence, as a rule, I repair to Kahira very early in the day, and even if nothing unusual happens I do not return to Mizr until the afternoon. Then I am almost dying with hunger. I find the antechambers filled with people, both Jews and Gentiles, nobles and common people, judges and bailiffs, friends and foes — a mixed multitude, who await the time of my return. I dismount from my animal, wash my hands, go forth to my patients, and entreat them to bear with me while I partake of some slight refreshment, the only meal I take in

[1] This combination of functions is now very rare, but among the delegates who attended Napoleon's Jewish conference in 1806 was the Rabbi-physician Grazziado Nappi.

the twenty-four hours. Then I go forth to attend to my patients, write prescriptions and directions for their various ailments. Patients go in and out until nightfall, and sometimes even, I solemnly assure you, until two hours and more in the night. I converse with and prescribe for them while lying down from sheer fatigue; and when night falls I am so exhausted that I can scarcely speak. In consequence of this, no Israelite can have any private interview with me, except on the Sabbath. On that day the whole congregation, or at least the majority of the members, come to me after the morning service, when I instruct them as to their proceedings during the whole week; we study together a little until noon, when they depart. Some of them return, and read with me after the afternoon service until evening prayers. In this manner I spend that day. I have here related to you only a part of what you would see if you were to visit me.

Now, when you have completed for our brethren the translation you have commenced, I beg that you will come to me, but not with the hope of deriving any advantage from your visit as regards your studies; for my time is, as I have shown you, so excessively occupied.[1]

Needless to state, the Church never reconciled itself to the reputation won by Jewish physicians, and the influence which it gave them over their patients. Efforts were constantly made to suppress these doctors, but the kings and popes themselves disobeyed the Church canons on the subject. When, however, the Christian Universities taught medicine scientifically, the Jewish and Arabian predominance died a natural death. Until this happened, however, there was scarcely a court or bishopric in Europe which did not boast its Jewish doctor.

Though the Jews of the middle ages were the first to appreciate the commercial advantages of permitting the loan of money at interest, Judaism as a religion cast a by no means favourable eye on the money-lender. When borrowers were the poor, men who required loans to meet their pressing personal wants and were not seeking capital to use at a profit, — and the borrowers of the early middle

[1] Translated by Dr. H. Adler, *Miscellany of Hebrew Literature* (London, 1872, vol. i.), p. 223; cf. Munk, op. cit. p. 30.

ages belonged largely to this class, — then the lending of money was only another form of relieving distress. The Church was certainly not more vigorous than the Synagogue against those who levied usury against borrowers of this type. 'A usurer is comparable to a murderer,' cries a Talmudical Rabbi,[1] 'for the crimes of both are equally irremediable.' This essential fact, that the Talmud as well as the Old Testament had the poor and needy in view where Jewish borrowers were concerned, but the commercial class where foreign borrowers appeared on the scene, accounts for the difference of attitude as regards taking interest on loans made to native Jews and foreigners. The Jews of the middle ages came to recognize the importance of this distinction while the Church was proving that interest generally was forbidden by Scripture as well as antagonistic to the laws of nature. Aristotle's strange plea that gold was barren was frequently repeated by the medieval Churchmen, who until the sixteenth century[2] drew no distinction between fair and extortionate interest, between loans to the poor and advances to capitalists. Interest was robbery whether the lender demanded five or fifty per cent. When the 'Monti di Pieta' were formed in Italy at a later date a more just distinction had, however, begun to establish itself in European public opinion. It is an interesting fact that some theologians stigmatized as usury the small charges exacted by these Monti di Pieta — instituted though they were with benevolent motives and as an antidote to the degenerate Jewish usurers of later times.[3]

Allusion has been made to the variation in attitude assumed by Jews towards the acceptance of interest from

---

[1] *T. B., B. Bathra*, 90; *B. Kamma*, 84. [2] Ashley, i. 154, ii. ch. vi.
[3] Lecky, *Rationalism*, ii. 259.

their brethren and from non-Jews. This distinction must be a little further discussed. It must not be forgotten that the Church drew a distinction of its own and connived at, if it did not formally grant, the right to Jews of accepting interest which they refused to Christians. Jewish tradition attempted to draw a similar distinction, and explained that the well-known text in Deuteronomy, which is usually taken to permit lending money to a foreigner at interest, refers not to the lender but to the borrower.[1] This interpretation was upheld by many medieval Jewish authorities, who maintained that, though the Bible allowed a Jew to *pay* interest to a foreigner, the *acceptance* of interest from a foreigner was unlawful. Jews did not for the most part act upon this principle, but so far as official Judaism is concerned, but a narrow line separated the obloquy attaching to the man who took interest from a fellow Jew and the discredit resting on him if his client were a non-Jew. 'If a usurer,' says the Jewish Code, 'is anxious to recover the privilege of being legally admissible as a witness' (a right of which his traffic deprived him), 'then he must of his own accord tear up the records of the debts due to him, he must entirely abandon his business, so that he never more lend money on interest *even to a non-Jew*, he must restore all that he has earned by taking interest, and if he cannot identify the parties he must employ the whole sum on public works.'[2] Older Jewish authorities

---

[1] The translation of Deut. xxiii. 20 would, in accordance with the Talmudic tradition (*B. Mezia*, 61 a, 70 b, 75 b), run thus: 'Thou shalt not *pay* interest to thy brother, interest of money, interest of victuals, interest of anything that is lent upon interest. Unto a foreigner thou mayest *pay* interest, but unto thy brother thou shalt not pay interest.' Cf. Mr. Arthur Davis in *Jewish Chronicle* (London), April 6, 1894, p. 9.

[2] Shulchan Aruch, המשפט חשן, xxxiv. 29.

were even more emphatic in applying to Jews who never accepted interest from non-Jews, the magnificent eulogy of Psalm xv.: 'He that putteth not out his money to usury shall never be moved,'[1] the phrase being applied by great Rabbis to interest taken from a non-Jew as well as from a Jew.[2] This high ideal was not maintained throughout the middle ages, for at the beginning of the thirteenth century some Jews distinguished and applied the verse only to their brethren in the faith. The transition is marked in another passage from the Jewish Code where we read, 'Our sages forbade the taking of interest even from a non-Jew[3] unless the loan were necessary for the livelihood of the borrower, *but now it is permitted.*'[4]

These last are very significant words, for they indicate an attitude towards trading in money which differs from the prejudice against it which Jews undoubtedly shared in the earlier centuries. The change was due in the first instance to the commercial instincts of the Jews which gave them an early insight into the true principles on which trade must be maintained. Probably the word *instinct* is a wrong one to use, for it is scarcely demonstrable that the ancient Jews had any conception of the value of international commerce. The intensity of their contempt for foreigners generally is hardly compatible with the existence of a large commercial class among the ancient Israelites.

---

[1] The importance attached to this Psalm may be seen from its inclusion in the service at the consecration of a Jewish house as well as at the laying of tombstones (*Authorized Daily Prayer-book*, ed. Rev. S. Singer, p. 300).

[2] Maimonides, Rashi, etc. Cf. the emphatic utterance of the Gaon R. Amram (Müller, *Mafteach*, p. 128), אסור להלוות לגוי בריבית.

[3] This was in the third and fourth centuries, e.g. (T. B. *Makkoth*, 24 a, and *Baba Metsia*, 70 b). [4] *Yore Deah*, 139, § 1.

Herzfeld indeed attempts to prove that the ancient Jews were a commercial people, [1] but M. Loeb is undoubtedly right in rejecting this supposition. King Solomon made a beginning of a commercial development, but this was so alien to the Jewish genius that the beginning led to no permanent results. After the return from the Babylonian exile the chief popular feasts in Jerusalem continued to be essentially agricultural. But, during the interval that elapsed between the days of Alexander the Great and the destruction of Jerusalem, numerous Jewish colonies were founded all over the world, and this dispersion must have given the emigrant Jews a taste for occupations which did not need long settlement on the soil. Moreover they did not obtain the right to hold land, and even if they had gained the right they would have been ignorant of the methods of cultivation prevalent in the various places to which they found their way. Up till the fifth century the Jews, however, remained agriculturalists in all their large colonies except Alexandria. After this period trade became the chief Jewish pursuit all over the world. The experience they gained developed that taste for commerce which supplied Europe with its industrial and commercial instruments until the Italian trading states became converted to the Jewish methods.

The Jews thus acquired a taste for finance, but the taste did not pass through a natural development. That money-lending had undoubted attractions for the Jews is certain, but how far this attraction would have gone cannot easily be decided. The whole policy of the Church in the middle ages forced the Jews to become money-lenders. Restric-

[1] This thesis, however, he only maintains in a tentative way. Cf. his *Handelsgeschichte der Juden* (ed. ii, Brunswick, 1894), p. 271 seq.

tions on their handicrafts, on their trades, were everywhere common. Even in Spain Jews were forbidden to act as physicians, as bakers, millers; they were prohibited from selling bread, wine, flour, oil, or butter in the markets; no Jew might be a smith, carpenter, tailor, shoemaker, currier, or clothier, for Christians; he might not sell them shoes, doublets, or any other article of clothing; he might not be a carrier nor employ or be employed by Christians in any profession or trade whatsoever.[1] Naturally these severe restrictions to a certain extent defeated themselves, but the constant pressure of the law gradually made itself felt. In other parts of Europe these restrictions were far more rigidly enforced than in Spain. It may safely be said that the Jewish trader in the later middle ages was bound hand and foot. In England money-lending was absolutely the only profession open to the Jew. On the continent, the Jews were taxed when they entered a market and taxed when they left it; they were only permitted to enter the market-places at inconvenient hours, and the Church ended by leaving the Jews nothing to trade in but money and second-hand goods, allowing them as a choice of commodities in which to deal new gold or old iron.

Forced into this position, the Jews found themselves in a peculiar relation to the law of the state which possibly was not without its fascinations. Money-lending was, throughout the middle ages, of doubtful legality; it was speculative and open to grave risks. It thereby provided to great Jewish operators something of the excitement attending the commercial enterprises of the middle ages when active participation in these was no longer permitted

---

[1] Depping, p. 371. These restrictions may be found in the Ordinances of Valladolid (1412). Cf. p. 410 below.

to the Jews. Jewish financiers were thus enabled to share
in great military undertakings; in the colonization of Ire-
land by Henry II and the discovery of America by Columbus, in the contests between Moors and Hidalgoes in Spain,
just as many centuries before they had been of similar
service to Julius Caesar in his world-wide designs.[1] The
middle ages lumped together the banker and the usurer,
regarding both with equal abhorrence. But looking back
with modern eyes, one can easily perceive that among the
Jewish medieval dealers in money there were many high-
minded and cultured men. Such a one was the noble
Yechiel of Pisa. This fifteenth century controller of the
money-market of Tuscany was a man of noble mind and
tender heart; he was deeply interested in literature, which
he generously patronized, and spent a large portion of his
wealth in works of enlightened benevolence. When the
Jews were expelled from Spain, Yechiel's sons spent their
wealth and health on the ransom of their afflicted brethren.
True, he charged twenty per cent on the loans that he
made, but this was the rate legalized and undoubtedly necessary under the existing conditions in Italy. As Bentham
proved, the mere attempt to fix the rate of interest by
law led, by natural causes, to an increase in the rates
charged. Undoubtedly the rates charged by Jews were
very high, but in every country where this occurred there
is overwhelming proof that the Jews were forced by the
rapacity of the governments to make exorbitant charges.
There is a constant consensus of statement in the authorities to the effect that the Jews were sometimes incom-

---

[1] Rosenthal, *Monatsschrift*, 1879, p. 321; Mommsen, iii. p. 549 (eighth
Germ. ed.); Manfrin, *Gli Ebrei sotto la dominazione romana*, ii. 192 (quoted
in Berliner, *Rom*, i. 17); Jacobs, *Angevin England*, p. 51.

parably more lenient creditors than those who belonged to another faith.[1] Thomas Wilson in his famous *Discourse upon Usury* has this striking passage :[2] —

'And for this cause they (the Jews) were hated in England, and so banyshed worthelye, with whom I woulde wyshe all these Englishemen were sent, that lende their money or other goods whatsoever for gayne, for I take them to be no better than Jewes. Nay, shall I saye : they are worse than Jewes, for go whither you will throughout Christendom, and deale with them, and you shall have under tenne in the hundred, yea sometimes for five at their handes, whereas englishe usurers exceed all goddes mercye, and will take they care not howe muche, without respecte had to the partye that bor- roweth, what losse, daunger, or hinderaunce soever the borrower sustayneth. And howe can these men be of God, that are so farr from charitie, that care not howe they get goods so they may have them.'

The excessive demands which were made upon the Jews by kings and princes absolutely forbade a fair rate of interest. All over Europe the same phenomenon manifests itself. The Jews were unwilling ' sponges,' by means of which a large part of the subjects' wealth found its way into the royal exchequer. The kings and princes of Europe were the arch-usurers of the middle ages. Their example was not lost on the lesser nobility, among which must be included some leading clerics, who entrusted sums of money to the Jews whom they protected, in order that the latter might earn profits for their lords.[3] Nowhere was this

[1] Cf. above, p. 103. See also Graetz (Eng. Trans.), iii. 571. Bernhard of Clairvaux said in 1146 : ' Pejus Judaizare dolemus Christianos foeneratores, si tamen Christianos, et non magis baptizatos Judaeos convenit appellare ' (Hahn, *Gesch. d. Ketzer*, iii. 16; Güdemann, i. 131).

[2] Ed. 1572, fol. 37 b.

[3] Cf. Ashley, *An Introduction to English Economic History and Theory*, i. pp. 203 seq; Trail, *Social England*, i. 471. The writer adds : ' The influence which the Jews exerted upon English commerce in the thirteenth century was undoubtedly of benefit to the civic population, since they served as a buffer between the native traders and the dominant landed interest.' Cf. B. L. Abrahams, *The Expulsion of the Jews from England in* 1290, pp. 21, 23, 45, etc.; and especially J. Jacobs, *Jews of Angevin England* (Introduction).

system more clearly exhibited than in England. Owing to the somewhat tantalizing vacillation of the English rulers, the English Jews in the twelfth and thirteenth centuries saw opening out before them attractive hopes that they might soon be permitted to own land and become as other Englishmen. But these dreams invariably ended in the sordid reality of the Exchequer of the Jews. This was not the worst, for owing to the competition of the Italian money-lenders in the reign of Edward I, the Jews were no longer necessary to him. It needs little imagination to conceive the fate awaiting an unnecessary Jew in the middle ages.

APPENDIX TO CHAPTERS XI AND XII

A

OCCUPATIONS OF THE JEWS OF ROME BEFORE THE FOURTH CENTURY [1]

Trading merchants.	Butcher.
Painter.	Tailor.
Actor.	Smith.
Poet.	Beggars.
Singer.	

B

OCCUPATIONS OF THE JEWS OF THE LEVANT, PERSIA, SYRIA, AND THE EAST GENERALLY (CHIEFLY UP TO THE TWELFTH CENTURY) [2]

Landowners (many).	Travelling merchants (travelled great distances).
Agricultural labourers (many).	
Millers.	General dealers.
Fruit-growers.	Clothiers.
Tree-planters.	Booksellers.
Vineyard owners.	Dealers in ship-stores.
Wine-sellers.	Goldsmiths (rare).
Corn-dealers.	Agents and brokers.
Builders.	Makers of water-clocks.
Slaveowners.	Soldiers.
Cattle dealers.	Owners of olive-presses.

[1] Berliner, *Rom*, i. (1), p. 98.

[2] The *Responsa* of Geonim, the *Itinerary* of Benjamin of Tudela, and other sources.

Dealers in houses.
Innkeepers.
Tanners.
Dyers (many).
Manufacturers of silk and purple
  cloth (Greece and Turkey).
Artisans (general).

Glass-manufacturers (Antioch and
  Tyre.
Ship-owners (Tyre).
Physicians (rare).
Musicians.
Scholars (of little note).
Pearl-dealers.

C

OCCUPATIONS OF THE JEWS OF GERMANY, NORTH FRANCE, AND ENGLAND[1]

Scholars.
Professional scribes.
Money-lenders (many).
Financiers.
Merchants (many).
Agriculturalists.
Vintners (many).
Smiths.
Sailors (rare).
Hunters (rare).
Soldiers.
Travellers.
Masons.
Tanners.
Bookbinders.
Card-painters.
Sculptors.
Armourers.
Coiners (many).
Stone-engravers.
Innkeepers
Doctors (comparatively rare).

Bakers.
Dairymen and cheesemakers.
Butchers.
Tailors.
Women-traders.
Goldsmiths.
Retail dealers in general stores.
Glaziers.
Grinders.
Turners.
Assayers.
Box-makers.
Cowl-makers.
Makers of mousetraps.
Barterers.
Booksellers.
Spice-importers (many).
Peddlers (especially dealers in
  ornaments such as gold-em-
  broidered gloves and head-
  cloths, furs, and dyes).
Salt-dealers.

[1] See chiefly Zunz, *Zur Geschichte u. Literatur*, p. 173 ; Güdemann, iii. 170 ; Berliner, *Aus dem inneren Leben*, 43, 47 ; Jacobs, *Angevin England* and the *Responsa* literature, e.g. Müller's *R. Meschullam b. Kalonymus*, p. 7. But few of these trades were carried on in England.

D

OCCUPATIONS OF THE JEWS OF SOUTH FRANCE, SPAIN, AND ITALY, BEFORE THE END OF THE FOUR-TEENTH CENTURY [1]

Physicians (very many).
Carriage-dealers.
Clerks of the Treasury.
Cloth-merchants.
Corn-dealers.
Fur-merchants.
Horse-dealers.
Leather-merchants.
Lion-tamers.
Jugglers.
Mule-sellers.
Bullion-merchants.
Surgeons.
Tailors.
Timber-merchants.
Upholsterers.
Wine-merchants.
Slave-dealers.
Goldsmiths.
Astronomers.
Pawnbrokers.
Apothecaries.
Farm-stewards
Finance ministers.
Majordomos.
Revenue officers.
Merchants.

Royal minters.
Soldiers.
Navigators.
Collectors of crops.
Founders.
Shoemakers.
Hide-dressers and tanners.
Silk-mercers.
Spice-dealers.
Silversmiths.
Weavers.
Peddlers.
Owners of vineyards.
Public officials (many).
Scholars and poets.
Metal-workers.
Mechanics.
Officers of Papal Household (before thirteenth century).
Gilders.
Carpenters.
Herdsmen.
Locksmiths.
Blacksmiths.
Basket-makers.
Curriers.
Makers of Scientific Instruments.

[1] J. Jacobs, *MS. Sources of the History of the Jews in Spain*, p. xxxvii, and the State documents printed throughout Lurdo's *History of the Jews of Spain*, and Amador de los Rios, *Historia de los Judios de España*, ii. 521; M. F. Fita, *Boletin de la real Academia de la historia*, iii. (Madrid), pp. 321 seq.

E

OCCUPATIONS OF THE JEWS OF PRAGUE IN THE SEVENTEENTH CENTURY[1]

Tailors (many cases).
Shoemakers.
Tanners.
Dyers.
Furriers.
Hatmakers.
Glovemaker.
Harnessmakers.
Saddler.
Butchers.
Carpenter.
Locksmiths.
Hatchetmakers.
Nailmaker.
Tinman.
Ironmongers.
Glaziers.
Potters.
Quiltmaker.
Upholsterer.
Candlemaker.
Writers.
Hospital nurses.
Domestic servants.
Cooks.
Citron importers.
Porters.
Innkeeper.
Pastrycooks.
Vintners.

Publicans.
Spirit-dealers.
Tobacconist.
Watchmen.
Street police.
Toll-keeper.
Woodcutters.
Timber-merchant.
Horse-dealer.
Charcoal-burner.
Architect.
Painters.
Musicians.
Singers.
String-maker.
Goldsmiths (many).
Pearl-setters.
Lace-maker.
Stone-graver.
Optician.
Glass polisher.
Wheelwrights.
Wagon-makers.
Doctors (many).
Barbers.
Apothecaries.
Midwives.
Printers (many).
Booksellers.
Bookbinders.

[1] From the epitaphs published by M. Popper in his *Die Inschriften des alten Prager Judenfriedhofes* (Brunswick, 1893); many of these artisans must have worked exclusively for the Jewish community.

F

PROFESSIONS OF THE JEWISH DELEGATES TO THE PARIS CONFERENCE SUMMONED BY NAPOLEON IN 1806

Landholders (several).	Ship-owner.
Merchants.	Cloth-merchant.
Clock manufacturer.	Leather manufacturer.
Silk-merchant.	Horse-dealer.
Tobacco manufacturer.	Officer in army.
Banker.	Municipal officials (several).
Rabbi-physician.	

G

JEWISH COMMERCIAL ACTIVITY IN THE MIDDLE AGES

M. Isidor Loeb arrived at the following conclusions as the result of his inquiries : [1] —

1. The Jews rendered conspicuous services to Europe by teaching it commerce ; by creating, in the teeth of the Church, that instrument of credit and exchange without which the existence of a State is impossible ; and by developing the circulation of capital to the great advantage of both agriculture and industry.

2. When the medieval Jews devoted themselves largely to commerce and money-lending, they were not obeying a natural taste nor a special instinct, but were led to these pursuits by the force of circumstances, by exclusive laws, and by the express desire of kings and peoples. The Jews were constrained to adopt these modes of obtaining a livelihood by the irresistible material and moral forces opposed to them.

3. Christian rivals in these branches of enterprise have not been unable to hold their own against the Jews, on the contrary the Christian operators have often crushed their Jewish rivals by the superior weight of their capital.

[1] *Réflexions sur les Juifs* in the *Revue des Études Juives*, t. xxviii. p. 19.

4. The trade in money rarely profited the Jews, who remained mostly poor or possessed of very moderate wealth; the real gainers were the kings, the aristocracy, and the towns.

5. The rates of interest demanded by Jewish money-lenders were, considering the scarcity of specie, and the extraordinary risks incurred, far from excessive, and were sometimes considerably lower than the rates exacted by Christian financiers. The Jews were not ' usurers ' in the modern sense of the term, but the outcries against Jewish usury were due mainly to the medieval ignorance of the elements of economics, while the prejudice against lending money for interest was derived from the Roman Catholic Church which both then and now regarded the practice as most blameworthy.

H

For an account of the modern occupations of Jews, see Joseph Jacobs, *Studies in Jewish Statistics* (London, 1891), pp. 22–40.

CHAPTER XIII

THE JEWS AND THE THEATRE

ABOUT thirty-five years ago a certain Solomon Benolicl built a theatre in Gibraltar with the intention of letting it for dramatic performances. Some scruples were felt as to the lawfulness of his conduct, and application was made to a foreign Rabbi for his opinion on the subject.[1] His reply was the reverse of favourable, but he allowed a distinction to be drawn between the performances of modern and ancient times. Many distinguished men, it was added, nowadays go to the theatre to while away an hour harmlessly. Exactly two centuries before, a Rabbi of Venice[2] expressed himself appalled at the establishment of theatres by Venetian Jews, wherein men, women, and children assembled to hear 'frivolous and indecent remarks.' He regretted that he had no hope of suppressing the obnoxious gatherings. But the opposition to the theatre from certain sections of Jewish opinion is even now so strong that in some Hebrew prayer-books, the words that a Talmudic sage uttered in the first century of the Christian era are still ordered to be recited every morning on

[1] See the שו״ת כרך של רומי, f. 3 b.
[2] Samuel Aboab, שו״ת דבר שמואל, § 4.

251

entering the synagogue : — ' I give thanks to thee O Lord, my God, and God of my fathers, that thou hast placed my portion among those who sit in the House of Learning, and the House of Prayer, and didst not cast my lot among those who frequent theatres and circuses.[1] For I labour, and they labour ; I wait, and they wait ; I to inherit paradise, they the pit of destruction.' It is well that these typical phenomena should be pointed out, side by side with the unquestionable fact that Jews are at the present day among the most devoted lovers of the stage. For the Puritanical sentiment which still keeps many thousands of English Christians from the playhouse is strongly shared by thousands of modern Jews.

It is superfluous to quote the opinions scattered through early Jewish literature, in which the circus and theatre are denounced. The Jewish objections to the theatre were fourfold. (1) The theatre was immoral and idolatrous. (2) It was the scene of scoffing and mockery. (3) It encouraged wanton bloodshed. (4) Attendance at the shows was an idle waste of time. The last argument is certainly open to question, and an opposite opinion is on record ;[2] but the other three were only too fully justified by indubitable facts. The ancient drama grew out of the pagan religious rites, and many of the performances in the circus were in origin unmistakably idolatrous. Nor is this all. In the Augustan age, as has been often pointed out, the favourite plays of the masses were not the masterpieces of Sophocles, Aeschylus, and Euripides ; were not even the comedies of Menander and Plautus. Actual scenes of

---

[1] This is the reading of the Jerusalem Talmud. The Babylonian Talmud (*Berachoth*, 28 b) reads : — יושבי קרנות, which may mean ' traders ' or ' idlers.'

[2] Midrash, *Genesis Rabba*, par. 80.

immorality were enacted on the stage, the loves of Jupiter
and Danae, of Leda and Ganymede, were exhibited in
detail by the mimes.   When Rome became Christian there
was little change at first, and we find heathen writers denouncing Christian actors for obscenity.[1]
There were other moral objections to the theatre.   No
Jew might listen to a woman's voice.   Even when some
concession was made in the fourth century, women might at
most join in choruses with men, but might not sing solos.[2]
Yet music was impossible without female co-operation, unless the men were particularly gifted.   There is, however,
no reason to doubt De Saulcy's view that the ancient Jews
were deficient in musical skill.[3]   Few, if any, of the Talmudic Rabbis are quoted as proficient musicians.   The
destruction of the Temple for a time made the Jews avoid
music and song, even at weddings.   But there gradually
intruded itself into Jewish thought a notion that instrumental music was un-Jewish,[4] and this notion — so opposed
to the clear language of the Bible — still so far dominates
'orthodox' Judaism at the present day, that the organ in
the synagogue is a symbol of reform.[5]   The Jews early
showed themselves intolerant of attempts to suppress their
musical instincts, and certain classes were permitted to
lighten their toil by singing choruses.   Curiously enough,
the classes favoured were ploughmen and sailors, who, even
to-day, are most given to accompany their work with
snatches of song.[6]   The general prohibition of music con-

[1] Smith, *Dict. Christian Antiquities*, arts. ACTORS and THEATRE.
[2] Cf. Löw, *Lebensalter*, p. 309.
[3] F. de Saulcy, *Histoire de l'Art Judaique*, p. 121.
[4] *Jer. Megilla*, iii. 2 ; *T. B. Gittin*, 7 a.
[5] The fervour of Jewish worship has gained by this antipathy.
[6] *Sota*, 48 a.

tinued in the middle ages, but it grew less forcible and effective, and was even removed by some authorities of note.[1]   Music was especially permitted on Purim and at weddings, while many Jews employed Christian and Mohammedan musicians to amuse them on the Sabbaths and festivals.[2]   Recent investigation has discovered in the Spanish records the names of Jewish lion-tamers and jugglers in Navarre.   Payments from the royal exchequers were made to both classes, and it is rather curious that among the Spanish-Jewish jugglers in the fourteenth century are the names of two sons of a noted physician, Samuel Alfaqui of Pamplona, who cured an English Knight, and received for his services the special thanks of the Queen Leonora of Navarre.[3]   But by the end of the sixteenth century, several communities possessed Jewish orchestras, which were often employed by Christians.   In 1648 the Sultan Ibrahim utilized the services of Jewish fiddlers and dancers, while in the reign of Mahomet IV (1675), at a royal banquet in Adrianople, Jewish dancers and mimics passed from tent to tent, performing tricks. In the same year, at the betrothal of Mustapha, a Jew and a Turk performed on a rope.[4]

A most remarkable feature about the change implied in such facts as these, especially as regards musical skill, must be noted.   While the Rabbis of the Talmud were not themselves proficient in the musical art, the *Bachurim* or Talmud students of the middle ages were often

[1] E.g. R. Tam.   Cf. מגן אברהם, cccxxxviii. 4.   Cf. Löw, op. cit. p. 311.
[2] See above, p. 197; below, ch. xxii.
[3] Jacobs, *Sources of the History of the Jews in Spain;* Kayserling, *Jewish Quarterly Review,* viii. p. 489.
[4] See the quotations in Schudt, *Merkwürdigkeiten,* i. 58.

accomplished musicians. The Jewish liturgy, so far as vocal music was concerned, grew more and more ornate. Medieval Rabbis of the widest reputation, like Jacob Molin, were noted lovers of vocal melody; and this fourteenth century Rabbi was the forerunner of a whole class of clerical musicians. The chazan or precentor became less a reader than a singer, less a singer than a spirited declaimer. He gave to his emotions an expression which can only be described as dramatic; he wept or was glad as the prayers called for it. The curious phenomenon of hymns in dialogue [1] must be mentioned in this connexion. The congregation and precentor prayed, too, in dialogue; the melodies differed for the two parts. The Torah or law was declaimed with sensative emphasis, and in many other ways the growth of the dramatic instinct is discernible. It is hardly surprising that a large proportion of successful opera-singers in modern times have been sons or daughters of Jewish precentors.

Despite the lingering opposition to which sufficient allusion has already been made, the moral and religious grounds of Jewish antipathy to the stage thus almost vanished in the middle ages. But another feature of the relation of Judaism to the stage remains to be unfolded, and this is of great significance in the story of medieval Jewish life. The stage has dealt hardly with the Jews in many ways. The Jew has been the object of an outrage and insult which has continued till our own times. In parts of Persia, whenever a provincial governor holds high festival, the *pièces de resistance* are 'fireworks and Jews.' The latter are cast into muddy tanks, and their efforts to extricate

---

[1] Cf. the specimens translated by Miss Nina Davis in the *Jewish Quarterly Review* for January, 1896.

themselves are the chief element of the fun.[1]   This may
be compared with the medieval pleasantries indulged in
at Rome during the Carnival.   From the fourteenth century the Jews had to contribute heavily towards the cost
of the public festivities.[2]   But in the fifteenth century a
more personal rôle was forced upon the Roman Jews.
' On Monday, the first day of the Carnival, at least eight
Jews were forced to present themselves to open the foot-
races.   Half clad, often amid heavy showers of rain,
whipped and jeered at, they were compelled amid the wild
shouts of the mob to cover the whole length of the race-
course, which was about 1100 yards long.   Occasionally
the poor victims succumbed to their exertions and fell dead
on the course.   On the same black Monday of the Carnival, the Fattori (lay heads), the Rabbis, and other leading
Jews were forced to walk on foot at the head of the procession of the senators from one end of the Corso to the other,
offering a ready butt for the insults and derision of the
assembled crowd.'   Such indignities must have been harder
to bear than the coarser cruelties of the ancient arena, in
which thousands of Jewish captives were flung by Titus as
victims to wild beasts.   In those old days Jews were forced
to fight one another under the eyes of their former sovereign, — a fitting sight for fitting eyes.   But this martyrdom
was less grievous than the petty irritations which in the
middle ages sometimes took their place.

The indignities which Jews suffered on the stage were
mostly of another type.   The ridicule of Judaism dates far
back in the history of the drama.   It is true that there is
no direct evidence that in Rome such insults were perpe-

---

[1] C. J. Wills, *Persia as it is*, p. 230.   [2] Berliner, *Rom*, ii. pp. 46 seq.

trated,[1] but if the Roman satirists, who used foreigners generally as the object of their wit, did not spare the Jews, it is not probable that the mimes were more generous to them. At all events, it is certain that in the Roman plays, as performed in Syria, a favourite topic for raillery was provided by Judaism. The clowns or mimes laughed at the Pentateuch and at the Jewish Sabbath.[2] Jewish women were publicly forced to eat swine's flesh in the theatre.[3] With such examples the medieval playwrights had no hesitation as to the use to be made of the Jews. In the Carnival plays and in similar comedies the Jews were uniformly reviled or laughed at.[4] Then the tale of abuse was taken up by the dramatists of all countries. The legend of the ritual murder of Christian children inevitably found its way on to the stage. It may almost be asserted that a convention was entered into, in accordance with which no Jew could be introduced upon the stage, except in a grotesque or odious character.

But from the outset a distinction must be drawn. The Jewess enjoyed an extraordinary immunity from attack;[5] she was as much lauded as the Jew was reviled. The stage Jewess was always beautiful, and was always intended to be loveworthy. Shakespeare's Jessica and Marlowe's Abigail were evidently drawn as foils and contrasts to Shylock and Barabas. Partly this sympathetic treatment was designed to lead up to the conversion of these Jewesses to Christianity, but one may feel justified in attributing the kindness

[1] Cf. Berliner, *Rom*, i. p. 100.   [2] *Echa Rabba*, Introduction.
[3] Philo, *In Flaccum*, sec. 11, ed. Mangey, ii. 529–531.
[4] Güdemann, iii. pp. 204 seq.
[5] Cf. M. Maurice Bloch's *La femme juive dans le Roman et au Théâtre* (*Revue des Études Juives*, number 46, 1892).

of dramatists to their generosity and gallantry. Even Scott reserves all his tenderness for Rebecca, and has none to spare for her father. With all his originality, Scott felt himself trammelled by the example of his predecessors.[1]

In England, on the other hand, as Mr. Sidney Lee has shown,[2] even in the sixteenth century some few dramatists gave favourable presentments of Jews.

In *The Three Ladies of London*, a tedious production which 'marks the slow transition from the morality-play to the genuine drama,' an Italian merchant, Mercatore, is harassed by a Jewish creditor named Gerontus. The Italian, to evade his debt, pleads that he has turned Moslem (the scene passes in Turkey), and 'has thus, according to a recognized Turkish law, relieved himself of his debts.' But while the merchant is repeating after the judge a formal renunciation of Christianity, the Jew interrupts —

> GERONT. Stay there, most puissant judge. Signor Mercatore, consider what you do.
> Pay me the principal; as for the interest, I forgive it you.
> MER. No point da interest, no point da principal.
> GERONT. Then pay me now one-half, if you will not pay me all.
> MER. No point da half, no point denier; me will be a Turk, I say.
> Me be weary of my Christ's religion.

'Gerontus,' continues Mr. Lee, 'confesses himself shocked by the merchant's dishonest conversion, and rather than be a party to it, releases him from the debt. Mercatore returns to his old faith, and congratulates himself on cheating the Jew of his money. The judge adds — " Jews seek to excel in Christianity, and Christians in Jewishness " — and

---

[1] That this is true may be seen from the fact that the subsidiary names of the Jewish characters in *Ivanhoe* are all borrowed from the *Jew of Malta*.

[2] *Elizabethan England and the Jews* (Transactions, New Shakespeare Society, 1888).

the episode closes.' It is noticeable that in this scene, in which the Jew plays no ignoble part, the Italian, and not the Jew, uses broken English. As a matter of fact, the Jews spoke a very refined and literary language until their style of expression became degenerate in the ghettos.

Besides this appearance of a Jew on the Elizabethan stage in a favourable light, Richard Brome wrote a play, now lost, entitled *The Jewish Gentleman* — a title which 'suggests an appreciative treatment of the Jewish character.' The incidental references made to Jews by Elizabethan dramatists were seldom complimentary, but in Beaumont and Fletcher's *Custom of the Country*, Zabulon, a Jew, plays a conspicuous rôle, and, in the opinion of Mr. Lee, 'an attempt is made there to do some justice to his racial characteristics.'

But Shylock has so completely dominated the English stage, that no great English dramatist since Shakespeare has attempted to introduce Jewish characters. So wonderful, however, was the sensation produced throughout the civilized world by the career of Moses Mendelssohn ('Nathan der Weise') and his friendship with Lessing, that even in England a small band of well-intentioned writers, headed by Richard Cumberland, set about doing justice to the Jew on the stage. This was towards the close of the eighteenth century.

CHAPTER XIV

THE PURIM-PLAY AND THE DRAMA IN HEBREW

THOUGH the Jews received rough treatment in the Carnival sports, they yet were not able to resist the temptation to imitate them. Purim, or the Feast of Esther, occurs at about the same time as Lent, and thus Purim became the Jewish Carnival. The Jewish children in Italy used to range themselves in rows, then they pelted one another with nuts; while the adults rode through the streets with fir-branches in their hands, shouted or blew trumpets round a doll representing Haman, which was finally burnt with due solemnity at the stake. Such uproarious fun was, however, neither new nor rare. In the Talmud may be found accounts of wedding jollities in which Rabbis would juggle with three sticks, throwing them up and catching them. So, too, at the feast of the Water-drawing during Tabernacles, Rabbi Simeon ben Gamaliel took eight torches and threw them up one after another without their touching. This species of merry-making was at its height in the medieval celebrations of Purim. On Purim everything, or almost everything, was lawful; so the common people argued. They laughed at their Rabbis, they wore grotesque masks, the men attired themselves in women's clothes, and the women went clad as men. This point, let me say in passing, was made a ground of objection to the theatre altogether. On the one hand, pious Jews would not listen to the voices of women, and, on the other, would not approve of dramatic performances in which men were dressed in women's attire. For it must be remembered that in ancient Greece there were no female actors, and the same thing applied to the later English stage. Shakespeare wrote his Juliet and Ophelia for *boys* who always performed the women's parts. So that on the whole one can understand that those who objected to disobeying the Biblical command, 'A man shall not put on a woman's garments,'[1] would necessarily set their faces against the theatre of the sixteenth and even seventeenth centuries. On this very ground, among others, the English Puritans succeeded in closing the theatres for many years during the Commonwealth.

But on Purim the frolicsomeness of the Jew would not be denied; and the demand for Purim amusements was loud and universal. Now, a demand is not long in creating the corresponding supply; hence the rise of a class of *Purim-Spiele* or Purim-plays.

Purim-plays, written in Jewish-German jargon, attained a very rapid popularity among Jews at the beginning of the eighteenth century. Previously to that period Purim was indeed the time of frolic and jollity in the ghettos, and there also seems to me some evidence that set plays were produced before the decade ending with the year 1710.[2] In the Gaonic age (ninth or tenth century) we read of Purim buffooneries and play-acting, and of a dramatization of the story of Esther. In the fourteenth cen-

---

[1] Cf. ch. xv. below.   [2] See the evidence in Löw, sec. viii.

tury the Jews of France and Germany were in the habit
of performing masquerades on the subject of Haman's
plot and penalty, but again the dialogue, if any, was
extemporized, and the chief fun was gained by men dressing up as women, wearing masks, and indulging in grotesque pranks. On Purim the Rabbis were not stern in
their expectations, and though they never encouraged,
nay often denounced, these infringements of the Mosaic
Law, they more or less turned their blind eye towards
such innocent and mirth-provoking gambols.

Indeed, 'Purim' and the 'Rejoicing of the Law' were
occasions on which much joyous licence was permitted
even within the walls of the synagogue. The former of
the two feasts, which falls in March, may be regarded,
from this point of view, as the carnival of European Jews.
The second, which occurs in October, was on the other
hand the carnival of the Jews who reside in the Orient.
The synagogical merry-making on these anniversaries
sometimes included dancing, the introduction of amusing
effigies, the playing of musical instruments, the burning of
incense, and even the explosion of fireworks. Pageants,
approaching very closely the real drama in its pantomimic
phase, thus early fell within the scope of Jewish recreations.[1]

Hence, though the Purim-play proper is a phenomenon
of the eighteenth, and the drama in Hebrew of the seventeenth, centuries, no account of the life of the Jews in the
middle ages would be complete without a reference to both
forms of art. The Purim-play was the natural develop-

---

[1] For dancing and burning incense on the 'Rejoicing of the Law' (to
some extent a post-Biblical feast) see Müller, *Mafteach*, p. 22. For the other
festivities cf. e.g. D. Pardo, *Responsa*, מכתם לדוד, § 19.

ment of a well-established form of Jewish recreation in the middle ages. Though set formal *plays* do not occur in the medieval Jewish records, the germs of the Purim dramas are easily discernible. The dialogue belongs to the beginning of the eighteenth century, but the characters and plots are traditional. Nothing marks the continuity of Jewish life more clearly than the survival of these Purim-plays into modern times. On the other hand, the dramas written in Hebrew are interesting for an opposite reason. They, to a certain extent, mark the coming close of the Jewish middle ages, or at all events they are signals of the approaching emancipation. The jargon plays for Purim show us the conservative side of Jewish life, the dramas in classical Hebrew show us Jewish life in its adaptability to changing circumstances. For, to put the same point differently, the jargon play is a product of the ghetto, while the Hebrew drama was only possible when the ghetto walls were tottering to their fall. The composition of dramas in Hebrew always synchronized with a new participation of the Jews in the national life of the European states in which they lived.

Strangely enough, the story of Esther and Haman was not the only subject that was represented at Purim time. *The Sale of Joseph*, and *David and Goliath*, enjoyed equal popularity with the 'Ahasuerus-play.' Bermann of Limburg was the author of a play on the first-named subject, and the first performance, of which a full record is extant, occurred, I think, in 1713. The play excited great interest, and many Christians were present, and two soldiers were employed to keep off the crowd. It was performed in Frankfort in the house 'zur weissen oder silbernen Rand,' then tenanted by Löw Worms. The landlord of

the house was David Ulff, Rabbi of Mannheim. The
actors were Jewish students from Prague and Hamburg.
There is nothing surprising in this, for the mystery and
morality plays were often performed in churches by priests.
The comic man of the piece was grotesquely named ' Pickle-
herring,' and in subsequent performances he no doubt introduced many 'gags' on topics of local and passing
interest. This character, Pickle-herring, was not a Jewish
invention, but figured as the funny man in other earlier
and contemporary dramas. The same comedy was acted
again at Metz in Lorraine, and several of the actors who
had previously played in it at Frankfort came to Metz for
the purpose. We thus already find a mention at that early
date of Jewish travelling companies. In confidence, says
Schudt, who gives us all these facts,[1] a Jew informed me
that they would never perform the play again even if better
times came for them, because shortly afterwards, a great
many more people died than usual; a sure sign of God's
anger, for he could not be pleased with Pickle-herring and
his foolish jokes, and God's word should not be added to,
but held in respect and fear. The compunction of the Jews
did not last very long, for in 1716, on May 18, the Jews of
Prague celebrated the birth of Leopold, Prince of Austria,
in ornate and pompous processions and performances; they
erected a triumphal arch, and for three days illuminated
their houses.

The 'Ahasuerus-Spiel,' the Purim-play *par excellence*, was
first printed in 1708. In the seventeenth century, Italian
Jewish dramas on the subject of Esther were current, but
the original jargon title-page of the Jewish-German version
is amusing enough to bear reproduction. 'A beautiful new

---

[1] *Jüd. Merkwürdigkeiten*, ii. 314.

Ahasuerus-Spiel, composed with all possible art, never in all its lifetime will another be made so nicely, with pretty, beautiful lamentations in rhyme. We hope that whoever will buy it will not regret his expenditure; because God has commanded us to be merry on Purim, therefore have we made this Ahasuerus-play nice and beautiful. Therefore, also, you householders and boys come quickly and buy from me this play; you will not regret the cost. If you read it, you will find that you have value for your money.'

Here is some of the dialogue freely rendered. Each character on his entrance, it will be noted, addresses himself to the audience.

HAMAN: Herr Haman I am named. In gluttony and debauchery I am an adept. Brother Scribe, let us sing a jolly song.

SCRIBE: That we will, till the furniture shakes with merriment.

HAMAN: Happy evening and happy time! You want to know why I am here? I couldn't stand the best of Jews even if I were compelled to leave the King's land. The best of Jews is worthy of being stabbed, and when my noble King enters I will complain against the wicked Jews. Come in, all who serve my gracious King.

HATACH: Bless you all, rich and poor. Do you wish to know why I am come? My name is Hatach, my mother knows me well. I ask the gentlemen present why they are armed with swords. I advise you to sing-in the King. You have never seen such a great King!

CHORUS: Noble, high-born King! Sir Father, step in! We have mead and wine, mead and wine, and hens and fish. In he comes, in he comes!

KING: God bless you, ladies and gentlemen, one and all. I am named Ahasuerus. And I gave a great feast to all, rich and poor. The Jews didn't eat, but they drank.

And so forth. Haman in the end is hanged and falls dead. Then the following revival occurs.

KING: Put a glass to his ears; perhaps he will come to life again.

HAMAN (rises): I have been into the next world and I have seen much money.

HATACH: Fool! Why didn't you take some?

HAMAN: I was afraid.

CHORUS: Here we stand around the purse. To ask you for ducats would be too much; we will be content with thalers.

Evidently a collection followed the performance.

The more recent imitations of these plays have been reverent reproductions of the Scriptural story of *Esther*, or secondly, adaptations of Racine's *Esther*, or thirdly, harmless parodies [1] of the Bible narrative.

Sometimes the Purim-play attempts a higher flight, and becomes a dramatized philosophy. One, written in Italy, in 1710, by Corcos, is the reverse of merry, for it is a very serious, not to say heavy, production.[2]   But for the most part, these Purim-plays, written in the vernacular jargon, belong to the class of folk-comedies. A literary Jewish drama hardly exists, for though Jewish poets composed meritorious plays in Spanish, the drama in *Hebrew* was a late exotic.   Yet it is an interesting enough phenomenon.   As we shall immediately see, the Hebrew drama fills a definite place in the social history of the seventeenth-century Jews.

There are indeed some historians who would carry the Hebrew drama back at least as far as the Hellenistic period.   The Song of Solomon is placed in that epoch by some prominent advocates of the theory that this Biblical love-poem is a genuine drama.   This is a fascinating and a not altogether improbable idea.   But Professor Budde has recently rendered it difficult and hazardous to retain the notion any longer.[3]   Budde goes so far as to assert that 'the entire Semitic literature, so far as we are yet acquainted with it, does not know the drama.'   But in Alexandria, a Greek drama was composed by a Jew,

---

[1] For *Purim Parodies*, see p. 383 below.

[2] *Discorso academico del Rabbi T. V. Corcos*, p. 10.

[3] See Budde's article in the *New World* (1894), pp. 56 seq., and the criticism of it by Russell Martineau, in the *American Journal of Philology*, vol. xvi. p. 435.   Luther was not the last to see dramatic form also in Job and Tobit.

Ezekiel, and it is quite in accordance with later phenomena that a Hebrew drama should have been created at that particular moment. The Alexandrian Jews were in the enjoyment of emancipation, they were proud of their new country, and they were anxious to show Judaism to be a *cultured* religion. We have here all the conditions requisite for the creation of a drama, and the wonder would be if a Jewish drama had *not* made its appearance in Alexandria.

The earliest Hebrew drama, of whose date we have certain information, belongs to the seventeenth century. Its composition is an interesting incident in Jewish social life. Hence the circumstances under which it was produced deserve some words of explanation.

Menasseh ben Israel, to whom the English Jews owed the favour shown to them by Cromwell, was still a young Rabbi in Amsterdam when he co-operated with the other leaders of the Jewish community there to establish a school for the study of Hebrew. This school was designed to meet the needs of certain Marranos, or forced converts to Christianity, who, finding themselves welcome settlers in Amsterdam, then the freest city in the world, desired to return to Judaism. But they could not read Hebrew. The children of these reverts to their ancestral religion were at all events now able to acquire the rudiments of Hebrew, or if they were so inclined they might, by passing through the seven classes into which the school was divided, leave the institution with considerable knowledge of the Talmud also.

To this school, soon after its foundation, went the boy Baruch Spinoza, and no doubt he looked with the customary awe of the new-comer on a rather older lad, fourteen or fifteen years of age, who then stood at the head of the

school.   This boy was Moses Zacut, afterwards famous as
a mystic, but interesting to us in this connexion as the
author of the first drama written in the Hebrew language
subsequent to the completion of the Canon.   The only
subsequent author of good Hebrew plays, Moses Chayim
Luzzatto (1707–1747), an imitation of the Italian Guarini,
was also a mystic, and also, like Moses Zacut, wrote his
plays in Amsterdam.   The first part of the coincidence
is certainly not accidental, for the Biblical Psalms already
prove that the poet and mystic are nearly allied.   The
most determined opponent of Jewish mysticism, Maimonides, was destitute of poetical power ; almost alone among
the great Jews of the middle ages he reasoned without
much rhyming.   With the medieval Jew the possession
of poetical imagination implies a tendency to mysticism as
surely as cause implies effect.   For such a Jew must let
his fancy play round the only real subjects of his thought,
round God and destiny, round the world and its spheric
harmonies ; he must, in fact, become a mystic because he is
a poet.   Both Moses Zacut and Moses Luzzatto wrote their
dramas in their youth, and became mystics later on ; both,
indeed, were dramatists before they were more than seventeen years of age.

To return, however, to the genesis of the drama in
Hebrew, which, as already remarked, took place in Amsterdam at the beginning of the seventeenth century.   At
that period Amsterdam was the centre of a national and
literary movement which gave Holland the greatest of her
patriots and her poets.   The Chambers of Rhetoric, with
their quaint, fanciful names and their old-world prize com-
petitions, made way for a national theatre, on whose boards
were re-enacted the deeds of the Dutch heroes of the past

and of the Hebrew heroes of Old Testament story. National feeling is at its highest and best when it creates a national drama, and England, like Holland, and almost contemporaneously with her, was aglow with national hopes, and, like her, England produced a series of dramatists since unrivalled. Holland, however, differed from England in an important point as regards the dramatic movement. In Joost van Vondel, the greatest Dutch writer of all time, Holland possessed a dramatist from whom Milton perhaps drew inspiration, for his finest plays dealt with Biblical subjects. In England the new drama was secular; in Holland it was, on the classical side, religious.

Now, it is hardly wonderful that under these circumstances the Jews of Holland should share the dramatic aspirations of their country to the full. Jewish dramatists had existed before in Spain, but they had written in Spanish.[1] Why did the Jews of Holland compose dramas in Hebrew and not in Dutch ? Does this not look rather as though the writers stood outside the national movement and not within it ? At first sight this seems an obvious inference, but, like most obvious inferences, it is altogether false. For had Moses Zacut written in his vernacular he must have used Spanish, which in Holland would have been trebly unpatriotic. The Jews of Amsterdam were slow to use Dutch as their language, just as the re-admitted Jews in England did not at once adopt English. It has further to be remembered that in Zacut's day no obscure Jewish dramatist would have had much chance of breaking through the barriers which the literary trade-union of Holland still kept up around the boards of the theatre. He would not have been able to gain a hearing. Being forced to write for his

[1] See below, ch. xx.

brethren, he wrote in Hebrew. But we have seen that Hebrew was not yet a familiar language with the bulk of Amsterdam Jews. The very force of their new patriotic emotions led them to cultivate Hebrew; they would put their best foot forward, they would prove to their fellow-countrymen in Holland that the sacred language lived, that it was a flexible and human tongue, that it was even capable of dramatic form.

But, beyond this mere patriotism, Moses Zacut was moved to write a drama in Hebrew by that same inspiring belief in his people's mission, which impelled Menasseh ben Israel to cross the channel and clear the way to a return of the Jews to Puritan England. In proof of this, I would point to the subject which Zacut chose for his *Yesod Olam*, the ' Foundation of the World.' Hebrew dramatists either restricted themselves to such incidents in Scripture as involved little of the supernatural, e.ĝ. the stories of Esther, of Joseph, of Saul, and of Samson, or, like Luzzatto, preferred to go outside the Bible in search of material. Most of the modern Hebrew plays, indeed, are morality plays, allegories in which God Himself is kept off the stage. Moses Zacut shows great skill here. He chose the Biblical story of Abraham, and yet managed to eliminate the supernatural, except in so far as Abraham is saved miraculously from Nimrod's persecutions. Zacut carefully welds together the Bible story with the Midrashic or traditional accretions to it, and thus what he lacks in original fancy he makes up by pictorial reminiscence. For, though the poet feels constrained to keep within the bounds of the records when he deals with the Bible, yet he includes in those records the Midrash also. But this help was not without its drawbacks. For just as the Jewish liturgical poets were inspired by the

Psalms, and at the same time hampered by their dread of departing from such great models, so the Jewish secular poets were trammelled by a desire to keep within the lines of the Midrash, from which they derived the accessory materials of their plays. This has always been a difficulty with the writers of Hebrew dramas.

Dr. Berliner, who first printed this play in 1874, thinks that the author's motive was to expose the Inquisition to scorn, and maintains that in Abraham's steadfastness against Nimrod, and in his legendary escape from the fiery furnace, were typified the Jewish fortunes in Spain. If the play was written for Purim evening, as Jewish plays so often were, this idea would be a natural enough one for a night on which Haman's crime and penalty are told again amid laughter and tears. But it seems to me that the opening scene, as well as several others in the play, shows a desire to portray the thought that the mission of Israel was for the world, to bear a light to the nations. Hence, Abraham's persistent attempts in the *Yesod Olam* to convert not only Terah, his father, but all who came within the circle of his influence. The very choice of Abraham for his hero suggests this, for had Zacut intended only to depict the fires of the Inquisition, why did he not take Daniel as his hero? Abraham was the very type of the universality of man, and Zacut, amid the world-emotions which moved him and Menasseh ben Israel too, turned back for the hero of the first Hebrew drama to the man in whom all the nations of the earth were to be blessed. Moreover, the most popular epic of Zacut's youth was the famous *Week* of Salluste du Bartas. This was translated into many languages, and Vondel spent some years of his life in turning parts of it into Dutch. It almost seems as if

Moses Zacut had this before his mind. Vondel produced a piece which he called *Noah, or the Destruction of the World*. Zacut appears to have said : ' I will prove the antithesis ; I will deal with Abraham and the Re-foundation of the World ; I will remind my country of Israel's still unfulfilled mission.'

Whatever the mission of Israel, however, may be, it is obvious that the production of dramatic masterpieces was no portion of it.

CHAPTER XV

COSTUME IN LAW AND FASHION

IT would be impossible to find in older Jewish literature a parallel to the Oriental proverb that 'the shirt does not change the colour of the wearer's skin.' On the other side, it is easy to philosophize too subtly on the subject of clothes, for it is a mere exaggeration to assert that costume is 'the impression and expression of a people's thought and feeling,' that 'dress mirrors forth a nation's pain and sorrow, its pleasure and its joy.'[1] Yet, in a more limited sense, dress is a measure of civilization, and progress only begins where a people has ceased to go unclad. To the Jew, costume was not a fashion at all; it was a direct consequence of his morality. Such a law as the Mosaic injunction which forbids men and women to dress alike, had a moral origin; and the Puritans showed themselves wise in retaining this restriction, though they abandoned the Mosaic regulation against the use of 'linsey-woolsey,' to cite the quaint sixteenth-century phrase.[2] Jews themselves have used a simi-

[1] A. Brüll in his excellent *Trachten der Juden* (1873), a work unfortunately still incomplete.

[2] Baker, the redoubted opponent of Prynne, cites the Puritan's retention of the prohibition against men wearing female attire (Deut. xxii. 5), but continues: 'But where findes he this Precept ? even in the same place where he findes also that we must not wear *Cloaths* of *Linsey-woolsey ;* and seeing that we *lawfully* now wear cloaths of *Linsey-woolsey*, why may it not be as *lawfull* for *Men* to put on *Women's* Garments ?'

lar discrimination, attaching great importance to the moral injunction, and neglecting somewhat the ritual one.

In the middle ages the dress-problem was always presenting itself for solution to Jews and Christians alike.[1] Luther declared that men might masquerade as women for sport and play, but not as a usual thing in sober, earnest moments. A great fifteenth-century Rabbi[2] maintained a similar attitude, and opinion was much divided on the question of the lawfulness of men and women commingling freely and wearing masks to avoid recognition on Purim and at wedding festivities. 'Every one who fears God will exhort the members of his household, and those who defer to his opinions, to avoid such frivolities,' says a medieval Jewish purist whose views were widely shared, though popular opinion took the opposite direction. But public opinion, as already pointed out, allowed this laxity if it were occasional and not habitual. Every effort was made by Jews to differentiate the ordinary attire of a man from that of a woman. The straps of the phylacteries used in prayer were never made of *red* leather, lest 'they would look like the dress of women.'[3] From a similar motive, the Jewish men in some localities abstained from donning garments of coloured wool or linen; dyed silks did not fall within the same category of forbidden stuffs.[4] But though there was great variety in local custom on all such matters, disguises which rendered it difficult to discern the wearer's sex might be freely worn on journeys for the protection of women.[5] Jewesses assumed false beards and girded themselves with swords

[1] Cf. p. 261 above.

[2] J. Minz, *Responsa*, § 17.   Cf. Shulchan Aruch, אורח חיים, ch. 696, § 8, and the באר היטב, ad loc. note 13.

[3] *Responsa* of Geonim, Müller (*Mafteach*), p. 125, in name of Amram.

[4] Op. cit. p. 227.   [5] ספר חסידים, §§ 200, 201.

during sieges to be mistaken for men, and thus be saved from insult. They also put on the characteristic garb of nuns to ensure a similar immunity.[1] Male Israelites were forced to adopt similar devices owing to the hazards which beset a Jewish traveller in the middle ages. They dressed as Christian priests, joined pilgrimages, and sang Latin psalms, to avoid betraying the dangerous fact of their Jewish identity.[2] Similarly, at a later period, Jews who resided under Islamic governors, wore white garments on their journeys in order to pass as Moslems.[3]

But moments of exalted joy or of pressing danger do not make up a lifetime. Under all ordinary circumstances the underlying motives which inspired Jewish ideas on costume were a sense of personal dignity and a keen regard for decency. The moral or ethical side of costume comes out strongly in all Jewish literature.[4] To go naked in the streets is to deny God and man : 'the glory of God is man, the glory of man is his attire.'[5] 'Put the costly *on* thee, and the cheap *in* thee,' said the Rabbinical proverb which set clothes higher than food.[6] Cleanliness and neatness in outward garb distinguished the *Talmid Chacham* or student of theology. 'It is a disgrace for a student to go in the streets with soiled boots;'[7] 'the scholar on whose robe is seen a dirt spot is worthy of death,' for wisdom, whose representative he is in the eyes of the world, is degraded by his slovenliness.[8] 'By four signs a scholar reveals his

---

[1] ספר חסידים, § 702.   [2] Ibid. § 220. Cf. Güdemann, i. p. 65.

[3] P. Cassel in Ersch und Gruber, II, xxvii, p. 236.

[4] Cf. A. Brüll, op. cit., which contains a fine collection of passages.

[5] *Jebamoth*, 63 b, *Derech Eretz Zutta*. Transparent garments, through which the body was visible in outline, were forbidden for use in prayer in the middle ages (*Responsa* of Geonim, Müller, pp. 32 and 268).

[6] *B. Mezia*, 52 a. Cf. *Chullin*, 84 b.   [7] *Sabb*. 114 a.   [8] Ibid. 114 a.

character : in his money, in his cups, in his anger, in his attire.'¹ Clothing, we have seen, took precedence of food among the necessaries of life. A curious practical turn was given to this moral principle. A poor man who sought public relief and asked for articles of clothing was at once satisfied without preliminary cross-examination as to his real need. If, however, he asked for food, he might be questioned in order to ascertain whether his was a deserving case.² Other Jewish authorities took the reverse view, but all agreed that if the petitioner had 'come down in the world' and had been used to wear fine and elegant attire, such was to be given to him now.³ With women dress was of even greater importance, and the Talmud treats their claims with marked generosity. A full year was allowed for preparing the bride's trousseau.⁴ After marriage, the husband was legally bound to provide his wife not only with dwelling and food, but with a head-dress, a girdle, a new pair of shoes, at each of the three great festivals, and other clothing items at ordinary times, at least to the annual value of fifty zuzim or shillings. This, says the Talmud, was exclusive of the voluntary gifts, chiefly of clothes, 'with which a man must rejoice his wife's heart.'⁵ Clauses to this effect were inserted in Jewish marriage contracts in the middle ages, and they still appear in all modern documents of the same class. Provision is specially made for 'garments for every-day wear as well as garments for Sabbath use.'⁶ The medieval Jews were most sensitive on this subject. 'Accustom yourselves and wives, your sons and

¹ *Derech Eretz Zutta ; Erubin*, 65 b.   ² *B. Bathra*, 9 a.
³ *Jerus. Peah*, viii. 7. A similar generosity was sometimes advocated with regard to the food supplied to the needy.
⁴ *Kethub.* 57 a.   ⁵ *Kethub.* 64 b; *Pesachim*, 109 a.
⁶ Cf. e.g. M. D. Davis, *Shetaroth*, p. 300.

daughters, always to wear nice and clean clothes, that God and men may love and honour you' — is the advice of a Jewish parent to his children in the fourteenth century.[1] Two centuries earlier, the famous translator of Maimonides wrote to his son : —

> Honour thyself, thy household, and thy children, by providing proper clothing as far as thy means allow, for it is unbecoming in a man, when he is not at work, to go shabbily dressed. Withhold from thy belly, and put it on thy back.

When, as we shall soon see, Jewish men were forbidden by civil and ecclesiastical law to dress as they pleased, they nevertheless attempted to exempt their wives from the indignities to which they were themselves subjected. The king of Castile once demanded of the Jews an explanation of the splendid attire, the silks and embroideries, worn by their wives and children.[2] The incriminated Jews replied : 'It is only our women who are richly attired ; we, the men, go clad in sober black as your Majesty has commanded. But we imagined that the sumptuary law applied only to us men, and that the king gallantly left our women at liberty to dress as they wished.' — 'It is not fair,' answered the king, 'that you should go like a coalman's donkey, while your wives prance about harnessed like the mule of the Pope.' It may well be conceived how bitterly Jews resented these intolerable interferences with one of their most sacred ideals, viz. the dignity of their women. No legal restrictions or sumptuary laws, however, succeeded in making the Jewish husband inattentive to his wife's dress. An irresistible desire

---

[1] See *Jewish Quarterly Review*, ii. 463, 464.
[2] This may be found in Ibn Virga's שבט יהודה.

of the men for finery in female attire continued a marked Jewish characteristic throughout the middle ages.

In another direction, religious scrupulosity determined an important Jewish fashion in dress. It is not easy to explain how the medieval Jews came to intensify and stereotype the custom of covering their heads, not only in worship, but when engaged in secular employments. Anciently, the habit was at most a piece of occasional etiquette, though it afterwards became a strict and general ritual ordinance. The Oriental code of manners showed respect by covering the head and uncovering the feet, in exact contradiction to the prevailing custom of Europe. In the early Rabbinical literature there is no trace, however, that such a custom was crystallized into a legal precept.[1] Slaves stood covered in the presence of their masters as a token of respect; the man of fearless courage, when he desired to display his valour, stood bare-headed.[2] This distinction seems not to have survived, for covering the head came to be a sign of respectful greeting. 'Rabina sat before R. Jeremiah of Diphte, and a man came in without covering his head. Then said Rabina: What an impudent boor it is!'[3] We see, however, the transition in a beautiful Rabbinical simile, which shows how the Jews, though reverent towards God, did not stand before Him in the attitude of slaves. 'A human king,' says the Midrash,[4] 'sends an edict to a province, and all the inhabitants read it, standing and uncovered, trembling with fear and anxiety. This, says God, I do not ask of you. I do not *trouble* you

---

[1] Cf. Löw, *Gesam. Schrift.* ii. p. 314 seq. St. Paul (1 Cor. xi.) also seems to imply that covering the head was not customary with the Jews of his time.

[2] It is noteworthy that the Targum Onkelos to Exod. xiv. 8 translates thus: 'the children of Israel went forth *with uncovered heads* (בריש גלי).'

[3] *Kiddushin*, 33 a.   [4] *Leviticus Rabba*, ch. xxvii.

to stand or *uncover* your heads when you read the *Shema.*'[1]
Thus the covering of the head in prayer was at once a
privilege, and a mark that the respect the Jew had to his
God was the reverence of a free man. If we add to this
the Oriental susceptibility to changes of temperature, we
shall not be surprised to find the custom of always appearing with covered head justified on hygienic grounds.
Rheumatism will come to the lazy wight who neglects to
cover his head, says the Midrash.[2]

The custom was a Babylonian rather than a Palestinian
one, and its local prevalence among the Persians must have
helped to convert what had been a merely personal act of
piety into a general rule for all Jews. In the middle ages,
the custom is first noticeable in Spain, under the Moors,
where again Oriental manners prevailed. In the twelfth
century, covering the head during prayer was apparently
not usual with the Jews of France. Maimonides general-
ized from the example of R. Huna, and laid it down that
no students of the Torah should go *bare*-headed,[3] for to do
so was a mark of immodesty and pride. But though other
great authorities supported Maimonides, it nevertheless
was not customary in France for even learned Jews to
habitually cover their heads,[4] but during the grace after
meals the person who said the blessing covered his head
with a cap or the corner of his coat.[5] In the thirteenth

---

[1] I.e. Deuteronomy vi. 4 seq.   [2] *Levit. R.*, ch. xix.

[3] *Hilchoth Deóth*, v. 6; *More Nebuchim*, iii. 52. That Maimonides wrote
under Moslem influence in Egypt, is clear from his adding that the Jew
should not go barefooted where the wearing of shoes was a customary sign
of respect. Löw, ibid. p. 321.

[4] The author of המנהיג, Laws on תפלה, § 45, says: לכן יתכן לו לאדם ללכת
בכיסוי הראש דרך צניעות ומוראת· מלכות העולם כמנהג כל אנשי ספרד יישר כחם.

[5] Ibid. *Hilchoth* סעורה, § 12.

century, boys in Germany and adults in France were called to the Law in synagogue bare-headed.[1] How certain it is that Jewish authorities did not regard praying with covered heads as an essential part of the synagogue rites, is shown by the attitude of the famous Solomon Luria on the question. He says that he knows no reason why Jews pray with covered heads, but he is especially disturbed that many Jews will never go bare-headed even in the secular pursuits, 'imagining that such is the Jewish law, and not merely an instance of superlative scrupulosity.'[2] Somewhat later the idea became fixed in the Jewish mind that to pray bare-headed belongs to those 'customs of the Gentiles'[3] which must not be imitated.

We shall have occasion to notice one or two other directions in which the desire to avoid imitating non-Jewish habits affected Jewish fashions in dress, but it may be asserted in general that there was no distinctive Jewish dress until the law forced it upon the Jews. The main element of distinctiveness which existed before the thirteenth century was produced by the migration of Jews from place to place. They often carried with them the fashions of one country to another, and continued to attire themselves in their new abodes as they had done in their old ones. Thus even before the Jews lost their political independence, they had begun to show cosmopolitanism in

---

[1] See דרכי משה to Tur, *Orach Chayim*, 282, note 3. Cf. *Or Zarua*, ii. 20, No. 43; Geiger's *Jüd. Zeitschrift*, iii. p. 142; and Löw, *Lebensalter*, p. 410, note 70: ואסור לקטן לקראת בראש וכו"ש גדול דלא כמנהג צרפת דקורין בראש מגולה. It may be further noted that in the *Kolbo*, p. 8 b, the two opposed views are both stated. R. Meir ben Baruch of Rothenburg says: אינו אסור לילך בגלוי ראש.

[2] מחמת חסידות. Luria, *Responsa*, p. 36 a. Cf. Brüll, *Trachten der Juden*, p. 11, note 2.

[3] חקות הגוים. Cf. טורי זהב to *Orach Chayim*, viii. 3.

dress, and the same phenomenon may be noted throughout Jewish history.

A very quaint custom compelled Jewish women to cover their hair on all occasions. In the Mishnah this custom is already described as a 'Jewish Ordinance,'[1] and the Jewess who went abroad with her hair exposed was liable to divorce. Later on the custom was explained by a reference to Numbers v. 18, 'And the priest shall set the woman before the Lord and let the hair of the woman's head go loose.'[2] This injunction was held to imply that in ordinary circumstances the Hebrew woman *covered* her hair. What may at first have been a modest etiquette grew into a scrupulous rule, and by the time of Tertullian Jewish women could be distinguished by the manner in which they hid their hair.[3] Indeed, if a Jewish girl went with uncovered head, it was presumptive evidence that she was unmarried.[4] A Jew might not pray in the presence of a woman whose hair was visible. In the middle ages the Jewesses who scrupulously cut or shaved off their own tresses, sought an antidote to the disfigurement by donning wigs. Jewish moralists protested against this innovation and pointed to the example of the Nuns as worthy of imitation by the daughters of Israel.[5] The preservation of this old habit in medieval life helped to confirm that distinctiveness in Jewish dress which grew out of the trans-

[1] *Mishnah Kethuboth*, vii. 6; *B. Kamma*, viii. 6; Tosefta, *Sota*, ix. See also St. Paul's remark in 1 Cor. xi. 5. For real origin see Conybeare, *J. Q. R.* viii.
[2] *T. B. Kethuboth*, 72 a; *Sifre*, i. 11.
[3] 'Apud Iudaeos tam solenne est feminis eorum velamen capitis, ut inde noscantur (*De cor.* iv.).
[4] *Mishnah Kethuboth*, ii. 10; *T. B. Berachoth*, 24 a.
[5] Samuel J. Katzenellenbogen דרישות, ed. Venice, 8 a. Quoted in Brüll's *Jahrbücher für jüdische Geschichte und Litteratur* (viii. 51), from which this paragraph is mainly derived.

ference of fashions from lands in which they were indigenous
to other lands in which they were foreign.   Towards the
end of the seventeenth century the Jews of Metz passed
what may be termed a resolution of 'transference,' so interesting from many points of view, that I cite it in full : —

ART. iii. All women must wear veils when they go to synagogue. Young
brides, aged twelve, thirteen, or fourteen years, are excused from this law
during the first year of their marriage; those who wed when fifteen years
old, are free from wearing a veil for three months.   At the service on Saturday
evening, on the evening when the festivals conclude, on week-nights, and on
Purim eve, all women are free to discard the veil.   The same law applies to
mantles.

Besides, however, this transference of fashion, the natural
tendency of Judaism towards conservatism in custom displayed itself in retaining the original costumes of various
nations after these had become obsolete.   Some such explanation as this accounts for the retention among the
Russian Jews of the *kaftan*, once a national Polish costume,
now, however, restricted to Jewish use.   In England the
three-cornered hat was retained in synagogue long after
it had ceased to be a general fashion.   'Change not the
customs of your fathers,' said many a Jewish moralist, with
special application to costume.   ''Tis measure for measure,'
cried Solomon Alami in 1415, in bitter resentment of the
Jewish *Badge*.   'Since we assumed the garb of non-Jews,
the latter have forced on us a garb which marks us out for
scorn.'   But the very words of this complaint prove that
there was no narrow bigotry against adopting the national
costumes of the various countries in which Jews dwelt.   On
the contrary, if the Jew remained old-fashioned in dress at
the one end of the scale, he became the leader of new
vogues at the other end.   Moreover, the more vigorous
traces of the agitation against wearing non-Jewish attire

belong to the sixteenth century, an age marked at once by the progress of the Protestant Reformation, and the initiations of the ghettos. A cleft between Jewish and Gentile life was then produced, which went far deeper than that caused by the enforced wearing of a Jew's badge three centuries earlier.

The one thing that is clear is that the growth of a specifically Jewish costume was the effect of external, and not of internal causes. It has already been pointed out that on journeys Jews dressed as Christian priests; this fact must not be pressed, however. But the underlying principle with medieval Rabbis was not that Jews must dress differently to others, but that they were forbidden to use any article of attire which the Christian or Mohammedan wore as a token of his faith. A similar remark applies to dressing the hair. Thus while the Jew would not wear the Mohammedan 'heaven-lock,' he was by no means cordially devoted to the love-lock pendant from his ears, which became in the middle ages a feature of the Jewish toilet. In northern Africa the Jews satisfied themselves by leaving a single hair to represent the 'corner.' [1] Shaving was common in Majorca in the fifteenth century, [2] and a similar state of things existed in Leghorn later on, where a *tekana* had to be introduced to enforce the use of scissors or a pilatory in preference to a razor. [3] It appears that the Jews resident in Moslem lands allowed their beards to grow without even trimming them, while in Christian countries, especially in Italy, trimming the beard was cus-

---

[1] *Responsa*, Tashbats, ii. 90. Elsewhere (iii. 93) Duran describes this custom of shaving the 'corners' as מכת המדינה, though in Algiers itself he succeeded in enforcing the custom of leaving the פאות untouched.

[2] Ibid. iii. 227.

[3] Chayim Azulai, שו"ת ספר חיים שאל, § 6.

tomary.[1] Parchon, the famous Jewish grammarian who wrote in southern Italy in 1160, condemned the Jews of Christian lands who refrained from cutting the hair of their head.[2] Here, again, it is clear that the Jews were endeavouring to assimilate their customs to local fashion, for, as hardly needs to be said, the retention of the beard was common to all Oriental peoples, and the Jews were most rigorous against shaving in the very countries where the removal of the beard was antipathetic to the sentiment generally prevailing. In Italy, Jewish parents cut their boys' hair in such a way that they left a curl on the top, after the common wont. They did this that their children might not be noticeable among Christian boys.[3] Jews did not display the small fringed garment which they wore in fulfilment of Deuteronomy. They refrained from walking through the streets without shoes on fast-days from a similar disinclination to make themselves conspicuously different to their neighbours.[4]

Naturally, Jews were divided as to how far this complacency might go. In Spain, where the relations between Jews and Christians were very cordial, Jewish savants wore the cope, which was really an ecclesiastical vestment. In 1526 Eliah Mizrachi, whose Rabbinical authority extended over the Jews of Constantinople, forbade Jewish savants and their pupils to wear such a cope thrown loosely over their shoulders, because he considered the garment

---

[1] Samson Morpurgo has a most interesting discussion of the whole subject in his שמש צדקה, p. 102 a. He mentions that in Salonica Italian travellers were sometimes forbidden by the Rabbis to cut their beards, though at other times the Jewish visitors in Constantinople, Adrianople, Smyrna, and Salonica were allowed to follow their own wishes in the matter.

[2] Parchon's *Machbereth*, Art. גלב; Bacher, in Stade's *Zeitschrift*, x, 143.

[3] J. Ayas, שו״ת בני יהודה, 95.   [4] See ref. note I, above.

to belong to the category of a specifically Christian costume. Many of these savants, who had migrated to Turkey from Spain after the expulsion in 1492, protested against this interference, on the pretext that as they had always worn the cope in Spain, they had an inalienable right to continue their old practice. Messer David Leon[1] was invited to give an opinion, and supported Mizrachi's view. But, apart from the fact that Mizrachi's prohibition referred specially to the Sabbath, his decision was not unanimously shared, and other authorities decided in favour of the cope.[2] The conflict which arose between these two sentiments — between a willingness to dress as non-Jews did and a natural repulsion against wearing the specific symbols of other religions — was solved with something very like a liberal use of common-sense. It must not be imagined that the difficulty only arose where Jews lived in a Christian society. Green veils were avoided by the Jews of Moslem countries, for these were the distinctive garb of the descendants of the Prophet. Prohibition came to the aid of common-sense, for while Christian rulers forbade Jews to wear the priestly *cappae*, the Oriental governments denied to Jews the right to wear green veils. But this point will recur later on. It remains to point out that the best Jewish authorities maintained that 'all colours not *exclusively* Mohammedan may be worn by Jews.'[3]

The religious scruples entertained by Jews against the free adoption of national costumes were thus mild in intensity and diminutive in extent. The Jews of the middle ages were in point of fact engaged in a constant crusade

---

[1] See S. Schechter in *Revue des Études Juives*, xxiv. p. 130.

[2] Cf. e.g. שו"ת כהונת עולם, § 74; besides Joseph Colon, שו"ת, § 88.

[3] Moses **Ha Kohen**, שו"ת כהונת עולם, § 75.

against the attempts — at first abortive, and in the thirteenth century all too successful—to force upon them a distinction in dress which they detested. The story of this degradation will soon be told. Some further evidence must first be adduced that, when left untrammelled by external law, the Jews dressed as their neighbours of other faiths. The Hebrew illuminated MSS. of the middle ages present a large number of Jewish costumes which, amid all their vagaries and anachronisms, in the main are identical with the national fashions of the country and time in which the MSS. were written.[1] Further, when Pope Innocent III introduced the Jewish badge in 1215, he distinctly asserted that theretofore the Jews had dressed like the rest of the

[1] Of the illuminated Hebrew MSS. in the British Museum, the following among others may be particularly noted: Add. 14,761, 26,957, 27,210; Or. 1404, 2737, and 2884. The third named is Spanish (early fourteenth century). All the men have their hair loose, and wear simple tunics of bright colours. These are sometimes prettily embroidered, and come to a point in front. The women wear an outer mantle which has no sleeves, but passes over the head, leaving the breast bare. The female hat is large, placed somewhat on one side; and while the back of the hat is bent up and elevated, the front is flat. This hat was common at the time in France and southern Europe. The men have a little circle shaved on the chin in the centre of the beard. In Add. 27,210 (also of the fourteenth century) a Greek style predominates, and the MS. probably emanates from Corfu. The women wear a long flowing Greek dress, rather tight-fitting, without waist, and fastening very high. MS. Add. 14,761 is French of the fifteenth century. Men wear a hood, long overcoat without sleeves and a cape. The musicians wear a parti-coloured dress. Earlier than the foregoing is Add. 26,957 (Roman rite, dated A.D. 1269). The women, with tight-fitting, low-necked dresses, and their close-drawn, jewelled hair fastened in nets and caps, are obviously Italian types; but it must be admitted that in clothing the men, the artist mingles every age and every nation. In Or. 2884 (fourteenth century) again the predominating costumes are French; in 2737 they are Italian. It is worth noting that these MSS. of the Passover Hagada, the *wicked son* is almost invariably depicted as a soldier in military dress. Could anything speak more feelingly regarding the relation in which the Jews of these centuries alone came to close quarters with soldiers?

population, with the result that intermarriages between Jews and Christians had often occurred.[1] The strenuous resistance offered by the Jews of Spain, Italy, and southern France to this attack on their liberty shows how keenly the Jews prized the right to follow the ordinary national tastes and fashions in dress. It is obvious that if there had been such a thing as a 'Jewish costume,' such a costume would have been common to the Jews of several countries. Of such an identity there is no direct evidence, and all the indirect evidence is entirely against it. In one part of the East, for instance, the Jews affected a military costume.[2] The head of the Jewish academy in Bagdad was 'clothed in golden and coloured garments like the king : his palace also is hung with costly tapestry like that of the king.'[3] The twelfth-century Jewish traveller, who gives us this information, was himself dressed differently to the ordinary Eastern Jews whom he visited.[4] In Europe the Jews, as was pointed out above, refrained from exhibiting the fringes which the Mosaic law prescribed on four-cornered garments.[5] Petachia was struck by the fact that the Persian Jews wore large and full outside wraps with fringes[6] — naturally this would be in keeping with the flowing robes of Orientals. Petachia noted that the Jews of Babylon prayed in synagogue bare-footed.[7]

[1] Graetz, *Hist. of Jews* (Eng. Trans.), III. ch. xv.

[2] Müller, *Mafteach*, p. 52.

[3] *Travels of R. Petachia* (ed. Benisch), p. 43. Cf. Benjamin of Tudela (ed. Asher), i. p. 101.   [4] *Petachia*, p. 11.

[5] In the eighteenth century it was with some Jews a mark of piety to exhibit one of these fringes outside the dress. (See יוסף אומץ, § 232.) But this was at a time when Jews were living in ghettos.·   [6] *Petachia*, p. 15.

[7] P. 45. As a further fact, I should mention that in Eastern lands the Jews often sit on the ground cross-legged at prayer. In the East generally there are no seats in the synagogues.

Such differences between the Jews of Asia and of Europe preclude a belief in the existence of a pronounced Jewish type of dress. The Jewish Rabbis and other synagogue officers wore no specific uniform,[1] but all Jews endeavoured to reserve a special suit for use in synagogue and on Sabbath. It must be remembered that many medieval Christians also had a special form of dress for use in church, indeed the clerical vestments were at first worn by all church-goers. Jews did not permit themselves to go to synagogue with an over-all thrown over their household dress, but put on a closely fitting tunic under the mantle which they mostly wore as well.[2] The outer mantle hence had a tendency to become *sleeveless*, and it seems to have been a feature of the Jewish *sarbel* or outermost garment that there was only one opening in it, viz. on the right hand side.[3] Even if he prayed at home and in private, the medieval Jew put on a better cap than the one habitually worn in the house in Germany.[4] The Jews declared for decency, simplicity, and cleanliness as well as for *alteration* in the garments worn in prayer and in study. In the thirteenth century Jewish students kept an entirely separate dress for use at their studies.[5] Even the poor made some changes in their attire for synagogue and Sabbath use. This was a Talmudical prescript also. R. Chanina says that ' every one must have two suits, the

---

[1] The ' geriffelte Mantel' worn by some aged Rabbis and other aged people (Güdemann, iii. 137) was only exceptionally used (ibid. p. 275).

[2] This seems to be the meaning of the *tekanoth* published by Güdemann, i. p. 261.

[3] Cf. Güdemann, i. pp. 137, 259. The Sabbath *sarbel* was closed on the right (יוסף אומץ, § 592) to restrain the right hand from easily breaking the Sabbatical laws.

[4] יוסף אומץ 3.   [5] See the חוקי התורה (p. 348 below), B § 3.

one for week-days, the other for Sabbaths.' Once R. Simlai
was lecturing on this subject, when some one in his audience
interrupted : ' Rabbi, alas! we are poor, and have no second
suits.' ' Then,' rejoined the Rabbi, ' arrange your one suit
differently.' [1] Similarly, the medieval German Jews wore
thick, heavy sandals over their feet, and on entering the
synagogue they removed these so as to avoid soiling the
floor of the synagogue.[2] Possibly they carried another
pair of shoes with them, which they substituted for the
others, or wore the other pair under the *holzschue*, as they
were named.[3]

On the subject of shoes more will be said anon, but
we will pass to some other indications that the Jews
favoured no particular fashions of their own in dress.
In the East, Jewesses dyed their eyebrows and hands after
the ordinary Oriental manner,[4] but they did not carry
the custom with them to Europe. In Europe, in the
eighteenth century, Jewish men powdered their hair[5] —
a thoroughly European habit, which was quite unknown
to the Jews of the East.

Amulets, again, were and are a common ornament among

---

[1] *J. Peah*, viii. 7; *B. Sabbath*, 113 a.

[2] Jews were always very punctilious about wearing decent shoes. ' It is
a disgrace for a student to walk in the streets with soiled boots' (*T. B.
Sabbath*, 114 a). Further, among the classes estranged from heaven are
' the man who has no wife and the man who wears no shoes' (ibid. 113 b).
The last remark was probably directed against the Essenes. ' A man shall
sell the beams of his roof to get money for buying shoes' (ibid. 129 a). It
may easily be conceived how deeply aggrieved the Jews were in those
Moslem lands in which they were forced to walk bare-footed whenever they
quitted the mellah or Jewish quarter.

[3] Güdemann, iii. 267. Cf. p. 18 above.

[4] *Responsa* of Geonim; Müller, *Mafteach*, p. 22, where the dyeing was only
forbidden on the Sabbath.

[5] Aryeh b. Chayim, שו"ת פני אריה 6.

the Jews of the Orient, where such trinkets were always popular with the general population.[1] In Europe, however, amulets, though not altogether unknown,[2] were so antipathetic to Jewish sentiment that in the eighteenth century a serious conflict arose out of the attempt to acclimatize a superstitious species of amulets and talismans in the European Jewries.[3] Amulets, in the form of inscriptions on the walls and doors for the protection of mothers and their new-born babes, were universal in the middle ages, and the inroad of mysticism into Jewish thought was responsible for strengthening if not creating a similar superstition among the Jews.[4] On the other hand, Abraham Ibn Ezra, who boldly maintained a sceptical attitude towards demons and spirits in the twelfth century, was one of the first medieval theologians of church or synagogue to denounce the popular belief in the ubiquity of minor representatives of the supernatural.

---

[1] Müller, *Mafteach*, p. 49.

[2] Cf. e.g. Solomon Luria, *Responsa*, 47.

[3] Graetz, *History* (Eng. Trans.), V. ch. vii.

[4] R. Judah Chassid, who, at the end of the twelfth and the beginning of the thirteenth century, was responsible not only for a splendid outburst of spirituality, but also for a deplorable accretion of these superstitions, was in the latter direction entirely opposed to the spirit of contemporary Judaism. See S. Schechter, *Studies in Judaism*, pp. 350 seq. and the references there given. Cf. Löw, *Lebensalter*, p. 77.

CHAPTER XVI

THE JEWISH BADGE

THE close alliance between Jewish and general costume in the middle ages is perhaps seen most clearly in the exaggerations of fashion which reached their climax in Italy at the beginning of the fourteenth century. It will be unnecessary to enter into much detail here with regard to the sumptuary laws on the subject of extravagance in dress, for incidental allusions have been already made to several such attempts to check the ruinous excess which the Italian States vainly sought to suppress with a strong hand. Jewish moralists and preachers shouted themselves hoarse in exhortations towards greater moderation.[1] 'Jews should don humble raiment and not flaunt coloured robes,' was already a Jewish maxim in the thirteenth century. 'Even on Sabbaths, when they may dress better, they should only wear simple dresses of camelot.' Linen might be worn close to the skin only on Sabbaths, on all other days a thick woollen garment was put undermost. This form of self-denial, when it took a moral form, did somewhat hamper the Jews from adopting national costumes, but it cannot be attributed to their sensitiveness as a fault that Jewish

---

[1] Cf. Güdemann, ii. p. 215, and the quotations in the same volume, p. 330.

authorities denounced the prevalent fashion of young Italian men wearing short tunics which left the legs bare.   Jewish preachers applied the scriptural verse : —

> 'Let not the foot of pride come against me,
> And let not the hand of the wicked drive me away,'

to the feet of those who wore shoes which left the upper part of the foot uncovered.[1]   But — and this is the interesting point — all the efforts of Jewish moralists were powerless against the contagion of national example.   It is true that Jewish sumptuary laws against extravagance in dress are old and widespread.   In the Talmudical code, litigants in civil cases were expected to dress alike so as not to influence the judges by their appearance.[2]   In criminal cases the accused dressed in black and let his beard grow wild in token of anxiety.   Similarly, an excommunicated Jew wore black for thirty days.[3]   White, on the other hand, was the colour of joy.[4]   The wearing of gold embroidery

---

[1] Ps. xxxvi. 11.   The second part of the verse was held by many to forbid the wearing of gloves during prayer.   The famous Jewish preacher, known as the 'Dubno Maggid,' to whom all good Jewish clerical stories are freely attributed, preaching on Ps. xxiv. on the verses 'Who shall ascend unto the hill of the Lord? . . . He that hath clean hands and a pure heart,' wittily remarked that this does not offer salvation as the reward of wearing gloves on one's hand or displaying a clean shirt over one's heart.   I greatly regret that space will not permit me to deal at greater length with the Jewish *Maggidim*.   Against appearing in public with unlaced shoes, see *Derech Eretz Rabba*, התיר מנעליו ויצא לחוץ הרי זה מגסי הרוח :.

[2] *T. J. Synhedrin*, iii. 9.   A similar instance of equality in dress was quoted p. 172 above.

[3] Cf. Josephus, *Antiq.* XIV. ix. 4.

[4] *T. B. Sabbath*, 114 a; *T. J. Rosh Hashana*, i. 3.   On the New Year and the Day of Atonement Jews wore white, originally as a sign of joy, but later on the custom came to be associated with the white shrouds worn by the dead.   Yet in olden times some Jews wore *coloured* shrouds (cf. first reference).

was regarded as a token of pride.¹ Throughout the middle
ages, this objection to gold trimmings continued, and plain,
modest black was the universal colour of the Jews, so far
as they had a favourite colour at all.² The Jews of all
countries wore black, in Spain, Germany, and Italy the
phenomenon was equally marked.³ Black being the colour
of grief, the Jews — 'mourners of Zion,' as they were called
— were no doubt strengthened in their predilection for black
on the score of modesty, by its applicability to their persecuted state.⁴ But, here again, it is obvious that the use
of black was not an anti-national choice, for in the Orient,
where black is antagonistic to the national sentiment, the
Jews avoided dark colours as scrupulously as they strove
to wear them in Europe.⁵ Unfortunately, as we shall see,
Jews were forced by many Mohammedan rulers to wear
black even against their inclination.

Luxury in dress, to return to my point, was not restricted
to the Jews of any one land. Often we find Jewish ostentation put forward as a ground for repression by the State.
The English chroniclers, in explanation of the frequent riots
against the Jews, were much struck by the display which
the Jews made of their wealth.⁶ Jews themselves at-

¹ *T. J. Yoma*, vii. 3.

² קו היישר § 82; Berliner, *Inn. Leben*, pp. 36, 37.

³ Cf. the strong insistence on the exclusive use of black in the *tekanoth*
published in Mantua in 1644.

⁴ In the mourning for Jerusalem, Jews were allowed by the Talmud to
wear black shoes (*Baba Kamma*, 59 b), though these were usually avoided as
a distinctively Roman custom. (Jews, however, borrowed from the Romans
the superstition that it was unlucky to put on the left boot first.) In the
middle ages there was a sect of Jews who continued to wear black as a
deliberate sign of mourning. Cf. Benjamin of Tudela (ed. Asher), i. p. 113.

⁵ Cf. the letter of Isaac Zarfati to the Jews of Germany, cited Berliner, op.
cit. p. 37.

⁶ J. Jacobs, *Angevin England*, pp. 339, 385.

tempted to curb their own ostentation from motives of prudence as well as of modesty. The two arguments are frequently combined. ' Luxury in dress must be avoided, for it rouses envy against us and is a mark of pride.'[1] This was written in Germany, and similar remarks occur in many Jewish books.[2]

But, strange to tell, the Jews excited no such envy in Italy, the home and fount of extravagance in the middle ages. Here the Jews imitated the national failing in a way which indicates how little the Jews really favoured a voluntary distinctiveness in their attire. If we can believe the Italian Jewish satirists of the fourteenth century, Italian Jews and Jewesses did not fall in the least behind their Christian brothers and sisters of Florence and the other republics. Sumptuary laws against extravagance were frequently enacted by the Italian governments, and the Jewish authorities were equally vigorous in attempting to restrain the ever-growing vitiation of taste. Severe repressive regulations were made over and over again, and, in the utmost detail, male and female alike were admonished what they might wear and what they must discard. In some cases these regulations were published on large posters and affixed to the walls of the synagogue.[3] These attempted to define the colour and style of male and

---

[1] R. Chanoch Henoch's ראשית בכורים (seventeenth century). Cf. Güdemann, *Quellenschriften*, p. 300.

[2] Cf. e.g. the Italian Jewish *tekanoth* quoted in the *Graetz Jubelschrift*, p. 58. These tekanoth date from the year 1416. A similarly powerful attack on luxury in dress emanates from Portugal in 1415. See Alami's אגרת מוסר, ed. Jellinek, p. 27.

[3] It is obvious that this is the case with a series of stringent laws printed in Mantua in 1644. This is printed on one side only. A copy of this poster is in the library of the British Museum.

female attire; the breadth of the veils; the number of jewels, 'precious or imitation,' that might be displayed; how necklets must be worn. 'Necklets or chains may be wound twice round the neck and not more, and the remainder must be well tucked inside the dress so as to be invisible. . . . Earrings may be worn with pearls, but not with precious gems. . . . No woman may wear more than three rings, the wedding ring included. . . . Brides, in their homes, may dress as they please.'[1] The penalty for infringement in this instance was : a male offender was ineligible to be 'called to the Law,' a female offender was to be denounced by name in all synagogues, once a month, until she yielded to the communal regulation and promised not to offend again. That such laws were ineffectual need hardly be said. The women obeyed them in letter but not in spirit, and the greater the details into which the *tekanoth* entered, the easier it became to evade them by inventing slight variations in fashion.[2] The sumptuary laws of all lands and peoples in all ages have invariably failed in their well-meant but unattainable objects.

So far, then, as the Jews were allowed a free choice, their costumes did not much differ from those of ordinary men and women. But at the beginning of the thirteenth century there dawned on the Jews of Europe a new era, dark with degradation and misery. The Church resolved

---

[1] It is very interesting to notice that in this code (Mantua, 1644) a special exception is made in favour of the Jewish physician, Benjamin Portaleone, who was allowed to dress as he liked so long as he avoided gold and silver jewellery. The exception is, however, quite in keeping with Jewish ideas. The *Kolbo* e.g. exempts Jews in official positions from the duty of not wearing garments considered to be emblems of non-Jewish religions. This relaxation was granted to save the officials from ridicule and degradation.

[2] That this was a common feminine device may be seen from the remark in the Metz regulations (*Annuaire d. Études Juives*, i. p. 98).

in 1215 that thenceforward Jews and Mohammedans must be marked off from their fellows by a badge prominently fastened to their outermost garment. The exact motive for inflicting this distressful stigma cannot be discovered, but, as the ostensible reason, Innocent III advanced the argument that the measure was imperative if intermarriage or concubinage was to be prevented between Christians and non-believers.[1] This desire to inhibit concubinage and perhaps intermarriage is repeated in many subsequent bulls, and may be regarded as the official justification of the badge which Jews were doomed to wear for several pitiful centuries. An attempt was indeed made to show that Moses had already commanded the Jews to wear a distinctive mark on their garments, but this application of the law of the fringes [2] to the law of the badge was an insult added to injury.

Clear and emphatic in its demand that the Jews must wear badges, the Lateran Council nevertheless avoided details. It left the definition of the size, colour, and character of the degrading mark to the taste of local governors and states. Rarely, the Jews themselves were left to their own devices, and were allowed to choose their own badges.[3] The shape

---

[1] 'Contingit interdum quod per errorem Christiani Iudaeorum seu Saracenorum et Iudaei seu Saraceni Christianorum mulieribus commisceantur. Ne igitur tam damnatae commixtionis excessus per velamentum erroris huiusmodi excusationis ulterius possint habere diffugium, statuimus ut tales utriusque sexus in omni Christianorum provincia, et omni tempore qualitate habitus publici ab aliis populis distinguantur' (Labbe, *Sacrosancta concilia ad regiam editionem exacta*, xiii. col. 1003 and 1006). Cf. the bull of Pope Alexander IV, in 1257; see Ulysse Robert's *Les Signes d'Infamie au Moyen Age* (ed. 1891), p. 8. This last-named book is an admirable collection of facts on the whole subject of badges and other medieval 'signs of infamy.'

[2] Numbers xv. 38.

[3] Scheid, *Joselmann de Rosheim* (in the *Revue des Études Juives*, xiii. 67 and 70). Cf. p. 299 below.

was by no means uniform, but the circular mark was undoubtedly the most usual. It is unnecessary to seek any deep significance in the choice of the circular form of badge. Some have seen in it a representation of a *coin*, in allusion to the financial pursuits of the Jews or to the thirty pieces received by Judas Iscariot as the price of his betrayal. Others have discerned in it the form of the Host, an emblem of Christianity which the Jews refused to accept, but which they were now forced to wear over their hearts. Yet a third explanation is worthy of mention. The badge was itself perhaps derived by Innocent III from the Mohammedans. If so, the circle or *full moon* would be an antithesis to the *Crescent* of Islam.[1]

Be this as it may, the circular form of badge, though the most common, was not the only one in use. Changes were effected in one and the same country, and it does not seem that the English design, imitative of the *two tables* of stone, was introduced into this country earlier than 1275. These tablets were apparently worn on the hem of the outer garment. On the other hand a badge, two inches wide and four inches long, was imposed on English Jews in 1222.[2] Similarly a modification was made in England with regard to the colour. Originally[3] the badge was white, but Edward I altered this to yellow and fixed seven as the age at which the badge became compulsory.[4] It does not appear that the English Jews were forced to wear distinctive garments as well as the badge, but in Austria in

---

[1] P. Cassel, in Ersch und Grüber, II. xxvii. p. 75.

[2] Tovey, *Anglia Iudaica*, p. 82.

[3] Tovey, p. 205.

[4] The Close Rolls of Edward I (10 Ed. I m. 8 d.) contains an entry entitled *Quod Iudeae portent tabulas sicut et Iudei*. Cf. B. L. Abrahams in *Jewish Quarterly Review*, viii. 360.

the thirteenth, and in Germany in the fourteenth and fifteenth centuries, the Jews were compelled to use a special hat, known as the 'Judenhut.' It was pointed at the top, and the brim was often twisted into the shape of a pair of horns.[1] Red was the favourite colour. It is not clear whether the Jews of Germany wore this hideous hat as a substitute for the circular wheel or in addition to it.[2] Other kings preferred other colours, thus in 1713 Frederick William imposed a green hat on the Jews of his realm.[3] It is certain that the wheel-badge was usual in Germany in the fifteenth century, the predominant colour being yellow or saffron. Jews fixed it on their breast, while Jewesses were obliged to bear two blue stripes on their veils or cloaks.[4] The size of the wheel varied, sometimes it was fixed at an inch in diameter, sometimes it was as big as a florin, sometimes it resembled a crown, sometimes it was as much as 100 millimetres across. Occasionally the letter S (= *signum*) appeared in the yellow circle. In Switzerland, in 1435, the badge took the form of a piece of red cloth, shaped like a pointed hat;[5] in 1508 it had become a wheel fixed on the back. In Crete, the obnoxious circular sign was also inscribed on the doors of houses occupied by Jews.[6]

---

[1] Weiss, *Kostümkunde*, p. 147.   [2] Cf. U. Robert, p. 91.
[3] Schudt, *Merkwürdigkeiten*, i. 5.
[4] These words occur in the bull dated 1452 (quoted by Schudt, vi. 244, 245): — 'Hinc nos prout in aliis nationis locis ordinavimus, praesentium tenore declaramus signum huiusmodi esse debere circulum de croceis filis visibiliter consutum, cuius diameter communis hominis digito minor non sit, ante pectus quoad masculos in veste extrinseca, ita quod omnium eos intuentium oculis appareat; et duae rigae blavei coloris in peplo mulierum in signum differentiae a Christianis discernantur.'
[5] Ulrich, *Sammlung jüdischer Geschichten in der Schweiz*, p. 463. Cf. Robert, op. cit. p. 100.
[6] Sathas, Ἑλληνικὰ ἀνέκδοτα, p. xxvi.

France may claim the honour of inventing the circular badge, which was already known in Paris in 1208.[1] In Marseilles, indeed, the Jews were permitted an alternative; they might wear either a yellow *calotte* or head-dress, or if they preferred they might adopt the wheel.[2] Here, too, the age at which the badge must be borne was fixed at seven years. In general, the rule in France was that Jew and Jewess alike wore the circular mark, though in the case of the women it was often replaced by a veil. Some variation occurs in the age at which Jews began to wear the badge. In Marseilles the age was seven, in Arles (1234) thirteen for boys and twelve for girls,[3] in Avignon the age was raised (in 1326) for boys to fourteen. In France the wheel was worn mostly on the breast, or at least above the waist; but sometimes a second circle was added, to be placed on the back, *retro in dorso*. Sometimes it was placed on the hat, or on the girdle; it might be pinned or sewn on to the garment which it disfigured. In other instances the badge was worn on the left shoulder.[4] As to the material used, no prescription existed, but the bull of Gregory IX (1233) probably represents the usual custom. If this be so, the badge must have been made of felt or cloth, and more rarely of cord, leather, or silk. In France, as elsewhere, the common colour of the badge was yellow; but occasionally the wheel was parti-coloured, white and red.

---

[1] Robert, p. 11.

[2] 'Statuimus quod omnes Iudaei a septem annis portent vel deferant calotam croceam, vel, si noluerint, portent in pectore unam rotam.' For references on the badge in France, see Robert, op. cit. pp. 14 seq. This charming booklet is naturally fullest in its treatment of the badges worn by the French Jews.

[3] This seems to have been adopted from Jewish custom, for these are the ages at which the *legal minority* ceases in Rabbinical law.

[4] Robert, p. 49.

More rarely still the circular mark was green. The same variations in size which were indicated above in the case of Germany and Austria occur in the French badges,[1] but on the whole the French badges were rather smaller than the German. It must be stated, to the honour of the Church, that though the clergy were responsible for the infliction of the badge, the secular authorities acted on their own initiative when they enforced the canonical regulation by heavy fines and penalties. Any informer received as a reward the garment from which the Jew had dared to omit the distinguishing mark.[2] In Nice, the town council and the informer divided the spoils between them. The threat of corporal punishment and the menaces of death seem, however, to have usually resolved themselves into monetary fines. Probably the Jews had to buy the badges from the public authorities, and Philippe le Bel devised the sale of badges as a fresh source of income for the royal exchequer.

It is unnecessary to enter into details with regard to the Jews of Italy and Spain. Here the same general facts present themselves; the motive and the manner in which the object was attained were identical with the motive and its execution in the rest of Europe.[3] The chief difference lay in this — that in Spain, Italy, and southern France the Jews were able to resist the infliction of the badge with more or less success for a considerable period.[4] Moreover,

---

[1] Robert, p. 27.

[2] 'Et si quis Iudaeus postmodum sine praedicto signo in publico inventus fuerit, inventori vestis superior concedatur.' Op. cit. p. 32.

[3] Innocent IV in his bull to Ferdinand III of Castile says : — 'Licet in sacro generali concilio provida fuerit deliberatione statutum ut Iudaei a Christianis habitu distinguantur, ne illorum isti vel istorum illi mulieribus possint dampnabiliter commisceri.'

[4] Graetz, *History of Jews* (Eng. Trans.), III. ch. iv.

many Jews in these more favoured lands were able to buy personal exemptions. The same remark applies to other countries, but the exemptions were most numerous in Spain and Italy. In Spain, moreover, Jews enjoyed in general a privilege only exceptionally granted elsewhere. They were permitted to discard the badge on their journeys. It is interesting to notice that when Bonami, son of Joce, settled in France after his expulsion from England in 1290, Philippe le Bel exempted him from the duty of wearing the badge, and temporarily allowed Bonami's son a similar licence.[1]

A few words must be added before this tale of infamy can be said to be complete. The previous narrative has dealt exclusively with Christian countries. How stood the matter in realms where Islam held sway over men's conduct? The answer is saddening. For, though they themselves were fellow-sufferers with the Jews in Spain, the Moslems felt little fellow-feeling for the Jew in the East and in the Levant. There was hardly a Mohammedan land in which the Jews were not compelled to live in a separate quarter and adopt some distinctiveness in dress. The difference was that the brand took a negative form where the Crescent ruled, and a positive one where the Cross prevailed. In other words, under Islam the Jews were forbidden to wear certain articles of dress, they were restricted in their choice of colours, they were forced to dress in black or yellow, and to appear bare-footed, as was pointed out above, but they were not compelled to bear on their breasts a peculiar badge of shame. This is sufficiently curious if the badge was originally a Moham-

[1] Langlois, *Formulaires et lettres du XIIᵉ, du XIIIᵉ, et du XIVᵉ siècle*, p. 18.

medan invention. The prohibition of colour was less irksome to the Jews, seeing that they themselves were in Europe at least inclined to regard bright colours with moral aversion. They wore small, black, brimless caps, being often forbidden the use of the red fez.[1] To don the turban became equivalent with the Jews of Turkey for conversion to Islam. Green, the Moslem colour *par excellence*, was avoided by Jews as well as prohibited. Where the turban was worn by Jews, it was mostly black and not coloured; occasionally, as in Tripoli, a parti-coloured turban marked the Jew. These restrictions, however, were not early, nor were they very stringently enforced. Hence the decay of taste and manners which occurred among the Jews of Europe was by no means paralleled in the Orient. Oppression almost invariably prevailed, but as Moslems were affected equally with the Jews, the latter did not suffer by contrast so much as they did in Christian Europe.

The effects produced by this system of branding the Jews as a pariah class were as deplorable as they were inevitable. The Jew became the mark for the meanest of insults. ' Beaten, reviled, scorned, abused by every one, . . . he was made to swallow abuse like water, he was not allowed to take offence at anything.'[2] He lost his old refinements. Of old, no people had paid more attention to accuracy and polish in speech, to decency and cleanliness in dress, to self-respect in their manners and bearing. A quarter of a century before the fatal edict of Innocent III, a Hebrew poet with sad premonition used metaphorically,

---

[1] Cf. Lancelot Addison, *The Present State of the Jews* (1675), p. 10.

[2] Leroy-Beaulieu, *Israel Among the Nations*, p. 197. Cf. Graetz, *History of the Jews* (Eng. Trans.), III. ch. xv.

with regard to persecuted Israel, language which but a little later became literally true.

> Erst radiant the Bride adored
> On whom rich wedding gifts are poured;
> She weeps, sore wounded, overthrown,
> Exiled and outcast, shunned and lone.

> Laid all aside her garments fair,
> The pledges of a bond divine,
> A wandering beggar-woman's wear
> Is hers in lieu of raiment fine.

> Chaunted hath been in every land
> The beauty of her crown and zone;
> Now doomed, dethroned she maketh moan,
> Bemocked, — a byeword, — cursed, and banned.

> An airy, joyous step was hers
> Beneath Thy wing. But now she crawls
> Along and mourns her sons and errs
> At every step, and, worn out, falls.

> And yet to Thee she clingeth tight;
> Vain, vain to her man's mortal might
> Which in a breath to naught is hurled;
> Thy smile alone makes up her world.[1]

Later on, this figure of speech developed into a portrait. The bitter resentment of the Jews shows itself in a growing use of the figure of the Law, attired in mourning garb as a woe-begone maiden, to typify desolate Israel. Meir of Rothenburg, whose birth almost synchronized with the invention of the Jews' badge, makes a powerful use of the figure in his fierce and heart-rending dirge on ' The Burn-

[1] Jacobs, *Angevin England*, p. 81 (the translation is by Mr. Israel Zangwill). The initials form the acrostic ' Elchanan,' the author's name. (Cf. Zunz, *Synagogale Poesie*, 249.)

ing of the Law.' [1]   Addressing the sacred mantled scroll
he cries : —

> Ah! sweet 'twould be unto mine eyes, alway,
>   Waters of tears to pour,
> To sob and drench thy sacred robes, till they
>   Could hold no more.
>
> But lo! my tears are dried, when, fast outpoured,
>   They down my cheeks are shed;
> Scorched by the fire within: because thy Lord
>   Hath turned and sped.
>
> .   .   .   .
>
> In sack-cloth I will clothe, and sable band,
>   For well-beloved by me
> Were they whose lives were many as the sand,
>   The slain of thee.
>
> Gird on the sack-cloth of thy misery
>   For that devouring fire,
> Which went forth ravenous, degrading thee
>   To ruins dire.
>
> .   .   .   .
>
> Even as when thy Rock afflicted thee
>   He will assuage thy woe,
> And turn again the tribes' captivity
>   And raise the low.
>
> Yet shalt thou wear thy scarlet raiment choice,
>   And sound the timbrels high,
> And glad amid the dancers shall rejoice,
>   With joyful cry.
>
> My heart shall be uplifted on the day
>   Thy Rock shall be thy light,
> When he shall make thy gloom to pass away,
>   Thy darkness bright.[2]

[1] 'When I was in France,' says Meir (*Responsa*, ed. Mekitse Nirdamim, p. 8, § 28), 'we used to wear wheels on our garments, for this was decreed against the Jews then.' This remark implies that, outside France, Meir did not wear the badge. Some, he tells us, made the badge a part of the garment, others made it of leather and stitched it on.

[2] From Miss Nina Davis' translation in *Jewish Quarterly Review*, vol. viii.

In this manner, by idealizing their sorrows, and by an imaginative transference of their woes to the Law and to God, the Jews contrived to resist the immediate deterioration which the badge threatened. In two countries the Jews were able indefinitely to postpone the incidence of the papal decree. These were Italy and Spain, and this respite had a valuable effect in mitigating the violence of the blow which the edict of Innocent III dealt. In the latter country several causes promoted toleration. The Moors had made Andalusia the home of a civilization which knew no distinction of creed. The air of Spain was fresh with breezes of perpetual intersectarian friendliness. Christian monarchs like Alfonso the Wise imitated and excelled the majestic, broad-minded culture of Abdulrahman III. Moor, Jew, and Hidalgo lived together in Christian Toledo or Moslem Granada on terms of an equality and toleration unparalleled in medieval history. Hence the Jews of Spain succeeded in resisting the bull of Innocent III, and for some two centuries were comparatively free from the restrictions with which their European brethren were laden. The happier lot of the Jews in Spain did much to preserve the rest of their brethren from demoralization. The French or German Jew who bore his badge could still hold up his head when he thought of Cordova, Toledo, Barcelona, and Seville. He himself might be dejected and degraded, but the mention of Spain revived his hope, re-aroused his pride. Thus we do not find that the bearing of the badge produced its worst consequences until the beginning of the sixteenth century. In the fifteenth century the Jews of Spain were subjected to trials which betokened the coming end. The Inquisition was established in 1391, and this event was almost simultaneous with the weakening of the power of the Moors. To these two events must be added the union of the crowns of Aragon and Castile under one rule. By this circumstance the rivalry of the two kingdoms was ended, and the Jews could no longer find refuge alternately in each from the persecutions of the other. In 1492 the blow fell, and the expulsion of the Jews from Spain temporarily annihilated Jewish dignity and self-reliance. This bright star in the dark-clouded Jewish firmament was set in an eternal eclipse, and the Jewish horizon grew blacker everywhere. Soon the ghettos were built to hold the sorrow-stricken race, pointed at by the finger of scorn as well as of fate. The effects of Innocent III's badges were completed by Paul IV's ghettos, and from the combined injuries which it thus received in the three centuries nearest to the one in which we live, the Jewish character was disfigured by those superficial deformities from which it is now endeavouring to free itself.

CHAPTER XVII

PRIVATE AND COMMUNAL CHARITIES. THE RELIEF OF THE POOR

LANCELOT ADDISON, in his entertaining account of the Jews of Barbary,[1] is at some pains to dispel the belief prevalent at his time that 'the Jews have no beggars.' He attributes this error to the 'regular and commendable' methods by which the Jews supplied the needs of their poor and 'much concealed their poverty.' The medieval notion that all Hebrews were rich, possibly owes its present vitality to this same cause. Deep-rooted in the Jewish heart lay the sentiment that poverty had rights as well as disabilities, and the first of those rights demanded that the poor need not appeal for sympathy by exhibiting their sorrows. In this characteristic the Jew was never Oriental, but struck out an original line of his own. Like Coriolanus, he might have exclaimed, against an alleviative or fraternal service bought by exposure and publicity : —

> Let me o'erleap that custom; for I cannot
> Put on the gown, stand naked, and entreat them,
> For my wounds' sake, to give their suffrage : please you,
> That I may pass this doing.

[1] *The Present State of the Jews* (London, 1675; a second edition appeared in the following year), ch. xxv.

No argument in favour of checking pauperism was held to justify the policy of putting the poor to shame. 'Better give no alms at all, than give them in public,'[1] and even those who in the middle ages thought that alms-giving under any and all circumstances had a shade of merit, declared that they who gave publicly and with ostentation would never get farther than the outskirts of paradise.[2]

Delicacy in the manner of giving was traced directly to the Scriptures, and many tender rules for sparing the blushes of the poor were derived in the Rabbinical literature of early centuries and of the middle ages from the verse :[3] —

> Blessed is he that considereth the poor:
> The Lord will deliver him in the day of evil;.

the stress being laid on the duty of *considerateness*. Consideration for the poor was sometimes one of the motives for severe sumptuary laws as regards the dress of the rich. But one of the chief forms which this considerateness assumed was to discountenance begging from door to door.[4] Nor were the poor to be forced to come and draw tickets from an urn before obtaining relief. Where the system of ticket-relief prevailed, the Parnass, or President of the congregation, and not the recipient of help, had to extract the tickets.[5] It is true that in larger Jewish congregations street and door begging became common when, in place of freedom to reside in any part of the town, Jews were restricted to certain streets or quarters. Within the ghetto,

---

[1] *T. B. Chagiga*, 5 a.

[2] Midrash גו״ן,.Jellinek, *Beth Hamidrash*, iii. 123.

[3] Psalm xli. 1.

[4] Lancelot Addison notices this feature; cf. יוסף אומץ, § 547.

[5] Judah Minz (fol. 14 a) orders that this must be done in Treviso, where the custom was introduced להוציא פתקין מן הקלפי in order to discourage begging.

the Jews formed one large family, and house-to-house begging wore a different look. Moreover, publicity in the sense that Christians would observe the beggar's progress, was no longer probable in the sixteenth and later centuries. But before the ghetto age, and especially in smaller towns, it might almost be asserted that there were no Jewish beggars at all. The fact that the Jews formed distinct communities in the midst of contemptuously indifferent or actively hostile environments, caused them 'to draw nearer and closer to each other, and tended to soften and bridge over the differences of poverty and position.'[1] Hence in most Jewish communities before the thirteenth century, though the inroad of itinerant mendicants was a grievous burden on Jewish benevolence, the number of settled, resident beggars was very small. The production of this result entailed much expenditure of money and care, but the highest form of alms-giving was reached, in the Jewish view, by taking such measures as made the poor self-supporting and enabled them to live by their own exertions.[2]

The Talmud alludes to a regular class of professional mendicants who practised self-mutilation in order to attract

---

[1] C. G. Montefiore, ' Hebrew Charity,' in *Jewish Chronicle* (London), May, 1884.

[2] Maimonides (מתנות עניים, ch. vii.) thus arranges the ranks of the givers of charity, (1) He who helps the poor to sustain himself by giving a loan or taking him into business with him; (2) He who gives to the poor without knowing to whom he gives, while the recipient is also ignorant of the giver; (3) He who gives secretly, knowing the recipient, but the latter remaining ignorant as to his benefactor's name; (4) He who gives not knowing the recipient, but the recipient knows from whom he obtains relief; (5) He who gives (both knowing) before he is asked; (6) He who gives after he is asked; (7) He who gives inadequately but with a good grace; (8) He who gives with a bad grace.

the sympathetic notice of passers-by. Such beggars were regarded with contempt and aversion, but this class no longer existed in the middle ages.[1] The system of house-to-house begging was occasionally favoured by wealthier Jews, but the ordinary middle class were opposed to it and their view carried the day.[2] In the seventeenth century the system was revived in another form, as we shall soon see, and, besides this, on Fridays and the eves of festivals, the Jewish poor went about from house to house gathering alms. In modern Jewish life this system became a full-blown abuse, and irrepressible crowds of pushing beggars assembled round the synagogue doors. But this grew out of the poverty which three centuries of ghetto-life produced. In the middle ages, life was simpler and its needs fewer, and men more enduring. Among the medieval Jews the public solicitation of alms was extremely rare.

Ostentatious pauperism was undoubtedly diminished by the complete measures adopted for relieving orphans and widows from want. The orphans were married and the widows pensioned. The provision of dowries for poor girls, even when their fathers were still living, was, and continues, a strong feature of Jewish benevolence. This was a religious duty, and as the bestowal of contributions to these dowries hardly fell within the category of alms-giving, so the acceptance of the dowries was not quite considered to be alms-receiving. It cannot be too strongly emphasized that

---

[1] The number of Jewish cripples and confirmed invalids cannot have been great, for we occasionally find in medieval records individuals described by such titles as ' Moses the invalid ' (המיוסר), or 'Samuel the Cripple.' (*Das Judenschreinbuch*, etc., published by the ' Historische Commission für Geschichte der Juden,' 1888, pp. 21 and 32.) These epithets would hardly have been *distinctive* had there been many to whom they would be applicable.

[2] Cf. Shulchan Aruch, יורה דעה, 250, § 5.

this relation between giver and taker was in itself a strong preventive to pauperism in the modern sense. But it is undeniable that it led to that insolence in the Jewish beggar which, growing out of the theory that the recipient of the gift was enabling the donor to perform a religious duty, and was, in a sense, the benefactor of the donor, made the *schnorrer*, or beggar, come to be a most persistent and troublesome figure in modern Jewish society.

The whole system of Jewish poor-relief was radically affected by the increase of travelling mendicants, whose numbers were recruited from the wholesale expatriations which followed in the wake of the Crusades. In the middle ages we find, for instance, an important change in habit. For while in the Talmudic period the distribution of relief in kind was a regular feature of Jewish charity, in the middle ages this was no longer a universal method of supplying the needs of the poor. The *tamchui* or daily distribution of food continued in many congregations,[1] but it was gradually superseded by three other methods, (*a*) the reception of poor travellers in the homes of the rich, (*b*) the provision for vagrants in communal hostelries or Inns, and (*c*) the benevolent activity of special societies formed for the succour and entertainment of the resident poor and of strangers. The relief in kind undoubtedly coexisted side by side with these arrangements. A favourite form of Jewish charity in the middle ages was the purchase of food to be retailed to the poor at cost price in times of scarcity.[2]

---

[1] 'Give of all thy food a portion to God. Let God's portion be the best, and give it to the poor' (*Ethical Will* of Eleazar ben Isaac of Worms, eleventh century). A similar sentiment occurs in the Will of Sabbatai Hurwitz: 'If a beggar comes to you, give him what you can, and do not put him to shame, for God stands at his right hand.' In the time of Maimonides the relief in kind had ceased to be general. [2] *Sefer Chassidim*, § 949.

Again, we read of a Jewish butcher in Prague who weighed his children three times a year and gave their weight in meat to the poor.[1] Another characteristic instance is furnished by an epitaph which is worth re-quoting for the insight it gives into the life of the Jewess. This particular lady lived during the Thirty Years' War, and died in 1628.[2] 'She supplied scholars with Bibles, and the plundered with prayer-books, she ran like a bird to weddings, and frequently asked the poor to dine with her in her own home; she clothed the naked, herself preparing hundreds of shirts for distribution among the poor.' Such personal efforts on behalf of the poor were always common with Jews; there was at least sentimental appropriateness in the long-continued rule that on fast-days food was to be distributed to the poor in provision for the evening meal.[3] But the daily distribution of food known as the *tamchui* gave way before other methods of poor relief.[4] In some forms relief in kind, however, remained universal in Jewish life. Such expensive but necessary luxuries as the *matsoth* or unleavened bread used on Passover, and the wine needed for various ceremonial rites, seem to have been regularly supplied to the poor. A similar remark applies to the

[1] Rabbinical parallels to this act are not wanting. The mother of Doeg ben Joseph weighed her child every day and distributed his increased weight in gold to the poor (*Echa Rabba*, ch. i.). Of a somewhat different form was the equally generous conduct of R. Tanchum. Whenever he purchased a pound of meat for his own use, he bought a second pound for the poor (Mid. ביום השמיני, Jellinek, iv. 138).

[2] Cf. Montefiore, loc. cit.

[3] Shulchan Aruch, *Yore Deah*, cclvi. § 2.

[4] The transition may be noted in such regulations as are contained in the Shulchan Aruch, יורה דעה 256, § 1, where the term *tamchui* is applied not only to contributions of food, such as bread or fruits, but also to *gifts of money*. The word *tamchui* thus came to mean the casual relief, as distinguished from the *kupah* or regular relief.

feast of Esther. But in this case, every Jew sent gifts of food and dainties to every other Jew, and the poor merely received a larger share of the affectionate attentions which fell to the lot of all. So thorough was the solidarity of Jewish social life, that it is impossible to draw a clear line between a friendly interchange of services and what we now should describe as deeds of charity.

None of the medieval methods of poor-relief adopted by the Jews were entirely unknown to the Talmud. In the Bible the system of poor-relief was intimately connected with the agricultural character of the national occupations. But in the Talmud, charity was not only the highest of virtues, it was also the broadest. Only one other virtue competed with it, and that was the study of the Law, which was higher only in this sense, that it included *all* virtues. No social code of morals ever took a wider view of the all-pervading claims of charity than the Talmud upholds on every page. The Talmud distinguished between *alms*, which meant a gift of money or property, and the *charity of love*, which meant a gift of one's self. In this higher sense, the Talmudic doctors included under the head of charity kindliness and fraternal love in all the social relations of life, in hospitality to the living and generosity to the dead, in visiting and nursing the sick, in words and works of mercy, in attendance at weddings.[1] This being the case,

---

[1] The following passage from the Mishnah (Peah, i.) occurs in the every-day morning service of the synagogue (*Authorized Hebrew Prayer-book*, p. 5) : — 'These are the things, the fruits of which a man enjoys in this world, while the stock remains for him for the world to come : viz. honouring father and mother, the practice of charity, timely attendance at the house of study morning and evening, hospitality to wayfarers, visiting the sick, dowering the bride, attending the dead to the grave, devotion in prayer, and making peace between man and his fellow; but the study of the Law is equal to them all.'

it may safely be said that all the most humane methods of poor-relief ever devised by the wit of man, may be found developed or at least adumbrated in the Talmud. In the middle ages the Jews, however, gave more prominence to some of these methods than they did to others.

For instance, the relief of travellers was a more pressing question in the twelfth century than in the fourth or fifth. In the Talmud, reference is made to public inns at which no money was taken. But the communal Inn[1] became a most necessary institution after the Crusading era, when the number of homeless Jewish poor greatly increased. Every Jewish congregation made arrangements of some kind for the lodging and feeding of poor or sick travellers. Sometimes the ordinary Jewish inn-keepers were paid from the communal funds, and tramps or wandering mendicants were freely entertained on the ground floor, while the more respectable, paying guests occupied the upper storey of the Inn. Sometimes, again, the poor traveller was lodged with a private family, in which case the latter offered gratuitous hospitality or received a fee from the communal revenues. This admission of the poor to the ordinary Jewish family life gave point to the metaphor which described the dining-table as the 'Altar of God.' Most marked change of all, however, was the growth of charitable associations. Certain difficulties were experienced with regard to those charitable duties which were felt to be incumbent on individuals and yet were beyond the means of individuals. Hence voluntary societies were created to meet these cases, which grew in number and variety as the conditions of life became more complex. This subject, however, must be deferred for a while, and a few words must be written on the methods

[1] Cf. above, p. 74; and see *T. B. Sota*, 10 a.

adopted for raising the *kupah* or general relief funds in various Jewish congregations in the middle ages.

The popular device for raising funds was the periodical assessment of the various members of the congregation by officials appointed as Charity Overseers. The duty was not usually entrusted to a single individual, but occasionally this was the case.[1] A dual directorate was mostly held desirable for *granting* relief. The distribution of charitable funds was always regarded by Jews as more onerous than the collection.[2] The administrators of poor-relief sometimes were the objects of much abuse from the poor,[3] but on the whole the overseers were men of the highest reputation and enjoyed the full confidence of their brethren. No enforced audit of their accounts was exacted, but they were expected in the sixteenth century to make a voluntary statement and to present a balance sheet.[4]

The total sum needed was approximately fixed by the treasurers, and each member contributed according to his reputed means. The collections for the *kupah* were made either weekly, monthly, or thrice a year. No one escaped from this duty,[5] even women and children contributed, though it was unlawful to accept large sums from them. The poor themselves were taxed for the relief of their own class, for charity was a universal duty which none must evade. While, however, the assessors were warned against demanding too much from willing but

---

[1] In the *Or Zarua*, i. p. 13, the author says: 'It is customary now to appoint only one treasurer, but I think that there should be two.' In the fifteenth century these officials were not identical with the treasurers of the ordinary communal funds. (Maharil, חול המועד ה"ח beginning.)

[2] *T. B. Sabbath*, 118 a.   [3] Maharil, ibid.

[4] *T. B. Baba Bathra*, 9 a; Shulchan Aruch יורה דעה 257, 2.

[5] *Kolbo*, 92 d.

straitened donors, they were armed with strong powers
against members who sought to underrate their own capacity
to give.   The assessors were licensed to make distraint on
the recalcitrant's property and to forcibly seize the amount
which, it was estimated, he ought to subscribe.[1]   It sometimes occurred that the civil authorities expressly conferred
on the Jews this right to distrain the goods of members of
the Jewish community who refused to share the duty of
providing for their poor.[2]

Side by side with the compulsory system, voluntary
methods of contributing flourished luxuriantly.   Bridging
over the two systems were the regular fines inflicted for
offences against communal *tekanoth* or regulations, such
fines being often appropriated to purposes of charity.[3]
Further, charitable offerings which were only partially
voluntary in essence though completely voluntary in form,
were the donations publicly announced in synagogue on
special occasions.

A very early instance of this form of benevolence has
lately been published by Dr. Neubauer.[4]   The place was

---

[1] For forcible charity see, אור זרוע i. p. 13; compare Shulchan Aruch,
Yore Deah, ch. 248. The various methods of estimating the sum to be
contributed by each individual Jew are thus summarized by R. Solomon
ben Adret (cf. *Beth Joseph* to *Tur Yore Deah*, § 250 end) : 'The amount of
a man's gifts must be proportionate to his means.   In some places, however,
each man gives as much as he pleases, in others he contributes in the same
proportion as he contributes to the royal taxes, but most blessed of all is he
who gives to the utmost of his power.'

[2] In Jan. 1759 such a power was granted to the Jews of Amsterdam (see
the interesting sheet of which a copy is preserved in the British Museum,
1982, b. 1).

[3] Cf. אור זרוע, i. p. 17 (§ 26).

[4] *Medieval Jewish Chronicles*, ii. p. 128. The ספר יוחסין from which this
is cited was written in 1055, in rhymed prose. It is interesting to note that
though the author describes in details those who were present in synagogue,

Kahira, the capital of Egypt, the occasion was the Day of Atonement. R. Paltiel was 'called to the Law' in synagogue. All the assembled congregation rose in his honour, but he bade all but the children to remain seated, threatening that otherwise he would not accept the office. When his reading was finished, he offered ' 5000 dinars, good, sound, full-weighted.' The sum he distributed as follows : 1000 for the school, 1000 for the poor of Jerusalem, 1000 for the college in Babylon, 1000 to various congregations for the general purposes of poor-relief, 1000 in honour of the law to purchase oils. Next morning he rose early to fulfil his promises, for he ever was quick to perform his word lest his second thoughts should prove less generous. He summoned a band of riders on horses and mules, and sent them with the caravan unto the desert, laden with the gold that he had vowed. At his death, his son distributed 20,000 drachmae on similar benevolent objects.[1]

Every Jew subscribed to the poor-box when he married, or on any occasion of joy, as well as on sadder anniversaries.[2] Such donations were so much a matter of rule, that they could hardly be termed voluntary, except in so far as the amount was concerned. Regular collections were made in synagogue on Purim, and on ordinary weekdays the prayers were interrupted in order to collect donations.[3] Many Jews made it a regular practice to contribute to the poor-box every morning before leaving the

naming the 'spiritual and lay heads, young men and old, lads, boys, infants and children,' the *women* are not mentioned. Evidently they were not present.

[1] Op. cit. p. 130.

[2] Gifts to poor accompanied the prayers for the dead (הזכרת נשמות). See אור זרוע, loc. cit.; cf. רוקח, § 217.

[3] *Machzor Vitry*, p. 7.

synagogue.   Similarly, private collections were made in the home on occasion of all family gatherings and festivities.[1]

Special taxes were sometimes apportioned to the cause of poor-relief, or the fines which accrued from the extravagant infringement of sumptuary laws were, in a spirit of poetical justice, reserved for the entertainment of the poor.   Of a more voluntary nature were the gifts bestowed on the synagogue as permanent funds for charitable uses. This would take various forms.   The donor might give a large sum of which only the interest was to be spent.[2]   Or he would buy a scroll of the Law and deposit it in the synagogue.   This scroll would be sold from time to time, still remaining the possession of the synagogue, but the new owner's name would be inscribed on it.   The sum so obtained would be used for the poor.[3]   Funds also accumulated from legacies, for rarely would a wealthy Jew die without bequeathing a considerable sum to the synagogue funds.

Even more interesting was a species of self-taxation, to which some medieval Jews resorted.   Thus a fifteenth-century Jew,[4] who was no ascetic, but was fond of a good dinner and a glass of wine, taxed his own pleasures, and gave a gold piece in charity for every extra glass of wine he drank.   This he also did at every opportunity, be the occasion 'the enjoyment of a tasteful dish, or a good bargain, or the birth of a child, or the marrying of a daughter.'   If he omitted reading the Sabbath Scriptural

---

[1] Communal regulations later on compelled such collections at all סעודות מצוה
(cf. e.g. תקנות הקהלה, Amsterdam, 1708, § 70).

[2] אור זרוע, i. p. 18, § 30.   [3] Cf. Lancelot Addison, p. 214.

[4] Cf. S. Schechter, *Studies in Judaism*, p. 167.

lesson thrice, he fined himself two gold pieces; if he failed to partake of three meals on the Sabbath, he paid half a gold piece. So with everything he bought, he 'salted his wealth with charity,' and if he indulged in an expensive garment the poor rejoiced with him.

The most important fact about this same fifteenth-century Jew's private charities, is the scrupulous care with which he set aside a *tithe* of his income for distribution to the poor. His own words on the subject are worth reproducing:[1] —

'I shall also, between New Year and the Day of Atonement in each year, calculate my profits during the past year and (after deducting expenses) give a tithe thereof to the poor. Should I be unable to make an accurate calculation, then I will give approximately. This tithe I shall put aside, together with the other money for a religious (charitable) purpose, to dispose of it as I shall deem best. I also propose to have the liberty of employing the money in any profitable speculation with a view of augmenting it (for the use of the poor). But all I have written above I shall not hold myself guilty if I transgress, if such transgression be the result of forgetfulness; but in order to guard against it, I shall read this through weekly.'

It will be seen that this benevolent individual must have devoted a large portion of his income to charitable purposes. The Talmud fixed the outside limit to which a generous man might go at one-fifth of his property.[2] As, however, the Talmud defines this limit with the desire of protecting the donor against his own excessive generosity, and implies that he who gives more than a fifth may impoverish himself,[3] there may have been many who exceeded these prescribed bounds, adequate though they were. The average Jew was always expected to give in all one tithe of his income.[4]

---

[1] S. Schechter, loc. cit. [2] *T. B. Kethuboth*, 50 a.

[3] On the other hand, a later Jewish moralist finely says: 'No man ever became poor through giving too much in charity' (Joel Shamariah's *Ethical Will*).

[4] Maimonides, מתנות עניים, vii, § 5.

But in the middle ages it was often felt desirable to make the tithe an exact charge, and not to rely on a rough and ready computation.[1] It remained a voluntary undertaking, however, and no congregation ever seems to have attempted to enforce the payment of the tithe in the case of unwilling donors. In fact the tithe continued to be a personal or family institution, the son promising to continue the father's custom, and only occasionally did a number of Jews bind themselves by a joint voluntary promise to give an exact tithe to the poor. This might happen on the initiative of a Rabbinical authority of great weight, such as the famous Asher ben Yechiel in the beginning of the fourteenth century. When he was still in Germany, his congregants all bestowed a tithe of their income on the poor. On settling in Toledo, he and his sons continued the practice. Gradually, however, they seem to have grown to the custom until, in the month of September, 1346, they entered into a formal promise in the following terms :[2] —

'We, the undersigned, accept an ordinance which we have in the handwriting of our father R. Asher, and which he worded thus : Hear my son the instruction of thy father, and do not forget the law of thy mother. Seeing that in the land whence we are come hither to Spain, our fathers and our fathers' fathers were wont to set aside for charitable purposes a tithe of all their business profits, in accordance with our sages' prescription,[3] we hereby undertake to follow

---

[1] Cf. אור זרוע i. p. 15; Maharil, שו״ת (Cremona, 1556, 56, etc.).

[2] *The Testament of Judah Asheri* (ed. Schechter), p. 15. He says : 'I add the form of promise lest perchance any one who sees it may desire to receive upon himself this same obligation.'

[3] *Pesikta R.,* xi.

in their footsteps, and have received upon ourselves the obligation to devote to the poor one-tenth of our profits earned in business, derived from the loan of capital or from commercial undertakings. Three-fourths of this tithe we will hand over to a kupah (or general fund), which shall be administered by two treasurers. This duty we undertake for ourselves and our children.'

Then follow the signatures of Asher and his sons, who on their part add that in giving the tithe they will include property which comes to them from every source, by inheritance, gift, or from marriage settlements. They further agree to pay the tithe within eight days of its falling due. The signatures of the children of the original covenanters are also added at a later date, and thus we see how a family tradition became fully established. The tithe, without ever becoming universal, must have been pretty common. In the fourteenth century it was in vogue in Germany, [1] and probably elsewhere.

Jewish charitable methods in the middle ages continuously tended towards differentiation. By the thirteenth century, philanthropic societies for various purposes make themselves apparent, but several centuries elapsed before the synagogue finally delegated most of its benevolent functions to semi-independent bodies. [2] In the sixteenth century the impoverishment of the Jews became most

---

[1] 'They shall give in charity *an exact tithe* of their property and shall never turn away a poor man empty-handed, but they shall give him what they can, be it much or little. If he asks for a lodging over night and they know him not, they shall supply him with money that he may pay an inn-keeper.' (*Ethical Will* of Eleazar the Levite of Mayence, who died in 1357.)

[2] The differentiation was anticipated by the practice of allotting certain proportions of the general charitable funds to definite objects.

marked, and the number of the poor increased.   In former times, Jewish kindliness had bridged over the gulf between wealth and poverty, now the gulf itself narrowed.   Perhaps it would be more accurate to say that wealth fell into far fewer hands, and thus the bulk of the Jews were all more or less unable to meet great demands on their means.   They compensated for the lack of money by the energy with which they rendered personal services, and the comparatively few rich men bore their burden manfully.

Another point must be noted.   In the ghettos, house-to-house begging might be carried on without publicity, so far at least as the Christian world was concerned.   Hence this system received a new impetus in the ghetto centuries, and re-established itself in Jewish life.   But the begging was restricted in time, and only occurred on Fridays and on the middle days of the festivals.[1]   Begging in the streets of the ghetto, or in front of the synagogue, was, however, sternly forbidden.[2]   In Rome the Fattori, or communal officers, continued to carry relief to the houses of widows and the sick in order to spare them the irksomeness of soliciting help in person.   As the number of Jews settled in Palestine increased, it became a pressing duty to provide for the settlers, and collections were regularly made for the purpose.   Envoys were dispatched from the Holy Land, and these were permitted to solicit help in every possible way.

Similarly, individuals, whether strangers or members of the local congregation, were allowed in special cases to make special appeals to the benevolent, though not in person. 'If a poor man,' says Leon di Modena[3] (1571–1648), 'has

---

[1] Cf. P. Rieger, *Geschichte der Juden in Rom*, ii. p. 315.

[2] Berliner, *Rom*, ii. 2, 56 seq.

[3] Cf. Montefiore, loc. cit.

occasion for extraordinary charity — as, if he has a daughter to marry, or would redeem any of his family that are slaves, whether he is one who lives with them or a stranger, 'tis all one, the overseers of the synagogue procure him a promise from every one; which is done thus. The chanter goes round and says to every one, calling him by name, " God bless so and so, who will contribute so much to such a charitable design." And because this is done on the Sabbath, upon which day they touch no money, every one promises by word of mouth what he thinks fit; and the week after every one readily pays what he promised to the overseer; and when they have gathered it they give it to the poor man.' Circular letters were also granted in such cases, and the father who had a daughter to marry or a relative to bury or release would readily obtain the succour he needed. Mostly, such circular letters had to be presented to the synagogal authorities at each stage of the itinerant collector's journey; for he needed a local licence before he could make a demand upon the purses of the benevolent. This system of travelling mendicancy may be traced as early as the end of the twelfth century.[1]

[1] *Sefer Chassidim*, § 955.

CHAPTER XVIII

PRIVATE AND COMMUNAL CHARITY (*continued*)

THE SICK AND THE CAPTIVE

It is obvious that if the charitable organization was to keep pace with the wants of the sick and the poor, special arrangements had to be made for meeting the various types of necessity. 'Societies' were already instituted at the end of the thirteenth century,[1] but a most luxuriant crop of benevolent agencies grew up in the sixteenth and seventeenth centuries. By that time the differentiation of charitable enterprises had reached its utmost limit. Elijah ben Solomon the Levite, who lived in Smyrna in the seventeenth century, and was the author of a very popular ethical code entitled 'the Rod of Reproof,' also compiled an elaborate treatise on charity. This book[2] contains nearly 2000 paragraphs, which take the form of learned comments on charitable maxims which occur in the Talmud and medieval Hebrew literature; the learning being interrupted by spirited homilies and striking anecdotes. At one point he stays

---

[1] Nissim Gerondi, writing circa 1350, enumerates five societies at Perpignan: for the study of the Law, visiting the sick, providing light, relief of the poor, and for burials (*Responsa*, § 84). Cf. Güdemann, i. 50.

[2] מעיל צדקה, 1731.

to enumerate the various charities to which pious Jews of his day were wont to subscribe. 'The list is very badly drawn up, and many particulars recur twice, and even three times; but after all due curtailment on the score of repetition, there yet remain seventy heads of charity, covering the widest field. First there are the charities given for particular objects, such as clothing the poor, paying for their education, paying dowries, paying burials, paying for doctor and medicine for sick persons and lying-in women, defraying the legal expenses of persons unjustly accused, paying nurses for orphan children, the travelling expenses of the poor, and so on. Then come charities given on particular occasions — for instance, on the Sabbath eve, on festivals, on fast days, on marriage, on recovery from an illness, beginning and end of a journey, during an epidemic, after a bad dream, and many more. Then there are the public charities, contributing to Kupah and Tamchui, to the societies for the ransom of prisoners, to collections at dinners, and to the maintenance of the public hostelries. Then there remain a number of miscellaneous charities, such as paying taxes for the poor, sending money secretly to persons who are unwilling to make their poverty known, lending books, and several other items too numerous to mention. The whole list,' adds Mr. Montefiore,[1] 'seems to show that the Talmudic ascription of charity to Israel, as a mark and token of his race, is not exaggerated or undeserved.'

This multiplicity of demands was met by the foundation of societies, which were almost as numerous as the various classes of charity which were enumerated above. Some of them possessed considerable property, which

[1] *Jewish Chronicle*, loc. cit.

accumulated as the years rolled by.   Rome in the seventeenth century may be taken as a typical instance.   The
benevolent societies in the Roman ghetto were grouped
under four heads:[1] (*a*) those for the relief of the poor,
(*b*) those which were concerned with the burial of the dead,
(*c*) those which provided for the aged, (*d*) those which served
religious and educational objects.   At this period seven
societies devoted their energies to the provision of clothes,
shoes, linen, beds, and warm winter bed-coverings for
young children, school children, the poor, especially women,
widows, and prisoners.[2]   Two societies provided trousseaus
and dowries for poor brides[3] — under which category was
sometimes included the loan of jewellery to those who
possessed none ; another society brought help to the
houses of those who met with sudden deaths, and yet
another was founded for visiting the sick.[4]   Other societies
performed the last loving services to the dying, conducted
the purification before interment, and attended to the burial.[5]
   The women of Rome had their own society, too, though

---

[1] Berliner, *Rom*, ii. (v) p. 184. In Hebrew these were societies for עוזר
דלים, גמילת חסדים, מושב זקנים and שומר אמונים, ישומר.

[2] Rieger, loc. cit. These societies were called מכסה ילדים, מלביש ערומים,
אורח חיים, שמחת הרגל, לב אלמנות ארנין, נוה שלום, מלביש עניי.

[3] Rieger, loc. cit. אליה הנביא and חברת בתולות. These societies were often
the cause of serious abuse. Indigent parents promised their daughters large
dowries, and when the bridegroom refused to proceed with the wedding unless
the dowry were forthcoming, the fathers went in tears to the managers of the
society and demanded help. In 1618 this society resolved that no father who
promised his daughter more than 200 scudi was eligible for help. It was also
found necessary to limit the number of cases dealt with annually to twelve.
In societies of this kind, the girls often drew lots to decide which should
receive dowries. The lucky maidens were in much demand with amorous
bachelors. Berliner, *Rom*, ii. (2) p. 57.

[4] Rieger, loc. cit., מחוק לנפש and ביקור חולים.

[5] Rieger, loc. cit., לוית מתים, אורח חיים, and רחיצה ח''ק.

even when this was not the case they were associated with the men in administering such charities as were concerned with the relief of their own sex.[1]   In addition to these societies, a special association devoted itself to collecting alms for the Holy Land.[2]   Eleven societies were engaged in promoting educational and religious aims.   One met for daily devotions and study, another for the same purposes on Sabbaths, a third for night prayers on the eves of the seventh day of Passover, the first day of the Feast of Pentecost, and the seventh day of Tabernacles.[3]   Two societies existed for providing the necessary legal *minyan*, quorum of ten adult males, at the memorial services held daily in the private houses of mourners, and another society supplied the *minyan* in the evenings.[4]   The Abrahamic rite was directed by a special society which also provided necessaries and dainties for the mother of the new-born boy ; yet another society busied itself with the prayers held on the evening which preceded the ceremony.[5]   In order to pro-

[1] In 1617 there was a חברת נשים in Rome (Rieger, p. 316).

[2] ח״ ארץ ישראל or ה״ ירושלים.

[3] These were called מנוחת אמה ואמונה ,ח״ עזרה בצרות and ח״ מקראי קדש (Rieger, p. 317).   The Societies for studying the Scriptures and Rabbinical literature were mostly called תלמור תורה ח״; the associations for prayer sometimes שומרים לבקר ח״.   On these last-named Societies, which date from the sixteenth century, cf. Steinschneider, *Jewish Literature*, p. 242.   Many of these societies were known by other, but similar, names to those noted above.   It is impossible to give the variants in anything like completeness.   A few may be added, ח״ק מגדלי יתומים ,ח״ק כלה גדולה ,ח״ק הכנסת ח״ק; חברת תועלת עטרת זקנים (for the relief of the aged); also משענת זקנים (for the same object); חברת מזל; גמילת חסדים עטרת תפארת (for Talmud); ח״ חנוך לנער; חברת הש״ס; בתולה; חברת עץ חיים (for educational purposes). See Zedner's catalogue of the Heb. books in Brit. Mus., pp. 48, 49, 92, 279, 447, 510, and 770.   In finding titles for such societies there was no limit to the fancy.   Every Bible phrase that was apt (or not apt) for the purpose was chosen at one time or another.

[4] These were the מנחם אבלים מכסה אלמנה, and מגישי מנחה Rieger, p. 318.

[5] Rieger, loc. cit.   They were named בעלי ברית ח״ and אליה הנביא.

vide the poor with the materials for fulfilling certain religious duties, such as the affixing to the door-posts of the *mezuzah* (Deut. vi. 9), the illuminations on the feast of Dedication and the kindling of the Sabbath-lights, three societies were established.[1] Lastly, there were two further associations in Rome formed for literary purposes of a religious character.[2]

Such a maze of societies, it is true, did not exist in every Jewish community;[3] but, on the other hand, this Roman list, elaborate though it be, is by no means exhaustive. Jewish benevolence was unbounded, and needed an incalculable number of outlets for its abundant energies. Besides, these benevolent societies performed a useful social function. The members met together at regular intervals to dine or to play, they prayed and studied together, and were united each to each in bonds of a peculiar friendliness. The synagogue as a body did not entirely dissociate itself from these philanthropic enterprises. On the contrary it aided them in various ways. The communal authorities appointed certain times at which public offerings or collections might be made in synagogues in favour of the various charities. Mostly the individual leaders of the synagogue were also very prominent in the management and support of the benevolent societies. Besides this,

---

[1] Their names were מדליקי חנוכה, שומרי מזוזות and מדליקי נר שבת.

[2] They were known as the מכברי תורה and קובע עתים לתורה.

[3] In 1630, in Mantua or San Martino seven charities are enumerated by Samuel Portaleone (see *Jewish Quarterly Review*, v. p. 514); several of these are generic terms which may, however, have included many subdivisions. The seven charities are: קופת גמילות חסדים, קופת תלמוד תורה, קופת ארץ ישראל, קופת שבויים, and קופת פרנסת עניים, קופה להשיא בתולה, קופת רחמים, i. e. (*a*) the box (fund) for the Land of Israel, (*b*) the box for studying the Law, (*c*) the box for burying the dead, (*d*) the box of Mercy, (*e*) the box for a maiden's dowry, (*f*) the box for maintaining the poor, and (*g*) the box for redeeming captives.

at all periods wealthy Jews expended large sums, either directly or through the communal organizations, in the support of poor students.

There were at least two acts of mercy which seem to have called a special machinery into existence at an earlier period of Jewish life. The first of these dealt with the sick and the dying. The Communal Hostelry may have served as an infirmary or hospital, but the medieval Jews preferred to treat each patient in his own home. The attendance on the sufferers from disease or bodily weakness was one of the most conspicuous duties which Jews of all times included under the general head of charity. This duty was incumbent on every Jew, rich and poor, and was extended towards patients of all classes and creeds. Though the Jews of the middle ages were strongly averse to accepting alms or other charitable services from any but their co-religionists, they felt no similar scruples in rendering such help.[1] On the contrary, Jewish charity knew no bounds of creed. Naturally, however, Jews were the chief recipients of Jewish charity.

Much tenderness was shown in visiting those who were confined to their houses by prostrating illness. After synagogue service on the Sabbath morning, the worshippers paid regular visits to the sick before returning home

---

[1] Cf. Shulchan Aruch, *Yore Deah*, ccli. 1, cccxxxv. 9; ccclxvii. 1; Maimonides, viii. and מלכים ה״, x. 12; מתנות עניים ה״; Isserles to *Yore Deah*, ccli. 1 and cxlix. 4; *Orach Chayim*, dcxciv. 3. These are but a small fraction of the numerous prescriptions (in Jewish authorities of all ages) which ordain the paramount duty of relieving non-Jewish poor with, and in preference to, the Jewish poor. For further passages see Hoffmann, *Der Shulchan Aruch*, etc. pp. 72 seq. As to the non-acceptance of gifts from others than Jews, cf. Müller, *Mafteach*, 131.

to partake of their meal.[1]   This general concern with
such matters partly accounts for the fact that so little
'parish visiting' was done by the Rabbis in the middle
ages; this function was performed by the laity in general
and by the lay-heads of the congregation in particular.
The Rabbi merely performed his share like other pious
members of the community.

The Jewish etiquette at such visits was almost beyond
praise.   It was thought bad manners for any but his most
familiar friends to call upon the patient too soon after he
fell ill, for such precipitancy might make him appear in
a worse plight than he actually was.   No visitor was to
become a nuisance by making too long a stay; nor was
he to present himself when the sufferer was in acute pain.
The patient was to be cheered, and not depressed by
conversation on dismal topics of death and misfortune.
A man's personal enemy was to refrain from visiting
the sufferer, for his presence might be misconstrued as
implying a desire to gloat over his foe's prostration.   An
essential of the visit was the prayer uttered on the patient's
behalf.   Women were notoriously tender to the sick, hence
their evidence was not accepted as to the inability of the
invalid to fast on the Day of Atonement.   Just as occurs
at the present day in our hospitals, Jewish men were
nursed by women, but the women were not nursed by men.

It does not seem that the community found it necessary
to make its own arrangements for the medical treatment
of the poor until a late period.   The Jewish physicians
attended the poor without charge,[2] a physician would
train his son to regard that as the proper course of

---

[1] *Or Zarua*, ii. p. 22.
[2] Cf. the activity of Maimonides, p. 235 above.

conduct,[1] and at all times Jewish doctors charged very moderately for their services. To add another to the instances cited in previous chapters, Saul Astruc Cohen, a popular physician and scholar of Algiers at the close of the fourteenth century, not only practised his art gratuitously, 'but spent his fortune in relieving both Mohammedan and Jewish poor.'[2] A medical officer was often attached to a benevolent society, which will soon be described. Such societies were chiefly called into existence by the various epidemics which devastated Europe in the middle ages. Under the strain of extraordinary needs, the usual methods for providing medical attendance broke down, and benevolent societies sprang into existence as rapidly as the demand for them arose.

It may be convenient to inquire at this point into the question whether the Jews were more or less subject to medieval epidemics than the rest of Europe. We may pass over as exceptional the serious cases of epidemic disease which affected the Jews when herded together in emigrant ships after their expulsion from Spain and Portugal. Under average circumstances, there is no doubt that it was generally believed that the Jews suffered less than the Christian populations from various forms of disease.[3] Their manner of life undoubtedly preserved them from those epidemics which depended upon controllable circumstances, or arose from causes to which the Jews were not subjected. Jews were free both from

[1] 'Thou mayest accept fees from the rich,' said Judah Ibn Tibbon to his son, 'but heal the poor gratuitously.' He adds: 'Examine thy drugs and medicinal herbs regularly once a week, and never apply a remedy which thou hast not thoroughly tested.'

[2] Graetz, *History of the Jews* (Eng. Trans.) IV. ch. vi.

[3] Cf. e.g. 'A. R.,' *A View of the Jewish Religion* (London, 1656), p. 399.

'Anglorum fames' and the 'Francorum ignis.' The standard of living was higher than the average with the Jews in the middle ages, and the famine-pestilences slew fewer victims in the ghettos than in the quarters inhabited by non-Jews. Agrarian epidemics, such as the 'Francorum ignis' or gangrene, were the scourge of the peasantry, not of the dwellers in towns. Leprosy was certainly less common among Jews than among Christians,[1] and again the explanation is reasonably simple. The medieval leprosy seems to have arisen from the large consumption of badly salted meat and fish, which, when eaten by the poor, was often in a semi-putrid condition.[2] Now the Jews, however poor, rarely ate any but fresh meat, and their religion prevented them from using it as food when it had become putrid.

Further, Jews seem to have suffered little from cholera and allied diseases. On the other hand, they were martyrs to malaria in the Roman ghetto, into which the Tiber constantly overflowed. Small-pox marked down a large number of Jewish victims.[3] In the terrible scourge known as the Black Death, which devastated the civilized world in the fourteenth century, the Jews were great sufferers. In the middle ages, the popular imagination invariably flew to *poisoning* as the explanation of epidemics, and the Jews were massacred by thousands during the outburst of fanatical madness which seized upon Europe in consequence of the Black Death. It is now known, however, that the Jews suffered equally with the Christians

---

[1] A myth that there were many Jewish lepers in France grew out of the identity in form of the badge worn by Jews and lepers in the middle ages.

[2] C. Creighton, *A History of Epidemics in Britain*, p. 110 seq.

[3] But see Schechter, *Studies in Judaism*, p. 360.

in Vienna, Goslar, Regensburg, Avignon, and Rome.¹
Many Jewish cemeteries were enlarged at this period to
receive the bodies of those who died from the plague or
fell martyrs to a foolish myth.²

Jewish burial societies, called 'Holy Leagues' (*chevra
kadisha*),³ have, with some plausibility, been traced back
as far as the fourth century. In the first century, the
interment of the dead was a duty undertaken by the whole
community. 'All who pass by when one is buried,' says
Josephus,⁴ 'must accompany the funeral and join in the
lamentation.' But outside Palestine the Jews did rather
more than this. Every Babylonian Jew ceased from his
work the moment that he was informed of a death, and
participated in the preparations for burial. 'Rav Hamnuna (died about 320) chanced to be in a town named
Darô. Suddenly he heard the note of a horn, and knew
by this signal that some one had just died. To his sur-
prise, he saw that some people continued at their work
as if nothing had happened (to need their immediate
attention). Hamnuna demanded: "Ought not these men
to be severely punished, since, knowing that a death has
just occurred, they still continue their ordinary avoca-
tions?" "There is an association in the town," he was

---

¹ R. Hoeniger, *Der Schwarze Tod in Deutschland* (Berlin, 1882), p. 42.
Cf. Haeser, *Lehrbuch der Geschichte der Medecin und der Volkskrankheiten*
(Jena, 1882), iii. p. 156.

² A 'thörichtes Märchen,' Hoeniger calls it (loc. cit.).

³ This title חברא קדישא was also used in a generic sense, of any society
formed for a religious purpose. One frequently meets in Jewish records
with ה"ק תלמוד תורה, and so forth. See e.g. Güdemann, *Quellenschriften*,
p. 301, where the Frankfort society, whose objects are educational, is
termed החבורה קדישא. Further, several benevolent societies in Amsterdam
were known as ח"ק (cf. Zedner, *Catalogue*, p. 49).

⁴ *Against Apion*, ii. 27.

told, " and therefore all men need not discontinue their work to attend to the dead." ' [1]

The general cessation of work when a death occurred continued in some Jewish congregations for many centuries. In 1730 all shops were shut in Sofia whenever a Jew died,[2] and throughout the middle ages information of a death was conveyed to every member of most congregations by methods already described, or by the pouring forth of all the water in the house wherein the dead lay unburied.[3] Still, the inconvenience and the dislocation of business caused by a general cessation from work must have powerfully helped forward the formation of Holy Leagues, which assumed the duties of tending the sick, supplying medicines and warm clothing, preparing the dead for burial, providing graves and tombstones, arranging for the celebration of the proper rites in the house of mourning, and relieving the immediate distress of those whom the funeral and the attendant loss of the wage-earners' income plunged into temporary want.

Epidemics were also a fruitful cause of the formation of these leagues or brotherhoods. At such periods the need of a special organization was much felt, and no fear of personal danger from contagion restrained the pious from

---

[1] *T. B. Moed Katon*, 27 b. This is the usual explanation of the passage (cf. M. Adler in *Jewish Chronicle*, Oct. 7, 1892), but it is by no means clear that the Talmud refers to a burial society. The phrase, חברותא איכא, may simply mean (as Rashi explains) that each *section*, חבורה, of the community attended to its own dead, and that the *whole* community did not need to concern itself with *every* funeral. For a possible reference to a burial society see *Semachoth*, ch. xii. It should be added that the correct reading in *Moed Katon*, 27 a, is the town Darô, and not the *south* (cf. *Dikduke Soferim*, ad loc.). [2] R. Meldola's שו״ת מים רבים, ii. 65.

[3] R. Nissim (to *Moed Katon*, 27 b) states that this was the usual signal of a death in his time.

devoting themselves to the task of affording decent and loving attention to the dying and the dead. Another occasional motive for the formation of such leagues was the distance of the cemeteries from the Jewish quarters. We have seen above that the cemetery was mostly near the ghetto, but this was not always the case. The cost and toil involved where the coffin had to be conveyed a great distance, led to unbecoming methods of transportation. In such case a Holy League would be created to provide for the decorous conveyance of the bodies and their interment in the distant cemeteries.[1] The members of these Holy Leagues enjoyed much respect and some religious and social privileges, for kindness shown to the dead was, in the Jewish view, the highest form of charity, in that it was rendered without possibility of gratitude or reward from the recipient.

Another imperative call was frequently made on Jewish generosity in the middle ages. Jews from the earliest periods regarded the duty of *ransoming captives* as one of their most pressing obligations.[2] The revolt against Rome resulted in the enslavement of a large number of the sons of Judah, many of whom were freed by their co-religionists. The cost of purchasing the freedom of Jewish slaves was always a first charge on the synagogical resources. At the end of the tenth century Moses ben Chanoch was carried to Cordova as a prisoner by the captain of the vessel in which he and his family had taken

---

[1] An interesting case of this kind is recorded by Joseph Sambary (Neubauer, *Anecdota Oxoniensia, Medieval Jewish Church*, i. p. 157). This occurred near the year 1500.

[2] Cf. Maimonides, מתנות עניים, viii. §§ 10–15; Shulchan Aruch, *Yore Deah*, § 252; *Kolbo*, 93 a. See also *Tosefta*, end of first chapter of *Shekalim;* and *Or Zarua*, i. p. 14. The duty is frequently referred to in the Talmud.

passage to Spain. The Cordovese Jews, little knowing the important rôle that the stranger was destined to play, ransomed him as a matter of course.[1]

In the course of centuries, however, the burden of ransoming Jewish prisoners became excessively onerous. The need of inter-communal action was severely felt, and independent Jewish congregations banded themselves together for the purpose. The scene of the worst experiences in this direction lay on the shores of the Mediterranean, in Spain and Italy. The Barbary corsairs of the eighteenth century had their analogues in the fifteenth. Heart-rending indeed were the sufferings endured by the Jews who fell into the hands of the bandits and pirates, who took advantage of the cruel necessity which drove the Jews from shore to shore in vain search for a friendly and peaceful resting-place. When towards the end of the eighteenth century Alfonso V of Portugal captured the African seaports, Arzilla and Tangier, he carried off 250 Jews of both sexes and every age, and sold them as slaves throughout the kingdom. The Portuguese Jews applied to Yechiel of Pisa, financier and philanthropist, and he generously assisted his brethren. Lisbon Jews formed a representative committee of twelve members, and the famous statesman-scholar, Don Isaac Abarbanel, himself travelled over the whole country and redeemed the Jewish slaves, often at a high price. 'The ransomed Jews and Jewesses, adults and children, were clothed, lodged, and maintained until they had learned the language of the country and were able to support themselves.'[2]

Soon, however, the Jews of Italy found their resources

[1] Graetz, *History of the Jews* (Eng. Trans.), III. ch. vii.
[2] Graetz, op. cit. ch. xi.

taxed to the utmost. The expulsion of the Jews from Spain in 1492 cast many thousands of exiles on the rest of Europe. Except in Rome, the Jews of Italy everywhere strained their fullest powers to provide for the burden thus cast upon them. In Naples, King Ferdinand behaved with the bravest humanity, and in the teeth of much popular opposition allowed the Jewish exiles to settle outside the town, and provided hospital accommodation for them. At Pisa the sons of the wealthy Yechiel fairly took up their abode on the quay,[1] to prevent delay in receiving and entertaining wanderers. In many places, moreover, the reception of the Jews was rendered the more costly, seeing that the fugitives had to be purchased by their Jewish benefactors. The captains of the vessels in which the Jews sailed frequently claimed the passengers as their slaves. In the Greek islands of Corfu and Candia, the Jews sold the gold from their synagogue ornaments to raise money for freeing such slaves. In Turkey, the Jews were received by the Sultan, Bajazet II, with extraordinary kindness, and the native Jews of his realm vied with their Italian brethren in the efforts they made to serve the Spanish exiles. Moses Kapsali, the most noted Turkish Rabbi of the time, travelled from congregation to congregation, and levied a tax on the native Jews to defray the cost of 'liberating the Spanish captives.' But it is unnecessary to add further details. The horrors of the expulsion from Spain are such, that a Jewish writer willingly refrains from repeating the oft-told tale of suffering and degradation. But the horrors are somewhat relieved by the superhuman efforts made by the Jews themselves to rescue their brethren from death or servitude.

[1] Graetz, op cit. ch. xii. Cf. p. 242 above.

The troubles of the Jews were not relaxed after the settlement in new abodes of those of the Spanish exiles who survived the perils of their expulsion. In the middle of the sixteenth century the vessels of the Italian republic or of African buccaneers captured many Jews and reduced them to slavery. The frequent oppressions in other parts of Europe produced similar but not such extensive results. Everywhere the Jews bestirred themselves to purchase the freedom of their brethren. Unhappily this readiness of the Jews to pay ransom, encouraged the man-stealers to further exertions. The capture of Jews was too profitable a business to fail of many willing and enterprising recruits. The Jews tried to protect themselves by refusing to pay too high a price for the freedom they so generously bought. Not often, however, were they able to resist the temptation to ransom their brethren at all costs. If they hesitated, the captors knew how to put on the screw, and the prisoners were maltreated, starved, and deprived of their wearing apparel until their price was forthcoming. To give a fillip to their co-religionists' pity, the prisoners were sometimes mutilated, their ears and noses being lopped off.[1] The Jewish communities were mulcted to a considerable extent, and their property squeezed from them. Occasionally, the ransomed prisoners were able to refund the sums paid for them : thus in 1543 a leading Jew of Algiers was ransomed for sixty or seventy crowns, and promptly repaid the amount.[2]

On regaining their liberty, many of these ransomed Jews

---

[1] Isidore Loeb, *Josef Haccohen*, p. 23.

[2] The need of 'ransoming captives' has been felt in Jewish congregations almost to the present time. A few years ago the Sephardic congregations in London retained the office of honorary superintendent of the fund for the 'Cautivos,' and possibly the office is still in existence.

were forced to beg to obtain the necessaries of life. The impoverishment of the Jews, which synchronized with the Reformation, rendered them less and less able to cope with the distress into which these miserable victims of medieval misgovernment were regularly plunged. The climax of Jewish impoverishment was reached at the beginning of the eighteenth century, but the dawn of a better day was visible before the close of that dark century in Jewish life.

CHAPTER XIX

THE MEDIEVAL SCHOOLS

THE Renaissance produced a violent transformation in the relative excellence of the Jewish and Christian systems of education in Europe. Before the revival of letters, the Jews were probably better educated than any other section of the European population. The average Jew could always read and write,[1] which is more than can be said of the ordinary layman in the middle ages. But at the Renaissance, Christian education not only took a vast stride forwards, but a backward blow was administered at the Jews, except those who dwelt in Italy, which left them far in the rear for some centuries. Moreover, the literary and religious upheavals which modernized the rest of Europe seem by a species of natural as well as deliberate reaction to have cast the Jews into their one real experience of medieval gloom. The Jewish middle ages began just when the medieval cloud vanished from Christian society.

Hence during the sixteenth, seventeenth, and eighteenth centuries — the ghetto centuries, be it noted — the Jews entirely lost the educational supremacy which they had previously enjoyed. During those centuries they were

---

[1] Zunz, *Zur Geschichte und Literatur* (1845), p. 177.

worse and not better taught than the rest of Europe, and the deterioration in educational method was accompanied by a diminution in the scope which Jewish culture embraced. That these evil effects were not more damaging was due entirely to the fortunate circumstance that the Talmudical school system was far in advance of its age.[1] The Jews, when thrown upon themselves in their dark ages, naturally turned to their Rabbinical traditions as their guide and norm. They endeavoured to obey the Talmudical prescriptions with regard to the education of children, and as these prescriptions were so fundamentally sound that they are not even now obsolete, the Jews of the ghetto period were preserved from anything like a complete intellectual collapse.

Reverting to the pre-ghetto period, the educational status of the Jews in various parts of Europe was by no means uniform. This, however, applies only to the acquirements of adults. Jewish children were educated much in the same way all over the civilized world, and the divergence only becomes apparent when the years of boyhood have passed. The term *boyhood* is employed designedly, for no regular provision was made for the education of Jewish girls. In the later medieval centuries, Christian women were far better equipped than their brothers and husbands, and thus the Jewish women would have suffered doubly by

---

[1] For an excellent account of the Talmudical views on education see Strassburger's *Geschichte der Erziehung bei den Israeliten* (Stuttgart, 1885). This book is not so useful for later periods, but this is the less regrettable seeing that the works of M. Güdemann are a complete armoury of information on the medieval period. To his *Geschichte des Erziehungswesens und der Cultur der Juden* (Vienna, 1880, 1884, 1888) must be added the same author's *Quellenschriften zur Geschichte des Unterrichts und der Erziehung bei den deutschen Juden* (Berlin, 1891).

comparison with their Christian sisters. But this neglect of female education by the Jews does not imply that the women were hopelessly ignorant. The Jewess married early, and even had she been provided with a school career, her years of study must have been very few. But with a large number of ritual prescriptions she was perforce made acquainted, and the just fulfilment of her ordinary household duties entailed a considerable knowledge of Biblical and Rabbinical law.

It is quite certain that a goodly number of Jewish women deserved the title of *learned.* This learning they acquired at home from the lips of their parents and brothers, for, as a medieval Rabbi naïvely remarks, though it be wrong to *teach* women, there is no reason why they should not obtain knowledge of their own initiative.[1] There is another important fact to be derived from a further statement of the same Rabbi. He asserts in so many words that many Jewesses in South Germany were, in the beginning of the fifteenth century, noted for their learning, a fact which is strengthened by many particular instances on record in the Talmud and in medieval annals of the Jews of other countries as well as Germany.[2] These women entered into learned discussions with famous Rabbis, and the opinions of 'Lady Rabbinists' were cited often with approval.

Jewish women did not as a rule learn to write, but occasionally they were accomplished scribes, assisted their husbands in their literary correspondence, and with their

[1] *Responsa*, Maharil (Cremona, 1556), 199.
[2] Some interesting cases are collected by Kayserling in his *Die Jüdischen Frauen* (Leipzig, 1879), pp. 134 seq., and Nahida Remy, *The Jewish Woman* (Philadelphia, 1896), passim. Cf. also Zunz, op. cit. p. 172.

own hands made copies of books of reference and of other learned works for them. Some of these copies, still extant, display a neat and clear hand, and — what is more — scrupulous accuracy. These women were adepts in other arts besides a knowledge of the Talmud. They were often musicians, and instructed their sisters in the tunes to which the synagogue hymns must be sung. The Jewish women were able to play on musical instruments, and would sing the verses which their husbands composed, with musical accompaniments.[1] Hence, when the eighteenth century saw a revival in Jewish culture, the women were the first to emerge into the new light. Wealthy Jews, subject to the disapprobation of rigidly orthodox Rabbis, engaged music-masters to teach their daughters the art of playing on instruments.[2] The phenomenal success of Jewesses as leaders of salons in the Mendelssohnian era of intellectual emancipation, was prepared by a long process of self-elevation which was steadily but silently developed in the female life of the ghettos.

Some of these Jewish women were even public teachers. Samuel ben Ali of Bagdad, one of the 'Princes of the Captivity' in the twelfth century, had no sons, but only one daughter. 'She is expert in the Scripture and Talmud,' says Petachia.[3] 'She gives instruction in Scripture to young men through a window. She herself is within the building, whilst the disciples are below outside and do not see her.' The same precaution was adopted by another Jewess who emulated Hypatia. This was Miriam Schapira,

---

[1] Cf. Kaufmann in *Jewish Quarterly Review*, iii. p. 298.
[2] See יוסף אומץ, § 890, מה מאור נחשב בעיני לאיסור גדול מה שהעשירים שוכרין לבנותיהם יודע נגן ללמדן כלי שיר.
[3] *Travels of R. Petachia* (ed. Benisch), p. 19.

the ancestress of the Loria family. She seems to have conducted a regular college, which was attended by many youths. She sat behind a veil or curtain while delivering her lectures.[1] Yet another woman, Dulcie, the daughter of Eliezer of Worms, held public discourses on the Sabbath. She supported her husband and family, and with her two daughters suffered a martyr's death in 1213 or 1214 at the hands of two Knights of the Cross.

If the Jewess made but rare appearances as a public teacher, she was present in every home as a private instructress. Several medieval Rabbis declared, in after life, that their first and best teachers were their mothers. The average Jewess was not equal to such a burden as this, but the education of her boys regularly fell on her shoulders until they attained their fifth year. Subsequently her part was that of the moral monitress rather than the intellectual guide. But this involved some important consequences. After the art of printing was invented, the favourite literature of Jewish women comprised simple ethical treatises which eulogized the domestic virtues and inculcated pure ideals. These she imparted to her sons and daughters. Moreover, the very fact that she did not know much Hebrew rendered it necessary for her to pray in the vernacular, and to teach her children to pray in the same language. The boy was early accustomed to easy Hebrew prayers, but he must have also become familiar with prayers in his ordinary language. Portions of the home ritual recited on the passover eve were translated by the father for the sake of the women and children.[2]

---

[1] Kayserling, op. cit. p. 138.

[2] אומר מה נשתנה ומתרגם לאנשי ביתיה (Müller, *Mafteach*, p. 110). Hymns in German and 'jargon' found their way into the same home rite at a later date.

The vernacular was also introduced into the synagogue for the benefit of the women. For their pleasure, an Arabic translation of the twenty-fourth chapter of Genesis was sung in the East on the Sabbath after a wedding.[1] In other congregations the lessons from the Prophets were on certain occasions translated into Spanish.[2] The old Aramaic paraphrase was, in fact, replaced quite early by a vernacular version.[3] The prophetical lesson for the Day of Atonement — the Book of Jonah — was read in Greek in those localities where Greek was the ordinary language in use.[4] Similarly, the tractate *Soferim* (beginning of the ninth century) lays it down as a duty to translate, for the women, the weekly readings from the Pentateuch and the Prophets before the close of the service. The translation was not read verse by verse after the Hebrew, but as one continuous passage.[5]

In the fourteenth century, the Book of Esther was read on Purim in Spanish from a translation, for the pleasure of the women, in various parts of Spain. The rigorous pietist, Isaac ben Sheshet, was scandalized to find this custom in force at Saragossa when, in the middle of the fourteenth century, he was appointed Rabbi to that

---

[1] Jacob ben Israel of Morea, שו״ת, § 82 (p. 174 b).

[2] This was done on the Passover, Pentecost, and the fast of the Ninth of Ab (cf. R. Meldola, שו״ת מים רבים, § 13). On the seventh day of Passover a boy sometimes acted as translator (*Machzor Vitry*, p. 304).

[3] *Responsa* of Geonim, Müller, p. 103. באיזה מקומות משנין וקורין ההרגום בשפה היהודעה לעם. The two habits were even retained side by side, for Simon Duran (*Responsa*, iii. 121) says that there were congregations in which the Aramaic translation was retained for the prophetical lessons of Passover and Pentecost, while the Song of Deborah was translated into Arabic.

[4] Judah Minz, *Responsa*, § 78.

[5] *Massecheth Soferim*, xviii. (ed. Müller, p. 35, and notes, p. 256). This custom of reading the translated passage *as a whole* was usual with the Byzantine Jews in the ninth century.

congregation.   Local Rabbis were more complacent than the new arrival, who set himself, with the aid of Nissim Gerundi, to crush the custom which had been in existence at Saragossa for a third of a century.   The ground of their objection is described by Graetz as ' sophistical,'[1] and it certainly deserves a harsh epithet.   They argued that as the reader understood Hebrew it was unlawful for him to read the Scroll of Esther in any other language, though the women, who did not understand the Hebrew, might lawfully hear it in Spanish.   Another argument was more weighty.   Isaac ben Sheshet questioned the accuracy of the translation.[2]   It seems as though his zeal triumphed, for we do not find any later references to the use of the vernacular on the Feast of Esther.

The incident just described is, however, very important. It shows that the vernacular was far more common in the medieval than in the modern synagogue.   Indeed, German hymns on the unity of God and the Thirteen Creeds, formulated by Maimonides, were so popular in the fourteenth century that they were the exclusive religious literature of many Jews.[3]   Jewesses had, however, ceased to pray in the vernacular by the end of the fifteenth century, for, in the words of a sixteenth-century writer, ' this beautiful and worthy custom ' was, to his regret, extinct when he wrote.[4]   But the eclipse can only have been local or of short duration.   John Evelyn in his *Diary* (anno 1641) tells us of his acquaintance, ' a Burgundian Jew, who had married an apostate Kentish woman. . . .   He showed

---

[1] Graetz, *History of the Jews* (Eng. Trans.), IV. ch. v.

[2] Isaac beŋ Sheshet, *Responsa*, §§ 388 seq.

[3] Maharil (in the לקוטים).   The Talmud permitted the use of the vernacular in some of the most important prayers (*T. B. Sota*, 32 a).

[4] S. Schechter, *Studies in Judaism*, p. 393.

me several books of their devotion, which he had translated into English *for the instruction of his wife.*[1] It is probable that similar concessions to women were made by other seventeenth-century Jews than those whose wives were born in a different creed. Translations of the Hebrew prayer-book into the vernacular grow very common in the course of the seventeenth century, and as these translations were sometimes printed without the Hebrew text, it may be inferred that some women, if not men, still prayed in the vernacular.[2] In quite modern times, on the other hand, there has been a remarkable increase in the number of Jewesses who are well acquainted with Hebrew.

Indirectly, too, the Jewish women rendered services to education in the middle ages. They were always proud of their reputation for zeal in encouraging their husbands and sons to study. In place of buying trinkets with their husbands' presents, they would purchase books. They would freely offer hospitality to poor travelling scholars. Wives would rise very early and retire to rest very late in order to welcome their husbands on their return from the *Beth Hamidrash*, or house of study.[3] The mothers, too, took their sons to school; and of the several reasons which made Jews prefer to employ married teachers, one was the constant presence in the schools of the mothers of the boys.[4]

Both the mother and father, indeed, participated in the important function of introducing the boy to school

[1] Evelyn's *Diary* (ed. Bray), i. p. 27.

[2] Thus Nieto's Spanish translation (London, 1740 and 1771) contains no Hebrew text; a similar remark applies to other Spanish and French translations (Amsterdam, 1648; Nice, 1776). Possibly these translations were used side by side with the Hebrew text.

[3] *Sefer Chassidim;* Maharil שמחות ה״.   [4] *Kolbo*, 88 b.

for the first time. This occurred when the boy was five, but it was deferred for a couple of years in case the child was weak or sickly. The ceremony of initiation was performed partly in a school and partly in the synagogue, and the favourite occasion was the Feast of Pentecost [1]— the traditional anniversary of the revelation on Mount Sinai. Early in the morning the boy was dressed in new clothes, and three cakes of fine flour and honey were baked for him by a young maiden. Three eggs were boiled, and apples and other fruit were gathered in profusion. Then the child was taken in the arms of the Rabbi or another learned friend first to the school and then to the synagogue, or vice versa. The child was placed on the reading-daïs before the Scroll, from which the Ten Commandments were read as the lesson of the day. In the school, he received his first lesson in reading Hebrew. On a slate were smeared in honey some of the letters of the Hebrew alphabet, or simple texts, such as ' Moses commanded us a law, an inheritance for the assembly of Jacob' (Deut. xxxiii. 4); and the child lisped the letters as he ate the honey, the cakes, and the other delicacies, that the words of the Law might be sweet in his lips. The child was then handed over to the arms of his mother, who had stood by during this delightful scene.[2]

The real school work then commenced, and was continued for at least seven years. For the most part boys who

---

[1] Sometimes the first of Nisan was the date selected. Cf. חוקי החורה (Güdemann, i. 267). From this early thirteenth-century code of education several of the details in this chapter are taken. Cf. Jacobs, *Ang. Engl.* 343.

[2] This account chiefly follows the *Machzor Vitry*, p. 628. For slightly different versions of the same custom see Güdemann, i. p. 50. In some cases the names of angels were invoked to open the child's heart and improve his powers of retention. Cf. Schechter, p. 368.

were not destined for professions, remained at school till they were thirteen or even fifteen. Elementary schools existed in every Jewish community, but were not all supported by public funds. The father was rightly thought by some to be disqualified from teaching his own children,[1] but he was bound to pay a teacher for them. The higher colleges for advanced pupils, or *yeshibas*, were only public in so far that they were supported by the community.

At these higher schools, to which mostly professional students repaired, the students lived together in the house of the principal or in a special building. But the elementary schools seem mostly to have been private in the sense that the teachers, though elected or authorized by the community, received their fees directly from the parents.[2] The teachers were not, however, left without control. The excellent Talmudical prescription,[3] that the number of pupils taught by one master must not exceed twenty-five, was rigidly enforced in the middle ages, and the pupil-teacher system was well developed. Thus if the class numbered forty, one qualified teacher and one pupil teacher were held sufficient. The pupil teacher was paid by the community.[4] In the advanced Talmudical schools these restrictions, however, had no relevancy. The teaching being by lecture, there was no reason why the audience should be limited in number.

The hours of instruction were long, and in winter the children went to school one or two hours before daylight.

---

[1] ספר הסירים, § 946. [2] Cf. S. Duran, התשב״ץ, i. § 64.

[3] *B. Bathra*, 21 a. Where there was any infringement of this rule, it was in the direction of greater severity. In the חוקי התורה, § vi., ten is the number of pupils assigned to each teacher.

[4] S. Duran, ibid., speaks of the תלמיד חריף שישמע עם התינ וקות מפי הרב וחוזר ומשגיר בפי התינוקות ובני העיר חייבים לתת שכר לאותו תלמיד.

Sometimes the signal for school was the jingling of the silver bells which fringed the mantles of the Scrolls of the Law.[1] The boys continued at their lessons until the time for morning prayer, when their teacher took them to synagogue, or had a private service in his own house. The children then went home for a hasty breakfast, after which lessons were resumed until eleven o'clock, when there was a break for the midday meal, all the pupils re-assembling exactly at twelve. There was another very short interval between two and three o'clock, and work was continued until the time for evening prayer, after which the children returned home. Night preparation was encouraged in the Jewish homes.

Corporal punishment was generally, though not quite universally, approved. 'At first the child is allured, in the end the strap is laid upon his back.'[2] But the punishment was not severe. It was a salutary rule that corporal punishment was a momentary expedient which should only produce momentary effects. No teacher was allowed to punish a child with sufficient vigour to leave marks or cause other injurious effects. A teacher with a violent temper was at once superseded.

The boys were first taught Hebrew reading, beginning with the alphabet, which absorbed a month. The teacher used a small wooden pointer, called in France a *tendeur*, with which he indicated the letters.[3] When the letters were known, the vowel signs were taken, to which another month was devoted, and lastly the pupil learnt the combination of consonants and vowels into syllables. Three months ap-

---

[1] Rashi on *Sabb.*, 58 b. The schools were quite near the synagogues, when not in the same buildings. Cf. ch. ii. above.

[2] *Machzor Vitry*, p. 628; against corporal punishment see חסידים ס״, § 306.

[3] ס״ הסידים, § 893.

parently sufficed for this difficult step. In the fourth month
the reading of the Pentateuch was started with the Book of
Leviticus. During the second three months the boy read
a portion of the weekly lesson in Hebrew. The following
six months were used in translating the weekly lessons into
the vernacular. By that time the boy was six years old.
Books were naturally scarce, but the teacher took a tablet
or slate and wrote on it three or four verses, or even whole
chapters, and this served as the week's lesson.[1] The words
were then rubbed off and a fresh section written on the
same slate.

In his next year's course the boy was taught the
Aramaic version of the Pentateuch, which he translated
into the vernacular; the next two years were devoted to
the prophetical books and the hagiographa. At the age
of ten the boy began the Mishnah, and by the age of
thirteen he had read a selection of the most important
of the smaller tractates of the Talmud.[2] Those who were

---

[1] The method is cited in the name of Maimon, father of Maimonides, by
Simon Duran (שו"ת התשב"ץ, § 2). The Hebrew inscribed on the slate was
written curiously ; not more than three words on one line and then two
on the next, while every word was marked with quotation signs, thus : —

ויד"בר ה' א"ל
.בי"ש"ה לאמ"ר

This bizarre method was intended to accustom the boy to the thought that
the text of Scripture, when written in the ordinary style, was not to be
deleted or tampered with. A remarkable method of learning Hebrew by
alphabetical tables or groups in Palestine and Egypt is described by Saadya
in his *Commentaire sur le Sefer Yesira* (ed. Lambert, p. 81; French translation,
p. 104). The children wrote the letter-groups in their exercise-books
(cf. Bacher, in *Revue des Études Juives*, xxiii. p. 247, note 1). 'When the
child,' says Saadya, 'has learnt these groups, he has also learnt to spell
everything.' Cf. Friedlander, *Proc. Soc. Bibl. Arch.* 1896; *J. Q. R.* viii.

[2] *Tractate Berachoth*, and the whole of the Order *Moed* (relating to the
Festivals).

destined to qualify as professional students devoted the next seven years to the greater tractates of the Talmud.

As the pupil grew older, greater importance was attached to *repetition*. The same lesson was delivered by the teacher three times, and the pupils repeated it at home in the evening. There were, in addition, regular recapitulations at weekly or monthly intervals. Equally important was the rule that the teacher was bound to instruct from the book and not by heart. It has already been mentioned that books were scarce and dear, a copy of the Pentateuch costing nearly as much as would pay four months' salary of the teacher.[1]   It followed that most Jews were unprovided with books in synagogue, and thus the precentor recited most of the service aloud, repeating the portions which, in accordance with the rubrics, he himself first said in silence. To this scarcity of books and the consequent habit of many craning their necks to look into the same volume, the Jewish habit of swaying the body in prayer has been with some plausibility assigned.[2]   The same cause, no doubt, increased the instinctive reverence with which Jews always regarded books in the middle ages.[3]

But unlike most modern bibliophiles, they were very willing lenders.   ' If *A* has two sons, one of whom is averse to lending his books, and the other does so willingly, the father should have no doubt in leaving all his library to the second son, even if he be the younger.'[4]   This twelfth-

---

[1] Such a book cost three marks in 1150, while the teacher's salary was then ten marks per annum. On the prices of books at various times see Zunz, *Zur Geschichte*, p. 211.   [2] *Cuzari*, ii. 80 (Cassel, p. 189).

[3] Some of the quaint remarks on this subject by the author of the *Book of the Pious* were translated into English by the Rev. M. Adler in the *Bookworm*, 1891, pp. 251 seq.

[4] The *Book of the Pious*, § 875.

century piece of advice comes from Germany; another, emanating at about the same period from Provence, contains the following directions from Judah Ibn Tibbon to his son: 'Take particular care of your books; cover your shelves with a fine covering, guard them against damp and mice. Write a complete catalogue of your books, and examine the Hebrew books once a month, the Arabic every two months, and the bound volumes once a quarter. When you lend a book to any one, make a memorandum of it before it leaves your house, and when it is returned cancel the entry. Every Passover and Tabernacles call in all your books that are out on loan.'

This love of books had an aesthetic influence on Jewish education, and on this point a short digression must be made. The Spanish Jews were dilettanti as regards accuracy in style and fine calligraphy. Literary polish was acquired by the habit of Hebrew verse-making, an art with which the Spanish and Provençal Jews were all familiar. To be unable to write verses was to argue yourself possessed of a 'barren soul.'[1] Classical models were strictly followed, for Spanish poets took rather less liberties with the Hebrew language than Kalir and the French school of Jewish liturgical versifiers allowed themselves. My present point is that this tendency towards a chaste style was a marked feature of the education of the young Jews in Spain. 'Use no strained constructions or foreign words,' writes Judah Ibn Tibbon to his son, 'endeavour to cultivate a concise and elegant style; attempt no rhymes unless your versification is perfect.' As will soon appear, the study of grammar went hand in hand

[1] Joseph Ezobi's *Silver Bowl* (written in Provence in the thirteenth century). See below, p. 354, note 2.

with this feeling for style, but the aesthetic element is the one which is now under consideration.

The charm of a beautiful handwriting was strongly felt by all Jews,[1] but most powerfully of all by those who lived in Spain and Provence. 'Improve your handwriting,' says the same father whom I have just quoted, 'for beauty of handwriting, excellence of pen, paper, and ink, are an index of the writer's worth. You have seen books in my handwriting, and know how the son of R. Jacob your master expressed his admiration in your presence.' Or again, to give an instance from the thirteenth century, another father thus addresses his son :[2] —

> And like thy father sing in tunefulness:
> Hark thou, a barren soul is profitless.
> Purge well thy soul, no stain therein to leave,
> Remove its grosser parts in virtue's sieve.
> When thou a letter sendest to thy friend,
> Is it neatly written? nay? 'twill sure offend;
> For in his penmanship man stands revealed —
> Purest intent by chastest style is sealed.
> Be heedful then when thou dost pen thy songs;
> To lofty strains a goodly hand belongs.

There is a note of intense love of external as well as internal beauty in books in another noble remark of Judah Ibn Tibbon : 'Avoid bad society,' he says, 'but make your books your companions. Let your book-cases and shelves be your gardens and your pleasure-grounds. Pluck the fruit that grows therein, gather the roses, the spices, and the myrrh. If your soul be satiate and weary, change

---

[1] In praise of Jewish calligraphy cf. Renan (and Neubauer), *Ecrivains juifs français du XIV* siècle, p. 393. On the different styles of character used see Zunz, *Zur Geschichte*, pp. 206, 207.

[2] Joseph Ezobi's *Silver Bowl*, cf. the Eng. Trans. by D. I. Friedmann in the *Jewish Quarterly Review*, vol. viii.

from garden to garden, from furrow to furrow, from sight to sight. Then will your desire renew itself, and your soul be satisfied with delight.'

A similar feeling dominates the scheme of studies prefixed by the Spanish Jew, Profiat Duran, to the Hebrew Grammar which he wrote before 1403. Though only a portion of his canons have an aesthetic application, I give a summary of them all, as they throw considerable light on the manner in which a cultured Jew studied. It will be noticed that his canons apply to men of business as well as to professional students.

(i) Work in conjunction with a fellow-student. (ii) Use works which are brief or systematic. (iii) Attend to what you read, and understand as you go. (iv) Use mnemonics as an aid to memory. (v) Keep to one book at a time. (vi) Use only books which are beautifully written, on good paper, and well and handsomely bound. Read in a pretty well-furnished room, let your eye rest on beautiful objects so that you may love your work. Beauty must be everywhere, in your books and in your house. 'The wealthy must honour the Law,' says the Talmud; let them do this by paying for beautiful copies of the Scriptures. (vii) Use eye and ear; read aloud, do not work in silent poring. (viii) Sing as you read, especially the Bible; in olden times the Mishnah, too, was sung.[1] (ix) See that your text-books are written in *square* characters, as these are more original and more beautiful. (x) Use books which are written in a large hand with firm strokes, rather than

---

[1] Singing during study was common to Jews everywhere. Cf. Güdemann, i. p. 54. On the singing of the Mishnah and Talmud cf. Steinschneider, *Jewish Literature*, p. 154, and the presence of musical accents in some MSS. of the Talmud, e.g. S. Schechter and S. Singer, *Fragments of Talmudical MSS. in the Bodleian* (Cambridge, University Press, 1896), Introduction.

thin and faint, for these make a stronger impression on the eyes and understanding. (xi) Learn by teaching. (xii) Study for the pure love of knowledge. (xiii) Study regularly at fixed hours, and do not say, Within such and such a time I will finish so and so much. If you are occupied in business all day, read at night when your day's work is over. (xiv) The road to knowledge lies through prayer; pray that God may grant you the knowledge that you seek.[1]

[1] These canons draw no distinction between the professional and the lay student. In the fourteenth century it was found desirable in Germany to institute the formal conferment of the *Morenu* diploma, which entitled the recipient to act as a Rabbinical *dayan* or judge. Previously, the title *Rav* or *Rabbi* had become quite general, and from the twelfth century every adult male was so designated, probably to distinguish the Rabbanites from the Karaites, who disputed the validity of the Rabbinical traditions. Hence the need of a distinctive Rabbinical diploma was felt. Its conferment was in no sense an 'ordination,' but merely a *venia docendi* from teacher to pupil. The new title conferred no authority beyond that which the reputation of the teacher and the will of the congregation allowed. (Graetz, IV. ch. iv.; Zunz, *Zur Geschichte*, 185 seq.; Güdemann, iii. 31 seq.)

CHAPTER XX

THE SCOPE OF EDUCATION

UP to the thirteenth year the education of Jewish boys all the world over was practically identical. Religion was the foundation of the school curriculum, and the training that the child received was designed to form his character as well as his mind. Herein lay the advantage of the medieval method, for the Bible was at once food for the mind and the heart. The Hebrew Scriptures were taught to children as language and as ethics concurrently.[1] Hence resulted the hallowing of knowledge — produced by the joint action of synagogue and school. It was customary in the middle ages for all Jews to spend a good deal of time in synagogue on festivals and Sabbaths for the purpose of studying the Bible and Rabbinical literature.[2]

There was no learned caste in Judaism, for every Israelite studied the Law. Boys about thirteen years old were often competent to read the prayers for the congregation,[3] but by no means all Jews were able to read Hebrew

---

[1] ספר חסידים, § 304.

[2] Natronai Gaon (*Responsa* of Geonim, ed. Lyck, 87). Cf. Müller, *Massecheth Soferim*, p. 257.

[3] Maharil. Cf. *Responsa* of Solomon ben Adret (Venice, 1546), § 450, whence it is clear that many Jews were capable of acting as readers, and that the appointment of an official precentor was partly intended to end the competition for the right to read the prayers.

— as it appears in the Scrolls used in synagogue — without vowel-signs or punctuation. Right through the middle ages, indeed, the never obsolete note, 'Ah, the good old times!' is sounded by Jewish authorities,[1] but the point is less important historically than practically. It is a warning to modern critics of the present that their lament for the loss of the good old times is no more reasonable than were similar regrets in the middle ages.

But though this same principle, viz. the combination of moral with intellectual training, ruled Jewish life everywhere, it was modified in some countries by rival tendencies. The study of Hebrew grammar is a typical case. In Spain and Italy, grammar was taught as a special subject in and for itself. Scientific Hebrew philology had been founded in the tenth century by Saadya, not, as has been commonly assumed, by the Karaites.[2] On the other hand, when the great German Talmudist, Asheri, went to Toledo in the fourteenth century, he confessed that his Hebrew grammar was so weak that he could not teach the Bible to the Spanish Jews. Hebrew grammar, however, was not entirely neglected in the Jewish schools of Germany and northern France, it simply had no independent place in the school curriculum.[3] It was learnt as a means

---

[1] For charges of ignorance see *Responsa* of Geonim, *Mafteach*, p. 25: Maharil, *Hilchoth Pesach*, עיה רבתה השכחה; *Responsa*, תשב"ץ, ii. 39, where he says 'all bridegrooms are ignorant, and cannot read the weekly portion from the Scroll'; Elia Mizrachi, מים עמוקים, 13; and S. Morpurgo, שמש צדקה, p. 102 c.

[2] Cf. W. Bacher, *Die Anfänge der Hebr. Grammatik* (Leipzig, 1895, p. 2): ' Bisher ist durch Nichts erwiesen, das schon vor ihm (= Saadya) der eine oder andere *Karäische* Lehrer unter der Einwirkung der arabischen Sprachwissenschaft zu ähnlichen Anfängen der hebräischen Grammatik gelangt wäre wie Saadya.'

[3] On the French and German Hebrew Grammarians of the middle ages, see Zunz, *Zur Geschichte*, pp. 107 seq.

to an end, that end being the true exposition of the Scriptures.

That grammar — in the practical sense — was not overlooked in these countries may be seen from this fact. In no part of the world did the medieval Jews speak a jargon. They spoke Arabic, Spanish, Italian, German, or French with accuracy, and wrote it with precision, though they probably employed Hebrew characters. Jewish jargons arose in the middle of the fifteenth century, and the phenomenon was due less to ignorance than to too much knowledge. The Jews were always bilingual, but in the fifteenth century there was hardly a congregation in which a large foreign element had not been forced to settle by continued expulsions from their native land. A jargon was inevitable, for as the only linguistic element common to all the Jews was the Hebrew, it came that many Hebrew words were introduced into the vernacular. Another source of the inroad of Hebrew words into the common speech of Jews was the practice of teaching young children the Hebrew names of ordinary domestic objects to improve their Hebrew vocabulary.

The Hebrew words introduced into *Ladino* were not, however, of this class. *Ladino* was a Jewish-Spanish dialect carried by the Jews from Spain into their exile. The Hebrew words which occur in this language are not the names of common objects. They are religious terms, sympathetic terms — such as the words for widow, father, pity, love — in which Hebrew is particularly rich, or they are emphatic ejaculations and colloquialisms.[1] It is worth noting that precisely these types of words are still common with Jews who otherwise speak the ordinary vernacu-

---

[1] M. Grünbaum, *Jüdisch-Spanische Chrestomathie* (Frankfurt, 1896), Intro., p. 2; on German jargon see his *Jüd.-Deutsche Chrest.* (Leipzig, 1882).

lars with purity and precision. The truth is that Hebrew possesses a wealth of emotional terms which find but feeble representatives in modern languages. Moreover, centuries of loving association have given to such Hebrew terms an intensity of meaning which the English and other modern equivalents lack.

But the fact must not be forgotten that the Jews always had a literary language as well as these jargons, and that language was the neo-Hebrew, which, despite the debasement to which it became subjected, remained on the whole chaste and pure, and only changed in the direction of greater flexibility and handiness. The Hebrew used by the Jews remained entirely free from foreign elements, for it must not be forgotten that the Hebrew poetry of the middle ages (as well as the Hebrew prose) was built entirely on literary and not on national instincts. This is a very rare phenomenon, the growth of a genuine poetry in a language which was not the language spoken by the poets.

Before the middle of the fifteenth century the Jews spoke the vernacular grammatically, even if they sometimes interlarded it with Hebraisms. Vernacular poetry was written by medieval Jews not only in Arabic and Spanish, but also in Latin, Italian, German, and French.[1] In the tenth century, Saadya translated the Bible into Arabic, the language no doubt more popular as a literary vehicle with Jews of Arabian Spain than other vernaculars were with the Jews of the rest of Europe. For the use of Jews in France and Germany the works, whether of Jews or Mohammedans, which were written in Arabic, were trans-

---

[1] Cf. Steinschneider, *Jewish Literature*, pp. 169 and 178. Leo de Modena in the sixteenth century had so much command of Italian that he was able to write lines which made good sense whether read as Hebrew or Italian.

lated into Hebrew. This, in passing, be it noted, implies that the French and German Jews were not altogether destitute of interest in extra-Biblical and Talmudical studies.

A paragraph or two more must be devoted to a few of the compositions written by medieval Jews in the various languages of Europe. Samuel the Nagid (died 1055) addressed King Habus of Granada 'in a poem of seven Beit, each of which was in a different language; and in several Muwasseh — poems in which the rhymes recur every seventh line like pearls in an elaborately arranged necklace — of Jehuda Halevi (twelfth century), the point of the whole consists in an Arabic distich. The oldest authority for the tradition of the *Cid* is his "officer," the apostate (Jew) Ibn Alfange. To the highly prized poets of Spain belong Abraham Ibn ol Fakkhar (died 1239?), Abraham Ibn Sahl (1200–1250), Ibn el Mudawwer, and the poetess Kasmune.'[1] Contemporaneously with these may be noticed a rarer spectacle, a German Jew in the guise of a Minnesinger. This was Süsskind of Trimberg. In the castle of the lord of Trimberg, which lay perched on the ridge of a vine-clad hill, and which threw its shadow into the winding Saale, or perhaps in the abodes of neighbouring knights, the Jewish lyrical poet, to the plaudits of knights of high degree and their beautiful dames, 'poured forth, lute in hand, his melodious strains, and the largesses which were showered on him proved his sole means of support.'[2] Süsskind was not quite alone in his love for the troubadour's art. Love-songs and ballads were read in the twelfth century by Jews, though the reading of the *Romance* was not recommended as a holy recreation.[3] The Franco-Jewish poet, Yedayah

[1] Steinschneider, *Jewish Literature*, p. 170.
[2] Graetz, *History of the Jews* (Eng. Trans.), III. ch. xiii.
[3] Güdemann, i. 32.

Penini, perhaps imitated the methods of the troubadours in his *Defence of Woman*, written in Hebrew in 1210.[1]

Another Jewish troubadour, Santob de Carrion, flourished in Castile in the fourteenth century. Of his *Book of Maxims*, written in Spanish in 1350 Ticknor says that 'the measure is the old *redondilla*, and is uncommonly easy and flowing for the age.' The poem still enjoyed considerable reputation in the fifteenth century for its 'quaint and pleasant' lines.[2] Much similar literature is recorded in Spain and Portugal, and the Jews of Germany, too, loved the legends of national heroes which they preserved in the vernacular, but sometimes in Hebrew characters.[3] Naturally, too, religious literature was cultivated in the vernacular. A Jewess of Regensburg, named Litte, wrote the *History of David* in the contemporary German dialect, using German rhymes interspersed with a few Hebraisms.[4] Later, a Jewess of Venice, Deborah Ascarelli, translated Hebrew hymns into elegant Italian verses.[5] Translations of the Bible, made by Jews in Spanish, were already printed at the first half of the sixteenth century. Some of these Jewish translations were apparently employed by the Protestants of Spain.[6]

A final word must be added with regard to the contributions made by Jews to the vernacular drama. The dramatic dialogues of Samuel Usque (1553) played a double rôle. Not only were they written in excellent Portuguese

---

[1] This suggestion of Professor Kaufmann is disputed by Renan (and Neubauer) in *Les Écrivains Juifs français de XIVᵉ siècle*, p. 25.

[2] Ticknor, *History of Spanish Literatur*, i. pp. 93, 95.

[3] Steinschneider, op. cit. p. 178.

[4] Zunz, *Zur Geschichte und Literatur*, p. 173.

[5] Graetz, op. cit. V. ch. iii.

[6] Ticknor, op. cit. pp. 48, 49.

by their author,[1] but they were translated into Italian. He himself rendered Petrarch into Spanish. But of the Jewish dramatists of this time the most famous was the Portuguese Jew, Antonio Enriques Gomez, the contemporary of Calderon. This gallant soldier, for he also won his spurs as a knight, composed some twenty-two comedies, some of which were received with much applause in Madrid.[2] His services to Mars and the Muses did not, however, win immunity for him. Persecuted by the Inquisition, he fled to France, where he enjoyed the friendship of Richelieu, and produced a vast array of epics and elegies in the vernacular. Finally, he found a resting-place in the then home of freedom, Amsterdam, where he heard, with grim satisfaction, that he had been burnt in effigy at an auto-da-fe in Seville. This was in 1660. The poet died in the same year.

But the chief drawback to the medieval Jews was their general dislike of Latin, the language not only of the destroyer of the Temple, but also the *religious* language of the medieval Church.[3] In Spain and Italy this repulsion was less keenly felt, and many a Jewish statesman in the Iberian peninsula conducted diplomatic correspondence in the Latin tongue. It is certain that at least in these countries Jews were quite familiar with Latin throughout the middle ages. The intellectual intercourse between Jews and Christians was therefore easier in Spain and Italy. An Italian Bible was regarded with something of the same

---

[1] Julius Steinschneider, in the *Festschrift zum X. Stiftungsfest des Akademischen Vereins für jüdische Geschichte und Literatur* (Berlin, 1893), has a long study on Samuel Usque's *Consolation of Israel.*

[2] Ticknor, op. cit. ii. p. 497.

[3] This was probably the reason why Latin is described by Jews as the *priestly tongue* (כתיבת גלחים). Dr. Güdemann (i. 229) holds that the designation implies that no one but the priests could read and write it.

reverence that was felt for the Hebrew text itself,[1] a feeling quite foreign to the Jews of northern France or Germany. Jews translated works by Christian writers into Hebrew, and cited them even in their Biblical commentaries. But their chief activity as translators was displayed in the realm of science and philosophy. It is not too much to say that Europe owed to the Jewish translators its knowledge of Mohammedan culture, which until the Renaissance included the Classical as well.[2]

The school curricula of the Jews of Spain and Italy in the middle ages were, to use the medieval phrase, *encyclopedic* in character. There was no early specialization as with modern systems, but all men of culture went through a wide and liberal course. In the case of Italy, indeed, it is hard to speak of a curriculum at all, for the very breadth of culture there, especially when it began to absorb the best blood of Spain, introduced an amazing variety into the educational notions. It should be remembered, too, that the Jews everywhere acted on the principle that particular cases must not be forced under general rules, and the idiosyncrasies of the individual pupil were carefully observed and respected.

But nowhere was there so much variety in the method of teaching as in Italy. This may account, too, for a certain free thought and laxity such as one seeks for in vain in the great Talmudical schools of the Rhine-lands, where, if the educational curriculum was narrower in extent, it was deeper in intent. After the thirteenth century, all the

---

[1] Güdemann, ii. p. 206.

[2] See the great work of Dr. Steinschneider, *Die Hebraeischen Uebersetzungen des Mittelalters* (2 vols., Berlin, 1893). For the services of Jews to the propagation of Folk-lore, cf. J. Jacobs, *Jewish Ideals*, pp. 135 seq.

original Talmudical work emanated from the French and German, not from the Spanish or Italian schools. Spain itself was Gallicized so far as its Talmudical studies were concerned by Franco-German emigrations of the thirteenth century, just as, three centuries later, Turkey and the rest of Europe were Arabicized by the accession of the Spanish exiles. The Jewish educational curriculum in Italy — and this, be it remarked, long before the Renaissance — included the whole domain of intellectual pursuits: Theology, Poetry, Philosophy, and Natural Science in all its branches. The curriculum in Arabian Spain is, however, even more important, as it dates from an earlier period than the Italian, and its broad lines could not have been paralleled outside Spain in the early middle ages.

The ordinary course of Hispano-Jewish study was, in the twelfth century,[1] Bible, Hebrew, Poetry (satirical, eulogy, and love-poem), Talmud, the relation of Philosophy and Revelation, the Logic of Aristotle, the Elements of Euclid, Arithmetic, the mathematical works of Nicomachus, Theodosius, Menelaus, Archimedes, and others; Optics, Astronomy, Music, Mechanics, Medicine, Natural Science, and, finally, Metaphysics. This wide and liberal curriculum was continued in later ages with unimportant variations, except in detail. In the middle of the thirteenth century, Jehuda ben Samuel Ibn Abbas[2] includes in the school curriculum Reading, Translation of the Pentateuch, the Historical Books of the Old Testament, Hebrew Grammar (treatises

---

[1] From the seventh chapter of Joseph ben Jehuda Aknin's Arabic work טב אלנפוס (Heb. מרפה לנפש); Steinschneider, *Hebr. Uebersetzungen*, p. 33; Güdemann, *Das Jüdische Unterrichtswesen*, etc. (Vienna, 1873), pp. 42 seq.

[2] In the fifteenth chapter of his יאיר נתיב, Steinschneider, op. cit. p. 35; Güdemann, pp. 147 seq. Cf. Abraham Ibn Ezra's *Yesod Mora*.

by Ibn Janach, Kimchi, Chayuj, Abraham Ibn Ezra), Talmud[1] (with Rashi's commentary and the additional glosses
known as Tossafoth), moral works such as Ibn Aknin's *Cure
of the Soul* and Honein's *Ethics of the Philosophers.* When
the religious curriculum was completed, the pupil 'tasted
the honey of science,' beginning, strangely enough, with
Medicine, for which a complete library of works are named.[2]
Next followed 'Indian' Arithmetic. The boy must have
been fifteen or sixteen before he began Arithmetic, but this
accounts for the fact that it was taught without the expenditure of much time over first principles. These would
already have been acquired during the ordinary intellectual
development of the youth. As Abraham Ibn Ezra's Arithmetic[3] was much used, it may be well to point out that the
order of subjects is a rather curious one: Multiplication,
Division, Addition, Subtraction, Fractions, Proportion,
Square Root. As, however, Addition starts with the sum-
mation of series, it is not so strange that it succeeds Multiplication and Division. After Arithmetic and other
mathematical subjects, including Music, the pupil commenced the study of Aristotle's Logic as interpreted by
Averroes. It is necessary to point out that the only
immediate disciples whom this great Arabian philosopher
inspired were Jews. Then the student took a systematic
course of Natural Science and Metaphysics.

The Spanish Jews were, as the result of this training,
men of the widest possible culture. One detects no note
of medievalism at all in their works and their lives, unless
it be the absence of special bent. Whatever their ultimate

---

[1] The order is the usual one: first Berachoth, then Moed, then the larger
Orders, Nashim, Nezikim, etc.   [2] Steinschneider, loc. cit.
[3] *The Book of Numbers* (ספר המספר), ed. M. Silberberg (Frankfort, 1895).

business in life was to be, the Jew of this liberal school was trained in all the arts and sciences of the day. The Rabbi, the financier, the man of letters, was also poet, philosopher, and often physician.

In contrast with this breadth, the acquirements of the medieval Jews in the rest of Europe shrink to insignificance. It is certain, however, that their culture was far higher than is usually supposed. Zunz, writing in the middle of the present century, when the struggle for enlightenment in Jewish educational methods was only half won, was scarcely just to the French and German Jews of the middle ages.[1] He agrees, however, that the Jews were better educated than their Christian contemporaries, but says with truth that a great deal of ignorance prevailed on natural phenomena, and that the Jewish atmosphere as well as the Christian was filled with demons and monsters. Birds grew spontaneously in the air on the trees,[2] and the Sea of Galilee flowed into the ocean.[3] Jews in the thirteenth century took omens from dreams like the rest of the world. The mystical movements of the middle ages were also the source of the admission into Jewish life of a good deal of ignorant superstition. Jews knew of men who had no shadows, of evil spirits lurking in caverns,[4] they feared the evil-eye, believed in witches and ghouls who devoured children, trusted to spells and incantations. In all this the Jews were in the same position as the Christians.

Admitting these and many similar facts, it still remains

[1] *Zur Geschichte* (1845), p. 177.
[2] Meir of Rothenburg, *Responsa* (ed. Lemberg), 160.
[3] *Raben*, 54. Cf. Güdemann, i. p. 117.
[4] Spanish Rabbis like Maimonides were remarkably free from such superstitions. Abraham Ibn Ezra even denied in set terms the existence of demons; a remarkable feat for the twelfth century.

clear that the intellectual attainments of the Jews of Europe, even outside the realms of theology, were by no means inconsiderable. Zunz remarks that a Rabbi like Samson of Sens had got no farther in his mathematical knowledge of a square than the certainty that 'the diagonal must be more than seven-fifths of the side.' But surely this was a very accurate approximation. Similarly, the great eleventh-century French Rabbi, Rashi, obviously knew no 'Indian Arithmetic,' but the calculations in his commentaries, though cumbersome, are completely accurate, and display a real grasp of first principles.[1] Some mathematical knowledge is displayed by the French Rabbi, known as *Rashbam*, in his famous Commentary on the Pentateuch.[2] It was, in fact, impossible to understand certain parts of the Talmud as the students in the great continental *yeshibas* did, without a considerable knowledge of mathematical principles, and it is instructive that in the seventeenth century we find appended to the legal decisions of a German Rabbi a list of propositions of Euclid needed for the elucidation of the Law.[3] The Jewish calendar, which the French and German Rabbis thoroughly understood, demanded some astronomical knowledge. It is the fact, too, that out of such a school there arose, in the eighteenth century, accomplished mathematicians like the so-called Gaon, Elijah of Wilna. Jewish children, be it remembered, in the middle ages were taught the meaning of numbers together with the alphabet.[4] The Jews of northern France

[1] See Rashi to *T. B. Succah*, 8 a; *Zebachim*, 59 b.

[2] See e.g. on Exodus xxvi. 9, etc.

[3] See the end of Jonah Landsofer's מעיל צדקה, where he proves Euclid I. 1, 9, 11, 22, etc.

[4] Cf. Güdemann, i. 118. They were taught that א = 1, ב = 2, ג = 3, and so forth.

were well acquainted with French, and transcribed it in Hebrew characters with phonetic precision.[1] Maharil, the great German Rabbi of the fourteenth century, was an adept at vocal music, and records many melodies.

Undoubtedly, however, the mass of the Jews failed to attain the lofty level of the Arabo-Spanish culture. The deficiency was great in volume, but greater in point of view. The difference was one of mental attitude rather than of mental attainments. To the Jews of Spain, Italy, and Provence, theology did not exhaust culture. Elsewhere nothing but the literature of religion was considered worthy of study. Theology absorbed the whole mind, and the dabbling of the young in metaphysics was not only considered useless, but also dangerous. It sapped faith and produced a divided allegiance to God. The violent reaction against philosophical inquiry which broke out, even in Spain and Provence, over the remains of Maimonides was not stayed in Jewish life until the era of the French Revolution. In the intervening centuries the Jews were driven in masses to the non-cultured lands of Europe, and the Universities were closed to them except by the road of baptism. The Jews were expelled from France and Spain, and the only cultured land left open to them was commercial Italy. For a long period the Jews of Turkey continued the Spanish tradition, and only lost their old culture in modern times under the stress of internal and external degeneration.

I have just said that the Jews of Italy and Spain did not bound their intellectual horizon on all sides by theology. Perhaps it would be more accurate to say, that while they

---

[1] Some of the oldest French extant is to be found in the glosses of Rashi. Cf. E. Renan (and Neubauer), *Écrivains Juifs français du XIVe siècle*, p. 389.

regarded Religion as the ultimate goal of education, they
still considered other subjects necessary as handmaids or
adjuncts to theology.   Joseph Ibn Caspi, in the early
decades of the fourteenth century, agreed that the fundamental principles of Judaism were not to believe but to
rationally know that God is, that he is one, that man must
love and fear him.[1]   'How can I know God and that he
is one, unless I know what knowing means, and what con-
stitutes unity?   Why should these things be left to non-
Jewish philosophers?   Why should Aristotle retain sole
possession of treasures that he stole from Solomon?[2]   No
one really knows the true meaning of loving God and
fearing him, unless he is acquainted with natural science
and metaphysics, for we love not God as a man loves his
wife and children, nor fear we him as we would a mighty
man.   I do not say that all men can reach this intellectual
height, but I maintain that it is the degree of highest
excellence, though those who stand below it may still be
good.   Strive thou, my son, to attain this degree; yet be
not hasty in commencing metaphysical studies, and constantly read moral books.'   It was undoubtedly a narrowing of religion to make Aristotle's works in Maimonized
form the only road to it.   Ibn Caspi's assumption would
inevitably restrict the number of those who can serve God
with truth, for the ordinary mortal is not a philosopher.
One can understand the vigour and temper with which
the non-philosophers resented this attitude and, throwing
themselves into the opposite extreme, asserted that metaphysics led not to, but from, God.

[1] Joseph Ibn Caspi's ספר המוסר in Eleazar Ashkenazi's טעם זקנים (1854).

[2] For the legend that Aristotle derived his philosophy from Solomon
on his supposed visit to Jerusalem with Alexander the Great, cf. my article
in *Mind*, July, 1888.   See also the Frankel-Grätz *Monatsschrift* for 1860.

Ibn Caspi was no doubt doing himself less than justice. He meant that there were other interests in life besides religion, but he asserted that these other interests were religious. Another Jew of the same school placed the matter in a clearer light. Yedaya Bedaressi (1280–1340), the poet-philosopher, was satisfied to prove that secular and scientific occupations were not inconsistent with a complete belief in God or devotion to the demands of religion. In his famous letter [1] to the half-hearted opponent of secular studies, Solomon ben Adret, he reveals the strength of his own convictions. He even adds : 'It is certain that if Joshua the son of Nun arose to forbid the Provençal Jews to study the works of Maimonides, he would scarcely succeed. For they have the firm intention to sacrifice their fortunes and even their lives in defence of the philosophical works of Maimonides.' The men who wrote in this strain would certainly have stood in the van of the literary Renaissance had not persecution laid its cold hand on their enthusiasm for knowledge.

Modern investigations make it clearer and clearer that the medieval Jews were kept from their share in the Renaissance by external and accidental causes. In Italy alone did they participate in the new expansion of men's minds. Elsewhere they were denied the chance. But they were, in truth, the pioneers of the Renaissance, whose fruits they did not share. As the Arab science dwindled and Latin learning took its place, the Jews of Provence at

[1] Cf. Renan (and Neubauer), *Les Écrivains Juifs français du XIVᵉ siècle*, pp. 31 seq. 'Comme tous les savants Juifs du moyen âge, Yedaya était universel. Nous aurons bientôt à apprécier le philosophe et le moraliste. Il s'occupa également des études talmudiques, notamment de la partie agadique, sur laquelle il fit des commentaires. Ajoutons qu'il était médecin, puisqu'il a fait des gloses sur le Canon d'Avicenne' (op. cit. p. 13).

the end of the thirteenth century were well equipped to lead the change. 'The Jews,' says Renan, 'ought to have played a great part in the work of the Renaissance. One of the reasons why France was slow in gaining by the great transformation is that, about 1500, France was quite destitute of a Jewish element. The Jews to whom Francis I was forced to have recourse for the foundation of his college, le Canosse, Guidacier, were Italian Jews.' [1]

When at last it did come, the Renaissance for which it had waited fell on Jewish life like a strong stream swollen by a long-gathered accumulation of waters. The sharpening of the mind produced by several centuries' devotion to Talmudical dialectics provided the Jews with a keen instrument for cultivating the fields fertilized by the rushing streams of emancipation. The postponement of the Jewish middle ages until the fifteenth century, and the late birth of the Renaissance at the end of the eighteenth, produced effects which could not vanish in a day. But because it came late, the Jewish Renaissance was all the more comprehensive. It will need, however, the lapse of at least another generation before its full effects, for good or evil, will have unfolded themselves.

[1] Renan, *Les Écrivains Juifs français du XIV⁰ siècle*, p. 393: 'À partir de la seconde moitié du xiiie siècle, l'arabe n'est plus connu des Juifs de Provence, à moins d'une étude spéciale; mais, d'un autre côté, ces Juifs provençaux, pour l'astronomié et la médecine, avaient des sources d'excitations toutes particulières. À mesure que la science arabe disparaissait, la science latine naissait; cette évolution nouvelle de l'esprit humain allait donner au travail israélite tout son prid. Les Juifs devaient avoir une part considérable dans l'œuvre de la Renaissance. Une des raisons pour lesquelles la France fut en retard dans cette grande transformation, c'est que, vers 1500, elle s'était à peu près privée de l'élément juifs. Les Juifs auxquels François Iᵉʳ dut avoir recours pour la fondation de son Collège, le Canosse, Guidacier, étaient des Juifs italiens.'

CHAPTER XXI

MEDIEVAL PASTIMES AND INDOOR AMUSEMENTS

A MERRY spirit smiled on Jewish life in the middle ages, joyousness forming, in the Jewish conception, the coping stone of piety. There can be no greater mistake than to imagine that the Jews allowed their sufferings to blacken their life or cramp their optimism. Few pastimes of the middle ages were excluded from the Jewish sphere. The Jew rarely invented a game, but he adopted a good thing when he saw it. The stern, restraining hand of religion only occasionally checked the mirth and light-heartedness with which the Jew yielded himself to all the various pleasures of which his life was capable.

We have already seen that the day of rest was not a day of gloom. To walk abroad in the fresh air on the Sabbath was a favourite delight of the Jews in the middle ages. On the festivals they strolled by brooks and streams, and watched the fishes disporting themselves in the water. They carried food with them which they threw into the streams, and derived a simple pleasure from the pastime, even though it was not strictly in accordance with Jewish ritual law.[1] The service in synagogue was not lengthened

---

[1] Maharil, הלכות חול המועד.

beyond measure, so as to 'preserve the pleasure of the festival.'[1]   Industrious as the Jewish women were, they had many holidays.   On the new moon they did no work, but amused themselves in ways to be described below, while the men and women, besides their other home-games, spent part of Purim in light and pleasant reading, in making preparations for a forthcoming wedding, or in embroidering gay garments for future wear.[2]

Joyous wedding parties and bridal feasts were held even on the Sabbath, — the day of peace, but not of repression, — singing and dancing occurred sometimes to the accompaniment of instrumental music, and, as we shall soon note, indoor amusements, such as chess and other table-games, were permitted on the seventh day.   The board was spread with the choicest viands that the husband's purse could buy, the wine flowed, and conversation tripped along, witty, religious, and cheery, interspersed with semi-religious songs set to merry tunes.   If the Jew visited his Rabbi, he heard many a humorous anecdote or quaint intellectual quip, told with a smile to a responsively smiling audience, who the more willingly applied the moral because they enjoyed the tale.   The Jewish observance of the Sabbath was strict but not sombre ; it was Judaic and not Puritanical — two terms far from identical in significance. Life was transfigured on the Sabbath day, and a tone of elevated joy was the prevailing note.

Religion did, however, seriously affect the Jewish amusements in two significant particulars.   These were the suppression of gambling and the interference with such

---

[1] See e.g. the interesting statement to this effect in the *Machzor Romania* (Constant. 1573), New Year, 30 a.

[2] כל דבר שאין צריך עיון, *Kolbo*, 46 b.

recreations as involved free intercourse between the two sexes. These points, however, will best be approached in the process of a general treatment of the favourite Jewish recreations of the middle ages.

Intellectual pastimes were far more common than physical as the middle ages advanced. But in the fourth century Jerome, when on a visit to Syria, saw 'large, heavy stones which Jewish boys and youths handled and held aloft in the air to train their muscular strength.'[1] At the same period, the Palestinian Jews were wont to practise archery, probably as a form of recreation.[2] Considerably earlier Tacitus, a hostile witness, says that 'the bodies of the Jews are sound and healthy, and hardy to bear burdens.'[3] Unhappily everything connected with the ancient gymnasia became distasteful to the Jews after the wars with Rome, and athletic exercises became a portion of 'foreign culture' which was tabooed.[4]

Jewish antipathy to another favourite sport — hunting — was much deeper. Already in the Bible the figures introduced as devoted hunters — Nimrod and Esau — are by no means presented in a favourable light. Herod is the first person described in post-Biblical Jewish history as 'a most excellent hunter, in which sport he generally had great success owing to his skill in riding, for in one day he once killed forty wild beasts.'[5] Herod was also a 'most straight javelin-thrower and a most unerring archer.' Now, as the

---

[1] On Zechariah, xii. 4.

[2] See Bacher, *Revue des Études Juives*, xxvi. pp. 63–68. The recreation is described by the phrase קורה חצים.

[3] *Hist.* v. 6: 'Corpora hominum salubria et ferentia laborum.'

[4] That athletics were included by the Talmud under חכמת יונית, 'Greek wisdom,' may be seen from *B. Kama*, 83 a, and *Sota*, 49 b.

[5] Josephus, *Wars*, I. xxi. 13.

Jews were frequently forbidden in the middle ages to carry arms, even in Spain, and as, moreover, Jews were never noted riders,[1] it is obvious that the moral objection to sports in which weapons and horses were necessary accessories must have gained overwhelming strength from compulsion. Hunting in particular was resented as cruel, and therefore un-Jewish. ' He who hunts game with dogs, as non-Jews do, will not participate in the joy of the Leviathan,' says a great medieval Jew.[2] The very vehemence of this prohibition prepares us to expect that, as a matter of fact, Jews did at least occasionally participate in hunting. Nor are indications wanting that this was the case, though rarely, throughout the middle ages. Zunz cites an instance.[3] In Provence, too, the Jews possessed trained falcons, and used them in hawking, themselves riding on horseback.[4]

Mr. Joseph Jacobs has unearthed an even more interesting case, which occurred in Colchester in 1267. ' A certain doe ' was started in Wildenhaye Wood by the dogs of Sir John de Burgh, and in her flight came by the top of the city of Colchester. ' And there issued forth Saunte son of Ursel, Jew of Colchester, Cok son of Aaron, and Samuel son of the same, Isaac the Jewish chaplain, Copin and Elias, Jews, and certain Christians of the said city. And these with a mighty clamour chased the same doe through the south gate into the aforesaid city, and they so worried her by their shouting that they forced her to jump over a wall,

---

[1] Nowack, *Lehrbuch der Hebr. Archäologie*, i. p. 367.

[2] Meir of Rothenburg, ש״ות (ed. Mekitse Nirdamim), p. 7, § 27. Cf. Talmud *B. Aboda Zara*, 18 b. The feast on the flesh of the Leviathan typified the joys of paradise.

[3] *Zur Geschichte*, p. 173.

[4] Berliner, *Aus dem inneren Leben*, p. 17.

and she thus broke her neck. . . . And there came upon them Walter the bailiff and Robert the Toller, beadle of the same city, and carried thence the game, and had their will of it.'[1] Evidently the Jews could not resist the instinct of joining in the chase when the animal crossed their path. But though other instances are on record, it may be doubted whether the Jews, even when their relations with Christians were friendly, could heartily participate in the chase, seeing that they could not eat the game so killed, in company with Christians.[2]

With more readiness, however, the Jews surrendered themselves to the pleasures of the tourney and other knightly exercises which involved no cruelty to animals. We have seen above that in their wedding festivities Jews often performed mimic fights. Jewish duellists were not unknown.[3] They would no doubt have been ready to join in martial sports had they been permitted. But in most places the Jews were not allowed to bear arms even in their own quarters and for self-defence. In 1181 it was enacted in England that 'no Jew shall keep with him mail or hauberk, but let him sell or give them away, or in some

---

[1] J. Jacobs, *Jewish Ideals*, p. 226. The narrative is from the Forest Roll of the county of Essex (1277). The Jews were severely punished for this breach of the forest laws.

[2] It will be noticed that in the Colchester case the Jews did not eat the doe, for an animal slain in the chase is unfit for the Jewish table. At a much later date Jews who indulged in hunting abstained from eating the hunted animal (S. Morpurgo, שו''ת שמש צדקה, p. 66 b). For other (late) references to Jewish hunters, see חתם סופר ד''י ח'', §§ 52, 53; J. Reischer, שבות יעקב, ii. § 63. The chief Jewish objection to hunting was based on its *cruelty*. Yet Isserlein mentions the cropping of a dog's ears and tail to improve its looks (פסקים וכתבים, 105). Cf. p. 128 above.

[3] Depping, *Les Juifs dans le moyen âge*, p. 182 : ' Judicatum est quod Calfot Judaeus poterit sequi Abraham Judaeum per duellum de Kemino ' (= in an open road). The date of this entry is 1207.

other way remove them from him.'[1]   Before that date sev-
eral English Jews seem to have ranked as knights.   The
Jews of Worms were practised in bearing arms,[2] while in
Prague this was even more notably the case.[3]

In Spain the Jews highly prized the privilege of wearing arms, styling themselves knights, and bearing stately
names.   Frequent attempts were made to prevent this,
especially towards the end of the fourteenth century.   In
1390 the Jews of Majorca were forbidden to carry arms in
their ghetto;[4] in 1412 the King of Castile resolved that no
Jews might 'carry swords, daggers, or similar arms in the
cities, towns, and places of my kingdoms.'[5]   In Portugal
as late as 1481 the following representations were made to
John II: 'We notice Jewish cavaliers, mounted on richly
caparisoned horses and mules, in fine cloaks, cassocks, silk
doublets, closed hoods, and with gilt swords.'[6]   The Jews
in Italy held sportive tourneys, in which the boys fought on
foot with nuts as pellets, while their elders rode on horseback through the streets, flourishing wooden-staves, and,
to the blast of horns and bugles, tilted at an effigy representing Haman, which was subsequently burnt on a mock
funeral pyre.[7]   Possibly the Jews actually took part in
real tourneys in the fourteenth century, and an instance
of such participation is recorded in Weissenfels in 1386.[8]

---

[1] Jacobs, *Jews of Angevin England*, cf. p. 75 with p. 260.

[2] *Rokeach*, § 196.

[3] G. Wolf, *Die Juden* (of Austro-Bohemia), p. 8.   Cf. ch. iv. above.

[4] *Revue des Études Juives*, iv. 38.

[5] The Ordinance of Cifuentes, § 7;   Lindo, p. 204.

[6] *The Cortes of Evora*, Lindo, p. 317.   [7] Kalonymos, מסכת פורים.

[8] Hecht, Wertheimer's *Jahrbuch*, iii. 169.   But compare Berliner, op. cit.
p. 16, and Zunz, *Zur Geschichte*, p. 184, from which it would seem that the
fight was not in sport, but earnest, and that the Jews merely defended themselves against the attack of a party of armed bandits.

The old religious objections to the classical gymnasia would probably have left little impress on medieval Jews had the latter been allowed a free choice.

Other amusements, of a more or less athletic nature, were also much favoured by Jews. They were extremely fond of foot-races. Both men and women frequently played games in which balls were used. The scene of this pastime was the street, or a public open space, and in France the game seems to have resembled tennis. Some authorities even permitted the game to be publicly played by women on festivals, others restricted the licence to children.[1] In place of a ball, round fruits, such as nuts and apples, or even eggs and spherical stones, were sometimes used. The nuts were placed in a heap, and the object of the player was to throw them down. This game was played both on the bare ground and on mats or carpets, women being particularly fond of it from very ancient times.[2] They also played a game which was something like skittles, a mark being set up to be thrown down by small stone pellets.[3] Sometimes victory in the *nut-game* was won by breaking the opponent's nuts. Another game with nuts needed a large urn, but the details of the game are not recorded.[4] The Jewish children also played at blind-man's-buff,[5] and enjoyed games in which sides were taken, such as the modern ' prisoner's base.' Each party

---

[1] דמשחקין בכדור שקורין פלו״שא בלע״ז בי״ט ברשות דרבים. Tossafoth to *Beza*, 12 a (near foot). In the Shulchan Aruch (*Orach Chayim*, 308, 45), ball-playing is forbidden on Sabbaths and festivals (but the note is added that some authorities permit it; cf. ibid. § 518, 1 note). In *Midrash Echa Rabba*, ii. 4, ball-playing on the Sabbath is cited as one of the causes of the destruction of the Temple.

[2] *T. B. Erubin*, 104 a; cf. *Kolbo*, 41 a.

[3] That is, I think, the game called אסקנדרי in the Talmud.

[4] Berliner, *Aus dem inneren Leben*, p. 12.   [5] Zunz, *Zur Geschichte*, 173.

appointed a chieftain or king, and the game consisted in endeavouring to capture the hostile representatives. So, too, they probably played at leap-frog.[1]

But by far the most popular athletic amusement of the Jews in the middle ages was *the dance*. Dancing, however, was not so much a personal pleasure as a means of rousing the enthusiasm of the assembled company. Hence gesticulations, violent leaps and bounds, hopping in a circle, rather than graceful pose or soft rhythmic movement, characterized the Jewish dances both of ancient and medieval times.[2] Apart from moral considerations, it is clear that promiscuous dancing between the two sexes was quite out of keeping with the style in which the art was performed by men. The women danced in line or circle, without any prescribed steps; but the leader would improvise a movement which the rest, striking cymbals the while, would attempt to imitate. They danced for the amusement, not of themselves, but of the onlookers, though naturally the two elements were not dissociated. How strongly dancing was beloved by the Jews has been indicated several times in the course of previous chapters.[3] But in the middle ages, despite the natural inappropriateness of promiscuous dancing already indicated, a tendency towards combined dances between men and women manifests itself. Against this innovation the voice of the Synagogue was unanimous. The Scriptural text (Prov. xi. 21) : —

> 'Hand to hand shall not go unpunished,'

was hurled with much effect at the offenders. 'Men and

---

[1] Löw, *Lebensalter*, p. 288.

[2] Cf. Nowack, *Lehrbuch der Hebr. Archäologie*, i. p. 279.

[3] Cf. above, especially the chapters on Marriage.

women shall neither rejoice nor mourn together,' said the
Jewish pietists of all ages.[1] Even young children only
played in the streets with their own sex.[2] The single
relaxation allowed was that a husband might dance with
his own wife, a father with his daughter, a mother with
her son, a brother with his sister.[3] This concession was
far from meeting the popular demands. Many Jews, especially young men and maidens, with some married couples,
disobeyed the Rabbinical rule, and not only danced together, but did so in the communal dancing-hall on the
Sabbath and festivals. The result was sometimes disas-
trous, for many Jewish husbands seriously objected to
their wives dancing with other men.[4] During the religious mania induced by the enthusiasm aroused by the
pseudo-Messiah, Sabatai Zevi, a good deal of temporary
licentiousness resulted from the indiscriminate dancing in
which the followers of Sabatai indulged.[5]

Another class of Jewish pastimes was of a more intellectual nature. Arithmetical tricks known as *gematria*

[1] ארחות צדיקים chapter on שמחה.

[2] The ספר חסידים, § 168, 9. Cf. against promiscuous dancing, op. cit. § 393;
הפרדס, 19 c; *Kolbo*, § 66; and other references in Zunz, *Zur Geschichte*,
p. 171.

[3] *Responsa*, David Cohen (1440?), § 14. Cf. too, C. Azulai, שו"ת יוסף אומץ,
§ 103, where this arrangement is described as 'an *ancient cherem*.'

[4] David Cohen, § 14. He raises no objection to the occurrence of dancing
on the Sabbath, but merely objects to the dancing of men with women
except in the cases already specified. Other authorities objected to amusements of this kind on the Sabbath altogether. Cf. the interesting discussion
in אבקת רוכל, § 206, whether 'young men of Toledo' located in Mayence
insisted on their right to amuse themselves outside the city in play-houses.
לטייל בשבת מחוץ לעיר במקומות מיוחדים לטייל. The custom of dancing, men and
women together, on festivals and to musical accompaniment survived later
on (cf. J. Steinhart, שו"ת זכרון יוסף, 17). Here, again, the objection was to
mixed dancing, not to the amusement as such.

[5] Graetz, *Geschichte*, x. 222.

were old favourites : perhaps instances of them are not unknown in the Old Testament.[1] At all events, they were very much fancied in the middle ages, and formed the recreation of great Rabbinical scholars. The Hebrew letters have a numerical as well as phonetic value, and thus endless entertainment could be obtained by the discovery that certain words had the same arithmetical equivalents as other words, which might then be connected with them for moral or humorous purposes. The Talmud, for instance, humorously says that a good Jew must drink wine on Purim until he can no longer distinguish between 'Blessed be Mordecai' and 'Cursed be Haman.' The point of this remark was derived from the numerical identity of the Hebrew words forming the two phrases.[2] Besides the gematrias, word-games were popular. One boy cited a Hebrew text, and the next player had to cap the quotation by another verse which began with the same letter which terminated the first quotation.[3] Somewhat of a similar nature was the *game of Samech and Pe*. These two Hebrew letters frequently appear in the Hebrew Pentateuch to mark two kinds of paragraphs. One boy chose *Samech*, the other *Pe*, and the book would be opened haphazard at any page. The game was decided by the number of times each letter occurred on the page thus turned up.[4]

There were three weeks in the year during which Jewish boys enjoyed a close time. Corporal punishment was forbidden between the 17th of Tammuz and the 9th of

---

[1] See Stade's *Zeitschrift* (1896), p. 122.

[2] The letters occurring in the sentences ברוך מרדכי and ארור המן each amount numerically to 502.

[3] *Book of the Pious*, § 644.　　　[4] Löw, *Lebensalter*, p. 289.

Ab — 'not even a strap may be used,' says the code,[1] ominous of what occurred at other periods of the year. During this happy period must be placed several boys' games, which could hardly have been perpetrated with impunity at other times. The *Rabbi game*, in which the boys donned the garments and affected the style of their teachers, was a delightful episode in the boy life of the middle ages. But their elders were not slow to participate in the fun, especially on that licensed day of the year, Purim. Men must laugh, and they laugh loudest at what interests them most. The more men's minds are full of their faith, the more ready they are to parody it and to get amusement out of it. To make sport of sacred things is by no means identical with irreverence. In the pre-Protestant ages, monks themselves connived at the buffooneries of the Lord Abbot of Misrule, the boy-Bishop, the President of Fools, or whatever else the mock representatives of the highest ecclesiastics were called. The Jews, too, on mirthful occasions, appointed scurrilous individuals gifted with a ready wit to act as pseudo-Rabbis, in whom was vested the inalienable right of laughing at sacred things, caricaturing the prayer-book, and ridiculing the real Rabbi, with his tricks of speech and gait and manner.

The most literary of these efforts were the Purim-Parodies,[2] which were of two types. Some caricature the Rabbinical style of argument, some parody the prayers, all are boisterous eulogies of the pleasures of wine. The

---

[1] Shulchan Aruch, אורח חיים, 551, § 18. Cf. *Rokeach.* § 309, and the ט"ז ad loc.

[2] For a bibliography of these parodies — of which some are as old as the fourteenth century — see Steinschneider, *Letterbode*, vol. vii. 1–13, and ix. 45–58.

former included 'Orders of Service for the Night of Drunkenness,'[1] which were far more legitimately amusing than were the imitations of the prayers.

Riddles were, however, the most characteristic of Jewish table-amusements in the middle ages.   In their origin, riddles were an attempt of early races to solve the mysteries of life; they were pieces of primitive science dependent on the discovery of somewhat remote analogies.   It is almost impossible to differentiate between the riddle and the metaphor.   But be their origin what it may, the ancient Hebrews were adepts in the construction and enjoyment of riddles.   The thirtieth chapter of Proverbs is a series of moral riddles, and the seventeenth chapter of Ezekiel unfolds a most beautiful and elaborate enigma with a moral signification.   In the Talmud and Rabbinical literature, a large number of famous sayings are put in the form of riddles.   Who is mighty?   Who is a fool?   Who is happy?   A whole class of popular phrases in the Talmud and Midrash are nothing more nor less than folk-riddles, the chief exponents being women-servants and children, but distinguished Rabbis also utilized this 'language of wisdom.'[2]   Ethical works of the middle ages, like Gabirol's 'Choice of Pearls,' abound in philosophical riddles.   Riddles found their way into the prayer-book for the passover eve.[3]   It goes without saying, therefore, that many Hebrew riddles of the middle ages were serious intellectual exercises.   The most famous instance of this type, as well as the most popular,

---

[1] ליל שמורים for ליל שכורים.

[2] Cf. on this whole subject, A. Wünsche, *Die Räthselweisheit bei den Hebräer* (Leipzig, 1883).

[3] The curious 'Who knows one? I know one,' etc.   According to Perles this hymn was imitated from a German folk-song (*Graetz Jubelschrift*, p. 37).

was Ibn Ezra's grammatical treatise, written in the form
of an enigma.[1] Every line of this riddle is full of point
and wit, but it is too technical for quotation. 'If you
want to know the answer,' says Ibn Ezra, 'ask the King
of Israel.' Now the Hebrew name of one of the kings
of Israel, Jehu,[2] does indeed contain the letters on which
Ibn Ezra was riddling.

Arithmetical puzzles set in the form of Hebrew acrostics were also a popular amusement with Jews of all ages.
Abraham Ibn Ezra was the author of several fine specimens, and many were subsequently composed, especially
for use on the Feast of Dedication.[3] These riddles are
a combination of *puns* and arithmetical niceties, but often
— especially in Ibn Ezra's hands — make very pretty play
with the *meaning* of the Hebrew letters. These are hard
to quote, as they need much citation of Hebrew for
their elucidation. 'There was a she-mule in my house :
I opened the door, and she became a heifer' — this is a
typical instance.[4] Strictly numerical riddles were also
constructed : 'Take thirty from thirty and the remainder
is sixty.'[5] To Ibn Ezra is, with some probability, ascribed
the famous arithmetical puzzle containing the device by
which the hero and his friends saved themselves from

---

[1] On the letters אהוי, often published and contained in many MSS., cf.
W. Bacher, *Abraham Ibn Esra als Grammatiker* (Jahresbericht of the Landes-
rabbinerschule, Budapest, 1881), p. 23.   [2] יהוא.

[3] These turn on the letters הנוכה (= Dedication), and are often *acrostics*.
A large number of such Hebrew riddles are extant in print and MSS. For
the use of puns in general, and in connexion with the word הנוכה in particular,
cf. Brüll's *Jahrbuch*, ix, pp. 18 seq.

[4] From Heb. פרדה (= *she-mule*) remove ד (pronounced דלח = *door*), and
there remains פרה (= *heifer*). Cf. for other instances Brüll, op. cit. p. 54,
and Jellinek, קונטרס הרמב"ם (2nd ed. Vienna, 1893), Appendix.

[5] From שלשים (= 30) take the ל (= 30), and the remainder is ששים (= 60).

being thrown overboard during a storm.   The same versa-
tile Rabbi is said to have written a pretty arithmetical
riddle on the subject of chess.

The poetical riddle also had its devoted admirers.
Most of the Jewish versifiers of the middle ages composed
riddles which display a considerable amount of fancy.
Some of the Hebrew riddles by Jehuda Halevi were
dainty beyond the average.[1]

Foreign riddles were early acclimatized on Jewish soil,
and thus some of the best known of the folk-riddles of all
lands were current in Jewish circles in the middle ages.
These imported riddles were often associated with interesting historical personages, such as King Solomon and
the Queen of Sheba, and the former sat in a crystal house
while the queen in vain plied him with mystic puzzles.
In the thirteenth century many of the riddles contained in
such folk-legends as *Solomon and Marcom* were already
known to the Jews.

The most Jewish type of this form of recreation was
the table-riddle.   The Greeks were no doubt adepts at this
form of wit, but in the middle ages the Jews and Arabs
were the chief admirers of it.   The thirteenth-century
Hebrew romances of Charizi and Zabara, the contemporary
social satires of Dante's Jewish friend, Immanuel of Rome,
abound in good table-riddles.   The Talmud also has some
fair specimens : 'Bake him with his brother, place him
in his father, eat him in his son, and then drink his father.' [2]
At all Jewish home festivities the flow of witty puzzles

---

[1] Some of these may be found in Mr. J. Jacobs' *Jewish Ideals*, p. 108.

[2] I.e. bake the fish in salt, its brother (for salt water comes with the fish
from the sea), place him in his father (= water), eat him in his son (i.e. the
juice or gravy), and then take a draught of water.   See *T. B. Moed Katon*,
11 a.

was ceaseless.   In this way, too, over the festive board, were retailed those folk-tales and Eastern myths in the diffusion of which to Europe the Jews played so great a part.   Cabalistic lore gave the children the 'Boy' Angel Sandalphon, the patron saint of youthful joys.   At their games the children addressed to him the invocation: 'Sandalphon, lord of the forest, protect us from pain.' [1] The Cabala, by many such loving touches, imparted new poetry to medieval life.

[1] Schechter, *Studies in Judaism*, p. 370.

CHAPTER XXII

MEDIEVAL PASTIMES (*continued*)

CHESS AND CARDS

THOUGH it is open to grave doubt whether the *game of chess* is referred to in the Talmud, it was already a well-known Jewish pastime in the twelfth century.[1] It seems to have first made its way into Jewish circles as a women's game; indeed most of the indoor games of the Jews in the middle ages started on their career under the patronage of the fair sex. It must be remembered that games were not played every day, but only on occasions of leisure, such as festivals. Women, as we have already seen, were privileged in this respect, and were allowed a licence denied to the men.[2] But the men also played chess on Sabbaths as the middle ages advanced, and no serious opposition was raised. In order to mark the honour of the occasion, the chessmen used on the Sabbath were made of silver,[3] and this habit became a stereotyped custom in the sixteenth century.

---

[1] Rashi, on Erubin, 61 a, explains the Talmudical נרדשיר to be identical with chess. Levy, *sub voce*, seems inclined to this view, but Löw, *Lebensalter*, p. 327, argues strongly against it. For the use of chess in the thirteenth century, see ספר חסידים, § 400, and Steinschneider, as cited below.

[2] Cf. in addition to the passages cited above, *Machzor Vitry*, p. 291.

[3] *Shilte Gibborim*, Erubin, 127 b.

No voice was raised against chess as a pastime until the
seventeenth century. Maimonides is sometimes quoted
as an opponent of chess.[1] But Maimonides only includes
chess under the category of forbidden pastimes if it
be played for money. The winning of money at any
amusement was rigidly denounced by many authorities
who had no objection to games of chance as such.
Maimonides, it is interesting to note, already refers to
a kind of chess in which the object was to force a mate,
and this is important for the history of chess, as the
variety is well known in modern times.[2] In the seventeenth century, some voices were heard against chess, on
the ground that it entailed a lamentable waste of time.
No doubt this complaint was well founded against passionate lovers of the mimic warfare, who, according to one
authority,[3] spent many hours daily at the game. 'They
say that they play to sharpen their intellects, but the study
of the Law would be a more efficient mental tonic. Moreover, I am not aware that when their minds have — as they
claim — been sharpened, these men display their keener
wits over serious intellectual pursuits.' As against this
rare opponent, many Jews favoured the game just because
it entailed so few evil consequences.

Some even taught their children chess to wean them

[1] Löw, *Lebensalter*, p. 328.

[2] Maimonides, *Commentary to the Mishnah*, Sanhedrin, iii. That chess was
played for a money-stake is clear from this, that some Rabbis, when formally
allowing the game on the Sabbath, stipulated that no money was to change
hands on that day (cf. Löw, *Lebensalter*, loc. cit.). Kalonymos, in his אבן
בוחן (ed. Lemberg, p. 28), also attacked chess when played for money.

[3] The שבט מוסר (ch. 42) disapproves of chess on any terms, whether
played for money or not. There were a number of Jews who objected *to
all games* under any and every condition, but these pietists failed to influence
the general action.

from cards and other games of chance.[1]   Similarly, anti-gambling laws in England were sometimes passed in the interest of better sports, such as archery.   At all events, some distinguished Jewish Rabbis of the twelfth century themselves eagerly played chess, and Jews of the four-teenth century wrote poems in its honour.[2]

> In crafty guise is their battle fought,
> With cunning art is their contest wrought.
> When these prevail o'er their foemen all,
> Behold, 'tis then that the dead men fall.
> Yet they from death may rise again,
> And cast their enemies amid the slain.[3]

Friendly as they were to chess, the Jewish moralists of all ages raised their protest in vain against games of chance. The ancient Israelites were ignorant of games of chance, and did not adopt *dice*, the most popular gambling game of antiquity, until the age of Herod.   The Mishnah de-clared dicing infamous, and excluded players of the game from the right to give evidence in a court of justice.[4] The money won at dice was dishonestly won,[5] and the gambler was occupied in a pastime 'not calculated to serve

---

[1] Schudt, *Merkwürdigkeiten,* ii.* 1.

[2] *Cusari,* v. 20; but cf. Steinschneider, p. 157.   A large proportion of the famous chess players of the present century have been Jews.

[3] Another Hebrew poem descriptive of the game of chess may be found translated into English in the *Jewish Chronicle,* Sept. 6, 1895.   The translator is Miss Nina Davis.   An unrhymed translation of Ibn Ezra's poem was also contributed to the same periodical by Miss Davis.   Steinschneider, in Van der Linde's *Geschichte und Litteratur des Schachspiels* (Berlin, 1874), vol. i. pp. 155 seq., argues, with too much emphasis, however, against the view that these Hebrew verses are by Ibn Ezra.

[4] R. Judah ben Ilai attempted to draw a distinction between those who played merely for amusement and those who used the game as a profession (Mishnah, *Synhedrin,* ii. 3).

[5] *T. B. Synhedrin,* 24 b.

the interests of society.'[1]   This, in the final resort, is the
only fundamental objection to gambling.   But dice and
several other gambling games were known to the medieval
Jews, especially in France and Germany, such as the games
of 'Odd or Even' (*ludere par et impar*), 'Whole or Half,'
'Back or Edge,'[2] betting on pigeon races, and lotteries
by means of the *teetotum* and similar toys.

In the fifteenth century, however, the game of cards
usurped the first place in the minds of all in search of
a pastime.   The origin of cards is still unknown, but it is
certain that the Jews were not among the first Europeans
to adopt the game.   From the year 1415, however, the
Jews fell under its strong fascination.

Despite frequent assertions to the contrary,[3] there is no
reference to cards in Jewish sources before the beginning
of the fifteenth century, by which time the game was
already known all over Europe.   At the beginning of the
fifteenth century the references are quite common.[4]   The
rage for the game rapidly spread.   As with contemporary

---

[1] *T. B. Synhedrin*, 24 b, לפי שאין עסוקין בישובו של עולם.

[2] Cf. Berliner, *Aus dem inneren Leben*, p. 12.   This game was played with
a knife, which apparently was thrown in the air, and the decision depended
on which side fell uppermost.   Probably the game was something like the
modern 'head or tail.'

[3] It is usually asserted (e.g. Löw, p. 329) that Kalonymos b. Kalonymos
alludes to cards in his אבן בוחן.   If this were true, this would constitute the
oldest clear reference to the game, as Kalonymos wrote in the year 1322.
As a matter of fact the reading קלפים (' cards '), which appears in the Lemberg
edition of the אבן בוחן, is an error.   The *editio princeps* (Naples, 1489) reads
כלי מצפיה הפצפצין וקוביא, and not הקלפים (MS. Brit. Museum Add. 19,948 has
the same reading as the *editio princeps*).   Kalonymos probably refers to
draughts, as I imagine פצפץ to be the same as פספס (= Greek ψῆφος).   קוביא
and פספס are associated in *T. J. Rosh Hashana*, as quoted in Levy, sub voce,
פסיפס.

[4] Cf. Löw, loc. cit.   Isserlein, in תרומת הדשן, ii. 186, asserts that Maharil
referred to cards in his sermons.

Christians, the passion did not manifest itself merely in
ignorant and uncultured minds.   The learned and the
great sometimes fell victims to its fatal spells.   One of
the saddest cases, that of Leon Modena, somewhat reminds
one of the experience of Charles James Fox.   Leon Modena
was a learned man and scientific thinker, and migrated to
Venice towards the close of the sixteenth century.   There
he taught and preached.   But a stumbling-block stood
in his path to success : his love for card-playing.   He was
fully aware of the evils of gambling, for at the precocious
age of fourteen he wrote against it a diatribe in dialogue,
which has been translated into several languages.[1]   Though
he often resolved to abandon the vice, of which he was
deeply ashamed, he never succeeded in doing so, even in
his old age.   The Rabbis of Venice published an order
excommunicating any member of the congregation who
played cards within a period of six years from the date
of the promulgation of the decree.   This was in 1628, and
was probably directed against him ; at all events, he successfully summoned all his learning and force to defeat
this attempt to fetter his freedom.[2]

Such efforts towards the suppression of card-playing
were almost as old as the game itself.   As Löw has pointed
out, the measures devised were threefold, (*a*) personal and
voluntary pledges, (*b*) communal *tekanoth* or restrictions,
and (*c*) literary and ethical satires and homilies.

Personal vows to abstain from games of chance took
a severely formal character.   The oath was registered and

---

[1] The הלמוד צחקן.

[2] Cf. Isaac Reggio, בחינת הקבלה, p. ix.   Leon Modena was unable to resist the
fascination of gambling because of his fatalism.   He believed that his acts
were predestined, and this weakened his efforts to amend.   Cf. also פתר יצחק
s. v. הרס.

signed in the presence of witnesses, often of Rabbis. In the year 1464, a Jew presented himself before the Notary of Arles and entered into a legal undertaking that he would not play dice or any other game except on his own or his brother's wedding-day or on three days during the feast of Passover. In penalty for any infringement of this promise, the Jew's hand might be amputated.[1] Such certificates of vows against gambling in general are sometimes found in the fly-leaves of Hebrew MSS. ;[2] they are alluded to in almost every ethical or ritual book dating from the beginning of the fifteenth century onwards.[3] One, signed at five o'clock in the morning of April 1, 1491, runs thus : — 'May this be for a good memory, Amen! At the twenty-third hour of the beginning of April, 1491, the undersigned received upon himself by oath on the Ten Commandments that he would not play any game, nor incite another to play for him, with the exception of draughts or chess,[4] and this oath shall have force for ten full years.' Then Jekuthiel, the son of Gershom, takes the oath before Abraham Farisol of Avignon. The second instance is even more emphatic. 'Ferara, Thursday Sivan 25, 1535. I have sworn before the Rabbis David Bensusan and Moses de Castro, and in

---

[1] Depping, *Les Juifs dans le moyen âge*, p. 326.

[2] Cf. Brit. Mus. Add. 4709 and Add. 17,053 (where such a document occurs on the last leaf). These instances were published by Dukes in the *Ben Chananja* (1864), cols. 682, 738. Cf. Löw, p. 331.

[3] Cf. Maharil (additions at end).

[4] This is probably what is meant by הטבלי, though perhaps the French game of *marelle* is meant. Cf. Güdemann's note, *Graetz Jubelschrift* (Heb. part), p. 63. There is much difficulty in identifying the games referred to in Hebrew sources, as medieval Jewish writers continued to employ the Talmudical term קוביא (lit. = κυβος or dice) to include all forms of games of chance.

the presence of the sons of the Rabbi Israel Ohab, *that I will never play any game in the world.'*

Thus the limit of the obligation depended on the will of the individual. So, too, he could exclude certain games from the circle of restricted pleasures ; thus chess was often excluded from the ban. Or he might permit himself the indulgence in games of chance on certain stated occasions. When once he had made the formal vow — and those cited above are by no means the earliest instances — the victim of his own abstinence would often be as eager to absolve himself from the oath as he had been to take it. Or he would evade his obligation if he could. He would play for money's worth if he might not play for money, and would substitute fruit for coins.[1] But for the most part the Rabbis were immovable, and the vow was held indissoluble by many authorities.[2]

A more important measure of repression was the *communal enactment* against gambling. Such enactments were most common in Italy, where indeed games of chance were very rife in the fifteenth century. An important instance of such a general undertaking occurred in Forli in the year 1416 :[3] —

'We also resolved that from this day forth and for ten years, no Jew shall assemble in his house or premises a party for gambling ; neither Jews nor Christians ; nor may any Jew play dice, or cards, or any other games of chance ; neither he himself nor any one else for him, nor

---

[1] Cf. the *Tekanah*, Güdemann, i. 260, which, however, permits it during the middle days of a festival.

[2] Löw, *Lebensalter*, p. 331, especially the stringent decision of R. Tam on the basis of *T. Jer. Nedarim*, v. 4, 8. R. Perez ben Elia of Corbeil, and R. Tobia ben Elia and others were more yielding. Cf. also p. 110 above.

[3] S. Halberstam, *Graetz Jubelschrift* (Hebrew section), p. 57.

he for others; neither with Jews nor Christians; neither in his own house nor in the house of others; except the game of draughts with dice, or chess without dice, provided always that these permitted games are never played for a higher stake than four silver bolognini. Also on fast-days, or if, God forbid, any one is sick, they may play cards to relieve their distress, but only on condition that they stake not more than one *quattrino* at any game.

'Whoever transgresses this resolution is a sinner, and he must pay one ducat as forfeit for every offence. If he refuses to pay, he shall be punished as follows: — He shall not count as one of the ten necessary to form a quorum for public worship, he shall not be permitted to read in the Scroll of the Pentateuch in synagogue, nor shall he be entrusted with the honour of rolling the Scroll — until he repents of his wickedness and pays the fine. If any one knows of another Jew dwelling in these cities who has done this wrong, he must denounce the offender, for if he fail and remain silent, he renders himself liable to the self-same penalties.'

This typical instance indicates four things: that the law was temporary;[1] that it was only binding on native Jews and not on immigrants or visitors—a most important point; thirdly, that Jews and Christians played together in Italy in the fifteenth century; and lastly, that on certain exceptional occasions card-playing was regarded as lawful. As regards the second point, there was much sensitiveness against interfering with local custom. Hence a foreign

---

[1] When no time-limit was fixed, the *tekanah* was nevertheless not held to be perpetual, 'because the custom was to fix a limit' (S. Duran, התשב"ץ, iii. 107).

visitor, who when at home lived in a town where games of chance were permitted, continued to enjoy the same privilege when he was staying in a place where a prohibitive policy prevailed.   But he was only allowed to play in private. With regard to the occasions on which card-playing was allowed, there was much difference of local habit.   Women were allowed greater relaxation than men, but the favourite occasions for allowing card-playing and other games of chance were — new moon, days on which no penitential prayers were said, the festivals of Chanucah and Purim, on the weekdays of the Passover and Tabernacles,[1] at weddings, and on the night before a boy was named. Sometimes, as was also the case with the Christian students of the Cambridge University in the age of Milton, card-playing was permitted by Jews at Christmas.[2]

There was a stronger weapon against gambling than compulsion.   Persuasion took the form of satire, moral exhortation, and private admonition of child by father. Kalonymos in his *Touchstone*[3] applied some scathing rebukes to those who filled their purses at the expense of less fortunate wights, whom they stripped of their attire and robbed of their lives.   Moral books, like the *Book of the Pious*, denounced gambling with hearty vigour, and

---

[1] *Responsa*, Israel Bruna, 136, and פחד יצחק s. v. חרם.   On the middle-days of Tabernacles cards were allowed only in the Tabernacle itself, not elsewhere; on Passover, some would not use cards as paste (i.e. leaven) was employed in their mounting (Isserlein, פסקים, 186).   Between the New Year and the Day of Atonement games were prohibited.   Cf. Berliner, *Aus dem inneren Leben*, pp. 10, 11.

[2] Masson, *Life and Times of Milton* (ed. 2), vol. i. p. 136.   Cf. W. H. Willshire, *A Descriptive Catalogue of Playing and other Cards in the British Museum* (1876), p. 6.

[3] I.e. אבן בוהן, ed. Lemberg, p. 28.   According to the satirist, all classes suffered from the passion for play, שם הם הטיילים בכל יום אם דל ואם עשיר.

regarded with abhorrence the ill-gotten winnings of the gamester.[1] Poets continued for centuries to write against gambling; and songs, in Hebrew and doggerel jargon, some composed by women, took up the same parable against the ruinous results both of winning and losing. But far earlier than this, Jewish parents imposed upon their sons the same moral aversion to gaming. 'At gambling,' said Maimonides, 'the player always loses. Though he may win money, he weaves a spider's web round himself.' 'Play no games for money,' said Judah Asheri to his son, 'for gambling is robbery.' 'As to gambling games,' says another — a fourteenth-century — father, 'I earnestly entreat my children never to play at them, except on festivals, and the women on new moon, but even then without money, and for stakes of food or eggs.'[2]

These well-intentioned efforts remained without serious effect. A curious case is recorded in 1520 which shows how popular cards must have been, for an official of the synagogue was a card-painter. In the year named, Joseph Jud brought a petition before the governor of a place near the Rhine about his son-in-law, Meyer Chayn, the *schulklopfer*, an official who, as we saw above, was commissioned to summon the congregation to the synagogue for morning prayer. This *schulklopfer* was a card-painter by trade, and he complained that his business was being spoilt by other Jews who imported cards made elsewhere.[3]

[1] Cf. also the *tekanah* against playing for money, quoted in Güdemann i. 260, and the references in note 6 of vol. iii. p. 139.

[2] This distinction was frequently made, but many refused to allow even this concession. Cf. ראשית בכורים, quoted in Güdemann, *Quellenschriften*, p. 300. For the quotations in this paragraph see *Jewish Quarterly Review*, iii. pp. 436 seq.

[3] Mone's *Zeitschrift für die Geschichte des Oberrheins*, xvii. 255. Reuchlin also refers to the incident. Cf. Berliner, p. 47.

As a general rule, the Jews established no independent standard of conduct with regard to their amusements. They played the same games as their Christian neighbours, and played them with the same rules and at the same tables.   This will lead us to the facts to be related in the following chapters.

CHAPTER XXIII

IF the legal status of the Jews were our sole criterion, the picture of their relations with medieval Christians would need to be painted in very sombre hues. Laws, however, were made to be broken, and the actual relations between Jews and Christians were for long periods far different to those which the Church Councils and, to a less degree, the Jewish ritual code tended to produce. Jews and Christians often defied the laws which sought to keep them asunder.

With but rare exceptions, the general trend of the Church influence on medieval legislation was towards the creation of barriers between Jews and Christians. Anti-social in the main, Church Council vied with Church Council in its proposals for marking off the Jews as a separate class, with ever-growing completeness. Periods and epochs can, however, be assigned for greater or less severity.

The great change occurred in the thirteenth century. Till the end of the twelfth century, the personal relations between Jews and Christians were on the whole friendly. In England the turning-point was the accession of King Richard I, in northern France the death of Louis VII.

With the exception of Italy and Spain, the Crusades, the thirteenth century heresies and monastic developments, the baneful influence of Pope Innocent III, the Black Death in 1349, the religious turmoils resulting in the Protestant Reformation, the ghetto legislation in the sixteenth century — these are landmarks in the history of Jewish repression all over Europe. For Spain, the critical moment came at the troubled year 1391, but its full consequences were delayed till the advent of Torquemada at the close of the fifteenth century.

For this curious phenomenon presents itself. Just as the Crusades produced no massacres in Spain or Italy, so it was almost a tradition with the popes of Rome to protect the Jews who were near at hand, however severely their official bulls condemned to persecution the Jews who inhabited more distant countries. The tradition was broken at the beginning of the thirteenth century by Innocent III, but even in later times, certainly till the end of the fifteenth century, the Jews — ill-treated as a class — enjoyed in the two countries named much personal respect and a certain degree of toleration.

Or the same fact may be put in another way. As will be soon pointed out, unfriendliness to the Jews flowed from the higher to the lower levels. Anti-Jewish prejudice originated among the classes, not among the masses. But this statement, true of the rest of Europe, is untrue of Italy. In the latter country such anti-Jewish feeling as was prevalent in the twelfth century was a *popular* growth. But because it emanated from below, it was controllable by those in authority. The priests in Italy were not fanatical instigators of the mob until the fifteenth century was all but passed. The Italian poets were far kinder to

the Jews than were the German, and the friendship between Dante and his Jewish imitator Immanuel was typical of this gentler attitude of the Italian muse. Again, in
Italy, trade was far from being entirely in the hands of the
Jews, and thus the commercial aristocracy of Italy could
— until trade rivalry embittered them — place themselves
above the prejudices elsewhere felt by the landed aristoc-
racies of Europe against the owners of wealth which was
not derived directly from the soil.

Moreover, the independence of the separate Italian republics made the Jews certain of an asylum in a neighbouring state, and thus enabled them to weather many
a temporary storm. It has already been shown that the
same immunity from crushing persecution was enjoyed
by the Jews of Spain while the kingdoms of Leon, Aragon,
and Castile were independent. A similar remark applies
to the independent principalities of medieval Germany,
before the era of the friars. The thought may be hazarded
that had the government in England been less centralized
than it was by the genius of Edward I, the Jews would not
have been expelled from the whole of England as they
were in 1290. An evil consequence of the independence
of parts of the same country was that the Inquisition found
it needful to obtain a strong footing in such states. At all
events, in the fourteenth and fifteenth centuries, identity
of culture overcame divergence of religion in Italy. Theology seemed to rule with a stronger hand as it drew further
from Rome. From the thirteenth century, Dissent had to
be crushed in proportion to its distance from the central
seat of Roman Catholicism, and in the campaign against
Dissent the Jews suffered with the Christian heretics. For,
as a whole, heresy was a reversion to Old Testament and

even Jewish ideals. It is indubitable that the heretical
doctrines of the Southern-French Albigenses in the beginning of the thirteenth century, as of the Hussites in the
fifteenth, were largely the result of friendly intercourse
between Christians and educated Jews.[1] In the bloody
measures against Raymund of Toulouse — the friend of
heretics, and the protector and employer of Jews — the
latter suffered severely from the anger of Innocent III. At
the Council of Avignon (September, 1209), Raymund and
all the barons of free cities were forced to bind themselves
by oath to entrust no office whatever to Jews, nor permit
Christian servants to be employed in their houses.

The indirect effects of the Protestant Reformation were
equally deleterious to the Jews. The popes themselves
were less fanatical than the agents on whom they relied
for the maintenance of their supremacy. The wandering
friars, as they passed further from Rome, became the
bearers of a fierce orthodoxy which could not tolerate the
Jews. Their efforts were seconded by Jewish apostates
to Christianity, some of whom felt themselves bound to
justify their secession by attacks on their former brethren
in faith. In the sixteenth century the Order of Jesuits
was founded, as a reaction to the Protestant movement.
Wherever these emissaries of Loyola penetrated, their
secret insinuations poisoned the minds of rulers and ruled
against the sons of Israel. In Poland, which in the fifteenth century was a haven of refuge for the exiled Jews
of Germany and central Europe, Casimir IV had bestowed
on the Jews social privileges such as they then enjoyed
nowhere else. Among minor points, Jews might bathe
together in the same river with Christians — a right fre-

[1] Graetz, *History* (Eng. Trans.), III. ch. xv.

quently denied them.[1] Further, any Christian who brought the baseless charge of ritual murder against a Jew, and was unable to substantiate his charge on credible testimony, was held punishable with death. But the inroad of the Jesuits into Poland changed all this. The spirit of the Polish heretics had to be crushed, and the Jesuits utilized the trade jealousies of the German dealers in Poland to rouse animosities against the Jews, which culminated in the cruelties which they suffered during the revolt of the Cossacks.[2]

From the Protestant side, the Jews received little better treatment. The ground for the Protestant animosity is not easily discerned. Possibly, it was that the ferments of the Reformation induced a leaning towards anti-Trinitarianism. That such a movement synchronized with the Lutheran and Calvinistic reformation is certain, and there is no doubt that the term *semi-judaei* was applied to its leaders. Be the cause what it may, Luther adopted a most unfriendly attitude towards the Jews, though — in the preparation of his German Bible — he made much use of Jewish assistants. It may be that Luther was unconsciously influenced by the notorious Catholic, John Eck, and could not allow himself to be behind his opponent in detestation of those who denied the Trinity.

At all events, Luther's pronouncements against the Jews had an effect which still persists. His utterances are the armoury of modern anti-Semitism just as, a thousand years before, Jerome's confession of faith had proved a continued source of intolerance. Jerome's instance is instructive.[3] He was closely connected with individual Jews from whom

---

[1] Lindo, p. 193. So, too, Jews were often forbidden to use the public promenades.   [2] Op. cit. V. ch. i.   [3] II. xxii.

he acquired a knowledge of Hebrew, and as a result he was suspected of heretical leanings. He accordingly purged himself of this suspicion and justified his faith by pronouncing his undying abhorrence of the Jews. This phenomenon frequently recurs in the middle ages on both sides of the account. The Jews, as a class, were often condemned by Christians, such as Wülfer and Wagenseil, who formed deep personal friendships with individual Jews, while the latter sometimes defended their friendly intercourse with individual Christians by descanting on their opposition to the special tenets of Christianity.

In defining the *practical* relations between Jews and Christians, it is important to consider the origin of the antipathy which undoubtedly existed throughout the middle ages and survived into modern times. In brief, popular prejudice against the Jews was an artificial creation. Medieval history displays no deep-seated, natural animosity, but at the most a latent suspicion which needed fanning from above if it was to blaze forth into a destructive conflagration. During the first Crusade, the masses in the Rhine-lands protected the Jews against the Knights of the Cross, but during the second Crusade the fiery eloquence of the monk Rudolph roused the masses to the desire of converting or annihilating the infidels.

It is instructive to remember what happened in France. Though Louis VII himself joined the second Crusade, and Peter of Clugny argued that it was useless 'to go forth to seek the enemies of Christendom in distant lands while the blasphemous Jews, who are worse than the Saracens, are permitted in our very midst to scoff with impunity at Christ,' though he counselled that the Jews were not to be slain but 'reserved for greater ignominy, for an existence more bitter than death ' — still in the kingdom of Louis VII the Jews had nothing worse to suffer than the confiscation of their property.

Bernard of Clairvaux stands out as a noble and adorable figure. At the risk of his own life he implored the people, excited by Rudolph, to show more humanity to the Jews. But Bernard was also an eloquent advocate of the second Crusade, and the monk Rudolph's influence was more powerful because he was more consistent. By the time Bernard could personally interfere, the people had got out of hand, as the indirect result of the crusading enthusiasm and the direct consequence of the powerful harangues of the monk, who went from town to town, and village to village, piteously appealing to his auditors with simple pathos and eloquent tears, moving them with the heart-rending story of the Passion and the Crucifixion. Wholesale massacres of Jewish congregations followed, but it cannot be said that the outburst was of popular origin. The same phenomena repeat themselves in all the great crises of Jewish life throughout their medieval history.[1]

From one point of view it may even be said that a competition arose between the Church and the Kings. The former (who sometimes succeeded and sometimes failed in carrying the masses with it) cried : ' *Expel the crucifiers.*' The Kings retorted : ' No ; we will let them remain, but will *make them pay for the privilege.*' It needed, however, a monarch of strong determination to resist the Church for long, and a Torquemada might always be sure of triumphing in the end over the scruples of an Isabella.

Another typical instance of the manner in which anti-Jewish feeling was propagated from above may be seen in

[1] Cf. Depping, *Juifs dans le moyen âge*, pp. 396, 397.

the action of scholasticism. With one hand, it has been well said, Albertus Magnus would turn with loving touch the pages of Maimonides, — in a sense a Jewish father of Christian scholasticism, — while with his other hand Albertus would endorse a decree committing the Talmud to the flames. Scholasticism treated practical questions from the point of view of pure reason, but its conclusions were applied by the masses without reason. Thomas Aquinas studied Jewish books, and regarded their authors with respect. He went far in friendly tolerance. He, unlike other scholastics, such as Duns Scotus, objected to forcible conversions of the Jews, and thought the latter should be allowed the free exercise of their religion. Necessary intercourse with Jews was quite permissible to pious Christians, provided that the latter were sufficiently firm in their faith to incur no danger of being shaken by familiarity with unbelievers.[1] But in his *De regimine Judaeorum* the whole weight of his authority is cast into the other scale, and Thomas of Aquino uses of the Jews language which must logically tend to their expulsion, robbery, and massacre. Scholasticism in fact treated the question of religious intolerance as an academic topic. So

---

[1] ' Primo ergo modo non interdicit ecclesia fidelibus communionem infidelium, qui nullo modo fidem christianam receperunt (scilicet paganorum vel Iudaeorum), quia non habet de eis iudicare spirituali iudicio sed temporali in casu, cum inter Christianos commorantes aliquam culpam committunt et per fideles temporaliter puniuntur. . . . Sed quantum ad secundum modum videtur esse distinguendum secundum diversas conditiones personarum et negotiorum et temporum. Si enim aliqui fuerint firmi in fide ita, quod ex communione eorum cum infidelibus conversio infidelium magis sperari possit quam a fide aversio, non sunt prohibendi infidelibus communicare, qui fidem non susceperunt (scilicet paganis vel Iudaeis) et maxime, si necessitas urgeat,' etc. *Summa Theologiae*, ii. 2, qu. 10, art. 9.   Cf. Guttmann, *Das Verhältniss des T. v. Aquino zum Judenthum*, p. 7.

treated, the problem has undoubtedly two sides, but the conclusions of scholasticism, harmless enough for the study, were terribly injurious for the street. Philosophy has often, undesignedly, seconded the enemies of progress through its inability to discriminate between political theory and practical politics.

The specific accusations on which the Jews were hated in the middle ages were also the creation of the leaders. The most awful of myths that embittered the life of the Jews, — the most prolific cause of the hatred and suspicion with which they were regarded, — viz. the charge of ritual murder, can always be traced to fanatical instigators who created an ill-feeling which did not otherwise exist. The mendicant friars fostered this ill-feeling, and so did the medieval poets of France and Germany. Usury undoubtedly helped to make the Jews unpopular, but here again the masses were less affected than the classes, as it was from the nobility and aristocracy that the Jews drew their most frequent clients.

The masses never charged the Jews with the fault most common in attacks on them, viz. lack of the social instinct. Observing that the Jewish dietary laws raised some obstacles to free intercourse, and observing further the unbending tenacity with which Jews refused to accept the religion of the dominant majority, it was the theologians who proclaimed the Jews anti-social and the haters of their kind. This supposed enmity of the Jews towards the human race was dinned into the ears of the masses until the calumny became part of the popular creed. The poets formulated the idea for the gentry, the friars brought it to the folk. If the people came to believe that the very blood of the Jews was black and putrid, that their ignoble and degraded estate was even perceptible by a disgusting odour which only baptism could remove : —

> Abluitur Iudaeus Odor Baptismate divo,
> Et nova Progenies reddita surgit aquis,
> Vincens Ambrosios suavi spiramine roras,[1]

— if the masses came to think the Jews poisoners of wells and sorcerers — the leaders of the Church and the aristocracy were responsible. The Church persecutions were no doubt often 'chastisements of love,' directed towards the absorption of the Jews within the embrace of the cross. But what could the average man think when he saw the most rigorous laws passed at every Church Council; when he saw the Talmud confiscated and burnt, and the Jews themselves slain by the Inquisition; when he heard papal bulls denouncing them, and warning faithful Christians to avoid them as a pest, to receive no services from them nor render services to them; when Jews and harlots were conjoined in the statutes as unclean and rendering unclean?[2]

As early as the reign of Constantine, the Council of Elvira forbade Christians to hold any communication with Jews. This anti-social policy was continued almost without a break until the date of the French Revolution. The mitigations of friendly popes and rulers were but small oases in a desert of arid repression. The worst feature in the unfriendly interference with the Church was that it mostly stepped in at the very moments when the masses were opening their hearts most freely to the Jews. In the fifteenth century the German population was rapidly recov-

---

[1] Bishop Venantius (end of sixth century), cited by Tovey, *Anglia Judaica*, p. 95. Schudt, ii. 344.

[2] 'Statuimus quod *Iudaei nec meretrices* non audeant tangere manu panem vel fructus qui exponuntur venales,' etc. Statutes of Avignon in Depping, *Les Juifs dans le moyen âge*, p. 323.

ering from the lurid effects of the Black Death scare. Friendly intercourse was again growing common. But the Church interposed, forbade 'bathing, eating, or drinking in common with Jews,' and enforced upon the masses the belief that the Jews were the enemies alike of God and of man.[1]

That these anti-Jewish and anti-social regulations needed constant confirmation is in itself an evidence that the mass of the Christian population, except in times of fanatical religious upheaval, or under the maddening impulse of mysterious epidemics, were not impregnated with a deep hatred of the Jews. That this was so, that, as we shall see, personal relations between Christians and Jews were at least on occasion friendly and intimate, was not the fault of the law. The law certainly left no stone unturned to prevent such friendships. It would be impossible to summarize the measures adopted with this aim, some of them — the institution of the ghetto and the infliction of the badge — have already been recorded at length. The chain of repression stretched over the eighth to the eighteenth century. When the French Revolution was well in sight, there was issued in Rome an *Edict against the Jews*, which forms a black page in the history of humanity.[2] This Edict, which merely recapitulates and codifies old enactments, is completely anti-social. Of its 44 Articles, the 31st runs thus : —

[1] Full accounts of the various anti-Jewish Bulls, dating from the energetic crusade of John of Capistrano in the middle of the fifteenth century, may be found in Graetz, *History of the Jews* (Eng. Trans.), Vol. IV. ch. viii. seq. I have given no references to incidents which may be found in the ordinary historical text-books or at greater length in Güdemann and Graetz.

[2] The Edict is translated (into German) in full in Berliner's *Geschichte der Juden in Rom*, ii. (2), 107.

Jews and Christians are forbidden to play, eat, drink, hold intercourse, or exchange confidences of ever so trifling a nature with one another. Such shall not be allowed in palaces, houses, or vineyards, in the streets, in taverns, in neither shops nor any other place. Nor shall the tavern-keeper, inn-keeper, nor shop proprietor permit any converse between Jews and Christians. The Jews who offend in this matter shall incur the penalties of a fine of 10 *scudi* and imprisonment; Christians, a similar fine and corporal punishment.

How stood the matter on the Jewish side? It may be answered that the Jews on the whole reciprocated the feelings with which they were regarded by the rest of the world. They retaliated on love with love and opposed hatred with contempt. As regards the manifestation of better feelings, however, a curious contrast reveals itself. Toleration in the Jewry came from above, the toleration of Christendom came from below. As I have endeavoured to show, the Christian masses were on the whole more tolerant than their priests and rulers. But the Jewish masses were less tolerant than their spiritual and intellectual heads.

The reason is not far to find. The Christian theologian was animated with a desire to convert the Jew, the Jewish theologian felt no similar desire to convert the Christian. In the medieval Jewish view, salvation might be reached by the Gentile by other roads than the one that led through the synagogue. Medieval Judaism being thus essentially tolerant, its leading spirits felt none of that anguish to proselytize which passes so easily into persecution and animosity. But, on the other hand, the neglect of proselytism engendered a good deal of race-pride on the part of the mass of those who stood within the privileged pale. Proselytism[1] was, of course, a dangerous enterprise in the middle ages — dangerous to the convert as well as to

[1] Cf. Alfonso's *Seven Codes* (1261), Lindo, pp. 92, 235.

those who received him. A single instance must suffice. In 1222 a Christian deacon was executed at Oxford for no other offence than his apostasy to Judaism.[1]

The expulsion of the Jews from Spain was largely due to the readmission into the synagogue of Marranos, or Jewish-Christians. At various periods in the middle ages conversion to Judaism occurred,[2] but the Jews were too much terrorized to seek conversions,[3] besides being free from any theological impulse to do so. The Jewish race thus remained fairly free from foreign admixture, and it retained a certain sense of its own superiority.

Another cause of prejudice on the part of Jews was produced by the ritual law. Many of the old ritual laws relating to 'idolaters' remained in the Jewish code books, and though the greatest Jewish authorities of the middle ages unanimously declared that the term 'idolater' did not include Christian or Moslem, many of these ceremonial laws remained in force with the masses and — in practice — with the very men who pronounced in theory that the followers of Christ and Mohammed were not idolaters! The conservatism of religious custom and, what is even more tyrannical, of religious *formulas*, was here a serious bar to Jewish enlightenment. The dietary laws were in themselves something of an obstacle in the way of social intercourse, but, curiously enough, this obstacle was not so insurmountable as one might imagine. But the knowledge that wine manufactured by a Gentile might not be used,

[1] Mathew Paris, *Chronica Majora* (ed. Luard, iii. p. 71).

[2] Cf. Graetz, *History of the Jews* (Eng. Trans.), III. ch. vi. (p. 172). The well-known story of the Arabian conversions (ibid. p. 62), and the conversion of the Chozars (p. 141), are but striking instances of a not infrequent phenomenon.

[3] Gregorovius, *Gesch. Rom*, vii. 492.

that food cooked by a Gentile might not be eaten, that the evidence of a Gentile was inadmissible in a Jewish tribunal, that the Gentile altogether stood on a lower moral level than the Jew — rules justly applied by the Talmud to 'idolaters,' but misapplied by the Jewish masses to all but the children of Israel — affected the uncultured Jew with a prejudice which was antagonistic to a spirit of respect and confidence.

Moreover, amid the massacres of the Crusades and the persecutions of the Inquisition, in the petty but perpetual restrictions to which they were daily subjected, the ordinary Jew beheld Christianity in its ugliest aspects. The cultured Israelite, on the other hand, knew other aspects of Christianity — knew it at its best as well as its worst. The Jewish tolerance towards Christianity accordingly emanated from the cultured classes, and to a large extent remained the property of the cultured.

CHAPTER XXIV

PERSONAL RELATIONS (*continued*)

LITERARY FRIENDSHIPS

SOME fine illustrations of this last phenomenon — namely, the power of great medieval Jews to rise above their personal experiences in order to form a fair estimate of another faith — will lead us to one of the most fertile causes promotive of personal intercourse between Jews and Christians in the middle ages. Maimonides was himself a sufferer from Mohammedan fanaticism, and his father and family fled for their lives from Cordova when the persecuting, if pure, Unitarianism of Ibn Tumart offered to heretics the Koran or the sword. But the fact that Islam persecuted Judaism was, in his view, no reason why Judaism should libel Islam. 'The Moslems,' he says, 'ascribe to God a perfect unity, a unity in which there is no stumbling-block.' He refused to describe as superstitious the customs — such as prostration in prayer, and the stone-throwing at the Kaaba — which Islam had taken over from paganism. Maimonides was as tolerant in regard to the doctrines of Christ as he was to those of Mohammed. 'The teachings of Christ, and of Mohammed who arose after him,' said Maimonides, 'tend to bring to perfection all mankind, so that they may serve God with one consent. For since the whole world is thus full of the words of the Messiah, of the words of the Holy Writ and the Commandments — these words have spread to the ends of the earth, even if any men deny the binding character of them now. And when the Messiah comes all will return from their errors.'[1]

This was written in the twelfth century; some fifty years earlier, Jehuda Halevi put the same thought in more poetical terms. 'The wise providence of God towards Israel may be compared to the planting of a seed of corn. It is placed in the earth, where it seems to be changed into soil, and water, and rottenness, and the seed can no longer be recognized. But in very truth it is the seed that has changed the earth and water into its own nature, and then the seed raises itself from one stage to another, transforms the elements, and throws out shoots and leaves. . . . Thus it is with Christians and Moslems. The Law of Moses has changed them that come into contact with it, even though they seem to have cast the Law aside. These religions are the preparation and the preface to the Messiah we expect, who is the fruit himself of the seed originally sown, and all men, too, will be fruit of God's seed when they acknowledge him, and all become one mighty tree.'[2]

This toleration towards Christianity was deep-seated. Jehuda Halevi uses Christian ideas and even phraseology,

---

[1] Maimonides, *Mishneh Torah*, ה״ מלכים, towards the end. Cf. also the quotations by L. M. Simmons in his paper on 'Maimonides and Islam' (*Publications of Jews' College Lit. Soc.*, London, 1887).

[2] Jehuda Halevi, *Cuzari*, iv. 23. 'Remember,' says Mr. J. Jacobs in commenting on this passage, 'that these words were spoken when Israel was being persecuted by both branches of the tree, and its noble tolerance cannot fail to strike you' (*Jewish Ideals*, p. 118).

the father of Maimonides employs Mohammedan theological terms with equal freedom. Indeed, some of his paragraphs sound almost like an echo from the Koran.[1] Bachya's famous moral treatise, *The Duties of the Heart*, lauds Christian monasticism with hearty enthusiasm.[2] Joseph Albo at the beginning of the fifteenth century shows, in his work on the Jewish religion, unmistakable evidence of Christian influence.[3] Isaac Abarbanel quotes, in his commentaries, Christian authorities such as Jerome and Thomas Aquinas with respect. This attitude was not confined to Spain. In the tenth century, a Jewish questioner of the great Babylonian authority, Hai Gaon, was unable to understand the meaning of Psalm 141, verse 5. Hai Gaon referred him to a Christian priest, who gave the Jew a satisfactory interpretation.[4] Such tolerance goes far back in Jewish history. 'He who communicates a word of wisdom, even if he be a non-Jew, deserves the title of wise.'[5] 'Christians are not idolaters' was the burden of many Jewish utterances: 'they make mention of Jesus, but their thought is to the Maker of heaven and earth.'[6] 'He who sees a Christian sage,' says the Shulchan Aruch,[7] 'must utter the benediction: "Blessed art Thou, O Lord, King of the World, who hast bestowed of Thy wisdom on man."'

[1] L. M. Simmons, *The Letter of Consolation of Maimun ben Joseph*, p. 4.

[2] Graetz, *History of the Jews* (Eng. Trans.), III. ch. ix.

[3] Graetz, op. cit. IV. ch. vii.

[4] Berliner, *Persönliche Beziehungen zwischen Christen und Juden*, p. 7.

[5] חכם, the usual designation of Talmudic Rabbis (*Megilla*, 16 a).

[6] R. Jerucham, xvii. 5, 159 c (cited, with many similar passages, by D. Hoffmann, *Der Shulchan Aruch*, etc., pp. 11, 16, 114, 115). This opinion was just as common with the Jews of the tenth as with those of the twelfth and thirteenth centuries (cf. op. cit. p. 67, note 21).

[7] *Orach Chayim*, ccxxiv. § 7.

The proverbial bitterness of the *odium theologicum* did not interfere with friendly intercourse between Jews and Christians until the thirteenth century. In the second century, intimacies occurred between Rabbis and representatives of the new religion. In the Talmud there are few violent polemics against Christianity, and a medieval controversialist like Jehuda Hadassi speaks with much tenderness of the person of Jesus.[1] The only theological controversies recorded in England were of an equally friendly character; they belong to the very end of the eleventh century.[2]

A new spirit was introduced by the zealous convert Donin on his entry into the Christian fold.[3] It was he who obtained, in 1239, the papal bull for burning the Talmud. These Jewish converts to Christianity became more Christian than the Christians, and originated that most cruel device — public theological controversies. The Jews in vain struggled to escape from the subtle net thus spread for them. They were forced to put in an appearance, and the result was inevitable. Theological passions were inflamed, popular prejudice grew, and each great controversy ended either in a massacre of the Jews or a confiscation of their religious books. The first real attempt to suppress the Talmud occurred in the thirteenth century as a direct consequence of the anti-Jewish zeal of the former Jew, Nicholas Donin.

Another baptized Jew, Pablo Christiani, was, however, the prime instigator of public discussions between repre-

---

[1] Cf. Neubauer, *Jewish Controversy and the Pugio Fidei* (*Expositor*, 3d series, vii. pp. 81 seq.).

[2] Before 1096. Cf. Jacobs, *Jews of Angevin England*, p. 7.

[3] Cf. Neubauer, loc. cit. and Graetz, Vol. III. passim.

sentatives of Judaism and Christianity. The Barcelona disputation in 1263, at which Pablo met a sturdy foeman in the noted Rabbi and mystic Nachmanides, was followed by what was worse than confiscation of the Talmud, namely, by its censorship by the Dominicans. It is a pity that space cannot be spared for a description of the mutilations to which Jewish books were subjected, for the matter has its humorous side. Nachmanides himself was banished from Spain for 'blasphemy,' and spent his last years a solitary exile in Jerusalem.[1]

In the following century the theological controversies became even more embittered. Every scrap of anti-Christian prejudice which the most malicious scrutiny could discover in Jewish books was collected and published broadcast by the foes of the Synagogue.[2] Jewish controversialists were not invariably fair or prudent, but never was bigotry or ignorance visited more severely on the heads of those who were guilty of them. In the year 1413, the most memorable of these public disputes was begun in Tortosa. It lasted for a year and nine months, and greatly augmented popular feeling against the Jews. Vincent Ferrer resorted to the most theatrical tricks; the cross was brought in amid sacred chants, and fiery exhortations were addressed to the Jews, entreating them to acknowledge the truth of Christianity. As in 1391, so in 1413, a large number of Jews were baptized, but the Marranos — as these half-hearted converts were named — proved a fertile danger to the Jews. Their constant relapses into Judaism strengthened the arm of the Inquisition, and finally led to the expulsion of the Jews from Spain.

The compulsory attendance of a contingent of Jews at

---

[1] Cf. above, p. 219.   [2] Graetz, IV. ch. vi. ; V. ch. v.

church to hear sermons against Judaism was more rigidly enforced as a result of the proselytizing zeal displayed at the beginning of the fifteenth century. This institution, so vigorously satirized by Browning in his poem on 'Holy Cross Day,' was much older than the fifteenth century, for in 1278 it was already known in Lombardy.[1] In the fifteenth century, however, the practice was much more general, especially in Italy. The ears of the Jews were examined on entering the churches, for they were suspected of stopping them with cotton. Overseers were appointed to ensure that the Jews remained awake during the two hours' sermon delivered to them.[2] The conversion of at least one Jew was a necessary part of the function in some instances. It is impossible, however, to go into further details, but a quotation from the bull of Benedict XIII, issued in Valencia in 1415, will suffice. This bull closes with the following paragraph : —

In all cities, towns, and villages, where there dwell the number of Jews the diocesan may deem sufficient, three public sermons are to be preached annually : one on the second Sunday in Advent ; one on the festival of the Resurrection ; and the other on the Sunday when the Gospel, 'And Jesus approached Jerusalem,' is chaunted. All Jews above twelve years of age shall be compelled to attend to hear these sermons. The subjects are to be — the first, to show them that the true Messiah has already come, quoting the passages of the Holy Scripture and the Talmud that were argued in the disputation of Jerome of Santa Fé ; the second, to make them see that the heresies, vanities, and errors of the Talmud prevent their knowing the truth ; and the third, explaining to them the destruction of the Temple and the city of Jerusalem, and the perpetuity of their captivity, as our Lord Jesus Christ and the other prophets had prophesied. And at the end of these sermons this bull is to be read, that the Jews may not be ignorant of any of its decrees.

But side by side with the theological conferences between

[1] Güdemann, ii. p. 235.

[2] Berliner, *Rom*, ii. (2), p. 87. His description is of a later period, but much the same arrangements were probably in vogue earlier.

Jews and Christians, there existed a number of literary friendships in which there was no admixture of evil motive. This remark applies with greatest force to Italy. Italy indeed was the scene in all ages of close literary friendships between Jews and Christians, such as no other country could show in the same profusion. In the tenth century, two Italians, the Jewish scholar-physician Donnolo and Nilus the Christian abbot, were affectionate friends from their youth upwards; they held literary converse with one another, and had a lively concern in each other's health.[1] The friendship between Anatoli and Michael Scotus, under the benign influence of the Emperor Frederick II, was a worthy pendant to the intimacy between Nilus and Donnolo.[2] From this, as from similar friendships, resulted some of those translations of Arabic works which brought to Europe the literature and science of ancient Greece. The Jews turned the Arabic into Hebrew, and helped their Christian friends to render the Hebrew into Latin.[3] The Italian Jews showed little originality, but their services were great as translators of medical, scientific, philosophical, and even folk-lore literature, such as the popular Kalila ve-Dimna.[4]

Of the literary intimacies between Jews and Christians in Italy, no more remarkable instance is recorded than that between Dante and his Jewish imitator, Immanuel of Rome. Before their time, the Hebrew satirist Kalonymos, and another co-religionist, Leo Romano, enjoyed the personal esteem of that princely friend of learning, Robert of Anjou, King of Naples.[5]

---

[1] Cf. Güdemann, ii. 23 ; Berliner, *Persönlische Beziehungen*, p. 4.
[2] On Anatoli's Christian friends, cf. Güdemann, op. cit. 226 seq.; Berliner, 10 seq. [3] Steinschneider, *Hebr. Uebersetzungen*, passim.
[4] See J. Jacobs, 'Jewish Diffusion of Folktales ' in his *Jewish Ideals*.
[5] Berliner, p. 13.

But Dante and Immanuel must have been bound in
the bonds of a more than ordinary affection ; for at the
former's death, the lawyer Bosone of Agobbio sent a
sonnet to Immanuel to console the Jew for the death of
the great Christian poet.[1] No theological prejudices stood
in the way of this mutual regard, for, as Immanuel himself
wrote in one of his rare Italian sonnets : ' Love has never
read the *Ave Maria*, Love knows no law or creed. Love
cannot be barred by a *Paternoster*, but to all who question
his supreme power Love answers, " It is my will." ' Some
centuries later, not even the old instinctive hatred of pagan
worship restrained Italian Rabbis from introducing—under
the impulse of the Renaissance — classical mythology into
their sermons just as Romanelli did into his Hebrew
dramas. David del Bene,[2] at the end of the sixteenth
century, dazzled his audiences by quotations from Italian
writers and the national poets. On one occasion he even
referred in a synagogue oration to ' quella santa Diana ' —
the holy goddess. Samuel Portaleone, a preacher of a
century later, used Italian proverbs to point a moral.[3]
The tradition of personal friendliness between Jews and
Christians was long and honourably preserved in Italy. It
is noteworthy that even Reuchlin's famous literary friendships with Jews grew up on Italian soil. At the end of
the fifteenth century he met Obadiah Sforno at Rome,
though another, and perhaps more momentous, intimacy

---

[1] See, on the question of the relations between Dante and Immanuel,
Geiger, *Jüdische Zeitschrift*, v. 268 ; Steinschneider, המזכיר, xi. 52, xiii. 115;
Graetz, *Geschichte der Juden*, v. 289; Güdemann, op. cit. p. 137.

[2] Cf. Kaufmann, *Jewish Quarterly Review*, viii. 511 seq.

[3] Cf. the quotations from MS. sources in the *Jewish Quarterly Review*,
v. 507.

with a Jew — the imperial physician Jacob Loans: was made at Frederick II's Court in Linz.

The fascination which drew Reuchlin to the Jews was not only his common interest with them in the Hebrew scriptures. The Cabala or Jewish mysticism charmed many Christian students besides Reuchlin to the feet of Jewish instructors. The most remarkable Italian figure of the latter part of the fifteenth century, the Count Giovanni Pico di Mirandola, found in the Jews Elias del Medigo and Jochanan Aleman, instructors in Hebrew and mysticism, and trusted personal friends. It is interesting to contrast what happened more than two centuries earlier in France and Germany. In the thirteenth century, mysticism formed a spiritual link between Judaism and Christianity in central Europe, but the personal relations between Jews and Christians were not improved by the common affection for mystical thought.[1] Never were the spiritual relations between Judaism and Christianity closer than in the era at which a deep cleft began to make itself permanently evident between their lives. In France and Germany, in the thirteenth century, mysticism (i.e. religion) bound the soul of a Jew to the soul of a Christian, but theology (i.e. dogma) divided their lives.

It cannot be said that interest in Judaism has always led to an equal interest in Jews. In seventeenth-century England this undoubtedly did occur, but it was chiefly in Italy that the two phenomena existed side by side. But at the very moment when Pico di Mirandola and crowds of other Christian youths were absorbing instruction from the lips of Jewish teachers in Padua and Florence, the Pope

[1] Güdemann, i. 153.

was excommunicating such Spanish Christians as regarded the Jews with friendly eyes.

Indeed, so keen and close was the learned and personal intercourse between Jews and Christians in Italy, that a curious controversy arose within the Jewish camp in the sixteenth century. The religious arguments between Rabbis and Cardinals were completely friendly. In the earlier periods they were of the nature of a mere interchange of witty questions and answers. As late as the beginning of the sixteenth century, Pope Clement VII (1523–1534) actually designed a Latin translation of the Old Testament, in which Jews and Christians were to co-operate.[1] But many Christians naturally undertook the study of Hebrew and of Jewish mysticism with the object of providing themselves with weapons of offence and defence against Judaism.

Under these circumstances, was it lawful for a Jew to teach a Christian the Cabala, and introduce him into the innermost recesses of Judaism? Naturally, some Jews were vigorous opponents of such a course. Maimonides, however, had taken his stand on the opposite side, and, with his usual tolerance, said, ' A Jew may teach the Commandments to Christians, for they admit that our Law is divine, and they preserve it in its entirety.'[2] The bigotry of those who opposed this view had no practical weight in Italy after the Renaissance. Besides the cases that have already been named, Abraham de Balmes was the teacher

---

[1] Berliner, *Geschichte der Juden in Rom*, ii. (1), p. 104.

[2] Maimonides, *Responsa* (ed. Leipzig, § 58). I quote the passage in full:
ויכול ללמד המצות לנוצרים והשכר והעונש כי יש כמה מהם שיחזרו למוטב והם אומרים
ומודים כי תורתינו זאת היא מן השמים היא הנתונה לנו על ידי משה רבינו ע״ה והיא
כתובה אצלם בשלי מוחה אך לפעמים יגלו פנים שאינם כהלכה וכמה מהם הם חוזרים למוטב
ואין מכשול לישראל.

of Cardinal Guinani, Guido Rangoni was instructed by Jacob Mantino, Lazarus de Viterbo corresponded on the Bible with Cardinal Sirleto (by the way, in Latin).

Perhaps the most noted instance was the activity of Elias Levita — the founder of modern Hebrew Grammar, and the teacher of many Christians. He, with Jacob Loans and Obadiah Sforno, must be allowed a large share in producing the Protestant Reformation.[1] Levita's relations with Cardinal Egidio were indeed of so touching a nature, and so well reveal the opposition already referred to, that room must be spared for a quotation from Levita's autobiographical preface to his principal work :[2] —

> Now I swear by my Creator, that a certain Christian (Cardinal Egidio) encouraged me and brought me thus far. He was my pupil for ten years uninterruptedly. I resided at his house and instructed him, for which there was a great outcry against me, and it was not considered right of me. And several of the Rabbis would not countenance me, and pronounced woe to my soul because I taught the law to a Christian, owing to the interpretation assigned to the words, ' And as for my judgements, they (i.e. the Gentiles) are not to know them ' (Ps. cxlvii. 20). . . .

> When the prince (i.e. Egidio) heard my statement, he came to me and kissed me with the kisses of his mouth, saying, ' Blessed be the God of the Universe who has brought thee hither. Now abide with me and be my teacher, and I shall be to thee as a father, and shall support thee and thy house, and give thee thy corn and thy wine and thy olives, and fill thy purse and bear all thy wants.' Thus we took sweet counsel together, iron sharpening iron. I imparted my spirit to him, and learned from him excellent and valuable things, which are in accordance with truth.

Though these literary friendships were almost entirely confined to Italy, some other causes of friendly intercourse were somewhat more general. Commerce brought the Jews into personal contact with Christians, and business

[1] Cf. Ginsburg, in his edition of Levita's *Masoreth Hamasoreth*, p. 38.

[2] Op. cit. Introduction (Ginsburg, p. 96). For other instances of similar friendship at various earlier periods in Italy, cf. Güdemann, ii. 228, 289; Berliner, passim.

partnerships were contracted in all parts of Europe, indeed of the civilized world, in the sixteenth as well as in earlier centuries. The evidence on this head is complete. We read of partnerships in Persia in the tenth century, of Jews employed by Christians, and of Christians by Jews.[1] Jews, at that time and place, employed non-Jews even to make the unleavened passover bread under Jewish supervision.[2] In France and Germany in the beginning of the twelfth century the same commercial toleration occurred, and Jews employed Christian builders, Christian postmen, and Christian laundry-men.[3] In the thirteenth century in Greece, Jews were in the employment of Christian masters.[4] In the Rhine-lands in the fourteenth and fifteenth centuries they worked together in the vineyards,[5] and Jews were permitted by their Rabbi to use the summer-houses of the Christian villagers as the booths prescribed by the Mosaic law.[6] It is even more important to know that such business intercourse continued in Germany in the fifteenth century, and in Rome in the sixteenth.[7]

The legislation of the middle ages seriously impeded these opportunities of friendly commercial intercourse, but never entirely suppressed them. The same remark applies to *social* intercourse. Up till the rule of Innocent III indeed, the social relations of Jews and Christians were close and cordial. We have already had several instances of Jews and Christians amusing themselves together. That this should have been so before the ghetto period is hardly

---

[1] See *Responsa* of Geonim (ed. Lyck), 66 seq. Cf. also Müller, *Mafteach*, p. 153.

[2] *Mafteach*, p. 219.   [3] *Machzor Vitry*, pp. 124, 288.

[4] Güdemann, ii. p. 311.   [5] Maharil, הלכות סוכה.

[6] Lev. xxiii. 42. Maharil, loc. cit.

[7] Isserlein, תרומת הדשן, 152; Berliner, *Rom*, ii. 20.

to be wondered at, for the Jews and Christians dressed alike, spoke alike, and were named alike.[1] Religious differences did not seriously restrict intercourse, for a most friendly desire to meet each other half-way may be easily discerned.

In the beginning of the eleventh century, the market-day was transferred from Saturday to Sunday in Lyons for the benefit of the Jews.[2] A German knight in the fifteenth century, who frequently received Jewish visitors, removed the Crucifix from his mantel on these occasions, so that the Jews might feel no hesitation in greeting him with a bow — a fine piece of courtesy. Christians made gifts to the synagogues, and Christian workmen built them;[3] Christians were present at Jewish religious ceremonies, and — even as late as the eighth and ninth centuries — observed the Sabbath in common with the Jews.[4]

On their side, the Jews were fully responsive. If there went on a process of Judaizing Christianity, the reverse action was equally noted, and Jews adopted many Christian habits and even interchanged superstitions. In 1193 a curious instance of this occurred in Canterbury. A Christian woman, Godeliva, 'was passing through the *hospitium* (inn) of a certain Jew, and entered it at the invitation of a Jewish woman ; for, being skilled in charms and incantations, she was accustomed to charm the weak foot of the Jewess.'[5] These attentions were returned, and a Christian knight would beg of a Rabbi a *mezuza*

---

[1] Zunz, *Zur Geschichte*, p. 174.   [2] Graetz, *Geschichte*, v. 219.
[3] Güdemann, iii. p. 151. Cf. *Orach Chayim*, ccxliv. (מגן אברהם), § 8.
[4] Op. cit. ii. 30 seq. Church Councils in 791 and 855 intervened to put an end to this state of things.
[5] Jacobs, *Angevin England*, p. 153.

or parchment-roll containing certain Hebrew texts, to act as a protective amulet for the walls of his castle.[1] The Jew gave gifts to Christians on the thirty-third day of the Omer (a Jewish religious feast midway between the Passover and Pentecost), on the Feast of Esther — occasions on which Jews exchanged gifts with Jews — and, what was even more friendly, sent gifts to Christians on the festivals of the Church.[2] A Jew would petition a judge on a Jewish festival to accept bail for the release of a Christian.[3] Jews visited Christians and drank wine with them, though this was against the weight of religious opinion. Some Jewish authorities, however, permitted it in order to encourage friendly intercourse.[4]

But it was chiefly their amusements that brought Jews and Christians together. Rabbis in the fifteenth century freely invited Christians to their houses, and visited them in their own abodes.[5] A Frankfort Christian, in the year 1377, would apply to a deceased Jew the friendly epithet *selig*.[6] The Jewish records, already quoted in the preceding chapters, prove conclusively that Jews lived in the same local quarters with Christians till the middle of the sixteenth century, while in Italy Jews and Christians played cards together, and ate, drank, and danced together.[7]

---

[1] Deut. vii. 9; Berliner, *Persönlische Beziehungen*, p. 16.

[2] Berliner, *Aus dem Inneren Leben*, 18; *Orach Chayim*, dcxciv. 3; Güdemann, iii. 135; Isserlein, op. cit. 195.

[3] Maharil, *Hilchoth Yom Tob*.

[4] Müller, חלוף מנהגים, § 10, *Mafteach*, p. 9; Güdemann, i. 48; Jacobs, op. cit. 269; and the references in Zunz, op. cit. p. 180.

[5] Maharil.

[6] Berliner, *Persönlische Beziehungen*, p. 17.

[7] Cf. also Berliner's *Aus dem Inneren Leben*, 33; Güdemann, iii. 139.

The same thing occurred in a modified degree everywhere else. Jews employed Christian musicians in Germany on the Sabbath, and played games of chance with them on all and every occasion. It is hard to conceive how closely this community in amusement might have drawn Jews and Christians but for the violent interference of external causes. An interesting and instructive case of this popular friendliness and external interference may be cited from an English record of the date 1286.[1] In that year, one of the chief Jewish families of Hereford gave a wedding feast, with 'displays of silk and cloth of gold, horsemanship and an equestrian procession, stage-playing, sports, and minstrelsy,' all in so magnificent a style as to induce many Christians to attend it, just as Christians attended Jewish weddings in Germany. Bishop Swinfield threatened to excommunicate any Hereford Christian who, on the occasion just referred to, dared to accept Jewish hospitality.

The bishop carried out his threat. Indeed, the Church very successfully raised barriers between Jews and Christians as the thirteenth century closed. At one time Jews were allowed to retain the services of Christians for performing necessary work on the Jewish Sabbath. Some Jews themselves objected to this on the religious ground that work which a Jew might not himself do on the Sabbath was forbidden also to any of his servants. But the Jews were not allowed a perfectly free choice in the matter, for they could only employ Christian servants on Saturdays or any other day by evading the stringent restrictive canons passed by various councils, or enacted in

[1] B. L. Abrahams, *Transactions of the Jewish Historical Society of England*, i. p. 141.

various papal bulls.[1]   Jews were prohibited from attending sick Christians and rendering them friendly services.
These measures were far too rigid to succeed.   They were
constantly evaded ; the popes themselves employed Jewish
doctors in the teeth of their own decrees to the contrary,
in Rome in the middle of the fifteenth century ; Christians
did cook and work for Jews on the Sabbaths and festivals.
Buxtorf — though he was fined 100 gulden for the offence
— attended at the naming of the eight-days-old son of a
Jew who had helped him in editing the Basel Bible, while
a Jew of Frankfort in the beginning of the eighteenth
century stood god-father to a Christian child.[2]   Another
Christian scholar, Johann Christoph Wagenseil, visited
the Rabbis of Vienna in 1650.   He attended synagogue
in order to observe the ceremonies performed there.   On
a certain Saturday a burning candle fell, and Wagenseil
promptly extinguished it, for he knew that the Jews were
unable to 'touch fire' on their day of rest.[3]

Instances of this mutual personal regard were more
common in the sixteenth and succeeding centuries than is
commonly believed.   But the continuous action of forces
devised against such friendly intercourse made themselves
very strongly and universally felt.   The ghetto's plague
and the garb's disgrace helped on the efforts of theologians to deny Christian fellowship to the outcast sons of
Israel.   The extraordinary fact is not that Jews and
Christians so rarely formed friendships in the seventeenth
and eighteenth centuries ; the marvel is that they formed

---

[1] Canons against Jews employing Christian servants began in the eleventh
century, but they become far severer in the thirteenth and fourteenth centuries.

[2] Schechter, *Studies in Judaism*, p. 354.

[3] Kaufmann, *Die letzte Vertreibung der Juden aus Wien*, p. 69.

such friendships at all. No more fitting close to this history suggests itself than a word of honour to those noble spirits on both sides, whom neither persecution on the one hand nor prejudice on the other could separate, for their hearts beat together in sympathetic aspiration towards all that strengthens the bonds of a common human brotherhood.

INDEX I

HEBREW AUTHORITIES

THIS list includes many, but not all, of the Hebrew works to which I have had direct resort in writing the previous pages. Books referred to, but not actually consulted, have been omitted from both Indexes. It will be noted that reference has been made to a large number of *Responsa*, but the list would have been much increased, had I included those which are cited merely as modern illustrations of statements in the text. The Hebrew *Responsa* literature contains a vast store of information, otherwise inaccessible, in the form of Responses by Rabbinical authorities to questions proposed to them for decision. In the course of their replies, much information is often given relating to far earlier periods. Thus, though Solomon Hakkohen wrote in the sixteenth century, he cites dated documents relating to the fourteenth century. So, too, the customs alluded to in the eighteenth and nineteenth century *Responsa*, are sometimes described as 'very old' — an epithet which is probably deserved. It must be remembered, too, that so far as the internal organization of Jewish life is concerned, no serious break with the middle ages occurred until the very close of the eighteenth century. I have added the century in which the authorities cited lived, only in those cases in which the date of the publication of the work differs considerably from the period at which the work was written. Here and there I have given no date owing to my own uncertainty. I have not cited *particular* editions of some works which have been very often printed.

INDEX II

GENERAL INDEX

Israel Abrahams was born in 1858. He was Reader in Talmudics at Cambridge and a distinguished representative of British Liberal Judaism. Abrahams was the author of *Studies in Pharisaism and the Gospels* and *Chapters on Jewish Literature* and was co-author (with C. G. Montefiore) of *Aspects of Judaism*.

Atheneum Paperbacks

TEMPLE BOOKS—*The Jewish Publication Society*

PHILOSOPHY AND RELIGION

Atheneum Paperbacks

STUDIES IN AMERICAN NEGRO LIFE